Economic Development, Crime, and Policing

Global Perspectives

International Police Executive Symposium Co-Publications

Dilip K. Das, *Founding President-IPES*

PUBLISHED

Examining Political Violence: Studies of Terrorism, Counterterrorism, and Internal Wars
By David Lowe, Austin Turk, and Dilip K. Das ISBN: 978-1-4665-8820-2

The Evolution of Policing: Worldwide Innovations and Insights
By Melchor C. de Guzman, Aiedeo Mintie Das, and Dilip K. Das, ISBN: 978-1-4665-6715-3

Policing Global Movement: Tourism, Migration, Human Trafficking, and Terrorism
By S. Caroline Taylor, Daniel Joseph Torpy, and Dilip K. Das, ISBN: 978-1-4665-0726-5

Global Community Policing: Problems and Challenges
By Arvind Verma, Dilip K. Das, Manoj Abraham, ISBN 978-1-4398-8416-4

Global Environment of Policing
By Darren Palmer, Michael M. Berlin, and Dilip K. Das, ISBN: 978-1-4200-6590-9

Strategic Responses to Crime: Thinking Locally, Acting Globally
By Melchor de Guzman, Aiedeo Mintie Das, and Dilip K. Das, ISBN: 978-1-4200-7669-1

Police without Borders: The Fading Distinction between Local and Global
By Cliff Roberson, Dilip K. Das, and Jennie K. Singer, ISBN: 978-1-4398-0501-5

Effective Crime Reduction Strategies: International Perspectives
By James F. Albrecht and Dilip K. Das, ISBN: 978-1-4200-7838-1

Urbanization, Policing, and Security: Global Perspectives
By Gary Cordner, Ann Marie Cordner, and Dilip K. Das, ISBN: 978-1-4200-8557-0

Criminal Abuse of Women and Children: An International Perspective
By Obi N.I. Ebbe and Dilip K. Das, ISBN: 978-1-4200-8803-8

Contemporary Issues in Law Enforcement and Policing
By Andrew Millie and Dilip K. Das, ISBN: 978-1-4200-7215-0

Global Trafficking in Women and Children
By Obi N.I. Ebbe and Dilip K. Das, ISBN: 978-1-4200-5943-4

Policing Major Events: Perspectives from around the World
by Martha Dow, Darryl Plecas, and Dilip K. Das, ISBN: 978-1-4665-8805-9

**Police Reform: The Effects of International Economic Development,
Armed Violence, and Public Safety**
By Garth den Heyer and Dilip K. Das, ISBN: 978-1-4822-0456-8

Economic Development, Crime, and Policing

Global Perspectives

Edited by
Frederic Lemieux
Garth den Heyer
Dilip K. Das

International Police Executive Symposium Co-Publication

CRC Press is an imprint of the
Taylor & Francis Group, an **informa** business

CRC Press
Taylor & Francis Group
6000 Broken Sound Parkway NW, Suite 300
Boca Raton, FL 33487-2742

First issued in paperback 2019

© 2015 by Taylor & Francis Group, LLC
CRC Press is an imprint of Taylor & Francis Group, an Informa business

No claim to original U.S. Government works

ISBN-13: 978-1-4822-0456-8 (hbk)
ISBN-13: 978-0-367-86864-2 (pbk)

Visit the Taylor & Francis Web site at
http://www.taylorandfrancis.com

and the CRC Press Web site at
http://www.crcpress.com

Table of Contents

Section III

**REFORMING POLICING TO IMPROVE
ECONOMIC AND SOCIAL DEVELOPMENT
IN EMERGING DEMOCRACIES AND NEW
INDUSTRIALIZED COUNTRIES**

Foreword

Few causes defended by the United Nations have generated more intense and widespread support than the campaign to promote development and rule of law, including that through violent crime prevention and reduction. The United Nations has helped to build a structure of internationally agreed on strategies, standards, programs, and goals to advance the cause of violence prevention and reduction, including the 2001 UN Program of Action to Prevent and Eradicate the Illicit Trade in Small Arms and Light Weapons in All Its Aspects, including an instrument on marking and tracing; Geneva Declaration on Armed Violence and Development (2006); Firearms Protocol; and Basic Principles on the Use of Force and Firearms by Law Enforcement Officials.

Eleven United Nations entities work on various aspects of the rule of law. Although there is no single entity in charge of the prevention and reduction of violence, various aspects of the challenge are part of the mandates of United Nations entities. For example, the United Nations Educational, Scientific and Cultural Organization works on education and culture of peace, Office for Disarmament Affairs on control of firearms and disarmament issues, Department of Peacekeeping Operations on the rule of law in the context of peacekeeping operations, United Nations Development Program in post-conflict situations, and United Nations International Children's Emergency Fund on children-related aspects. The United Nations Women focuses on gender-related aspects.

The cornerstone of this structure is the General Assembly Resolution 63/23 adopted in 2008 on Promoting Development through the Reduction and Prevention of Armed Violence. In this resolution, member states reaffirmed their commitments to creating an environment conducive to development and the elimination of poverty and stressed the need for a coherent and integrated approach to the prevention of armed violence, with a view to achieving sustainable peace and development.

Violence affects all societies to different degrees, whether they are at war, in a postconflict situation, or suffering from everyday forms of criminal or political violence. The human toll of armed violence is severe and now by far exceeds violence in wars and armed conflicts. The World Health Organization (WHO) estimates that 600,000 deaths due to violent intentional injuries occurred in 2004 versus 184,000 deaths through violent injuries due to war and conflict.

Each human life is precious and each death is a tragedy, but statistically for each death resulting from wars and civil strife there are three deaths resulting from violent crime in nonconflict situations. No region is immune to the damage caused by violent crime, but the highest concentration of homicides is found in Africa, Central America, and South America. The percentage of homicides ranges from 77% in central Africa to 19% in western Europe.

Violent crime has a significant and enduring impact on individuals, families, communities, and societies. Reports of the Geneva Declaration Secretariat and the WHO show that violent crime is among the top five leading reasons of death for adults. According to current research, in the United States one in five intentional gunshot wounds is fatal. Physical injuries require long hospitalization and have long-standing psychological and social consequences. Violent crime destroys families and divides communities. People fear violence in the community so much that they decide to carry their own weapons for protection, increasing the potential that they may become perpetrators of a violent act, but for societies the human costs of violent crime are even higher. Armed violence disrupts access to education, health, and social services and reduces the capacity of social and human resources by disseminating insecurity and fear. It can lead to large-scale displacement; restrict mobility; and contribute to illicit markets, economies of violence, and power structures, which undermine governance and state stability.

Violent crime also has substantial negative impact on national economies and constrains the achievement of the Millennium Development Goals. It has a negative impact on the socioeconomic development of all societies but disproportionately severely affects those in low- and middle-income countries. A 2008 study of the Geneva Declaration Secretariat estimated that across 90 countries the cost of lost productivity from nonconflict or criminal violence alone ranges from USD 95 to 163 billion and decreases the annual growth of an average economy by around 2%. This is without counting health costs, which are substantial: for example, in El Salvador only hospitalization of victims of violence is estimated to be in excess of 7% of the country's health budget and in South Africa only abdominal firearm injuries have been assessed at about 4% of the national health budget.

Of course, each country experiences the impact of violence differently. For example, North America experiences the highest loss in productivity, whereas Latin America suffers from the highest impact in terms of gross domestic product. Moreover, it leads to the destruction of property and infrastructure and also undermines the effects of local and foreign investments. These are resources that are diverted away from essential health and social services and poverty eradication.

There is no single cause of violence but rather a wide range of factors that interact at different levels making certain individuals, groups, and communities disproportionately more affected by violence. At the individual level, such factors include behavioral problems, age, gender, educational level, substance abuse, and a past history of experiencing violence. For example, young males with low educational level are particularly at risk of committing or being victims of violent crime. Even the exposure to violence in the past—whether this has occurred at the national level (political violence) or at the familial level (domestic violence)—is a typical risk factor.

Risk factors related to community and society include social, political, and economic exclusion; unemployment/underemployment; rapid and unregulated urbanization; weak governance structures; an oppressive and ineffective security sector; and demographic youth bulges and resource scarcity (like access to necessities of life or basic goods and services). Additional risk factors are easy and unregulated access to small arms, alcohol, and narcotics because they can often act as a trigger and turn a nonviolent situation into a lethal encounter.

Preventing and reducing violent crime and promoting sustainable development are priorities for governments. Governments have the primary responsibility to ensure public safety, and they have an interest in providing human security and development to their citizens. In particular, reducing access to firearms and preventing them from falling into wrong hands by controlling their sale, purchase, and use is the direct responsibility of governments. Statistically, countries with more restrictive firearms policies and lower firearms ownership tend to experience lower levels of firearms violence.

Concrete work based on United Nations Resolution 63/62 on the Consolidation of Peace through Practical Disarmament Measures continues in particular through the meetings of the so-called Group of Interested States in Practical Disarmament Measures in New York. Governments recognized the seriousness of the escalating levels of armed violence. They agreed to work on practical measures to promote socioeconomic development that aim at reducing violence. Furthermore, they acknowledged the importance of cooperation between governments and subregional, regional, and international organizations to prevent and reduce violence and to promote measures that enhance prospects for sustainable and equitable development. The same resolution encouraged nongovernmental organizations (NGOs) to collect and destroy firearms and ammunitions. Although some progress has been made to recognize the problem and sensitize public opinion, we have a long way to go before achieving the goal of an armed violence-free society.

To tackle the problem of criminal violence, comprehensive and coherent approaches are needed at the international, national, and local levels. There are many proven key prevention strategies that address underlying risks of violence in general. They include reducing access to lethal means of violence, reducing the availability and abuse of alcohol, disrupting illegal drug markets, improving life skills and enhancing opportunities for children and youth, promoting gender equality and empowering women, changing cultural norms that support violence, improving criminal justice systems, improving social welfare systems, reducing social distance between conflicting groups, and reducing economic inequality and concentrated poverty.

Multidimensional and multisectorial approaches across health, security, justice, and education have to be developed and implemented in countries suffering from the negative impacts of criminal violence, aiming at reducing the level of violence within these societies. There is no one-size-fits-all solution, and each local community and country will have to assess their own risks and vulnerability and plan their initiatives to prevent and reduce violence accordingly.

Also, governments by themselves cannot defeat criminal violence. NGOs, the private sector, academia, and local authorities are the frontline actors in finding local answers to these global challenges. The challenges we face in this fight are of such magnitude that no government can overcome them alone. All actors—civil society, the private sector, government, and international organizations—need to join their forces. Indeed, when we see the prevention and reduction of violent crime in action it is often through concrete initiatives on the ground. Sometimes, small as they appear, these programs have three-pronged approaches: they are comprehensive and combine a range of prevention strategies to address risk factors, involve partnerships of law enforcement and criminal justice agencies with NGOs and local authorities to target youth crime and violence, and address the economic and social needs of a community. They are designed and implemented from the bottom up, with long-term needs in mind not stop-gap solutions. Fully embracing these partnerships and collaborative relationships with civil society enables much better results than what governments and United Nations entities can achieve on their own. And they are the way forward.

Finally, I would like to stress the importance of working to understand the root causes of criminal violence and its impact on development and public safety, so that our efforts can go beyond the reactive and focus on the forces that underpin this behavior, as well as on its symptoms and consequences. Our work must be integrated and holistic, rather than disconnected and fragmented. We must assess the impact of existing strategies so that successful interventions and preventive measures can be supported and replicated. We must ensure that measures of accountability are introduced, which emphasize individual, community, and national responsibility for preventing and reducing armed violence. Most importantly, we must work to ensure that sufficient resources are allocated for prevention and intervention with respect to all forms of criminal violence.

Andrei Abramov
Chief of the NGO Branch
United Nations Department of Economic and Social Affairs

INTERNATIONAL POLICE EXECUTIVE SYMPOSIUM
Co-publication Preface

The *International Police Executive Symposium* (IPES) was founded in 1994 to address one major challenge, i.e., the two worlds of research and practice remain disconnected even though cooperation between the two is growing. A major reason is that the two groups speak in different languages. The research is published in hard to access journals and presented in a manner that is difficult for some to comprehend. On the other hand, police practitioners tend not to mix with researchers and remain secretive about their work. Consequently there is little dialogue between the two and almost no attempt to learn from one another. The global dialogue among police researchers and practitioners is limited. True, the literature on the police is growing exponentially. But its impact upon day-to-day policing, however, is negligible.

The aims and objectives of the IPES are to provide a forum to foster closer relationships among police researchers and practitioners on a global scale, to facilitate cross-cultural, international and interdisciplinary exchanges for the enrichment of this law enforcement, to encourage discussion, and to publish research on challenging and contemporary problems facing the policing profession. One of the most important activities of the IPES is the organization of an annual meeting under the auspices of a police agency or an educational institution. Now in its 17th year, the annual meeting, a five-day initiative on specific issues relevant to the policing profession, brings together ministers of interior and justice, police commissioners and chiefs, members of academia representing world-renown institutions, and many more criminal justice elite from over 60 countries. It facilitates interaction and the exchange of ideas and opinions on all aspects of policing. The agenda is structured to encourage dialogue in both formal and informal settings.

Another important aspect of the meeting is the publication of the best papers presented by well known criminal justice scholars and police administrators who attend the meetings. The best papers are selected, thoroughly revised, fully updated, meticulously edited, and published as books based upon the theme of each meeting. This repository of knowledge under the co-publication imprint of IPES and CRC Press-Taylor & Francis Group chronicles the important contributions of the International Police Executive Symposium over the last two decades. As a result, in 2011 the United Nations awarded IPES a Special Consultative Status for the Economic and Social Council (ECSOC) honoring its importance in the global security community.

In addition to this book series, the IPES also has a research journal, *Police Practices and Research: An International Journal* (PPR). The PPR contains research articles on police issues. It is an international journal and is distributed worldwide. For more information on the PPR visit **http://www.tandf.co.uk/journals/GPPR**

This unique volume, titled, *Strategic Responses to Crime: Thinking Locally, Acting Globally*, includes selected articles that were originally presented by police executives and scholars from several countries who attended the 13th Annual Meeting of the International Police Executive Symposium held in Ayvalik, Turkey, in 2006. However, the articles have been updated and several papers outside of the conference have been added to capture the theme of the book. The volume is divided into four sections, each of which includes perspectives of police administrators and members of the academia from different countries. These chapters encompass topics in law enforcement from operations to organizations including pervading issues that the police confront both locally and globally. The chapters provide a comprehensive survey of police practices across police jurisdictions. This book is a useful reference for practitioners and researchers.

IPES advocates, promotes, and propagates that POLICING is one of the most basic and essential avenues for improving the quality of life in all nations; rich and poor; modern and traditional; large and small; as well as peaceful and strife-ridden. IPES actively works to drive home to all its office bearers, supporters, and admirers that, in order to reach its full potential as an instrument of service to humanity, POLICING must be fully and enthusiastically open to collaboration between research and practice, global exchange of information between police and academics in every country, universal disseminations and sharing of best practices, generating thinking police leaders and followers, and reflecting and writing on the issues challenging to the profession.

Through its annual meetings, hosts, institutional supporters, and publications, IPES reaffirms that POLICING is a moral profession with unflinching adherence to the rule of law and human rights as the embodiment of humane values.

—Dilip K. Das
Founding President, *International Police Executive Symposium*, www.ipes.info

Book Series Editor for:

Advances in Police Theory and Practice, CRC Press-Taylor & Francis Group

Interviews with Global Leaders in Policing, Courts, and Prisons, CRC Press-Taylor & Francis Group

PPR Special Issues as Books, Routledge-Taylor & Francis Group

Founding Editor-in-Chief, *Police Practice and Research: An International Journal*, PPR, http://www.tandf.co.uk/journals/GPPR

Preface

This book is the product of the 22nd annual meeting of the International Police Executive Symposium that was held at the United Nations Plaza, New York, from August 5, Sunday, to August 10, Friday, 2012. The theme of the meeting was "Economic Development, Armed Violence and Public Safety," and the meeting was chaired by Dr. Garth den Heyer, Charles Sturt University, Manly, Australia, and Police Foundation, Washington, DC. The symposium focused on the nexus and linkages between economic development, armed violence, and public safety and, as a result, current practices and challenges of these topics were a feature of the presentations and discussions. The delegates, from 30 nations, believed that policing is one of the most basic and essential avenues for improving the quality of life in all nations, rich and poor, modern and traditional, large and small, as well as peaceful and strife ridden.

The meeting heard presentations from police leaders and police researchers from a number of countries subject to these conditions and other attendees who had worked under these conditions. Although a range of views were presented, there was a shared concern for the need to understand the links between the police, the broader criminal justice systems, and the larger social context in which policing occurs. These views culminated in the drafting of a meeting resolution by Associate Professor Darren Palmer, Deakin University, Australia. The resolution of this conference was that reforms to police and public safety in areas undergoing economic development and/or experiencing criminal violence must

- Be based on sound research, utilizing multimethod approaches with access to key stakeholders and quantitative data.
- Avoid "off-the-shelf" policing models and ensure that any ideas or concepts are adapted to local contexts.
- Be informed by the need to uphold the rule of law and protect and foster respect for human rights.
- Include accountability mechanisms and protection against undesirable conduct.
- Be fully evaluated to ensure that these reforms do not produce unacknowledged or unintended consequences.

The book presents these issues by organizing its chapters according to their regional perspectives: global, modern democracies, emerging democracies, and newly industrialized countries. This categorization provides an opportunity to shed light on the existing regional contrasts related to the interrelations and underlying factors between policing, fluctuations in socioeconomic development, and crime. The first section of this book addresses international trends related to crime, economics, and social challenges that can directly influence the response of police. The second section of this book focuses on strategies deployed by law enforcement and justice systems to improve economic and social development in advanced democracies. The third section addresses strategies deployed by law enforcement and the justice system to improve economic and social development in emerging democracies and newly industrialized countries.

The conclusion chapter offers an overview on the dynamics and effects of police reforms through the lens of the contributions included in this book but will also expand on other related considerations that are critical in understanding the underlying forces that build police reforms. The relation between socioeconomic developments, violent crime, and policing is complex and characterized by a plurality of factors that may impact police reforms. More precisely, the conclusion addresses the sources of police reform, types of reforms, factors influencing the dynamics of police reforms, and impact of such reforms as well as the challenges that emerge in postreform eras.

As a concluding remark, we would like to point out that the book provides strong insights into foundational elements for a research agenda on police reform and on its impact on economic developments and armed violence. First, this field needs a more systematic international comparative analysis on the impact of reform in law enforcement on economic development and violence, for example, measuring the effect of adopting a specific model of policing or implementing a particular technology on reduction of violence, cost of crime, and efficiency of public policing. The field of policing and public safety lacks, in general, international comparative research. Second, it is critical to produce a body of evaluative research that assesses, with methodological rigor and systematic analytical processes, the impact of police reform on economic development and violence. Third, there is a need to adopt a case study approach to scrutinize in more depth change management strategies used in police reforms and implantation of strategic initiatives in law enforcement and the justice system. Finally, as several chapters in this book have pointed out issues with the political leadership in implementing reforms in law enforcement and the justice system in general, it would be essential to support research aiming at understanding better how police leaders and senior public officials manage the politics of reform. Such research would be instrumental in generating knowledge about effective leadership under pressure and effective policy development in organizations facing crisis.

We hope that you will enjoy reading this book and appreciate the important contributions made by the contributors.

Frederic Lemieux
Garth den Heyer
Dilip K. Das

Editors

Frederic Lemieux is a professor and director of police science and Security & Safety Leadership Programs at the George Washington University, Washington, DC. He received his PhD in criminology from the University of Montreal, Canada, in 2002. Dr. Lemieux's research has focused on social control and policing. He is currently conducting studies on transnational drug trafficking enforcement and on the function of criminal intelligence as a formal social control tool. Dr. Lemieux has also published three books and various journal articles examining crime control during major disasters, counterterrorism and intelligence agencies, and police cooperation.

Garth den Heyer is an inspector with the New Zealand Police. He is also a senior research fellow with the Police Foundation in Washington, DC, and lecturer with the Australian Graduate School of Policing and Security. He received his doctorate in public policy from the Charles Sturt University, Manly, Australia, in 2006. Dr. den Heyer's research has focused on police service delivery effectiveness and police reform in postconflict nations. He is currently conducting research on the cost-reducing strategies adopted by police agencies to maintain effective and efficient delivery of services. Dr. den Heyer has also published three books and various journal articles examining police structures and performance, policing in developing nations, and the police's role in countering terrorism.

Dilip K. Das has years of experience in police practice, research, writing, and education. After obtaining his master's degree in English literature, Dr. Das joined the Indian Police Service, an elite national service with a distinguished tradition. After 14 years in the service as a police executive, for example, as a chief of police, he moved to the United States, where he achieved another master's degree in criminal justice and a doctorate degree in the same discipline. Dr. Das is a professor of criminal justice, a former police chief, and a human rights consultant to the United Nations. He is the founding president of the International Police Executive Symposium (IPES), where he manages the affairs of the organization in cooperation with an appointed group of police practitioners, academia members, and individuals from around the world. Dr. Das is also the founding editor-in-chief of Police Practice and Research: An International Journal. He is author, editor, or coeditor of more than 30 books and numerous articles. Dr. Das has received several faculty excellence awards and was a distinguished faculty lecturer.

Contributors

James F. Albrecht is presently working as a professor of criminal justice at the University of New Haven, Connecticut. Jimmy has also held a number of executive practitioner positions, including police chief of criminal investigations in the joint European Union/U.S. police in Kosovo (former Yugoslavia), and he retired as New York Police Department captain and regional commander after serving 22 years. Jimmy served 3 years as graduate professor of criminal justice leadership at St. John's University, New York; continues to serve as a graduate professor of homeland security at the Pace University, New York; and is completing his PhD in criminal justice at the University of New Haven.

Johanna Berning is a senior lecturer at the University of South Africa, in the Department of Police Practice. She was a member of the South African Police Service from 1976 to 1990. Berning possesses a national diploma in police administration, national higher diploma (honors) in postschool education (in 1991), national higher diploma (honors) in policing, and masters in forensic investigation. Berning is currently registered for her doctoral degree in police science. Berning's research interests are policing, police management, and forensic investigation.

Johan Bertilsson is a firearms and tactics instructor. Since 2005 he has been chief self-defense instructor at the Skåne County Police Department, Swedish National Police Force, and since 2009 he has held a PhD student position at the Department of Clinical Sciences, Lund University, Sweden. His research interests include perceptive, cognitive, and motor skill performance depending on the effects of internal and external pressures like pretraining, psychological, and physical stress.

Setlhomamaru Dintwe holds a Bachelor of Criminal Justice (NWU); Bachelor of Technology in Policing (TSA); Master of Technology in Forensic Investigations and Doctor of Literature and Philosophy (UNISA). He was a member of the South African Police Service for 5 years, where he worked at the Boitekong Detective Branch in Rustenburg as an investigator. He was promoted to a position of principal investigator and transferred to the Anti-Corruption Command of the Independent Complaints Directorate. His responsibilities included investigating corrupt activities of the members of the South African Police Service and the Municipal Police Services/Metro Police nationwide. He was promoted to the position of provincial manager: investigations in Nelspruit, Mpumalanga Province, South Africa.

Per-Anders Fransson received a PhD in medical science from Lund University, Sweden, in 2005 and the degree of associate professor in 2009. He presently holds a position as senior researcher at the Department of Clinical Sciences, Lund University. His research interests include the human central nervous system; sensory and motor systems; and function decline or adaption of these systems as an effect of physical and psychological stress, drugs, and new training paradigms.

Peter Fredriksson has, professionally, previously worked as both a firefighter and a paramedic before he started working as a police officer. He presently holds a position as a self-defense instructor at the Skåne County Police Department, Sweden, and as a developer of strategies concerning tactics, firearms, self-defense, and training in the Skåne County Police Department. His research interests include performance when under pressure and ways to conceptualize the adaptation needed for different, common, or dangerous situations.

Jonas Hansson has been a police officer since 1993. He has mainly been a patrol car police officer and is an instructor at the Basic Training Program for Police Officers at the Umeå University, Sweden. Hansson is also currently a PhD student at the Umea University.

Peter Johnstone is a professor of criminal justice at the University of North Texas, Denton, Texas. He holds a BA with honors, an LLM (master of law in international criminal law), and a PhD in comparative law. Peter came to the United States 11 years ago. His last appointments in the United Kingdom were as reader-in-law and jointly research fellow at the Institute of Advanced Legal Studies, University of London. Peter has written several books and more than 70 scholarly articles. Recent books include *The History of Criminal Justice* (5th edition) with Mark Jones (2011), *Drugs and Drug Trafficking* (2012), and *Crime and Policing Crime* (2013).

James Lewis holds a bachelor's degree in electronic systems and a master's degree in educational technology. He has written and published books and training manuals for corporate, academic, and law enforcement in the fields of cyber defense and computer and digital forensics. He teaches computer and digital forensics and cyber crime investigations for Baker College and is the state director for the Center for System Security and Information Assurance. He is also the founder and state director of the Michigan Collegiate Cyber Defense Network.

Mans Magnusson received an MD in 1981 and a PhD in 1986 from Lund University, Sweden; became associate professor in otorhinolaryngology in 1988; and received a full professorship in 1999. He presently holds a position as senior consultant and head of the division of Otorhinolaryngology and is head of the section of Senses, Neuroscience and Psychiatry of the Department of Clinical Sciences, Lund University. His research interests involve inner ear and vestibular disorders, postural control, and orientation.

Kim McLandress is the executive director of Chilliwack Restorative Justice, British Columbia, Canada. Kim has been with the organization since January 2000. She has a bachelor of arts degree in criminal justice from the University College of the Fraser Valley, British Columbia, Canada, and a master of arts degree in criminal justice with a focus on school-based restorative practices from the University of the Fraser Valley.

Moses Montesh was a member of the South African Police Service from 1993 to 2004. He joined the University of South Africa in February 2004. He holds a national diploma in public management, BA in police science, BA honors in police science, masters in public administration, and DLitt et Phil in police science. Professor Montesh has appeared on national television debating policing and criminal justice issues in South Africa. He has also appeared in Parliament presenting papers on matters relating to policing and has published papers on policing, public administration, and the military.

Stephen B. Perrott is a professor of psychology at the Mount Saint Vincent University, Nova Scotia, Canada. He obtained his doctorate in clinical psychology from McGill University in 1991 after previously serving as a member of the Halifax Police Force located in Nova Scotia, Canada, for 10 years. His research focuses on the psychology of policing, including police culture, stress, workplace violence, and community policing. Perrott is a frequent media commentator on criminal justice matters and is a lecturer and consultant to the Halifax Regional and Royal Canadian Mounted Police. His international efforts include work with the Philippine National Police in a sex tourism project in that country and a stint teaching psychology in The Gambia.

Lars-Folke Piledahl is a district police commissioner. He received the position as chief of staff of Skåne County Police Department, Sweden, in 2005, and since 2011 he has held the position as chief of South Skåne Police District. He is interested in education and strives to expand science and experience-based knowledge aimed at enhancing the safety of police officers by improving their skills through better training methods and equipment.

Darryl Plecas is the Royal Canadian Mounted Police university research chair in the School of Criminology and Criminal Justice at the University of the Fraser Valley, British Columbia, Canada. He is a recipient of the University of the Fraser Valley's Teaching Excellence Award, and in 2003 he received an Innovative Excellence in Teaching, Learning and Technology Award at the Fourteenth International Conference on College Teaching and Learning. He has served as an associate of the International Centre for Criminal Law Reform and Criminal Justice Policy at the University of British Columbia and as an expert observer to the 10th United Nations Congress on the Prevention and Treatment of Offenders.

Keith Robinson Superintendent Keith Robinson was transferred to the Upper Fraser Valley Regional Detachment, British Columbia, Canada, in

March 2007. In May 2008 he was appointed acting officer in charge of the Upper Fraser Valley Regional Detachment, and in 2009 he was appointed as the officer in charge of the Upper Fraser Valley Royal Canadian Mounted Police. Superintendent Robinson has extensive practical policing experience and has served as a general duty investigator.

Colette Squires is an organizational consultant and mediator, advising charities and nonprofit organizations on sustainability through effective program development and evaluation processes, restorative justice practices, and conflict services for individuals and organizations. She is a sessional faculty member at the Justice Institute of British Columbia and a researcher at the University of the Fraser Valley, British Columbia, Canada, where she completed her MA in criminal justice.

Adki Surender is a reader and the head of the Department of Public Administration at Vivek Vardhini College of Arts and Commerce, affiliated to the Osmania University, Hyderabad, India. Adki completed his master of philosophy and doctor of philosophy in public administration at the Osmania University. He worked on the topic "Traffic Administration and Role of Police" for his doctoral award, and his area of specialization is urban traffic administration.

Christopher Vas is Academic Director at the School of Management and Governance, Murdoch University-Perth, Australia. Previously, he was Program Director at the Crawford School of Public Policy at the Australian National University leading the Productivity and Policy Futures Program. He has extensive public policy experience having worked extensively in the Australian government, including the Australian Federal Police.

Acknowledgments

First of all, we express our deepest gratitude to all contributors who made this project possible. We want to thank all of the authors for the originality and the high quality of the work they produced. This book represents a major contribution to the field, and achieving this objective demanded patience as well as flexibility. We want to thank Andrei Abramov, chief of the NGO Branch at United Nations Department of Economic and Social Affairs, for his support in hosting the International Police Executive Symposium (IPES) at the United Nations. Also, we were delighted to work with Carolyn Spence and her team at CRC Press. The confidence they had in the book and their judicious advices were instrumental to the realization of this book. Also, we want to thank Dr. Melchor C. de Guzman, associate professor of the College at Brockport and book editor for the IPES who coordinated with the editors for the finishing of this book and James Albrecht for his work behind the scenes and for the New York and NYPD site visits and tour. Dr. Ana Mijovic-Das, MD, who designed and organized the entertainment provided to the spouses while delegates attended the symposium and the cultural program, deserves our heartfelt thanks. We extend our thanks to Minite Das, IPES director of public relations, who superbly managed the logistics for the meeting. Finally, we thank Captain Mark Hoffman, director of security at United Nations, for his diligence with security requirements and facilitating the logistics during the meeting.

In Memoriam

Jan Wiarda, *chief of police in the Netherlands, died on February 6, 2013 at the age of 72. Jan was a member of the board of the International Police Executive Symposium (IPES) from 1996 to 2013. Jan was a striking personality who made efforts throughout his life to improve police performance. His starting point was legitimacy above efficiency. Citizens should be able to trust that the police will always obey the rules applicable to them. An important motivation for him was meeting the wishes and expectations of citizens as much as possible. For Jan, this determined the effectiveness of the police. Close, problem-oriented cooperation with other organizations and especially citizens on the basis of good insight into underlying causes of safety problems was the main method we followed. This inspired his great interest in scientific knowledge in the field of policing. Jan's contributions to the debates on the IPES board were characterized by a great extent of erudition and social involvement and an innovative intellectual capacity. Jan was a policeman at heart and soul. After he retired—and until his death—Jan remained an active promoter of the legitimacy of police, for which he used his extensive network of authoritative experts. We miss Jan sorely.*

Introduction

Relations between Policing, Socioeconomic Developments, and Crime: An Introduction

This book regroups the work of several academics and police professionals who gathered at the 22nd International Police Executive Symposium in August 2012, which convened at the invitation of the United Nations Department of Economic and Social Affairs NGO Branch. The theme of the meeting was "Economic Development, Armed Violence, and Public Safety." The participants believed that policing is one of the most basic and essential avenues for improving the quality of life in all nations, rich and poor, modern and traditional, large and small, as well as peaceful and strife ridden. The delegates also noted that there are considerable challenges confronting the maintenance of public safety in areas undergoing economic development and/or experiencing armed violence. During the meeting, there was a shared concern for the need to understand the links between the police, the broader criminal justice systems, and the larger social context in which policing occurs. Focusing solely on any one topic or placing too much emphasis on one topic to the exclusion of another is, at best, unlikely to produce any sustainable improvement of public safety and may indeed be counterproductive.

Therefore, the book explores the interrelations between policing, socioeconomic development, and crime. More precisely, the project places an emphasis on these complex interrelations by providing worldwide perspectives and case studies. In relation to these three central topics, authors contributing to this book address specific issues, such as youth violence in society, economic downturn and global crime trends, restorative justice and recidivism, community-based policing, investigation techniques applied to financial crimes, policing gang violence, implementation of the rule of law in postconflict countries, and policing transportation infrastructures. All of these issues are by-products of changes that occurred at socioeconomic, policing, and criminal levels. Also, the book presents these issues by organizing its chapters according to their regional perspectives: global, modern democracies, emerging democracies, and newly industrialized countries. This categorization provides the opportunity to shed light on existing regional contrasts related to the interrelations between and underlying factors of policing, fluctuations in socioeconomic development, and crime.

This introduction chapter explores the theoretical and conceptual frameworks related to the topics of this book by breaking them down into three sections. In the first segment, we explore classic and new literature that is relevant to the relation between socioeconomic development and crime. More precisely, we examine how socioeconomic changes affect deviance and crime, as well as how phenomena such as industrialization, urbanization, socioeconomic policy, business cycles, and political instability might affect crime trends. At first sight, one might consider these elements as being only loosely related to policing; but, in fact, they are critically connected because they have the power to transform the society and consequently require reforms in police mission, strategy, and practice. The second section addresses the relation between socioeconomic developments and policing by focusing on the impact of socioeconomic conditions on the transformation of policing and the evolution of its mission. We pay attention to phenomena such as the professionalization of police, bureaucratization and expansion of police activity, commodification of public security, and globalization of security assemblage. The third segment of this chapter focuses on the relation between policing and crime by describing the evolution of police management models and development of strategies to address crime and public expectations of law enforcement effectiveness. Finally, the last section proposes a brief overview of the organization of the book.

Socioeconomic Developments and Crime

The relationship between the economy and crime is a complex one, which demands a careful review of individual, cultural, and structural factors that are at play. First, Durkheim (1982/1895) studied the impact of significant change in societies on social pathologies and crime. Macrosociological transformations such as population growth, immigration flux, urbanization, and industrialization—which are often associated with economic development—can influence interactions between groups within the society to provoke a breakdown of common norms and values (anomie). According to Durkheim, these structural changes tend to alienate individuals by putting them into ill-suited situations, such as social isolation and poor working conditions, which incite the individuals to take self-corrective action to cope with unhappiness. At the collective level, such actions can translate into social disorders. At the individual level, these actions can take the form of deviant behaviors, such as suicide or crime. A thought-provoking statement made by Durkheim (1982/1895) about crime is that it is "bound up with the fundamental conditions of all social life" (p. 98). The author further asserts that crime or criminals should not be considered as an evil that must be suppressed but should rather be considered as an inevitable or normal social function to express a need for change or a reaction to change.

Second, thriving or depressed economic conditions in a given country have an impact on individuals' environments by modifying the nature of opportunities available to those who are socially encouraged, such as access to employment and their ability to achieve personal aspirations. According to strain theory, at the individual level criminal or deviant behaviors arise when individuals experience adverse conditions in attempting to achieve valued goals of a society, such as economic success or at least financial sustainability. For example, Merton (1968) argues that in some societies legitimate means to achieve material success are not uniformly distributed among social classes or institutions, a discrepancy that generates strain and pressures disadvantaged individuals to adopt nonlegitimate coping strategies. Agnew (1992), who focuses more on emotions and norms instead of cultural values, contends that an individual's failure to achieve valued goals (financial success), the removal of positive-valued stimuli (salary), and the potential of facing negative stimuli (social rejection) will lead to strain. It is important to note that strain can be related to a unique but overwhelming event (unemployment or handicap) or to small annoyances that can accumulate over time leading to frustration, dissatisfaction, resentment, and anger—critical emotions for the perpetration of some crimes (Akers, 2000). Also, the author suggests that individual characteristics and the nature of strain-related events are central in explaining how economics can influence an individual's motivation to engage in criminal activities.

Third, Messner and Rosenfeld (1994) revisit Merton's theory of anomie to refocus on the criminogenic influence of social institutions in American society (e.g., polity, family, school, and church) and assert that society is failing to achieve its socialization mission because it is promoting individualistic and pecuniary objectives. More precisely, Messner and Rosenfeld (1994) contend that "education is regarded largely as a means to occupational attainment, which in turn is valued primarily insofar as it promises economic rewards" (p. 78). Messner and Rosenfeld's anomie theory implies that cultural pressure to secure monetary rewards, combined with weak controls from non-economic social institutions, fosters inevitable criminal activity.

In an attempt to test this new theoretical framework, studies have examined if a governmental policy of income redistribution might temper the pursuit of private economic interests and also have a negative impact on crime rates in the communities receiving the redistributed resources. Messner and Rosenfeld (1997) and Savolainen (2000) have examined the "welfare-state" index comprising both the relative and the absolute wealth distribution expenditures made by each country. In their analyses, they study several countries, including the country's homicide rates, relative prosperity, and income disparities in homes for both the majority and minority communities. Their results show that economic inequality between individuals has a positive correlation with homicide rate, but this is only in those countries in which government spending for "social security" is very weak (relative to the wealth of the society as a whole and the country's level of economic development). Other studies have demonstrated that the per capita rate of juvenile homicides in the 39 most economically developed countries varies inversely to the relative spending that their governments invest in citizens' social welfare (Fiala & LaFree, 1988). Another study testing the per capita rate of homicide (for both sexes and all age groups) in 18 economically developed countries devoted to wealth distribution also found that the relationship varies inversely (Pampel & Gartner, 1995).

Several studies have scrutinized the impact of economic cycles, which affect economic development (Deaton, 2010), on crime rates throughout the past 40 years. Some researches suggest that although significant economic downturns can result in an increase in crime rates, such an increase is not always the case (Cook & Zarkin, 1985; Chiricos & Delone, 1992; Bushway, Cook, & Phillips, 2010; Smith, Devine, & Sheley, 1992). On the one hand, Cantor and Land (1985) found that an augmentation of unemployment rates might lead to an increase in crime rates in uncertain conditions. On the other hand, the work of Lafree (1998) shows that the cycle of economic expansion in the United States coincides with a significant increase in crime and delinquency rates. Conversely, Blumstein and Wallman (2006) showed that the 1990's economic growth corresponded with a 30-year low in crime rates. During the same period, two critical economic growth cycles provoked contradicting effects on crime rates. Although several commonly considered indicators of economic adversity do have effects on crime rates, these effects differ depending on the rates of inflation and levels of objective risk (Baumer, Wolff, & Rosenfeld, 2013).

It is true that in several countries stagnation and rising crime rates can be attributed to failing economic reform or programs. However, in other countries—such as those in Africa and South America—the causes are more diverse, although some common features do emerge. Studies conducted by Azam, Berthelemy, and Calipel (1996); Easterly and Levine (1997); and Temple (1998), as well as Collier and Gunning (1999), investigated the influence of economic growth in Africa, and they all found that violence and unrest affect economic growth negatively. Ayres (1998) reports similar results for Latin America and concludes that crime and violence are considered as major obstacles to development in Latin American and Caribbean countries. Kaufman (2004) performed a limited analysis on the Executive Opinion Survey (EOS) concerning the report by firms on costs of terrorism, common crime, and organized crime to business, as well as their reports on the prevalence of money laundering through the banking and nonbanking (informal financial) sectors. The research shows a close association between both organized crime and common crime and the quality of domestic institutions. Kaufman found a strong correlation between the quality of police organizations and the economic harm caused by organized crime in a given country.

Studies conducted by Stewart and Fitzgerald (2001) and Stewart (2001) examine the relationship between economic development and insecurity— broadly conceptualized as political violence and violent crimes—among several undeveloped countries from Africa, Asia, and South America. One of Stewart's main observations is that economic development is almost always negatively affected by armed violence and that specific sectors such as agriculture, manufacturing, and exports are often the most adversely affected. Other economic studies point out that armed violence tends to be greater among countries with lower per capita incomes, lower life expectancy, and lower economic growth (Nafziger & Auvinen, 2000; Collier & Hoeffler, 2000). Also, studies have shown that armed violence occurs more frequently when wealth distribution is highly unequal and when this inequality increases among ethnic or religious groups over time (Stewart, 2001).

Finally, some studies found that violence can result from a failure of the state to implement or maintain an established social contract that interrupts the delivery of social services and economic benefits (Addison & Murshed, 2001; Nafziger & Auvinen, 2002). In such a context, an increase in poverty and a diminution of public services can impact the rate of violence, especially if the state's benefits only reach a small number of individuals (e.g., regime supporters). Countries where economic development is nonexistent, such as failing or failed states, also represent a serious challenge for the security of their people and more broadly human security (United Nations Development Program, 1994). Failed states cumulate a series of heavy disadvantages such as limited options and progress in areas such as education, employment, health, and technology. In these cases, most of the missing state infrastructures, services, and benefits distribution have been destroyed. These conditions foster vicious cycles of imbalanced development and generate conditions for armed violence that spurs from organized crime activities or political violence. According to Alkire (2003), economic development and human security share three fundamental components: (1) both are people centered, which means that individuals should be empowered agents in security and economic processes; (2) development and human security should address the individual's dignity and reduce vulnerabilities; and (3) both concepts consider poverty and inequality to be the root causes of an individual's vulnerability to violence and fear.

Economic Development and Policing

Throughout the centuries, the evolution of policing and police power has been affected not only by the nature of political systems but also by economic forces. For example, an increase in commercial maritime activities on the Thames River at the end of the eighteenth century and a sharp augmentation of stolen cargo on the London Docks and piracy activities on the Thames River led to the establishment of the Thames River Police (Critchley, 1967; Walsh, 1994). The foundation of this unit paved the way to a more professionalized and structured police force in England by introducing the first full-time salaried police officers. This newly established police force was also a response to the shortcomings of the Bow Street Runners, who were working based on stipends and not necessarily assigned to patrol work. This approach had cost benefits in terms of the economic consequences of criminal activity in the London Pool, and the possibility of effectively preventing these crimes by having a more reliable police force eventually became a source of inspiration to Sir Robert Peel three decades later (Critchley, 1967).

The emergence of modern policing coincides with the industrialization era and the subsequent development of new technologies. Between 1770 and 1880, several Western countries experienced significant demographic and sociopolitical changes as a result of the Industrial Revolution. This unprecedented economic development generated a broad population migration from rural areas toward cities and towns that soon became new economic centers. However, this socioeconomic phenomenon also generated strong waves of disorder, larceny, and various misconducts (such as public drunkenness, fights, prostitution, and theft) that prompted the creation of public police forces (Shelley, 1981). Moreover, criminal activities rapidly spread due to the new transportation sectors of the Industrial Revolution, where criminals were more common on roads, railways, and canals. This crime expansion made police forces diversify their crime prevention strategies and create new specialized divisions. Also, the emergence of social movements such as labor and women's movements (Blumer, 1990) occurred in the industrialization eras. Between 1850 and 1914, urban police forces were confronted with large-scale strikes organized by workers and civil disobedience actions conducted by women. Both movements were able to challenge the relevance of police crowd control tactics and understanding of protesters. The violence emanating from the confrontations between these social groups and the police forces became a highly politicized issue that led to political contentions and police reforms (Walker & Katz, 2012).

During and after World Wars I and II, most Western countries experienced what Johnston (1992) called the "rebirth of private policing." During the two wars, fear of sabotage and espionage encouraged corporations and states to increase security throughout private security firms. After 1960, private security continued to emerge due to the need for more customized and distinctive protection for individuals and their properties: the commodification of security (Loader, 1999; Shearing & Stenning, 1981; Shearing & Wood, 2007). The need was primarily generated by an expansion of the economy, an increase of government regulations in different industry sectors, and a significant augmentation of crime rates over the same three decades. Crime prevention became the core business strategy of the private security sector in the booming economy of the second half of the twentieth century. Also, since the 1980s the public debt of most Western countries skyrocketed, forcing several local and national governments to downsize their activities, including policing. On the one hand, the downsizing of police resources coincided with the large-scale inception of computer technology and more sophisticated approaches, such as CompStat, to fight crime from a problem-solving perspective (Weisburd, Mastrofski, McNally, Greenspan, & Willis, 2003). On the other hand, the diminution of public security services also contributed to the creation of a vacuum that was rapidly filled by the private sector in the form of outsourcing. In other words, the state simply let private firms become the sole source of security providers in certain industry sectors.

More recently, the economic downturn of 2008 had a direct impact on North American law enforcement agencies at three levels: (1) reduction of police staffing though layoffs, mandatory furloughs, staffing attrition, and reductions in the ratio of police officers by population served; (2) change in organizational management through consolidation of local police departments (mergers); and (3) transformation of the delivery of services, such as integrating more civilian personnel, recruiting volunteers, incorporating technology to operational decision making, and enhancing collaboration between the police and the private sector (Community Oriented Policing Services, 2011). Some public police organizations have been mandated to find ways to reduce their operational costs or to find alternative sources of funding. Several police agencies in North America have therefore developed à la carte services for which police work is now remunerated by a third-party agency to accommodate special security needs, such as highway escorts for oversized freight, urban festivals and concerts, and VIP protection, among others (Gans, 2000; Gabrosky, 2004; Ayling & Shearing, 2008). Despite the fact that the commercialization of public security services raises concerns related to accountability and impartiality of security providers (Loader & Walker, 2006; Stenning, 2000), the private security industry has expanded at the global scale to become in the twenty-first century a multibillion-dollar industry by selling alarm system protection, providing risk analysis, and offering armed guard protection, among other services (Jones & Newburn, 2006; Loader, 2000; Manning, 2006).

Today's global security assemblages (Abrahamsen & Williams, 2009)—boosted by the globalization of markets—contribute directly to the reconfiguration of the governance of security at the national level by modifying the relationship between security provisions and states' sovereignty. For example, the research by Abrahamsen and Williams (2009) shows that in Nigeria and Sierra Leone the diversity of "security agents and normativities interact, cooperate and compete, to produce new institutions, practices, and forms of security governance" (p. 1). Also, the creation of new economic regions, like trade zones, can have a direct impact on police reform (Anderson, den Boer,

Cullen, Gilmore, Raab, & Walker, 1995; Dorn, 1996; Busch, 1988; Fijnaut, 2004; den Boer, 2008). The establishment of the European Union and its impact on the restructuring of regional economies into common markets increased drastically the internationalization of police activity due to the reconfiguration of border surveillance; partial reform of legal systems to allow transnational policing to take place in several countries; and creation of new structures such as Europol, Eurojust, and Frontex (Benyon, 1994; Bigo, 1996; Bigo, 2002; Deflem, 2002; Lemieux, 2010a).

Finally, it is critical to address the complex relationship between economic development and policing in emerging democracies and transitioning countries. According to Bayley (1990), in developing countries the security regime orientation of police forces results in shifting resources from general safety considerations to the preservation of political elites and to the achievement of their narrow, self-serving agendas. Police are used for the repression, rather than protection, of individuals, increasing the fear of being victimized. Weak economic opportunities and low wages expose police institutions to rampant corruption that compromises citizens' safety and security. When the state faces resource limitations and fails to meet the material needs of police organizations, a lower incentive for police officers to provide broad security is generated and more protection-focused, service-oriented forms of policing are favored. In these particular cases, weak police institutions can accentuate an already dysfunctional economy by not creating a safe environment where merchants and consumers can conduct their transactions, not enforcing contractual laws, and not investigating public funds embezzlement.

Also, police organizations with postcolonial origins retain a long-standing influence of imperial models in their development. Policing in weak states is influenced by foreign development aid and military assistance. Developing countries are particularly vulnerable to the agendas of wealthier foreign states, corporations, and institutions. Several regimes are accepting military and law enforcement assistance in return for influence over domestic policy or access to resources (Job, 1992; Goldsmith, 2002). Foreign interventions can also take the form of private security agencies deploying mercenary troops or by simply protecting Western interests, such as embassies; resource extraction industries; and the protection of industry and critical infrastructures such as seaports, airports, and pipelines.

Crime and Policing

It is widely acknowledged in the literature that police strength is not only determined by crime rates but also by the population density, cultural heterogeneity, social inequality, territorial extent, and particular security issues associated with aggressive social groups (Bayley, 1990). In North America, studies have shown that police strength tends to evolve over time, mainly due to socioeconomic factors (Ruddell & Thomas, 2010; McCarty, Ren, & Zhao, 2012; Zhao, Ren, & Lovrich, 2012). Also, a recent cross-national study demonstrated that political factors, such as corruption and the presence of a black market, are significantly associated with police strength or lack thereof (Ruddell & Thomas, 2009). Finally, police agencies facing actual or potential social conflicts emanating from ethnic, religious, and nationalistic struggles tend to have the highest level of strength measured in terms of surveillance and intrusive measures. For example, Lemieux (2008) showed that police organizations evolving in hostile environments tend to develop more proactive and intrusive capabilities through undercover activities and intelligence collection.

In general, crime that is judged less serious, such as several types of property crimes and fraud, is less prioritized by police agencies, which prefer to focus on more serious crimes that generate a greater harm to the community and have a better chance to be successfully prosecuted. In response to environmental pressures, police focus on developing a proactive doctrine, which makes it possible to coordinate crime-fighting operations and the allocation of resources (Crawford, 1997). During 1970–1980, two proactive models surfaced: "community-oriented" and "problem-oriented" policing (Goldstein, 1979; Skogan, 2004). These complementary policies focus on crime prevention by increasing the accessibility of police officers to citizens and by addressing community concerns through the identification and analysis of underlying problems related to disorder and crime. Most of the strategies employed by law enforcement were focusing on crime prevention in "hot spot" areas by addressing a wide array of issues ranging from auto theft and robberies to youth delinquency and gang violence.

During the 1990s, we witnessed the expansion of criminal analysis techniques as the result of disillusionment regarding the effectiveness of the earlier crime prevention approach in the 1980s, that is, the inability of police to anticipate and understand crime displacement, skyrocketing crime rates, and organized crime activities. The many scandals concerning interrogation techniques, failed surveillance of repeat offenders, and actions committed by "prolific" criminals also contributed to the development of "intelligence-led policing" (Audit Commission, 1993; Home Office, 1989; Home Office, 1995; Maguire, 2000). In the 1990s, it was also noted that a relatively low number of offenders were responsible for a substantial number of crimes reported to the police. Efforts were therefore made to dissuade or neutralize these individuals to reduce overall crime rates and to generate a greater impact on specific crime-related problems. Lemieux (2008) shows that certain criminal phenomena, such as serial crimes, repeat offenders, and violent organized crime activities combined with an amplification of media coverage, and growing concerns among populations contributed to a shift in the police management model and to a new security policy toward more surveillance and proactive policing. Focused law enforcement activities on particular forms of crime as well as the monitoring of ethnic communities, street gangs, and high-profile criminals were considered as the core elements of a strategic thinking approach and knowledge-based policing (Ratcliffe, 2009; Williamson, 2008). However, the intelligence-led policing approach can create frictions within a community if implemented incorrectly due to racial profiling practices related to searches and frisks, civil rights violations, and privacy issues.

At the international level, law enforcement agencies are now using networks of officers to facilitate police cooperation by exchanging intelligence on transnational crime and international criminal organizations (Robertson, 1994). These networks enable police agencies to identify specific criminal activity within specific criminal groups and to develop a knowledge-based approach about actual or potential criminal activity not necessarily because it took place within their jurisdiction but because it occurred in another country, which has made investigation results available to foreign colleagues. International police cooperation allows police operations to disregard national boundaries to operate on an international scale and to develop a more informed approach, which can guide the prioritizing and targeting of criminal groups (Lemieux, 2010b). According to Nadelmann's (1992; 1993) work, a path-finding study in the fight against drug trafficking, agents from the U.S. Drug Enforcement Administration assigned to Latin America employed four tactics to avoid dealing with corrupt police organizations in the region: (1) collaboration with the least corrupt police departments and/or a rotation between police services; (2) establishment of relationships based on trust and friendship with local officers; (3) exploitation of the competition between different national law enforcement agencies; and (4) implementation of extensive operations during regime changes, when the spread of corruption is typically at its lowest point.

However, police cooperation and law enforcement in general are virtually nonexistent in postconflict and unstable countries, mainly due to the fact that police organizations have been decimated by armed violence and crippled by years of underfinancing. Also, police organizations and national security agencies often face insurmountable challenges in restoring trust and establishing their legitimacy due to the atrocities that rogue elements of the security forces may have committed against the civilian population or against the state during the conflict (Robin, 2009). Further, some of the policing tasks in a postconflict environment regularly require military support, which can often confuse or exacerbate already tense relations between police and citizens (O'Neil, 2005). Even with international support, it can take several years to achieve a complete reform of security forces due to the inadequacy of training, low wages and/or corruption, lack of infrastructure (lack of police stations), lack of equipment, and lack of trustworthy human resources (Stodiek, 2006). Reestablishing confidence and legitimacy in police organizations in postconflict countries cannot happen without visible success in combating crime and ending the climate of impunity toward the regime (Stanley, 1999; Stodiek, 2006). The expected role of police is also to foster the conditions necessary for the reconciliation and reconstruction of the community by ensuring fairness in the enforcement of laws and contributing directly to make the environment safer (Mani, 1999). Reinstating or replacing security organizations in transition times is complex and depends on a broad range of social, political, economical, and organizational factors that are conducive to a successful reform of police.

Outline of the Book

The previous sections provide a comprehensive—but certainly not exhaustive—conceptual framework that helps to better understand the foundations of each chapter included in this book. The relationships between economic development, crime, and policing are critical to better interpret how this dynamic affects the evolution of the need for more or less public safety. We clearly saw in this chapter that societies face different challenges relevant to the dynamics of the economy, crimes rates, and nature of policing. Figure I.1 helps to conceptualize these interactions between the central elements of this book. In this introduction, we have scrutinized the existing literature that mostly pertains to the overlapping areas corresponding to the overlapping areas of numbers 1, 2, and 3. The chapters of this book address in detail the

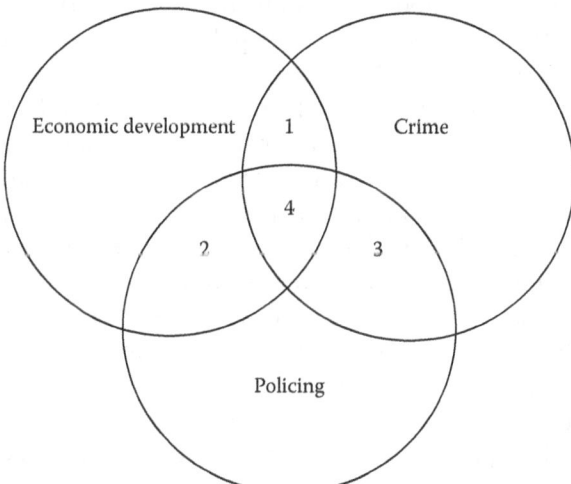

Figure I.1 Areas of interaction between economic development, policing, and crime and armed violence.

implications for each of these overlapping areas. As a collective effort, this book in its entirety will generate conclusions that are related to the overlapping area number 4, which corresponds to the combined effects of economic development, crime, and policing that are most likely to lead to potentially crucial reforms of police systems.

The chapters of this book are organized into sections according to a regional perspective where the focus of the study emanates from and an overall global perspective, from advanced democracies, emerging democracies, and newly industrialized countries. The first section of the book addresses international trends related to crime, economics, and social challenges that can directly influence the response of police. In the first chapter, Frederic Lemieux analyzes the relationship between economic recession and homicides in globalized cities. More precisely, the author explores several research propositions regarding the relationship between the globalization of cities and the impact of a recession on local economies, globalization and local inequalities, and globalization and local homicide rates. The implication of this chapter is mainly connected to area 1 of Figure I.1; but it also has direct implications for public safety (area 2) as economic downturns have negative impacts on police organizations, as demonstrated in the section "Economic Development and Policing" of this introduction. In the second chapter, Christopher Vas reflects on the implications and opportunities for criminal justice policy makers in continuing to be proactive and at the same time transforming their policies to better prepare for future social challenges. More precisely, the author argues that there is a need for a transition from the traditional reactive approaches of law enforcement toward preempting and preventing crime by adopting a technology-driven response associated with a societal network-based modus operandi. This chapter primarily addresses issues related to the relationships between policing, social control strategies, and crime (area 3 presented in Figure I.1).

The second section of this book focuses on strategies deployed by law enforcement and justice systems to improve economic and social development in advanced democracies. In this section, Chapters 3 and 4 provide more of a strategic understanding and application of change in policing tactics, whereas Chapters 5, 6, and 7 have a more applied or operational perspective. In Chapter 3, Peter Johnstone scrutinizes the assertion that Sir Robert Peel and the Metropolitan Police Act of 1829 had an overwhelming influence on the U.S. police and criminal justice system. The author suggests that the influence of Peel is precedential but represents only one part of a far more complex policing history for the United States. Peter Johnstone argues that the U.S. police system is the product of several modern developments in conjunction with public and private law enforcement responses of greater antiquity that were transported, in stages, and absorbed into the policing landscape of the United States. The chapter focuses mainly on the evolution of policing in the United States in conjunction with sociopolitical and socioeconomic changes (area 2 in Figure I.1). In Chapter 4, Stephen B. Perrott explores the discrepancy between the claim that many police officials adhere to the community-oriented policing model and to the implementation of strategies that are significantly removed from this model, which is more aggressive and less community oriented. The author argues that an erroneous rationale is offered as to why police forces are motivated to adhere to the community-based policing mantle despite there being evidence to the contrary. Perrott reflects on the value of community policing and the necessity to move on a consent-based type of policing consistent with the values of Western democracies. The chapter focuses mainly on the political rhetoric about police–community relations and managerial discourse of crime prevention that have shaped policing strategies in the past decades (area 3 in Figure I.1).

In Chapter 5, Keith Robinson, Darryl Plecas, Colette Squires, and Kim McLandress examine the impact of restorative justice on recidivism and police resourcing. More precisely, the authors analyze shoplifting cases from a Canadian restorative justice program and discover that precharge restorative justice may have greater efficacy for repeat and adult offenders compared to first-time youth offenders only. This chapter presents a useful scenario of how some justice programs oriented toward offenders can evolve to address concurrent issues related to police resources (area 3 in Figure I.1). In Chapter 6, James Lewis explores the evolving nature of criminal activities that emanates from the exploitation of new information technologies, such as cyberespionage. More precisely, the author adopts a demonstrative approach in which he displays how different types of cyberespionage can be committed and concealed. This chapter focuses on the evolution of crime and how police techniques, as well as investigative strategies, can be adapted by learning from past experiences related to similar offenses (area 3 in Figure I.1). In Chapter 7, Colette Squires and Darryl Plecas examine a case study related to strategies deployed to suppress local gang activities. More precisely, the authors provide a detailed analysis of the multidimensional gang deterrence strategy implemented by the Abbotsford Police Department in British Columbia, Canada. The chapter proposes an exhaustive description of the history, rationale, methods, and lessons learned from the program named "Death by a Thousand Cuts" (area 3 in Figure I.1).

In Chapter 8, Jonas Hansson examines traditions and fundamental elements in basic police training programs. More precisely, the study focuses on police training in Sweden and scrutinizes police students' opinions about the teaching and lessons that they receive during basic training. This study aims to contribute new knowledge about teaching and learning in police training. The chapter addresses a broader issue related to the creation of professional identity, culture, and relevance in a society where social, political, and economic developments constantly challenge police knowledge and redefine the role of law enforcement (area 2 in Figure I.1). In Chapter 9, Johan Bertilsson, Peter Fredriksson, Lars-Folke Piledahl, Mans Magnusson, and Per-Anders Fransson discuss the opportunities, experiences, and challenges of having research collaborations between police authorities and universities. Acknowledging a growing complexity of social upheaval, which in turn presents a number of challenges to police authorities around the world, the authors suggest that collaborations between police authorities and universities can provide a base for mutual exchange of recent scientific discoveries and instigate new research projects within areas of special relevance for law enforcement and society. According to the authors, such cooperation provides opportunities for law enforcement personnel to gain experience in general scientific methods and procedures. Again, this chapter focuses on how police can develop a better understanding of the overall society through knowledge from the academia and learn from changing disciplines and domains (area 2 in Figure I.1).

The third section addresses strategies deployed by law enforcement and the justice system to improve economic and social development in emerging democracies and newly industrialized countries. In Chapter 10, James F. Albrecht proposes an evaluation of the challenges in policing a postconflict developing democracy. More precisely, the author examines the case of Kosovo through the lenses of justice administration and rule of law. He argues that despite the establishment of functioning professional police, the local Kosovo Police and international law enforcement professionals are still plagued by overwhelming caseloads involving government-sustained organized crime, war crimes, and corruption. By analyzing the successes and challenges in establishing and coordinating the rule of law in Kosovo, the chapter provides insight into similar issues faced by other postconflict developing democracies across the globe. Finally, the chapter proposes a number of recommendations that aim at moving Kosovo into a more effective democratic future (area 3 in Figure I.1).

In Chapter 11, Setlhomamaru Isaac Dintwe proposes to examine the effectiveness of anticorruption programs in South Africa. More precisely, the author analyzes the consequences of anticorruption programs introduced after the democratization of the country. The aim of this study is to establish whether the anticorruption program employed by the South African government encapsulates the internationally accepted elements reminiscent of anticorruption programs worldwide and whether this strategy is effective enough to thwart public corruption in South Africa (area 1 in Figure I.1). In Chapter 12, Johanna Berning and Moses Montesh scrutinize the role and action taken by anticorruption agencies after the enactment of several acts, programs, and strategies in South Africa. The authors examine the roles and functions of several agencies, such as the police, Asset

Forfeiture Unit, Special Investigating Unit, auditor general, Public Service Commission, Directorate of Special Operations, and Directorate for Priority Crime Investigation. This chapter mainly focuses on the enforcement of relatively new anticorruption laws and the implementation of strategies to combat pervasive corruption activities (area 3 in Figure I.1). In Chapter 13, Moses Montesh and Johanna Berning propose to analyze the outcomes of the 1996 National Crime Prevention Strategy (NCPS), as well as suggesting a separate Youth Crime Prevention Strategy for South Africa. More precisely, the authors identify the shortcomings of NCPS related to youth delinquency and demonstrate that without a proper crime prevention strategy adapted to juveniles the South African police and criminal justice system will not be able to effectively address this type of crime alone (area 3 in Figure I.1). Finally, in Chapter 14 Adki Surender explores how police organizations in India address the consequences of urbanization and rapid population growth on the safety of infrastructure. More precisely, in the light of the United Nations' Global Plan for the Decade of Action for Road Safety 2011–2020, the author discusses the implications of the police's role in road management, road and vehicle safety standards, and population education on responsible behaviors on roads (drivers, passengers, and pedestrians) in the metropolitan area of Hyderabad, India. This chapter mainly focuses on the establishment of new initiatives and the enforcement of road regulations to improve safety on motorways and to reduce the number of casualties related to car accidents (area 3 in Figure I.1).

In conclusion, the editors of this book are providing a comprehensive review of fundamental elements related to police reform and how it might affect society, as well as the role of society in reforming police systems. The conclusion also highlights how the chapters of this book apply to these fundamental elements and how they are related to the area number 4 in Figure I.1. Finally, building on the chapters included in this book and from a larger body of literature, the editors suggest new directions for the elaboration of such a broad research agenda.

References

Abrahamsen, R., & Williams, M. (2009). Security beyond the state: Global security assemblages in international politics. *International Political Sociology*, 3, 1–17.

Addison, T., & Murshed, M. S. (2001). *From Conflict to Reconstruction: Reviving the Social Contract.* (WIDER Discussion Paper 2001/48). Helsinki, Finland: WIDER.

Agnew, R. (1992). Foundation for a general strain theory of crime and delinquency. *Criminology*. 30, 47–88.

Akers, R. L. (2000). *Criminological Theories: Introduction, Evaluation, and Application.* (3rd ed.). Los Angeles, CA: Roxbury Publishing.

Alkire, S. (2003). *A Conceptual Framework for Human Security*. Centre for Research on inequality, Human Security and Ethnicity (CRSE), London, United Kingdom: University of Oxford.

Anderson, M., den Boer, M., Cullen, P., Gilmore, W. C., Raab, C., & Walker, N. (1995). *Policing the European Union*. Oxford, United Kingdom: Clarendon Press.

Audit Commission. (1993). *Helping with Enquiries. Tackling Crime Effectively*. London, United Kingdom: HMSO.

Ayling, J., & Shearing, C. (2008). Taking care of business: Public police as commercial security vendors. *Criminology & Criminal Justice, 8*(1), 27–50.

Ayres, R. L. (1998). *Crime and Violence as Development Issues in Latin America*. Latin American and Caribbean Studies, Washington, DC: World Bank.

Azam, J. P., Berthelemy, J. C., & Calipel, S. (1996). Risque politique et croissance en Afrique. Revue economique (Economic Journal), 3, 819–829.

Baumer, E. P., Wolff, K. T., & Rosenfeld, R. (2013). Are the criminogenic consequences of economic downturns conditional? Assessing potential moderators of the link between adverse economic conditions and crime rates. In R. Rosenfeld, M. Edberg, X. Fang, & C. Florence. (Eds.), *Macroeconomic Effects on Youth Violence*. New York: NYU Press.

Bayley, D. (1990). *Patterns of Policing: A Comparative International Analysis*. New Brunswick, NJ: Rutgers University Press.

Benyon, J. (1994). Policing the European Union: The changing basis of cooperation on law enforcement. *International Affairs, 70*(3), 497–517.

Bigo, D. (1996). *Polices en réseaux: l'expérience Européenne*. Paris, France: Presse de science Po.

Bigo, D. (2002). Border regimes and security in an enlarged European community. In J. Zielonka (Ed.), *Europe Unbound: Enlarging and Reshaping the Boundaries of the European Union* (pp. 213–239). New York: Routledge.

Blumer, H. (1990). *Industrialization As an Agent of Social Change: A Critical Analysis*. Livingston, NJ: Transaction Publishers.

Blumstein, A., & Wallman, J. (2006). The crime drop and beyond. *Annual Review of Law and Social Science, 2*, 125–146.

Busch, H. (1988). Von Interpol zu TREVI: Polizeiliche Zusammenarbeit in Europa. Bürgerrechte und Polizei/CILIP, 30, 38–55.

Bushway, S., Cook, P., & Phillips, M. (2010). *The Net Effect of the Business Cycle on Crime and Violence*. Duke Department of Economics Research Paper. Retrieved on August 4, 2014 from http://ssrn.com/abstract=1655741.

Cantor, D., & Land, K. C. (1985). Unemployment and crime rates in the post-World War II United States. *American Sociological Review, 50*, 317–332.

Chiricos, T., & Delone, M. (1992). Labor surplus and punishment: A review and assessment of theory and evidence. *Social Problems, 39*(4), 421–446.

Collier, P., & Gunning, J. (1999). Explaining African economic performance. *Journal of Economic Literature, 37*(1), 64–111.

Collier, P., & Hoeffler, A. (2000). Greed and grievance in civil war. World Bank, 30(11), 1845–1864.

Community Oriented Policing Services. (2011). *The Impact of Economic Downturn of American Police Agencies*. Washington, DC: U.S. Department of Justice Office of Community Oriented Policing Services.

Cook, P. J., & Zarkin, G. (1985). Crime and the business cycle. *Journal of Legal Studies*, *14*(1), 115–128.

Crawford, A. (1997). *The Local Governance of Crime: Appeals to Community and Partnerships*. Oxford, United Kingdom: Clarendon Press.

Critchley, T. A. (1967). *A History of Police in England and Wales*. London, United Kingdom: Constable.

Deaton, A. (2010). "Understanding the Mechanisms of Economic Development," *Journal of Economic Perspectives, American Economic Association*, *24*(3): 3–16.

Deflem, M. (2002). *Policing World Society: Historical Foundations of International Police Cooperation*. Oxford, United Kingdom: Oxford University Press.

den Boer, M. (2008). Governing transnational law enforcement in the EU: Accountability after the fuse between internal and external security. In M. den Boer & J. Wilde (Eds.), *The Viability of Human Security* (pp. 63–78). Amsterdam, the Netherlands: Amsterdam University Press.

Dorn, N. (1996). The EU, Home Affairs and the 1996: Intergovernmental convergence or federal diversity? In N. Dorn, J. Jepsen, & E. Savona (Eds.), *European Drug Policies and Enforcement* (pp. 153–170). New York: St. Martin's Press.

Durkheim, E. (1982/1895). *The Rules of Sociological Method*. New York: Free Press.

Easterly, W., & Levine, R. (1997). Africa's growth tragedy: Policies and ethnic divisions. *Quarterly Journal of Economics*, *112*(4), 1203–1250.

Fiala, R., & LaFree, G. (1988). Cross-national determinants of child homicide. *American Sociological Review*, *53*, 432–445.

Fijnaut, C. (2004). Police co-operation and the area of freedom, security and justice. In N. Walker (Ed.), *Europe's Area of Freedom, Security and Justice* (pp. 241–282). Oxford, United Kingdom: Oxford University Press.

Gans, J. (2000). Privately paid public policing: Law and practice. *Policing and Society*, *10*(2), 183–206.

Grabosky, P. N. (2004). Toward a theory of public/private interaction in policing. In J. McCord (Ed.), *Beyond Empiricism: Institutions and Intentions in the Study of Crime* (pp. 69–82). Advances in Criminological Theory, Piscataway, NJ: Transaction Books.

Goldsmith, A. (2002). Policing weak states: Citizen safety and state responsibility. *Policing and Society*, *13*(1), 3–21.

Goldstein, H. (1979). Improving policing: A problem oriented approach. *Crime and Delinquency*, *25*(2), 236–258.

Home Office. (1989). *Criminal and Custodial Careers of Those Born in 1953, 1958 and 1963*. Statistical Bulletin, London, United Kingdom: Home Office.

Home Office. (1995). *Criminal Careers of Those Born between 1953 and 1973*. Statistical Bulletin, London, United Kingdom: Home Office.

Job, B. (1992). *The Insecurity Dilemma: National Security of Third World States*. Boulder, CO: Kumarian Press.

Johnston, L. (1992). *The Rebirth of Private Policing*. London, United Kingdom: Routledge.

Jones, T., & Newburn, T. (2006). The United Kingdom. In T. Jones & T. Newburn (Eds.), *Plural Policing. A Comparative Perspective* (pp. 34–54). London, United Kingdom: Routledge.

Kaufman, D. (2004). *Corruption, Governance and Security: Challenges for the Rich Countries and the World*. Munich, Germany: Munich University Press.

Lafree, G. (1998). *Losing Legitimacy: Street Crime and the Decline of Social Institutions in America*. Boulder, CO: Westview Press.

Lemieux, F. (2008). A cross-cultural comparison of intelligence-led policing. In T. Williamson (Ed.), *The Handbook of Knowledge Based Policing: Current Conceptions and Future Directions* (pp. 221–240). Chichester, United Kingdom: John Wiley.

Lemieux, F. (2010a). *International Police Cooperation: Emerging Issues, Theory and Practice*. Cullompton, United Kingdom: Willan Publishing.

Lemieux, F. (2010b). Tackling transnational drug trafficking effectively: Assessing the outcomes of the Drug Enforcement Administration's international cooperation initiatives. In F. Lemieux (Ed.), *International Police Cooperation: Emerging Issues, Theory and Practice* (pp. 260–280). Cullompton, United Kingdom: Willan Publishing.

Loader, I. (1999). Consumer Culture and the Commodification of Policing and Security. *Sociology, 33*(2), 373–392.

Loader, I. (2000). Plural policing and democratic governance. *Social and Legal Studies, 9*(3), 323–345.

Loader, I., & Walker, N. (2006). Necessary virtues: The legitimate place of the state in the production of security. In J. Wood & B. Dupont (Eds.), *Democracy, Society and the Governance of Security* (pp. 165–195), Cambridge, United Kingdom: Cambridge University Press.

Maguire, M. (2000). Policing by risks and targets: Some dimensions and implications of intelligence control. *Policing and Society, 9*, 315–336.

Mani, R. (1999). Contextualizing police reform: Security, the rule of law and post-conflict peacebuilding. *International Peacekeeping, 6*(4), 9–26.

Manning, P. K. (2006). The United States of America. In T. Jones & T. Newburn (Eds.), *Plural Policing. A Comparative Perspective* (pp. 98–125). London, United Kingdom: Routledge.

McCarty, W., Ren, L., & Zhao, J. (2012). Panel analysis of the determinants of police strength during the 1990s. *Crime & Delinquency, 58*, 397–424.

Merton, R. K. (1968). *Social Theory and Social Structure*. New York: Free Press.

Messner, S., & Rosenfeld, R. (1994). *Crime and the American Dream*. Belmont, CA: Wadsworth.

Messner, S. F., & Rosenfeld, R. (1997). Political restraint of the market and the levels of criminal homicide: A cross-national application of institutional anomie theory. *Social Forces, 75*(1), 1393–1416.

Nadelmann, E. A. (1992). The DEA in Latin America: Dealing with institutionalized corruption. *Journal of Inter-American Studies and World Affairs, 29*(4), 1–39.

Nadelmann, E. A. (1993). *Cops Across Borders: The Internationalization of U.S. Criminal Law Enforcement*. University Park, PA: Pennsylvania State University Press.

Nafziger, E. W., & Auvinen, J. (2000). The economic causes of humanitarian emergencies. In E. W. Nafziger, S. Frances, & R. Vayrynen (Eds.), *War, Hunger and Displacement: The Origin of Humanitarian Emergencies*. Oxford, United Kingdom: Oxford University Press.

Nafziger, E. W., & Auvinen, J. (2002). Economic development, inequality, war and state violence. *World Development, 30*(2), 153–63.

O'Neill, W. G. (2005). *Police Reform in Post-Conflict Societies: What We Know and What We Still Need to Know*. New York: International Peace Academy.

Pampel, F. C., & Gartner, R. (1995). Age-structure, socio-political institutions, and national homicides rates. *European Sociological Review, 11*(3), 243–260.

Ratcliffe, J. (2009). *Strategic Thinking in Criminal Intelligence*. Sydney, Australia: Federation Press.

Robertson, K. G. (1994). Practical police cooperation in Europe: The intelligence dimension. In M. Anderson & M. den Boer (Eds.), *Policing Across National Boundaries* (pp. 106–118). London, United Kingdom: Pinter.

Robin, S. (2009). Whose voices? Understanding victims' needs in transition. *Journal of Human Rights Practice, 1*(2), 320–331.

Ruddell, R., & Thomas, M. (2009). Does politics matter? Cross-national correlates of police strength. *Policing: An International Journal of Police Strategies & Management, 32*(4), 654–674.

Ruddell, R., & Thomas, M. (2010). Minority threat and police strength: An examination of the Golden State. *Police Practice and Research, 11*(3), 256–273.

Savolainen, J. (2000). Inequality, welfare state, and homicide: Further support for the institutional anomie theory. *Criminology, 38*(4), 1021–1042.

Shearing, C. D., & Stenning, P. (1981). Modern private security: Its growth and implications. In M. Tonry & M. Norval (Eds.), *Crime and Justice–An Annual Review of Research* (pp. 193–245). Chicago, IL: University of Chicago Press.

Shearing, C., & Wood, J. (2007). *Imagining Security*. London, United Kingdom: Willan Publishing.

Shelley, L. (1981). *Crime and Modernization: The Impact of Industrialization and Urbanization on Crime*. Carbonade, IL: Southern Illinois University Press.

Skogan, W. H. (2004). *Community Policing: Can It work?* Belmont, CA: Wadsworth.

Smith, M. D., Devine, J. A., & Sheley, J. F. (1992). Unemployment and crime: Age and race effects. *Sociological Perspectives, 35*(4), 551–572.

Stanley, W. (1999). Building new police forces in El Salvador and Guatemala: Learning and counter-learning. *International Peacekeeping, 6*(4), 113–134.

Stenning, P. C. (2000). Powers and accountability of private police. *European Journal on Criminal Policy and Research, 8*(3), 325–352.

Stewart, F. (2001). Horizontal inequalities as a source of conflict. In F. Hampson & D. Malone (Eds.), *From Reaction to Prevention*. London, United Kingdom: Lynne Rienner.

Stewart, F., & Fitzgerald, V. (2001). *War and Underdevelopment: The Economic and Social Consequences of Conflict*. Oxford, United Kingdom: Oxford University Press.

Stodiek, T. (2006). *The OSCE and the Creation of Multi-Ethnic Police Forces in the Balkans*. (CORE Working Paper 14.) Hamburg, Germany: Center for OSCE research.

Temple, J. (1998). Initial Conditions, Social Capital and Growth in Africa. *Journal of African Economies. 7*(3), 309–347.

United Nations Development Program. (1994). *Human Development Report*. New York/Oxford: Oxford University Press.

Walker, S., & Katz, C. (2012). *Police in America*. (8th ed.). New York: McGraw-Hill.

Walsh, D. (1994). The obsolescence of crime forms. In R. Clarke (Ed.), *Crime Prevention Studies*: Vol. 2 (pp. 149–163). Monsey, NY: Criminal Justice Press.

Weisburd, D., Mastrofski, S. D., McNally, A. M., Greenspan, R., & Willis, J. J. (2003). Reforming to preserve: COMPSTAT and strategic problem solving in American policing. *Criminology & Public Policy*, 2, 421–456.

Williamson, T. (2008). *The Handbook of Knowledge Based Policing: Current Conceptions and Future Directions*. Chichester, United Kingdom: John Wiley.

Zhao, J., Ren, L., & Lovrich, P. (2012). Political culture versus socioeconomic approaches to predicting police strength in U.S. police agencies: Results of a longitudinal study, 1993 to 2003. *Crime and Delinquency*, 58(2), 167–195.

International Perspectives on Economic and Other Social Challenges Facing Police Reform

I

Economic Recession and Homicide Rates in Globalized Cities
A Cross-Sectional Analysis

1

FREDERIC LEMIEUX

Contents

Introduction

According to common wisdom, a deteriorating economy is certain to spur a rise in crime rates. The perspective on crime and economic difficulties has been inspired by Becker's model (1968), which states that an individual would commit a crime if the benefits of committing the crime outweigh the costs of committing the crime. Applied to an aversive economic environment, this model suggests that income-generating crimes such as theft and burglaries will become more attractive because an increasing number of people are becoming unemployed. However, historical data on arrests and unemployment show that there is no clear relationship between crime and unemployment—a common measure of economic difficulties. According to the economist, Philip Cook, who recently examined the course of crime rates in urban areas of the United States in recent decades: "the statistical evidence indicates that the 1990s crime rate decline, like the crime surge that preceded it, has not been clearly correlated with changes in socioeconomic conditions."

Recently, several media outlets have reported a significant decrease in crime rate throughout the United States, despite the unprecedented 2008 recession, since the great depression of 1929. *The Economist* reported in June 2011 (citing FBI's Uniform Crime Report statistics) a 5% drop in violent crimes and 4% decrease in property crimes between 2008 and 2010. However, it was also reported that the decline in crime rates seems to not happen evenly across America and tends to be more important in small towns than in large cities such as New York and San Antonio, where crime rose during the same period. According to Eurostat, European Commission, the declining trend of crime rates over the past two decades has considerably slowed down between 2006 and 2009 in most member states of the European Union (Tavares, Thomas, & Bulut, 2012).

These statistics show that crime rates do not fluctuate evenly according to the size of city and the region of the world. These statistics should not be a surprising finding because it is most likely echoed the variation in socioeconomic opportunities reflecting local and regional realities. The partial collapse of the financial system had devastating consequences such as rising unemployment and surging poverty. It is also a reality that some countries and cities have been affected differently due to differences in economic vigor, labor market, social policy, institutional strength, and exposure to global trade system.

In regard to the recent economic situation, several questions related to the economy/crime association emerge: Did the international recession of 2007/2008 influence violent crime rates in the globalized cities, worldwide? For instance, can the *globalized character* of a large city amplify the negative impact of an international economic downturn and increase crime rates due to unemployment and economic inequality? Can the *globalized nature* of a large city decrease or stabilize crime rates by maintaining a high level of economic opportunities compared to less globalized cities? How much are crime rates in globalized cities influenced by macroeconomic trends like the 2008 great recession and how can other noneconomic factors affect the distribution of crime in globalized cities (domestic/international social policies, crime deterrence, mobility and transportation, etc.).

Economic Cycles and Crime Rates

In a classic work published by Cook and Zarkin (1985), the authors stated that "business cycles have pervasive effect on the structure of economic opportunity and hence on behavior" (p. 115). Research analyzing the correlation between crime rate and economic cycles are derivate from two main theoretical approaches. The first one, developed by Becker (1968), stipulates that there is a positive correlation between unemployment and property crime. More precisely, this economic model suggests that during periods of recession people may turn to illegal activities because of the lack of opportunities for legitimate income. The second one, inspired from Cantor and Land (1985), proposed a different theoretical approach based on motivation to commit crime and opportunities available to commit crime. According to them, crime rate is more likely to rise in economic growth phases and decline in contraction phases.

Several decades of research scrutinizing the relationship between economic cycles and crime rates have produced interesting if not counterintuitive set of results presenting large disparities in the magnitude of the correlation between unemployment and the property crime rate (Levitt, 2004). Putting aside the few studies showing loose relationship between the lack of economic opportunity (unemployment) and crime (Garrett & Ott, 2009), most researches have described an asymmetrical or inverse relation according to economic phases. In other words, during the second half of the twentieth century, studies have shown that crime rates tend to surge during phase of economic growth and decline during economic contraction period. For example, both studies realized by Levitt (2004) and Raphael and Winter-Ebmer (2001) found that 1% decrease in the unemployment rate was associated with a 2% decrease in the property crime rate. However, this finding is valid only short term and is not consistent over a long period (Gould, Weinberg, & Mustard, 2002). This caveat in the findings offers an analytical basis to study immediate impact of drastic structural change in the economy such as recession on crime rates.

Several studies scrutinizing the relation between crime rates and national and regional economies have been conducted in the United States and few European countries. For instance, Pyle and Deadman (1994) have illustrated throughout time series analysis, covering the period of 1946–1991, that crime rate is strongly related to economic activity and business cycles in England and Wales. A study realized by Krisberg, Guzman, and Vuong (2009) incorporated three indicators to measure crime: reported crime data, arrest data, and prison data from 1970 to the present. National data were reviewed along with data for the five most populous states: California, Florida, Texas, New York, and Illinois. The findings show that there is no clear association between economic recession and crime rates over the past 4 decades. Another study of violent crime trends in 100 U.S. cities realized by Butts (2008) found that only 9 cities saw a definitive increase, whereas nearly all others saw a decline in violent crime. The research conducted by Detotto and Otranto (2012) shows that most of the crime types appear to be countercyclical behavior with respect to the overall economic performance in Italy. According to them, only a few crime categories have an evident relationship with the business cycle. For instance, bankruptcy, embezzlement, and fraudulent insolvency seem most likely to anticipate business cycles.

Finally, the work of Nilsson and Estrada (2009) analyzed relation between levels of criminal victimization over time among groups whose well-being and financial situation changed during the period of 1988–1999 in Sweden due to recession. The results show that the levels of victimization vary in relation to the presence and seriousness of financial problems as well as group composition effects (most disadvantaged socioeconomic groups). Also, some studies have demonstrated the existence of a relationship between unemployment, recession, and incarceration rates. For instance, Box (1987) examines cross-sectional and longitudinal British and U.S. studies that have explored the relationship of unemployment and income inequality to crime and imprisonment. His findings show that relationship between crime and unemployment is inconsistent. However, a significant relationship exists between the unemployment rate and the imprisonment rate. According to the author, this relation exists because of the tendency of criminal justice personnel to deal more harshly with unemployed persons. In a more recent study, Cox (2010) analyzes the impact of the 2007/2008 recession on the incarceration of African–Americans. The findings show that the 2008 economic downturn has amplified the unemployment rates among the black community, explaining partially the prevalence of high incarceration rates among that community.

At the macro level, crime rates are influenced by a wide range of factors unrelated to macroeconomic trends and the static nature of Becker's model does not take into account other factors such as crime deterrence, evolution of public policies, changes in legislation, and demography (Levitt, 2004). According to Rosenfeld (2009), macroeconomic conditions do indeed have a strong influence on crime rates. Globalization of economic trends can be associated to cross-national crime rates. For instance, the works of Rosenfeld and Messner (2009) suggest that the U.S. and European crime declines occurred in tandem because they were both brought about by upturns in the economy. To verify this assumption, the authors did a pooled cross-sectional time series analysis of burglary rates in the United States and nine European nations between 1993 and 2006. The results show that burglary declines in the United States and Europe were associated with rising consumer confidence.

Research conducted by Lafree and Tseloni (2006) shows that violent crime rates are highest for transitional democracies and homicide rates gradually increased in the second part of twentieth century for full democracies mostly because of the brutalizing effects of the market economies that so far have universally accompanied democratization and the modernization of countries. The authors analyzed the data from 44 countries from 1950 to 2000. Finally, the work of Buendia (1989) points out the correlation between economic growth and the increasing crime rates in eight countries: Thailand, Colombia, Nigeria, Kenya, Costa Rica, Singapore, Japan, and Poland. According to the author, the global economic development has generated massive urbanization and occupational changes worldwide that diminish the cohesiveness of traditional societies and influence crime rates.

Globalized Economies and Recession

The definition of recession, from the National Bureau of Economic Research, is "a significant decline in economic activity spread across the economy, lasting more than a few months, normally visible in real GDP, real income, employment, industrial production, and wholesale-retail sales." For the purpose of this paper, "Globalization is understood as major rises in worldwide trade and exchanges in an increasingly open, integrated, and borderless international economy" (Intriligator, 2003, p. 2). According to a report published by the Milken Institute, globalization of economy is the culmination of a plurality of national and international circumstances (Intriligator, 2003). First, technological advances have significantly lowered the costs of transportation and communication and dramatically lowered the costs of global exchanges. Second, trade liberalization and other forms of economic liberalization have led to reductions in trade protection and to a more liberal world trading system. Third, globalization of economy could be induced by the transformation of institutions, the expansion of their international reach, and wide-ranging horizons of their managers that are empowered by advanced communications. Fourth, there is a worldwide convergence of beliefs in the value of a market economy and a free trading system. Fifth, there are cultural developments inspired by globalized and homogenized media, the arts, and popular culture and with the widespread use of the English language for global communication.

Despite the numerous advantages of a globalized market, there are several downsides as well. One of them relates to the potential of regional or global instabilities stemming from the interdependencies of economies on a worldwide basis. There is the possibility that local economic fluctuations or crises in one nation could have regional or even global impacts. A worldwide recession or depression could lead to calls to break the interdependencies that have been realized through the globalization process (Intriligator, 2003). This particular downside materialized in 2007/2008 with the global spread of the U.S. recession accelerated by the financial meltdown of Wall Street. According to Islam and Verick (2011), the United States was the epicenter of the crisis and its economy was hit directly by the meltdown in the subprime mortgage market along with the repercussions of the financial crisis and the ensuing credit crunch. As a consequence, the U.S. economy fell into recession in December 2007 and is estimated to have shrunk considerably in 2009 (–2.7%). However, this contraction was smaller than most G20 countries and smaller than the average for advanced economies (–3%). According to International Monetary

Fund report (2009), the impact of the crisis on developing countries has been far from universal. The most severely affected are middle-income countries, especially in Central and eastern Europe. Because of its links with the United States, most of Latin America fell into a deep recession with Mexico being hit harder. However, most low-income countries were able to evade the recession despite a considerable slowdown of their economic growth (World Bank Group, 2010). In Organization for Economic Cooperation and Development (OECD) countries, the unemployment rate has increased from 5.7% in the third quarter of 2007 to 8.6% in the third quarter of 2009, representing an increase of 10 million individuals without jobs (OECD, 2009).

However, globalization is not only based on national economies but relies also on the vitality of large urban areas that are connected to international trade routes. Cities are at the heart of a new regional geography where the centrality of an urban-based and region-wide system of capitalism is often overlooked as international nodes or regional gateway global economy. In the past decades, foreign investment and trade growth have centered on and been organized among the continental leading cities or *globalized cities*. Globalized cities are also the major air and sea transport hubs and regional industrial exportation is often organized from downtown offices there generating a local cosmopolitan economy. National and regional investment flows to shopping malls, industrial estates, hotel and resort developments, and residential development are planned and directed toward globalized cities. The globalized cities are also critical to regional information flows, cultural exchange, the shaping of regional fashion and taste, and the media production.

The influence of globalized cities on crime rates in the midst of an international great recession has been overlooked. First and foremost, the lack of study can be mainly explained by the extraordinary nature of the phenomenon. The scope and consequences of this great recession is unprecedented since 1929. Second, globalized cities and cosmopolitan economies are relatively new concepts that have not necessarily been studied by or integrated to other disciplines such as criminology and sociology. Finally, from a methodological perspective, data related to crime and recession indicators can be really difficult to access on a local basis increasing the difficulty of conducting such international comparative analysis. This study will scrutinize crime rates in globalized cities in the wake of an international recession. More precisely, this research will attempt to verify the following four propositions:

Proposition 1: In the aftermath of the 2007/2008 great recession, the more a city is globalized the more it will experience the negative consequences of the economic downturn.

Proposition 2: In the aftermath of the 2007/2008 great recession, the more a city is globalized the more the socioeconomic inequality will be important.

Proposition 3: In the aftermath of the 2007/2008 great recession, the more a city is globalized the higher the homicide rates will be.

Proposition 4: Controlling for the negative impact of the great recession and the discrepancy in wealth distribution, the level of globalization will influence homicide rates.

Methodology

This research offers an international comparative analysis of crime rates in 60 large cities in the world during the year of 2008. The methodology will be based on a quantitative approach, using data compiled by local and national public authorities, international organizations (IOs), and nongovernmental organizations. The cross-sectional analysis, or analytical design for this research, uses homicide rates as the dependent variable. Murder was selected for this research for one reason only: this crime is the most likely to be reported by public authorities. During the data collection phase, it was clear that categories such as property crime and violent crime are vague and can comprise different types of incidents that differ from one country to another. Because of its quasi-universal prohibition, the murder crime category is most likely to be reported by states as well as IOs. It is true that recession is often related to property crime but, as mentioned in the review of literature, several studies have also established the link between business cycles and homicides. Economic strain and deprivation can increase the level of frustration of those who do not have access to economic opportunity, which can raise the number of violent crimes such as armed robberies, domestic violence, and violent outbursts.

For instance, a recent study conducted by McCall, Land, and Parker (2011) on U.S. cities found that large cities with high levels of deprivation and concentrated poverty, high income inequality, high percentages of divorced males, high unemployment rates, higher percentages of youth, higher percentages of the Hispanic population, and higher numbers of police per capita are also cities that are more likely to be in a higher rather than a lower homicide trajectory group. Greater percentages of the population enrolled in higher education and locations in states with higher incarceration rates are characteristics of cities associated with membership in a lower homicide trajectory group. Unfortunately, data used to operationalize all variables are not reported evenly at the international level. Most of this information is available at the national level but is near to impossible to access from the city-level perspective.

A central concept in this study is the globalized nature of cities and to provide a reliable measurement of this independent variable, the analysis will be relying on the 2008 A.T. Kearney's Global Cities Index. This index ranks metropolitan areas according to 24 metrics across five dimensions:* (1) business activity, (2) human capital, (3) information exchange, (4) cultural experience, and (5) political engagement. This ranking offers the opportunity to compare a large number of cities using stable and reliable measurements. Finally, for economic metrics this study is using unemployment rates per city to measure the impact of labor market opportunity in each city and the Gini index, which in part, measure socioeconomic inequality values related to levels of income. The coefficient varies from zero (perfect equality) to one (maximal inequality). The use of this index is relevant for this study because the coefficient is related to the size of urban areas (U.S. Census Bureau, 2011). Also, a study realized by Cole and Gramajo (2009) on cross-national analysis of homicides points out Gini index is a better predictor of homicides than poverty factor. However, according to these authors, the effect of socioeconomic inequality on homicide rates remains modest. Finally, the analysis includes population density in metropolitan areas, because it can highlight the likelihood of interpersonal violence based on the increase of interpersonal contact. Also, this variable is included in most cross-sectional research on homicides as a control variable (Hansmann & Quigley, 1982; Avison & Loring, 1986; Neumayer, 2003).

Analysis

According to a United Nations report, the trend of homicide rates shows a sustained decline for a majority of countries located in the Americas, Asia, Europe, and Oceania in the past decade. However, some exceptions exist in Central America and the Caribbean where murders are increasing mainly due to transnational drug trafficking and gang activity (United Nations Office on Drugs and Crime [UNODC], 2011). The report shows that the number of homicides worldwide was estimated at 468,000 in 2010. About 36% of these homicides occurred in Africa, 31% in the Americas, 27% in Asia, 5% in Europe, and 1% in Oceania region. The report also points out interesting findings relevant to this study. First, the analysis establishes a clear link between homicides and development. More precisely, countries with large income disparities are four times more likely to be plagued by violent crime than more equitable societies. Moreover, the results show that economic slowdown is also related to homicides. For instance, the report states that in selected countries the murder rate went up during and after the economic

* For more details regarding the exact metrics used by the study, please consult the 2008 Global Cities Index Report at http://www.atkearney.com/index.php/Publications/the-2008-global-cities-index.html (accessed on July 24, 2012).

crisis of 2008/2009 after a sharp decline of national indicators such as gross domestic product, consumer price index, and unemployment.

As interesting and relevant as these findings are, they only address the national level of homicides and do not measure the possible relationship with the globalization of local economies. To find out if the findings at national level can be replicated at the local (city) level, correlation analyses have been performed between homicide rates and the independent variables: socioeconomic inequality, population density, and unemployment levels. The results show that there are no statistically significant relations. This first set of findings suggests that homicide rates may not be influenced by the same factors at local and national levels. However, it is important to note that some important studies find a positive correlation between the Gini coefficient and violent crime rates (Krohn, 1976; Krahn, Hartnagel, & Gartrell, 1986; Bourguignon, 2001; Fajnzylber, Lederman, & Loayza, 2002), whereas others do not find a strong correlation (Neumayer, 2005). In other words, the relation can be somewhat ambiguous. As for unemployment or labor market indicators in general, it seems that the relation between homicide or crime rates varies significantly according to regional or local characteristics and is more often associated to violent crimes over time (longitudinal analysis) as opposed to cross-sectional analysis, again due to local differences. Regarding the density of population, the lack of correlation is not a surprise because existing literature previously found the absence of relation with violent crimes (Neuman & Berger, 1988).

A second set of results of analysis between the city globalization index and socioeconomic inequality or unemployment levels show mixed correlation measures. The findings suggest that the more globalized a city is, the lower the unemployment rate ($r = -0.29$; $p < .05$). However, this correlation between the globalization index and the Gini index is not statistically significant. These preliminary results suggest that the globalized character of a city can reduce the negative impacts of economic adversity (unemployment level). However, the globalization index does not seem to be related to a reduction or increase of socioeconomic inequality.

Finally, the last correlation analysis intends to verify the third proposition, which states: "in the aftermath of the 2007/2008 great recession, the more a city is globalized the higher the homicide rates will be." The result shows a strong and significant correlation ($r = -0.37$; $p < .01$) indicating that the more a city has an elevated index of globalization, the lower the homicide rate. To make sure that the findings are not distorted by an overrepresentation of globalized cities location, the sample shows a balance between the number of cities in modern economies ($n = 27$) and the number of cities in emerging economies such as Brazil, China, India, Nigeria, and Venezuela ($n = 26$). This precision is critical because the report published by United Nations (2011) mentioned that homicide rates vary substantially from one world region to another.

To this point, the analytical design has only involved models based on measures of association and shows some interesting results relevant to the design of the next analytical model. The last analysis is based on a multivariate approach that verifies if the level of globalization will influence crime rates when controlling for unemployment and socioeconomic inequality (proposition 4). To specify the regression model, the analysis must take into account the previous findings and exclude independent variables that are correlated with each other. For instance, it has been demonstrated that the index of globalization seems to be strongly associated with density of population and unemployment level, which generates multicollinearity problems.* Therefore, to avoid an unstable statistical model (and because the aim of the fourth proposition is to verify the existence of possible influence of globalization index on homicides), two regression models have been generated. In Model 1, all the dependent variables have been entered except the global index. The multiple regression model with the three predictors produced an r^2 of 0.12 but the model is not statistically significant ($p = .10$). However, the model does suggest that the Gini index is a predictor of homicide rates and for that reason will be included in the second model.

The unemployment and density variables have been removed from the regression Model 2 and only the Gini index and globalization index have been included. The multiple regression model with the two predictors produced an r^2 of 0.13 and, therefore, the model is statistically significant ($p < .01$). As shown in Table 1.1, the globalization index has significant negative regression weights, indicating cities with higher globalization index are expected to have a lower homicide rate, after controlling for the socioeconomic inequality index. The Gini index has a nonsignificant negative weight, indicating

Table 1.1   Summary of Multiple Regression Analysis for Variables Predicting Homicide Rates ($N = 52$)

Variables	B	SE(B)	Beta	t test	Sig.
Model 1[a]					
Gini index	43.107	18.98	0.324	2.271	0.028
Density	0	0	0.068	0.484	0.631
Unemployment	0.085	0.479	0.025	0.177	0.86
Model 2[b]					
Gini index	−25.891	25.251	−0.138	−1.025	0.31
Globalization index	−0.102	0.044	−0.315	−2.333	0.024

[a] Model 1 summary: $r^2 = 0.12$, $p = .10$.
[b] Model 2 summary: $r^2 = 0.13$, $p < .05$.

* Multicollinearity occurs when two or more predictors in the model are correlated and provide redundant information about the response.

that the variable did not contribute to the multiple regression model. In other words, the multiple regression model shows that 13% (r^2) of the homicide rates variance is explained mainly by the city globalization index. According to the analysis, globalization of cities seems to be the best predictors among all the other variables included in both models. However, the impact of globalization on violent crimes, such as homicide, remains modest.

Conclusion

This study aimed to examine the relationship between international economic trends and crime rates in large urban areas. More precisely, the study examined the influence of the 2008 world economic recession on violent crime in globalized cities. The findings suggest that the higher the index of globalization, the lesser is the unemployment levels and homicide rates. When controlling for population density, unemployment levels, and socioeconomic inequalities, it appears that the globalization index is the best predictor of the variation of homicide rates across cities. The outcome of this research provides a better understanding of the influence of the macroeconomic phenomena (international recession and globalization) on homicide rates in large cities. Moreover, to define guidelines for future public policies, this research scrutinized the factors associated to the globalized nature of selected large cities, which could affect directly or indirectly violent crime rates during or after a recession period. According to this economic perspective, homicide rates can be considered as a performance measure, which could be used to assess the aptitude of local governance to curb down the negative impacts of an international economic downturn by developing global initiatives and opportunities at the local level. Again, these findings are modest and must be interpreted with caution.

Because the study shows modest results, the next phase of this research will include two additional years: one year before the economic crisis and the second year after 2010. The purpose of a comparison before, during, and after the event will give more perspective on both the evolution of indicators and on the dependent variable (homicide rates). Also, the likelihood of a *lag effect* regarding the negative impacts of the 2007/2008 recession is not negligible. Therefore, it is possible that some cities were affected more rapidly than others by job loss or stayed in the recession for a longer time. The same is also true for homicide rates; it is possible that the variation in violent crimes was delayed due to preventive factors such as social programs (for instance access to unemployment benefits). Consequently, new regression models should be enhanced and include variables related to social policies of respective countries or cities. Finally, it would be pertinent to test new regression models on different but still highly relevant dependent variables such as property crime and imprisonment rates.

References

Avison, W. R., & Loring, P. L. (1986). Population diversity and cross-national homicide: The effects of inequality and heterogeneity. *Criminology, 24,* 733–749.

Becker, G. (1968). Crime and punishment: An economic approach. *The Journal of Political Economy, 76,*169–217.

Bourguignon, F. (2001). Crime as a social cost of poverty and inequality: A review focusing on developing countries. In S. Yusuf, S. Evenett, & W. Wu, *Facets of globalization: International and local dimensions of development* (pp. 171–191), World Bank Discussion Paper No. 415. Washington, DC: World Bank.

Box, S. (1987). *Recession, crime, and punishment.* Totowa, NJ: Macmillan.

Buendia, H. G. (1989). *Urban crime: Global trends and policies.* Tokyo, Japan: United Nations University.

Butts, J. A. (2008). Violent Crime in 100 U.S. Cities. Chicago, IL: Chapin Hall Center for Children at the University of Chicago.

Cantor, D., & Land, K. C. (1985). Unemployment and crime rates in post-World War II United States: A theoretical and empirical analysis. *American Sociological Review, 50,* 317–332.

Cole, J. H., & Gramajo, A. M. (2009). Homicide rates in a cross-section of countries: Evidence and interpretations. *Population and Development Review, 35*(4), 749–776.

Cook, P. J., & Zarkin, G. A. (1985). Crime and the Business Cycle. *Journal of Legal Studies, 14*(1):115–128.

Cox, R. (2010). Crime, incarceration, and employment in light of the great recession. *The Review of Black Political Economy, 37*(3–4), 283–294.

Detotto, C., & Otranto, E. (2012). Cycles in crime and economy: Leading, lagging and coincident behaviors. *Journal of Quantitative Criminology, 28*(2), 295–317.

Fajnzylber, P., Lederman, D., & Loayza, N. (2002). Inequality and violent crime. *Journal of Law and Economics, 45,* 1–40.

Garrett, T. A., & Ott, L. S. (2009). City business cycles and crime. Retrieved from SSRN: http://ssrn.com/abstract = 1222979; http://dx.doi.org/10.2139/ssrn.1222979.

Gould, E. D., Weinberg, B. A., & Mustard, D. B. (2002). Crime rates and local labor market opportunities in the United States: 1979–1997. *Review of Economics and Statistics, 84*(1), 45–61.

Hansmann, H. B., & Quigley, J. M. (1982). Population heterogeneity and the sociogenesis of homicide. *Social Forces, 61,* 206–224.

International Monetary Fund (IMF). (2009). *Annual report 2009—Fighting the global crisis.* Washington, DC: International Monetary Fund.

Intriligator, M. (2003). Globalization of the world economy: Potential benefits and costs and a net assessment (no. 33). Los Angeles: University of California.

Islam, I., & Verick, S. (2011). *From the great recession to labour market recovery. Issues, evidence and policy options.* International Labor Organization/Palgrave Macmillan. Houndmills, England.

Krahn, H., Hartnagel, T. F., & Gartrell, J. W. (1986). Income inequality and homicide rates: Cross-national data and criminological theories. *Criminology, 24,* 269– 295.

Krisberg, B., Guzman, C., & Vuong, L. (2009). *Crime and economic hard times.* Oakland, CA: National Council on Crime and Delinquency.

Krohn, M. D. (1976). Inequality, unemployment and crime: A cross-national analysis. *The Sociological Quarterly, 17*, 303–313.

Lafree, G., & Tseloni, A. (2006). Democracy and crime: A multilevel analysis of homicide trends in 44 countries from 1950 to 2000. *The ANNALS of the American Academy of Political and Social Science, 605*(1), 25–49.

Levitt, S. D. (2004). Understanding why crime in 1990's: Four factors that explain the decline and six that do not. *Journal of Economic Perspectives, 18*(1), 163–190.

McCall, P. L., Land, K. C., & Parker, K. F. (2011). Heterogeneity in the rise and decline of city-level homicide rates, 1976–2005: A latent trajectory analysis. *Social Science Research, 40*(1), 363–378.

Neuman, W. L., & Berger, R. J. 1988. Competing perspectives on cross-national crime: An evaluation of theory and evidence. *The Sociological Quarterly, 29*, 281–313.

Neumayer, E. 2003. Good policy can lower violent crime: Evidence from a cross-national panel of homicide rates, 1980–97. *Journal of Peace Research, 40*, 619–640.

Neumayer, E. 2005. Inequality and violent crime: Evidence from data on robbery and violent theft. *Journal of Peace Research, 42*, 101–112.

Nilsson, A., & Estrada, F. "Criminality and Life-Chances in a Welfare State: A Longitudinal Study of Childhood Circumstances, Crime and Living Conditions up to Age 48." *Paper presented at the annual meeting of the ASC Annual Meeting, San Francisco Marriott, San Francisco, California.*

Organization for Economic Cooperation and Development (OECD). (2009). *OECD Factbook 2009.* Paris, France: Organization for Economic Cooperation and Development.

Pyle, D. J., & Deadman, D. (1994). Crime and the business cycle in post-war Britain. *British Journal of Criminology, 34*, 339–357.

Raphael, S., & Winter-Ebmer, R. (2001). Identifying the effect of unemployment on crime. *Journal of Law and Economics, 44*(1), 259–283.

Rosenfeld, R. (2009). Crime is the problem: Homicide, acquisitive crime, and economic conditions. *Journal of Quantitative Criminology, 25*, 287–306.

Rosenfeld, R., & Messner, S. F. (2009). The crime drop in comparative perspective: The impact of the economy and imprisonment on American and European burglary rates. *British Journal of Sociology, 60*, 445–471.

Tavares, C., Thomas, G., & Bulut, F. (2012). Crime and criminal justice, 2006–2009. Eurostat.

The Economist. (2011, June 2). Good news is no news. Accessed online on June 15, 2012. Retrieved from http://www.economist.com/node/18775436.

United Nations Office on Drugs and Crime (UNODC). (2011). *The 2011 global study on homicide.* New York: United Nations.

U.S. Census Bureau (2011). *U.S. neighborhood income inequality in the 2005–2009 period.* Washington, DC: Department of Commerce.

World Bank Group. (2010). *Annual report 2010.* Washington, DC: World Bank Group.

Generating Insight from Foresight

Emerging Challenges for Law Enforcement Policy Makers

2

CHRISTOPHER VAS

Contents

Introduction

This chapter adopts a forward-looking *foresight* approach to shed some light on the uncertain domain within which crime patterns are emerging. In a global system that is connected, multifaceted, and at the same time accentuates uncertainty (Innes, 2006; Bammer & Smithson, 2008; Ransley & Mazerolle, 2009) the use of linear approaches to solve complex crime is becoming less optimum. As discussed in this chapter, it is plain to note how traditional crime patterns are either flat lining or dropping, while new network and technology driven crime patterns are on the rise. This changing nature from traditional to networked crime is giving rise to a growing trend of what has been termed *borderless crime* (Wilson, 1996; Broadhurst, 2010). It is hence no longer adequate to use strategies that accentuate a silo approach in tackling new crime that is increasingly being dominated and underpinned by networks, both socially and in the use of technological infrastructure. Law enforcement and the criminal justice system at large need to reposition itself not as a mechanism that only fights crime, but as a value-laden networked system that proactively addresses socio-economic issues that give rise to criminal activity. This requires a transformation to take place from within before external forces dictate and impose changes on it.

The chapter is structured into two parts. First, using a futurist approach I leverage studies conducted on long-term global socioeconomic issues to identify emerging trends and patterns. These trends are analyzed for its implication on the law enforcement and criminal justice system. An effort is made to link the macro trends with societal changes by interrogating some of the quantitative data from developed countries and then further contrasting it with a case narrative from India. This helps provide a rich source of quantitative and qualitative material that forms the essence of discussion and analysis in the second part of the chapter.

Acknowledging the growing complexity and uncertain nature of socioeconomic development, the central argument within this chapter is for the need to transition from traditional approaches of law enforcement to a state where preempting and preventing crime forms the core by adopting a technology-driven societal network-based modus operandi. The secondary objective of the chapter is to challenge existing mental models that rely on singular disciplinary approaches as opposed to multidisciplinary perspectives that can harness insights and new ways of thinking to tackle emerging crime issues.

Emerging Trends: Linking Global to Society

This section brings together the macro developments evident at the global level with developments emerging at the societal level. Figure 2.1 accurately

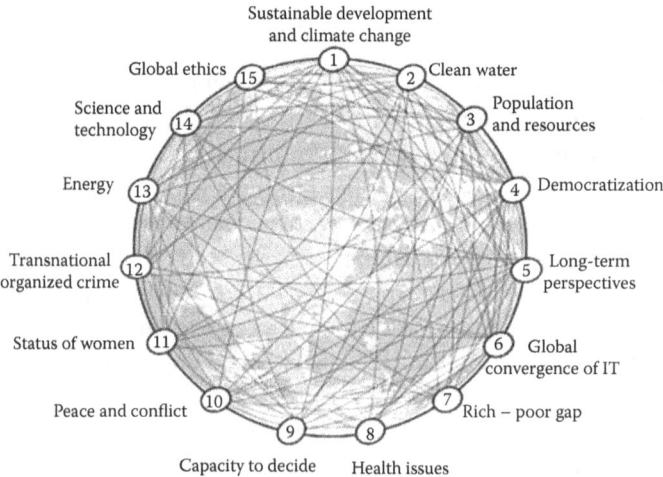

Figure 2.1 Global challenges. (From The Millennium Project, Global Futures Studies & Research. [2009]. Global Challenges for Humanity. http://www.millennium-project.org/millennium/challeng.html.)

depicts the challenges we face today among which crime is only one. As with the essence of this chapter, the growing interconnectedness of issues is what we focus on, so that a more holistic understanding of issues can be derived on how global and societal issues linkages can impact crime levels.

In doing so, this section discusses the geostrategic and geopolitical changes, especially the alleged movement of power from the West to the East; how these changes are impacting socioeconomic issues within national boundaries and how this is creating opportunities for new crime, especially technology-related organized crime. This section takes a quantitative and qualitative approach by analyzing data on traditional crime and also discussing a case study to enable a rigid discussion and its implications on law enforcement policy making.

Geostrategic Uncertainty and Its Influence on Social Construct within Society

Armed conflict and trade: The growth of burgeoning economies such as China and India are not global sensations anymore. Indonesia along with the commonly known BRIC nations (Brazil, Russia, India, and China) is also showing signs of a fast-paced economic growth trajectory. All things being equal, the rise of these economies overtaking some Western economies in the coming decades is very real. With such rise what is also evident is the increasing proportion of national spend on boosting military capability and power. This is evident through the data in Table 2.1, which outlines the gross domestic product (GDP) spend on military by a snapshot of developed and emerging economies.

If we only look at China and India, the significant growth in military expenditure is evident equating to almost 65% and 45%, respectively. In

Table 2.1 GDP Spend on Military Capabilities

	2007	2008	2009	2010
Russia	$44,579,907,733	$58,129,623,567	$53,307,458,652	$58,608,114,962
China	$71,628,146,868	$91,793,093,953	$109,807,640,948	$119,203,642,363
India	$28,737,847,030	$30,357,595,797	$36,476,332,154	$41,434,363,426
Indonesia	$5,100,157,506	$4,898,347,670	$4,694,345,644	$7,151,071,089
Australia	$16,112,664,207	$19,851,609,548	$17,837,010,186	$22,971,948,376
Canada	$17,373,601,899	$19,234,284,001	$19,394,875,776	$22,709,377,184
Japan	$40,078,229,529	$46,067,476,949	$50,854,929,833	$54,335,323,308
United Kingdom	$65,821,267,298	$65,371,688,672	$57,758,870,512	$59,224,929,538
United States	$555,679,640,000	$619,961,480,000	$668,225,520,000	$697,794,930,000

Source: World Bank data (calculations by author).

Western economies, the highest growth is seen in Australia equating to roughly 43% but still much less than what China and India spend in actual dollar terms. No doubt, the current dollar spend by the United States is still massive, which still outshines all other economies. In that respect, China's spend equates to more than the combined spend of Australia, Canada, and the United Kingdom. This is quite apparent in the case of China with its enhancements of naval capabilities to further strengthen its influence beyond the borders of the South China Sea—a significant sea-trading route for most Pacific economies. For China, this boosting of military capability is vital as East Asian economies like South Korea, Japan, Taiwan, Singapore, and Philippines are geostrategic allies of the United States. Russia on the other hand is also enriching its nuclear and submarine capabilities using wealth generated from its commodity trading in hydrocarbons. Russia is attempting to increase its footprint in Asia by becoming the largest supplier of weapons in the region. The United States is also using technological advances—evident in its Global Posture Review—to continuously influence its allies thus enhancing its geostrategic power base. This geostrategic imbalance or competition has been a cause for an increase in transnational security issues rising through terrorism, organized crime, and cyber warfare. For instance, the involvement of the West in the rising tensions in the Middle East is a case in point (Bisley, 2009). This growing multipolar world with power dynamics shifting from the West to the East brings with it a high level of uncertainty and a heightened possibility of conflict among nations. It is unlikely that a full-blown military conflict will arise despite the increased investments in boosting military capabilities but a conflict based on trade relations can be real.

Set against the backdrop of growing economic uncertainty, a trend that sees economies move from globalization to protectionism could be likely. According to the Department of Agriculture, Fisheries, and Forestry in Australia, food exports in 2011 increased by 10% to $27.1 billion as a result of increasing demand from Asia. Food exports now constitute about 12% of Australia's total exports. Given the burgeoning middle class in Asian economies, its society is driving up demand for better quality food. Australia is well positioned geographically to be at the apex of Asia's food supply chain, which is why former Australian Prime Minister Julia Gillard referred to the country as becoming a "Global Food Superpower." One part of this strategy is to allow foreign investment and ownership of Australian agricultural lands. However, despite the Government's ambition of becoming a food superpower, 80% of Australians are against any foreign investment in Australia's agricultural land (Burke, 2012). This displays the level of disconnect that exists between government planning versus the sentiment and views of people expressed at the societal level and why a trade standoff could become a potential future scenario driving up concerns around food security.

International governance and society: Moving away from the (re)-positioning of global economic powers and trade relationships, if we turn to international governance issues—renowned scholars such as Kishore Mahbubani in his books *"The New Asian Hemisphere: The Irresistible Shift of Global Power to the East"* and *"Can Asians Think?"* has for a long time argued about the declining power of global international institutions such as the International Monetary Fund and the World Bank. Given the dominance by the American and European power brokers within these institutions, they have failed to recognize the importance of emerging nations such as China and India as equal partners. It is this limitation from such global governing institutions—of continuing to view emerging economics as unequal partners—that have exacerbated the uncertainty and tensions between the West and the East. This has created a geostrategic disparity between neoliberalism and conservatism. Despite the benefits of Western democratic governance and market driven systems, State-level intervention and authoritarian regimes have also proved valuable. We only have to look at the global energy sector, which shows a large percentage (in excess of 70%) of energy organizations being owned and controlled by the State.

No doubt, improved governance of State and non-State actors is becoming a dominant trend in many regions across the globe for many reasons including tackling crime and corruption. The research conducted by Gopal and Najam (2012) analyzing over 300 pieces of information from *Searchlight* nodes of the Rockefeller Foundation, show why better governance frameworks are critical in Africa and Latin America. Gopal and Najam have identified 11 categories (Figure 2.2) to assess emerging trends and their importance within the regional context. Better governance to tackle corruption and to conduct fair elections, gender inequity, public health, increasing influence from China, sustainable development to address food insecurity, poverty, and education challenges are emerging issues for the African region. China's increasing investment in the African resources sector is seeing mixed responses from communities. Despite such views, a growing trend of higher Chinese investments in the region is visible. Governance and inequality continue to be major issues for countries in this region, which give rise to levels of crime. Asian economies, on the other hand, are seeking improved governance frameworks to enhance access to education, opportunities for societal development, and infrastructure development as a means to better provide for their communities. In the case of Latin American countries, a very high level of emphasis (much higher than what is seen in the Asian and African regions) is placed on governance issues to tackle issues of corruption, social inclusion, freedom of expression, and to improve regional cooperation. As depicted in Figure 2.2, it is evident how important issues around governance and societal development have become in these regions.

Africa   Asia

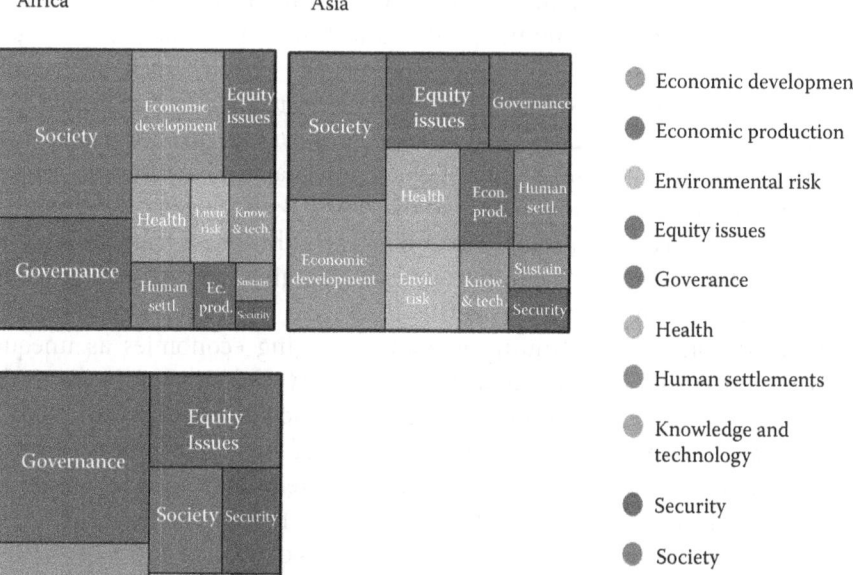

● Economic development

● Economic production

● Environmental risk

● Equity issues

● Goverance

● Health

● Human settlements

● Knowledge and technology

● Security

● Society

● Sustainability/provision (natural resources)

Latin America

Figure 2.2 Eleven categories of trends in Africa, Asia, and Latin America, respectively (size of the box denotes its dominance). (From Connecting the Dots (Gopal, S., & Najam, A., *Connecting the dots: Information visualisation and text analysis of the searchlight project newsletters*, Boston University, Boston, MA, 2012.)

In Asia, technology is becoming an important tool and lever that is being harnessed to address such systemic issues and to stimulate grass-root movements such as the Hazare anticorruption movement in India, the Arab uprisings against authoritarian political regimes, and so on. With over 42% of the global online users living in the Asian region (Broadhurst, 2010) and a fast growing population that get connected to network technology on a daily basis, it is palpable to see how this will create many more future changes in how the region is governed. Technology will drive faster responses to governance issues. However, there are numerous systemic and legislative challenges that can complicate these responses, further leaving room for crime opportunities as a result of new social movements. Societal conflicts caused by rising inequality and unemployment are also increasing in developed countries that are heavily reliant on other economies such as China for manufacturing, and India and Philippines for services. The aging population problem in the West, growing inequality, poverty, and uneven wealth distribution—there are real social challenges that are either front and center in many economies or on the periphery as minor trends that are likely to emerge as global patterns in the coming decades.

Technology Crime versus Traditional Crime

Technology crime: The pace of technology development evident in the creation of superior products and services has certainly improved productivity of organizations and individuals alike. Today more tasks can be attended to and executed in lesser time. For example, the use of mobile phones and applications that allow access to email servers has created a culture that imposes on people a mindset of being connected to work constantly. This is further supported by evidence where Facebook—only after 7 years of its launch—was being used by over 50% of the online population in the United States and India, and much higher proportions in countries such as Chile, South Africa, and Indonesia (Carbone & Nauth, 2012). Of note, is the growth of Twitter—which in 2007 had approximately 500,000 tweets in the first quarter and in 2010 had over 4 billion tweets in the same period (Deibert & Rohozinski, 2010). There is little doubt about how interconnected national and global systems have become using such technology developments. This high level of connectedness has created elements of *critical infrastructure* that has the network structure as its backbone and is hence very valuable to protect. Using the Dutch context, Sommer and Brown (2011) neatly depict this level of interconnectedness (Figure 2.3).

This interconnectedness of systemic elements and productivity improvements has also resulted in the growing nature of technology crime. For instance, the increase in sexual abuse especially of minors by virtue of a thriving international business model supported by the spread of the Internet and related imagery technologies is widely known. Likewise, financial crime relating to the misuse of credit cards and money laundering has also been on the increase. Figure 2.4 is an extract from the report provided by the Australian Crime Commission, which depicts the increase in electronic fraud in Australia.

However, the instances of such crime being reported is still probably not very high as Moulton (2012) points out, following his analysis of the data reported in the Canadian context. He argues that until the system is capable of attending to and effectively prosecuting criminals in a timely manner, the rate at which technology-driven or technology enabled-crime gets reported will be relatively low. Geoff Slocombe and Kym Bergmann in the 2012 edition of the *Asia Pacific Defence Review* discuss the growing levels of *Cyber Warfare*, indicating heightened state of transnational conflict or espionage using electronic methods. Cyber Warfare is one extent of crime that threatens national security. *Cyber Terrorism*—orchestrated by a group(s), *Cyber Crime*—orchestrated for personal gain, and *Cyber Hacks*—unauthorized use

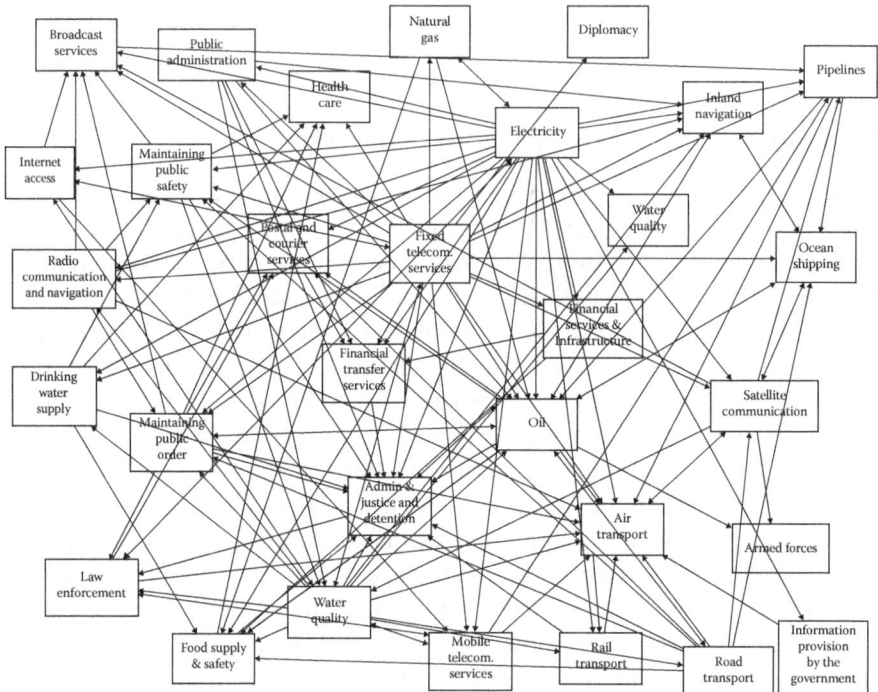

Figure 2.3 Dutch critical infrastructure network. (From Sommer, P., & Brown, I., *Reducing systemic cybersecurity risk*, OECD/IFP Programme, Paris, France, 2011.)

FRAUD AS OCCURENCE PER 100,000 TRANSACTIONS

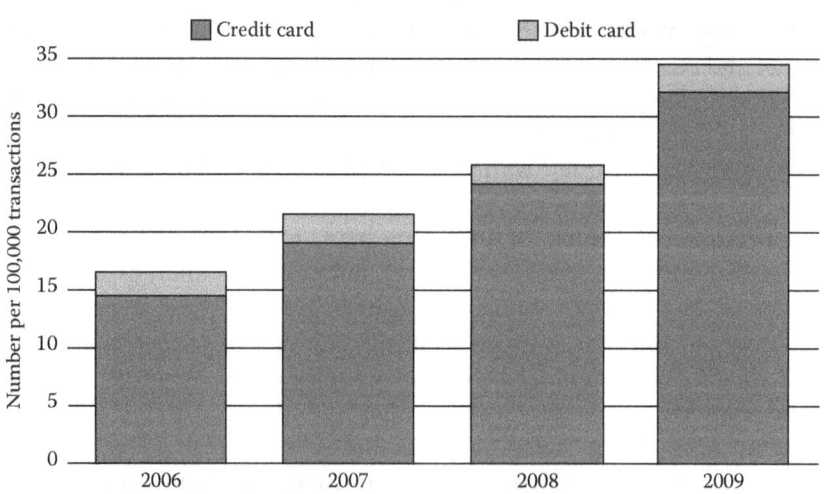

Figure 2.4 Electronic fraud in Australia. (From Australian Crime Commission, *Organised crime in Australia*, Australian Crime Commission, Canberra, Australia, 2011.)

of computer systems, are other dimensions that add to the nature of cyber-security. Three cases clearly demonstrate this trend—the pro-Russian attack that shut down Estonian electronic infrastructure in 2007 for over 3 weeks using the Distributed Denial of Service approach; the 2010 Stuxnet attack—a sophisticated virus code that damages a central controlling system also called Supervisory Control and Data Acquisition—that was believed to have caused harm to Iran's Natanz nuclear facility specifically to its uranium centrifuge controlling system; and the 2011 security breach on the European Union Emission Trading Scheme, which controlled about 92 billion euro of the global market (Slocombe, 2012). Followed by this are the 2012 incidents, wherein millions of individual passwords were stolen from Sony and LinkedIn systems. This shows how technology and network infrastructure has become the backbone of many political and socioeconomic functions today and hence the resultant increasing trend of cybersecurity problems. Such situations become even more complicated when government systems are compromised by engaging in direct government to citizen or government to business services. Although this can provide efficiencies of scale as opposed to outsourcing it to contract organizations, an overdependence on government services can leave it open to cyber attacks if repetitive problems are not addressed. In doing so, governments must acknowledge that risks exist at multiple levels and manage them appropriately. These risks can vary from human errors to the compromise of physical networks and infrastructure architectures that result in information vulnerabilities through phishing, spamming, and application security vulnerabilities (Sommer & Brown, 2011; World Economic Forum, 2011). The good news is that careful research and analysis carried out by Sommer and Brown suggest that it is unlikely in the coming decade for any single cybersecurity incident to create a *global shock* that could cripple the entire global network. However, there is no doubt that localized cyber attacks against institutions and individuals will continue to occur.

Traditional crime: If we contrast these growing technology-related crime trends with data on traditional crime, using crime data recorded in the United States, the evidence shows a decline or flat lining of violent and property-related crime. Also gleaning from the Canadian system, the crime data reported by Statistics Canada suggests that per capita crime reporting has been on the decline for the last decade (Figure 2.5).

Generally, such reduction in crime would be a welcome sign for law enforcement and the criminal justice system. However, when analyzed thoroughly, what this might reflect is the reduction in capability of the legal system to respond effectively to crimes, which has resulted in the lower number of crimes being reported. Moutlon (2012) uses the Funnel Theory to expose the system's inefficiencies in Canada. Despite an approximate 20% reduction in the crime reported, Moulton points to the significant

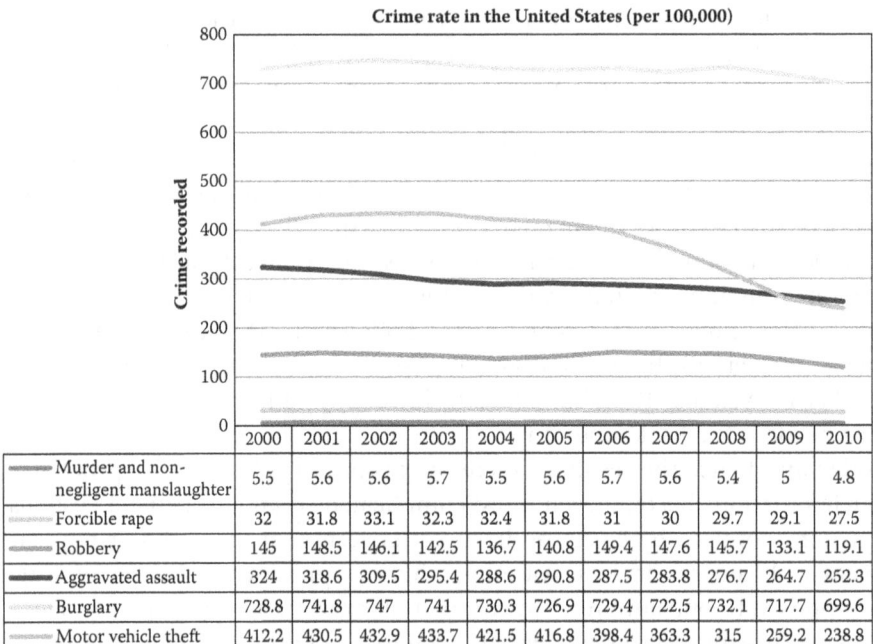

Crime rate in the United States (per 100,000)

	2000	2001	2002	2003	2004	2005	2006	2007	2008	2009	2010
Murder and non-negligent manslaughter	5.5	5.6	5.6	5.7	5.5	5.6	5.7	5.6	5.4	5	4.8
Forcible rape	32	31.8	33.1	32.3	32.4	31.8	31	30	29.7	29.1	27.5
Robbery	145	148.5	146.1	142.5	136.7	140.8	149.4	147.6	145.7	133.1	119.1
Aggravated assault	324	318.6	309.5	295.4	288.6	290.8	287.5	283.8	276.7	264.7	252.3
Burglary	728.8	741.8	747	741	730.3	726.9	729.4	722.5	732.1	717.7	699.6
Motor vehicle theft	412.2	430.5	432.9	433.7	421.5	416.8	398.4	363.3	315	259.2	238.8

Figure 2.5 Crime rate in the United States. (From Uniform Crime Reporting Statistics, U.S. Department of Justice.)

increase in costs of the legal system—court expenditures 20.9%, corrections expenditure 58.9% at the provincial and 44.7% at the federal level, policing expenditures 92% with personnel increase of only 3%. Moulton also points to the drastic increase of about six to eight times, over the last 3 decades, in the time required by the police to respond to a report of crime and the subsequent 22.7% increase over the last decade in the time required by the criminal justice system to finalize criminal cases. This has subsequently resulted in society developing its own alternatives to the criminal justice system. For instance, between the period of 2001 and 2006 Canada saw a 15% increase in private policing personnel when the public system grew by only 3%. These indications reflect the reality of the situation with the legal and criminal justice system. It is vital that adequate mechanisms be put in place to address problems that relate to boundary-specific traditional crime, as the cyber challenge that awaits the criminal justice system is borderless and boundary-spanning.

Societal Change

Earlier in this chapter, I briefly touched on elements of societal implications as a result of global repositioning, international governance and trade issues. Treverton, Lempert, and Kumar (2012) in their report *How*

Americans Will Live and Work in 2020 explore the implications of four societal trends specific to the United States: demographics, lifestyle, economic, and the workplace. They point to the changing nature of roles for the public and private sector in shouldering equal societal responsibility given the economic and fiscal uncertainty and depleting government revenues. Despite this change, an emerging trend has also been taking center stage wherein income and wealth inequalities between American whites and minority communities have been increasing significantly. The high birth rate in the Latino and generally non-white communities has resulted in over 50% of the new births (ending July 2011) taking place in non-white communities. This has further exacerbated the polarization of income and wealth inequalities. This is not typical just for the United States. As depicted in Figure 2.6, the OECD's *Future of Families to 2030* report also projects a sharp increase in the number of single person and single parent households in OECD countries.

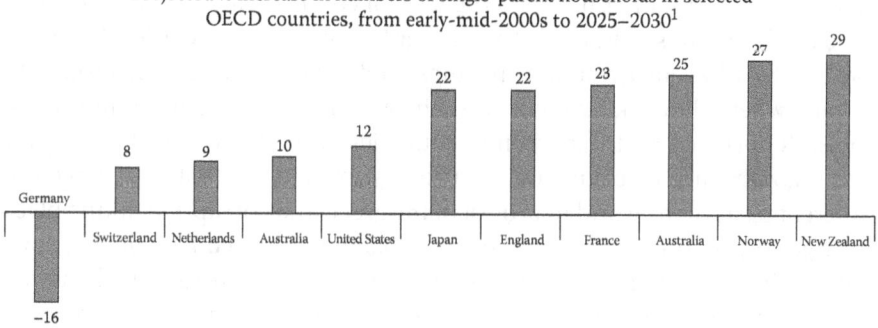

1. The periods over which changes are projected are as follows: Australia (2006–2026), Australia (2007–2030), France (2005–2030), Germany (2007–2025), Japan (2005–2030), Korea (2007–2030), Netherlands (2009–2030), New Zealand (2006–2031), Norway (2002–2030), Switzerland (2005–2030), United Kingdom (2006–2031) and United States (2000–2025)

Figure 2.6 Projected increase in single person and single parent households. (From Organization for Economic Cooperation and Development, *The future of families to 2030*, OECD, Paris, France, 2011.)

Should such projections eventuate especially in the single parent category, it is likely that income and wealth inequalities will continue to rise. There is substantial research evidence that suggests single parent households and poverty levels, and poverty and crime levels are linked (DeKeseredy, Alvi, Schwartz, & Tomaszewski, 2003; Western, 2006; Western & Wildeman, 2009). The increase in single person households can also alter the social fabric of society. Given the already high levels of Internet connectivity with youth in OECD countries (Broadhurst, 2010) and its occasional negative influence, which limits youth engagement with society, this could segregate and dismantle the very nature of being connected with society. This can result in issues such as higher youth unemployment, an increase in mental health issues resulting from individuals being less connected to society and feeling less part of a community, which could force them to take on criminal activities.

In an employment context, the polarization of low- and high-skilled workers—given the hollowing out of mid-level roles to technology and information infrastructure developments—is also becoming a societal problem given the rising rate of unemployment. This has resulted in an increase in a focus on education for higher order skills and subsequent increase in workforce participation by specific cohorts such as women and older people. Although these participation rate increases are seen as positive societal change, there are clusters that are distancing themselves from such challenges by increasing their dependence on government welfare. Furthermore, a higher proportion of people are using technological advancements to become engaged in political movements and activities. On one hand, this has motivated governments and political parties to enter into dialogues with communities and the society in decision-making. On the flip side, multiple views, perspectives, and ideologies clash when government attempts to achieve consensus and this raises the level of conflict within specific societal stakeholder groups. Although this has enhanced engagement levels within society, this has also resulted in quick mobilization of activist groups to extents where they take the law in their own hands. Cases in point are the society's uprisings that were seen in countries of the Middle East calling for better governance mechanisms, the Occupy movements that were staged in different parts of the world in protest of the greed and corruption taking place in large corporations and even the 2011 riots in the United Kingdom following a police shooting, which in a span of a few days spread quickly across most major cities. Such movements have clear implications for new types of crime that are emerging through social networking and the compounding challenges for the law enforcement system. Despite such wide-ranging multifaceted societal problems that are exacerbated by technology use, there are also deeply entrenched law enforcement-related systemic issues that warrant discussion. The following case study puts these issues into perspective. Let us consider the case of policing in India, in the state of Andhra Pradesh (AP).

Reflecting on Systemic Issues and Evidence from India: A Case Narrative

In speaking* with the police commissioner and senior officers in the state of AP the magnanimous scope of crime was evident. AP is India's fourth largest state with a population of over 84 million. Providing suitable law enforcement and prevention options for its metropolitan region that houses over 7 million people within an area of 250 km² is no easy task when the state has to contend with a rising number of criminal offences in economic crime, theft, burglary, and dacoits. Extending beyond the metropolitan region, the five deputy commissioners manage between five and eight districts—each of which comprises approximately 3 million people. Given the rising poverty levels and growing inequality in this society, the crime arena is a social challenge, turning into a profession of keeping individuals occupied and employed. This has resulted in growing expectations from the community on law enforcement officers in maintaining law and order to such an extent, wherein even maintenance of basic infrastructure and sanitation are perceived to be the responsibility of these officers. This is not unique to the Indian situation. As Ransley and Mazerolle (2009) have discussed, even in Australia police are being looked on to play an extended role in society by responding to entrenched social issues such as those within the Indigenous communities. Facilitating health checks, preventing excessive alcohol consumption, building new infrastructure, and encouraging school education have become part of the responsibility of the Northern Territory Police in Australia. In India, in AP specifically, addressing societal issues has become a compounding challenge with a lesser number of new recruits joining the police force, limiting wages and working conditions that include 14–16-hour shifts. In addition, the meager facilities offered to police officers in terms of housing, salary, allowances, and promotional opportunities make plain as to why it is difficult to attract individuals to the policing profession. One of the officers I interviewed also talked about his tenure of 21 years within the service during which time he was promoted only once. These are difficult working situations for officers.

In relation to criminal investigations, the senior station officer discussed the extensive political influence in the investigation of certain criminal cases.

* January 2010. Interview with the author, Hyderabad, India.

Because of an ever-increasing workload, as a result of scale and population, the ability of officers to communicate and engage effectively with society and display empathy for people's problems is constantly challenged. The officer also discussed the debilitating state of operational affairs in maintaining his station. For instance, the monthly allowance of 100 L of diesel only meets half the station's operational needs; a daily meal allowance per prisoner of 7 Indian Rupees is nowhere enough to even purchase a loaf of bread. Such issues have forced the station to make dubious deals with nearby gas stations, bars, and restaurants to meet the station's shortfall and in return these outlets are allowed to operate beyond the normal stipulated working hours. From a perspective of warranting corrupt practices, the officer also discussed how a junior officer is tasked with maintaining the books to record illegal resources including money that were being received by the station. Although most of these resources are utilized for operational purposes any under spend in the month gets distributed among officers to compensate for the shortfall in officer incomes. Such acts have never impacted on the manner in which crime reports are lodged and matters investigated. The senior station officer notes that every crime gets recorded irrespective of the situation. In terms of the duration taken for the investigation, this varies especially if the complainant withdraws from the case fearing the cumbersome court procedures or criminals themselves. In some cases, complainants themselves pay hefty bribes to either delay the investigation of the case or for closure altogether. People also have a preconceived mindset in terms of having to bribe police officers for the work they perform even if not specifically asked for. This has created a perception within the community that the work remains incomplete if a police officer is not bribed. Despite such conditions, the senior station officer talks about his long service within the police service. On being asked as to why and how he has survived in such harsh conditions within the police service for 21 years, he says the opportunities that existed when he joined the force were minimal despite having earned bachelor-level qualifications in science and education. He speaks of the immense respect he is able to command from society as the senior police officer in the jurisdiction, which he says is greater than what the local politician can also command. He takes pride in detailing instances where he has had to help mend relations between bickering neighbors, spousal disputes, and the like. He concludes by saying that he secures immense satisfaction from working with the community.

This case clearly depicts the grim picture for law enforcement officers and the issue of *forced* systemic corruption. The interplay between the officers who are instated to uphold the law and prevent crime are forced to operate in harsh conditions without requisite resources and support, which drives further disengagement from the system and heeds systemic corruption. Combined with the increasing demands from an institution that is squeezed to the maximum, the challenges on officers is massive to be able to work within the constraints of the system despite external power, influence, and pressure imposed on investigation matters. Although this narrative provides a context for systemic issues in India, the broader challenges may not be very different if experiences are compared from across the globe especially in states that have weak governance systems.

Systemic Implications and Opportunities

Having outlined the myriad challenges emerging from changes taking place at the global to the societal level, it is vital that some attention is provided to understanding its implications on the criminal justice system and avenues to leverage new opportunities as either a response mechanism or a deterrent.

Policy transfer convolution: The merit of policy transfer—specifically, crime prevention and control—across jurisdictions either regional or global is never direct. Although it is important to learn about what works and what does not across jurisdictions, the balance of this relationship is seldom linear (Legrand & Vas, 2014). A major impediment in straightforward policy transfer is the specific context of each region underpinned by its own crime landscape. For instance, *zero-tolerance policing* was adopted in the province of Ontario in Canada based on the positive results that emerged from its implementation in New York. However, this does not suggest that such a policy approach would be just as successful in other regions or in tackling different crime types. Research has shown that crime rates can drop in regions that do not adopt tougher criminal laws (Pollard, 1997). This suggests that linkages to increasing crime levels can be many and very often do not emerge from just one source. As DeKeseredy (2009) points out, the changes made by Ontario Premier Mike Harris to policies during his tenure until the early 2000s in health care, employment insurance, and welfare resulted in the rise of homeless people and unemployed youth flowing into the streets. Similarly, the election of Progressive Conservative Member Stephen Harper—a dedicated law and order advocate—as Canadian prime minister in 2006 saw incarceration rates in Canada increase by 3%, while at the same time homicide rates decreased by 10% from 2005. It was around this time that the poverty rate in cities like Toronto, Canada's poverty capital, was on the rise despite higher levels of employment (Monsebraaten & Daly, 2007). This suggests that policy complexity exists and linear ways of adopting cross-jurisdictional policies including crime prevention policies can sometimes result in negative consequences. This is not to suggest that policy transfer is an approach that must be avoided. In fact, it is quite the contrary. The only caveat is that any transfer of crime prevention policies must be matched with the contextual situation of the particular region.

Legislative complexity: If policy is one side of a coin called *trial and tribulation*, legislative complexity is the other side of the same coin. For instance, McNicol and Schloenhardt (2012, pp. 369, 385) have discussed the complexities that exist in dealing across borders when dealing with the issue of child sex tourism offences. The Australian Government in 2010 introduced a new Division 272 into the *Criminal Code* (Cth) to criminalize a range of sexual activities with children by Australians. Despite this introduction, prosecution and collection of evidence is still fraught with challenges when mutual assistance treaties and memoranda of understanding do not exist, for example, with Vietnam. Further on, the time it takes for government to introduce necessary legislation to tackle such criminal offences can be very long—as outlined in this context by McNicol and Schloenhardt noting that the introduction of Division 272 was a result of "extensive consideration of sexual offences internationally over the past decade" (p. 379). Notwithstanding even such an origination, the new offences create challenges for law enforcement agencies in terms of obtaining convictions due to the breadth of such new offences and also amplifying the possibility of wrongful convictions (McNicol, 2012, pp. 388–389).

In combating borderless and technology-related crime, which is a substantial challenge for legislation today, the question as Deibert and Rohozinski (2010) poses is not whether or not to regulate, but how to regulate. They equate cyberspace to a mob model where there is a constant tussle between "public and private authorities, civic association, criminal networks and underground economies" (Diebert & Rohozinski, 2010, p. 44). In such situations, effective coordination through public–private partnerships, regional cooperation, and reassessing of international governance relationships are mechanisms that must be orchestrated efficiently if legislation to tackle such complex and transnational nature of crime is to be successfully implemented (Alzab, 2012). This, as Broadhurst (2010) and Grabosky (2007) have argued, can prevent the use of safe havens and jurisdiction shopping.

Societal networks and partnerships: Despite such challenges, it is vital for law enforcement organizations to work much more closely with the community and relevant societal organizations, including businesses in tackling and preventing crime. Communities need to be empowered and trusted as partners in crime control actions not just at the local level but at all levels that can even extend to national security. Given the dominance and prominence of technology platforms and the increasing cybersecurity issues for our time, there is a need to build on—from "officer-driven street patrols" to "community-driven cyber patrols" tasked with ensuring and safeguarding communities, online and offline. For instance, the Government of India, through the Ministry of Home Affairs, is working closely with the fisheries community to gather intelligence and where required using these communities in extreme situations in actual armed confrontations. This is evident through the press release put out by the Minister of State of Home Affairs to its Parliament, which states:

> The fishermen are also being used as 'eyes and ears' to get valuable information relating to national security for intelligence gathering. Indian Coast Guard is regularly conducting community interaction programmes in the fishermen dominated villages along the coast to get valuable information relating to national security.... Coastal Security is a multi agency responsibility that involves surveillance, intelligence gathering, dissemination of information and actual armed confrontation (Press Information Bureau, Government of India, 22 May 2012).

Such sentiment of working collaboratively with societal partners has been reiterated by many, if tackling complex crime is to be successful. The level of government engagement and its ongoing relationship with society and citizens must be transformed. The World Economic Forum (2011) in its report *The Future of Government: Lessons Learned From Around The World* points out that governments need to continuously adapt and evolve to a changing citizenry, a society whose expectations are constantly developing. It is hence important that governments create new networks across the public, private, and the third sector to *coproduce public value* and subsequently transform itself into becoming flatter, agile, streamlined, and tech-enabled (FAST). Vas and Lenihan (2012) have used the public engagement initiative of New Brunswick to discuss in detail how such societal–government partnerships can be created and sustained. Extrapolating their study to the law enforcement context will be no different in its approach. This partnership can be created by governments, first understanding the complexity and multidimensional nature of crime specific to the community followed by a deeper engagement process with the community to identify alternatives and work collaboratively toward effectively implementing the planned action. Underpinning such a process is the need for government and society to reach a position of trust and commitment.

Research partnerships and analytics: Finally, it is vital that law enforcement organizations continue to enhance their partnerships with research institutions and related entities that have built expertise in synthesizing large amounts of data and information. In a world where there is no dearth of information and the rapid pace at which new data is created, it is critical for law enforcement officers to create information networks that can help demystify the data, reduce information complexity, and subsequently identify emerging trends and patterns that can tackle crime in a proactive manner. Just as Goldstein (2003), Johnston and Shearing (2009), Bradley and Nixon (2009), Cordner and White (2010), Weisburd and Neyroud (2011), and many others have pointed out, there is a weak relationship between the availability of information and knowledge, and its use in operational policing—a disconnect in having a "shared academic-practitioner infrastructure" (Fyfe & Wilson, 2012). This needs to be rectified. It is no more the case where such networks are only a value-added organizational benefit. Partnerships with researchers and analytics can significantly aid law enforcement organizations in many other ways too, which include enhancing data analytics capability in law enforcement officers, supporting the identification of new data and information sources, making sense of such material for law enforcement purposes, and proactively examining emerging crime trends and patterns. This helps tremendously in reducing uncertainty and converting elements of uncertainty to risk elements to which appropriate risk management strategies can be created. Another benefit of such partnerships, which is most often overlooked, is the aspect of getting stakeholders outside the law enforcement arena as partners to better understand the complexity and boundaries within which the system functions. This can create further goodwill and increased levels of trust, which can result in new societal partnerships and networks to flourish, forming a vital part of a networked criminal justice system.

Conclusion

This chapter has argued for the need to adopt new ways of thinking to tackle the changing nature of crime. It is no longer optimum to use silo approaches to comprehend the connected nature of criminal offences taking place at the societal level without understanding the changes taking place at the macro global levels.

This chapter has discussed global challenges in the context of geostrategic imbalances given the perceived shift of economic power from the West to the East and the boosting of military capabilities and related trade competition. In drawing out the economic growth dichotomy with societal challenges, better governance to tackle issues of systemic corruption and increasing inequality in society is a key emergent trend that is being witnessed across different regions of the globe. The growing reliance on technology is also impacting negatively on crime trends especially with regards to organized financial and technology-enabled crime. Despite such external factors of influence on crime, this chapter shows that systemic issues still exist within law enforcement institutions, especially in economies with weak governance frameworks.

Given such trends and heightened levels of uncertainty, there is a need to transition from the current state where criminal offences are reacted and law enforced, to a new state where crime can be preempted and prevented. It is crucial that the societal divide that exists with the criminal justice system is bridged and the community is made an important partner within the network. To do so, it is also vital that such societal networks leverage the benefits of technological platforms to enable better use of social media to garner participation.

Such a networked system must thrive on societal engagement and partnerships that can help reduce uncertainty and subsequently enhance the capability of the criminal justice system and the individuals who serve within it.

References

Alzab, M. (2012). International regulation urgently needed to protect citizens against cybercrime. Regulatory Institutions Network (RegNet)—ANU College of Asia and Pacific. Retrieved from http://regnet.anu.edu.au/news/international-regulation-urgently-needed-protect-citizens-against-cybercrime, accessed on July 26, 2012.

Ashdown, N. (2012). Straw poll: Fiji begins preparations for democratic elections. *IHS Jane's Intelligence Review, 24*, 4, 26–31.

Australian Government (2011). *Organised crime in Australia.* Canberra, Australia: Australian Crime Commission.

Bammer, G., & Smithson, M. (2008). *Uncertainty and risk: Multidisciplinary perspectives.* London, England: Earthscan.

Bisley, N. (2009). Geopolitical shifts in Australia's region toward 2030. *Security Challenges, 5*(1), 15–36. Kokoda Foundation, Australia.

Bradley, D., & Nixon, C. (2009). Ending the dialogue of the deaf: Evidence and policing policies and practices, an Australian case study. *Police Practice and Research: An International Journal, 10*(5–6), 423–435.

Broadhurst, R. (2010). A new global convention on cybercrime. *Pakistan Journal of Criminology, 2*(4), 1–10.

Burke, J. (2012). Over 80% of Australians against Chinese investment in agricultural land. *Foodmagazine.* Retrieved from http://www.foodmag.com.au/news/over-80-of-australians-against-chinese-investment, accessed on July 28, 2012.

Carbone, C., & Nauth, K. (2012). From smart house to networked home. *The Futurist: Forecasts, Trends and Ideas About The Future, 46*(4), 29–31.

Cordner, G., & White, S. (2010). Special issue: The evolving relationship between police research and police practice. *Police Practice and Research: An International Journal, 11*(2), 90–94.

Deibert, R., & Rohozinski, R. (2010). Liberation vs control: The future of cyberspace. *Journal of Democracy, 21*(4), 43–57.

DeKeseredy, W. (2009). Canadian crime control in the new millennium: The influence of neo-conservative US policies and practices. *Police Practice and Research: An International Journal, 10*(4), 305–316.

DeKeseredy, W., Alvi, S., Schwartz, M., & Tomaszewksi, A. (2003). *Under siege: Poverty and crime in a public housing community.* Lanham, MD: Lexington Books.

Fyfe, N., & Wilson, P. (2012). Knowledge exchange and police practice: Broadening and deepening the debate around researcher-practitioner collaboration. *Police Practice and Research: An International Journal, 13*(4), 306–314.

Goldstein, H. (2003). On further developing problem-oriented policing. In J. Knuttson, *Problem-oriented policing: From innovation to mainstream. Crime prevention studies* (Vol. 15, pp. 13–47). London, England: Sage.

Gopal, S., & Najam, A. (2012). *Connecting the dots: Information visualisation and text analysis of the searchlight project newsletters.* Boston, MA: Boston University, The Frederick S. Pardee Centre for the Study of the Longer-Range Future.

Grabosky, P. (2007). The internet, technology and organised crime. *Asian Journal of Criminology*, 2, 145–162.

Innes, M. (2006). Policing uncertainty: Countering terror through community intelligence and democratic policing. *Annals of the American Academy*, 605, 222–241.

Johnston, L., & Shearing, C. (2009). Special issue: New possibilities for policing research and practice. *Police Practice and Research: An International Journal*, 10(6), 415–422.

LeGrand, T., & Vas, C. (2014). Epistemic Policy Transfer: The Case of the OECD and Skills and Workforce Development Policy in Australia. *Journal of Comparative Policy Analysis: Research and Practice*. DOI:10.1080/13876988.2014.910909.

McNicol, J., & Schloenhardt, A. (2012). Australia's child sex tourism offences. *Current Issues in Criminal Justice—Journal of the Institute of Criminology*, 23(3), 369–393.

Monsebraaten, L., & Daly, R. (2007). Toronto families slip into poverty. *The Toronto Star*. Retrieved from http://canadianimmigrationreform.blogspot.com.au/2007/11/toronto-fast-becoming-canada-povery.html, accessed on July 16, 2012.

Moulton, E. (2012). Myth and reality: Interpreting the dynamics of crime trends: Lies, damn lies and (criminal) statistics. *Police Practice and Research: An International Journal*. doi:10.1080/15614263.2012.674300.

Organisation for Economic Cooperation and Development. (2011). *The Future of families to 2030*. Paris, France: OECD.

Pollard, C. (1997). Zero-tolerance: Short term fix, long term liability? In N. Dennis, *Zero-tolerance policing in a free society*. London, England: Institute of Economic Affairs.

Ransley, J., & Mazerolle, L. (2009). Policing in an era of uncertainty. *Police Practice and Research: An International Journal*, 10(4), 365–381.

Slocombe, G. (2012). Cyber security—Web war II. *Asia-Pacific Defence Reporter*, 38(4), 28–41.

Sommer, P., & Brown, I. (2011). *Reducing systemic cybersecurity risk*. Paris, France: OECD/IFP Programme.

The Millennium Project, Global Futures Studies & Research. (2009). Global Challenges for Humanity. http://www.millennium-project.org/millennium/challeng.html.

Treverton, G., Lempert, R., & Kumar, K. (2012). *How Americans will live and work in 2020*. Santa Monica, CA: RAND Corporation.

Vas, C., & Lenihan, D. (2012). Innovating government through public engagement: The case study of New Brunswick. In D. Lenihan, *Rescuing policy: The case for public engagement*. Ottawa, Canada: Public Policy Forum.

Weisburd, D., & Neyroud, P. (2011). *Police science. Toward a new paradigm. New perspectives in policing*. Cambridge, MA: Harvard Kennedy School and National Institute of Justice.

Western, B. (2006). Punishment and inequality in America. New York: Russell Sage Foundation.

Western, B., & Wildeman, C. (2009). The black family and mass incarceration. *The ANNALS of the American Academy of Political and Social Science*, 621(1), 221–242.

Wilson, R. (1996). Using international human rights law and machinery in defending borderless crime cases. *Fordham International Law Journal*, 20, 1606–1636.

World Economic Forum. (2011). *The future of government: Lessons learned from around the world*. Geneva, Switzerland: World Economic Forum.

Reforming Policing to Improve Economic and Social Development in Advanced Democracies

II

Real Influence of Sir Robert Peel on Twenty-First Century Policing in America

3

PETER JOHNSTONE

Contents

Introduction

Influences on policing in the United States are as diverse[1] as the pattern of policing within the country. It was perhaps inevitable that given the influence of Britain on the early development of the United States there would be adoption of established criminal justice practices from Britain, especially those from England and the Common Law. Consequently the English criminal justice lexicon; sheriff, constable, "Hue and Cry," magistrates, justices of the peace, circuit judges, and a concept of what it means to "police" are all largely, but not exclusively, informed by England. However, a closer inspection of the informing factors reveal that much of what occurred in policing in England throughout the Middle Ages and into the eighteenth century was not exclusively a domestic creation. Subsequently what transferred to the United States as an English system was in fact a concomitant of Anglo-Saxon[2] and Nordic customs with influence from France in the eleventh century and then again, significantly, the eighteenth century.

"The office of sheriff is the one secular dignity generally known in English-speaking lands which for more than nine centuries has maintained a continuous existence and preserved its distinguishing features."[3] Variously known as the shire-reeve, sheriff, or *scirgerefa*[4] and eventually elevated to the title vice-count or viscount[5] in some instances, the sheriff[6] is a well-known feature of the common law criminal justice landscape, which has a history that can be traced back to at least the reign of Ine[7] as a royal appointee with local administrative functions.[8] Over time the responsibilities of the shire-reeve increased and his role developed into, *inter alia*, those of tax collector, jailer, and court administrator.[9] The task of securing felons and then holding them until the arrival of a court was a responsibility assigned to the sheriff from the period of Alfred the Great.[10] "Moreover he was a royal steward and was associated with the king's *tun* by the fact that he fed the king's prisoners there."[11] Securing the attendance of suspects before a trial court remains a primary function of the office of sheriff today. In his role as the chief law officer for a shire, the sheriff held authority to demand assistance from local village people. Over time various appointments were made to provide a level of local rudimentary protective services that from modest beginnings as watchmen and vigilantes[12] would eventually form the basis of a professional police force for England. In London, we have specific references to the official powers of the sheriff in the laws of King Athelstan,[13] "For this district the reeve has apparently been holding a folkmote, within it he takes pledges for the observance of the peace, and in London region its men are to be led by him in pursuit of the thief."[14]

William the Bastard,[15] conqueror and first Norman king of England significantly increased the responsibilities of the sheriff. Within the first few years of his reign he appointed numerous fellow countrymen to the county shire-reeves position to ensure that there was a close watch on the fiscal as well as local feudal responsibilities.[16] Importantly, though local and new French sheriffs did not lose any of the previous responsibilities of the office "Among these may be named his powers connected with peace and with police."[17] Whereas in the pre-Norman period the sheriff had authority to preside over a hundred court hearings, to uphold the king's peace and to apprehend suspected criminals, under William these functions were formalized and positively encouraged.

The office of constable also existed prior to the arrival of the conqueror. At the time of the invasion sheriffs were ordered by Harold of England to "… appoint constables in the hundreds, townships and neighbourhoods. All were to obey the head constable of the shire in matters 'ad defensionem regni et pacis conservacionem contra alienigenas, vel contra quoscunque alios pacis perturbatores'."[18] Aside from his famous dispute with Thomas Beckett, Henry II was responsible for many legal innovations. The Assize of Clarendon, 1166, has frequent references to the sheriff[19] in their policing role and in their custodial role: "And when a robber or murderer or thief, or harbourers of them, shall be taken on the aforesaid oath, if the Justices shall not be about to come quickly enough into that county where they have been taken, the sheriffs shall send word to the nearest justice through some intelligent man, that they have taken such men; and the Justices shall send back word to the sheriffs where they wish those men to be brought before them: and the sheriffs shall bring them before the Justices."[20] King John signed the Magna Carta 1 year before his death. This famous document contains 63 clauses, 27 of which relate to the role and functions of the sheriff. Clause 47 states that "We will not make men justices, constables, sheriffs, or bailiffs, unless they are such as know the law of the realm, and are minded to observe it rightly."[21]

By the time of Henry III,[22] roving felons were a significant problem and constables were regularly assisting sheriffs in providing patrols within villages and across the countryside to ensure safe passage between villages and to market towns.[23] Henry III also increased the remit of his peace officers to take responsibility for patrolling the English coastline and vulnerable fortifications.[24] Toward the end of Henry's reign the sheriffs and their assistants, the constable, had accumulated significant powers including the provision of protection to inland castles. To counteract this encroachment on their "bailiwick,"[25] the barons collaborated and managed to reaffirm themselves as the primary custodians of the shire. This marks the end of shrieval dominance in county peacekeeping albeit a number of the newly appointed shire and region keepers were themselves former sheriffs.[26] Under the new system, sheriffs were still responsible for apprehending and securing the attendance of felons and in real terms the new shire keepers often served under the sheriff when he exercised policing powers and functions. It was not the case, however, that the shire keepers would answer to the constable who remained a lower level "peacekeeper" answerable to the authority of the sheriff. By the close of this century, the "shire keeper's" role had developed into a regional responsibility,[27] which in some respects had the effect of restoring the primary policing function within the bailiwick back with the sheriffs[28] and constables. The elevated office of shire keeper remained and gained in stature to become the primary administrative functionary of a county. It still exists in England today as the, largely ceremonial, Lord Lieutenant[29] who is served by his assistant the High Sheriff.[30] As Professor Raymond Moley of Columbia University once stated, "Today in England the sheriff is a dignified and gentlemanly nonentity who guarantees for one year the proper performance of work in which he plays no part. An under-sheriff performs legal routine chiefly in relation to civil proceedings such as the summoning of jurors, the execution of civil judgments, and the returns of the results of parliamentary elections."[31] The first person to hold the office of sheriff in America was William Stone in 1634 in the County of Accomack, Virginia.[32] One visible policing aspect of being sheriff was the ability to require that local citizens assist in the apprehension of offenders. This right to demand help existed in medieval England as well as colonial America. The formation of a posse[33] gained greater actual, as well as fictional, notoriety during westward expansion in the United States. It has also been attributed to the development of vigilantism and private policing during the eighteenth and nineteenth centuries.[34] In terms of policing models, the sheriff is one of the only examples of centralized policing ever to occur in England. Its transposition to the United States alongside decentralized city forces gives the United States uniqueness lost to England centuries ago.

In England, the night watchmen, beadle, and constable limped through protecting citizens and apprehending criminals for the next 500 years. In France, the king had created a policing presence, the *Maréchaussée*, as far back as the early 1100s. This was followed by a larger military police response from 1337[35] onward. Between 1536 and 1544, King Francis I implemented a range of measures to formalize policing across the nation. The "Sun King" Louis XIV reigned in France from 1643 to 1715. He was renowned for his work on legal reform largely instituted and executed by his minister Jean Baptiste Colbert.[36] In October 1666, Louis ordered Colbert to design a plan for a Paris police force. By March of the following year, Louis authorized the creation of the office of Prefect of Police for Paris,[37] followed in 1699 by a royal decree that authorized the establishment of Prefecture of Police for each major city in France.[38] The range of policing responsibilities was very broad and extensively beyond the activities associated with contemporary policing in the United States.[39] Over the period of the next 150 years, the role and function of the city police of France expanded. In particular, that of the Prefecture of Police and his officers who assumed judicial responsibilities unfamiliar to sheriffs and constables in England. In one instance the "police court" at *Le Châtelet*, Paris, heard 200 cases in a 3-hour period. Forty-five women and 16 men were sentenced that day, May 25, 1759.[40] The sentencing powers of the police court were also extensive. Benjamin Dechauflour was tried for sodomy on May 24, 1726. He was convicted the same day and sentenced to death by burning. The punishment was carried out the following morning.[41] As the pending revolution gained momentum in France, so too did the anxiety of the monarchy and Paris slid into a period of sinister policing where spying became the main thrust of police work within the capital. Often quoted but never verified, Gabriel de Sartines, Lieutenant-General of Police from 1759 to 1774, reportedly told the king that wherever three persons speak to one another on the street, one of them would be one of his police spies.[42] Undoubtedly, the pre-Revolution Paris police[43] represents a well-organized body of law enforcement personnel that had specialist skills and responsibilities far beyond those represented in England during the same period. The cities of France had a formal civilian police presence and the smaller towns and villages had the protections provided by a military police. By 1788, there was one police officer for every 193 residents of Paris.[44]

After the tumultuous events of the revolution, the *Maréchaussée* managed to remain in form but were renamed the *Gendarmerie Nationale*.[45] "With the accession of Napoléon Bonaparte as first consul in 1799 the trend towards centralization of police was reinvigorated."[46] The Napoleonic Codes brought order to the legislation of previous regimes and provided a comprehensive body of all applicable law to all citizens. Application of the new codes rested with the existing civilian police forces and a redesigned and higher profile military police force to be called the *Gendarmerie Nationale*. Drawn from the ranks of serving military personnel, the *Gendarmerie Nationale* would comprise of well-trained, well-resourced, well-paid military men who would live in barracks[47] and provide police services to the citizens and the highways of rural France. As "the man who would restore order to a society plagued by crime, violence and uncertainty,"[48] Napoléon created a military police force that was copied throughout continental Europe. His less famous civilian police continued to employ dubious spying methods under the directorship of Joseph Fouché[49] but combined together, the military country police and the civilian city police provided a comprehensive and effective policing response for France that was superior to every other nation state in the world at the time. All that remained was to ensure effective supervision within those towns of smaller populations and this was achieved through the creation of the *Commissaire de Police.* The commissaire reported to the Prefect of the Département but with the ability to circumvent this line of authority if needed. "This made the *commissaire* a very powerful and influential figure locally. Thanks to his 'direct-line' to powerful figures like Fouché and Savary,[50] he was often able to outflank not only the prefects[51] and mayors of his department, but even the judiciary and the gendarmerie, when it came to identifying common criminals, political subversives or wayward, allegedly corrupt local officials." In 1829, the same year that Sir Robert Peel finally managed to convince the British parliament to authorize a police force for London,[52] France reestablished the *sergent de ville.* A uniformed civilian appointment that had been present in a variety of forms across Europe for more than 200 years,[53] the renaissance version was charged with providing a police presence in the smaller towns of France, which would supplement the work of the *Commissaire de Police.*[54] Much like Dickens' ridicule of the beadle and watchman of London[55] the *sergent de ville* did not escape the critical tones of Victor Hugo in the role of Javert[56] in Les Misérables. Notwithstanding the comedy of policing the combination of a military gendarmerie and a civilian police force across all of France positioned the country to be at the forefront of policing in the later years of the eighteenth and the early years of the nineteenth centuries. "Perhaps the highest compliment ever paid to the Napoleonic *Gendarmerie* came from Britain, the arch-enemy of Napoleonic France, when in the 1820s, the secretary for Ireland, Sir Robert Peel, chose it as his model for the new Royal Irish Constabulary. Even Napoléon's bitterest enemies came quickly to acknowledge the usefulness of this particular institution."[57]

In eighteenth-century England the word police was virtually unknown.[58] When the word was introduced "...it was regarded with the utmost suspicion as a portent of the sinister force which held France in its grip."[59] As Edward Burt wrote in 1720, "...Soon after his arrival in London, he had observed a good deal of Dirt and disorder in the Streets, and asking about the *Police,* but finding none that understood the Term, he cried out, Good lord! How can one expect Order among these people, who have not such heard a Word as *Police* in their Language."[60] London was reeling under a crime wave and the local watch and beadle system was woefully incapable of dealing with the organized serial felon. The constable system was still a reflection of medieval England and the night watchmen were old, inept, and frequently asleep or drunk on duty.[61] In 1792, the Middlesex Justices Act created the establishment of a police office within London. In reality much had been achieved before passage of this legislation and a recognizable police force had been in existence in a number of manifestations for the City of Westminster and the river Thames for many years. "In fact, there were a number of police offices, all rather similar to the Bow Street police office which had been functioning for 30 years."[62] In the early years of the eighteenth century, Thomas de Veil was appointed as magistrate to the City of Westminster. Over the course of the next 17 years, he established his Bow Street office as one of the most efficient within the metropolis. In 1748, De Veil was succeeded by the novelist Henry Fielding and his half brother John Fielding.[63] Henry soon authored *An Enquiry into the Cause of the Late Increase of Robbers* and to the surprise of some of his contemporaries Fielding immersed himself into writing about[64] and practicing the establishment of a police force for the City of Westminster and Middlesex County from the Bow Street residence. Over time the mixed bag of assistants that Fielding managed to employ proved themselves to be reliable thief catchers with an in-depth knowledge of the criminals within the immediate vicinity of Bow Street.[65] His associates were soon nick-named the Bow Street Runners,[66] their official title was Principal Officer of Bow Street.[67] The Bow Street Police office was far from an ideal solution to the London crime problem. What it represented was a practical move toward a permanent police force for the metropolis. Regency England was still plagued with reward systems and general mistrust of a permanent force that might in any way appear to represent a standing army. Sir Leon Radzinowicz described the Bow Street office as "The headquarters of a closely knit caste of speculators in the detection of crime, self-seeking and unscrupulous, but also daring and efficient when daring and efficiency coincided with their private interest."[68]

The combined efforts of De Veil, the Fielding's, and Patrick Colquhoun all amount to a significant influence on policing London. Armed officers patrolled the main streets of London during the nighttime,[69] the highways into and out of the metropolis were "policed" by 68 patrols,[70] and on the eve of the 1829 Act uniformed officers patrolled the central streets during daylight hours.[71] In 1792, a Scottish-born merchant who had spent a number of years in Virginia was one of the first appointees under the new legislation that created stipendiary magistrates.[72] Patrick Colquhoun[73] immediately took up the issue of providing London with a regular, paid, full-time police force. He anonymously published *A Treatise on the Police of the Metropolis* in 1795 in which he estimated that the indigent population of London was so great that there was in existence a class of habitual criminals, 50,000 in number, who had no alternative but to engage in crime.[74] He even suggested that the French police[75] were a suitable model[76] for adoption in England.[77] Needless to say these views won him no friends in the British parliament and his strenuous attempts to bring about the adoption of legislation that would establish a London police force were repeatedly defeated.[78] Undaunted by the intransigence of the British ruling elite Colquhoun persisted and he can certainly be credited with playing a significant role in the establishment of a full-time police force for the river Thames.[79]

By the late eighteenth century, more than 13,500 vessels were competing daily for space on the river Thames.[80] Crime was rampant and the merchants of London united in supporting the establishment of a permanent protection force.[81] In June 1798, the merchants of London established a Marine Police Establishment[82] with a permanent staff of 80[83] and a reserve of more than 100. By the end of the year, *The Times* reported that "It is astonishing the effects the institution has already achieved in the preventing of piracies and robberies....."[84] In 1800, the British government endorsed the private policing enterprise and a Police Bill[85] was passed to formalize and make public policing of the river Thames. The main proponents of the Bill[86] were John Harriot,[87] Patrick Colquhoun,[88] and Jeremy Bentham.[89] There can be no doubt that London now had a permanent, uniformed police force that operated as a "public institution, regulated by statute and designed to safeguard commercial and other property on the river."[90]

Views about the impact of the Fielding's and Colquhoun are varied. Emsley refers to them as a "veritable holy trinity" in the eyes of Whig historians,[91] whereas Critchley considered their achievements meager.[92] In a sense both opinions are correct. The Fielding's undoubtedly moved the policing agenda forward to the point at which, small though it was, London had a group of paid, permanent police officers. Colquhoun, although personally frustrated by the lack of recognition he received for his attempts to change the hearts and minds of the British parliament, he too raised the level of awareness and the volume of discussion as well as achieving the personal satisfaction of ensuring that a marine police force was established, which still exists within the Metropolitan Police today. If we attribute the introduction of the word "police" to the Fielding's then it is to Colquhoun that we owe thanks for its absorption into the English lexicon. What the "holy trinity" did not achieve was to convince the British public that a permanent police force would be anything other than a foreign invasion. This sleight of hand was left to a politician, Sir Robert Peel, and another round of crime waves in the early 1800s.[93] However, one of the great achievements of this trio, whether by design or default, was that they managed to change the negative perception of foreign policing to a uniquely English entity that focused exclusively on maintenance of the peace and the prevention and detection of crime.[94]

Opposition toward a full-time land force for London was still strong in the early years of the nineteenth century. Britain was at war with France and anything that had the slightest resemblance of a *Gendarmerie* was repeatedly rejected, by the populous, the press, and the parliament.[95] "The necessities of time, emphasized by the crime wave and frequent riots, created the stage for London police reform; however, little could have been accomplished without the political skills of Sir Robert Peel."[96] Peel[97] was promoted to chief secretary for Ireland in September 1812. His responsibilities included the maintenance of law and order in the country and to this effect he was responsible for the Peace Preservation Act 1814,[98] which established the Irish Peace Preservation Force,[99] a forerunner to the Royal Irish Constabulary of 1822.[100] Public disturbances had become a regular feature of life throughout Ireland and the government frequently faced the task of quelling public disorder. "Peel's arrival coincided with a lull in banditti activity, but it was his job to muster the forces of authority in anticipation of the inevitable trouble to come."[101] Peel was much impressed by Napoléon's *Gendarmerie*; he approved of the military rigor and the utilization of a barrack system to house members of the force. And whereas he might not have been as enamored as Colquhoun who had referred to the French police as having "The greatest degree of professionalism,"[102] he certainly recognized the value of having a countrywide paramilitary policing response that was answerable to a central authority. Peel was pleased with his creation and wrote somewhat prematurely, "Although the police bill has been but a few weeks in operation, the effect is already such as to justify the most sanguine expectation of its ultimate success."[103] Peel retired from his post as chief secretary for Ireland in 1817 and returned to England. His departure from Ireland was lamented in many quarters[104] and it has been, perhaps generously said that he may have intentionally created the Peace Preservation Force to help alleviate the "'pitiable condition of Ireland'"[105] by providing a source of employment. Peel left Ireland with the blueprint for a Common Law Gendarmerie that was to be exported around the globe to almost every former British colony. It was considered by some as, "Being without parallel in its semi-military organisation, with exception, perhaps, of the French gendarmerie...."[106] In 1822, Peel was elevated to the position of home secretary where he would now have the opportunity to grapple with the police issue back in England.[107]

"Coloring the entire discussion was the example of an efficient and repressive system of police in France, where extensive intelligence networks caught ordinary criminals as well as those who spoke and acted in ways that undermined the stability of the regime...."[108] Peel had become an astute and cautious politician, he recognized that to move forward he would need to advocate a moderate approach that emphasized preventative measures and crime detection provided for by a uniformed but distinctly civilian force.[109] A compromise was inevitable. One significant factor for Peel was the strong opposition voiced by the financial "City of London."[110] He decided not to attempt to bring the "Square Mile" into his new plans[111] and on Tuesday September 29, 1829[112] the first uniformed officers of the London Metropolitan Police commenced evening patrol across the metropolis to save the City.[113] Their uniforms were carefully chosen to reflect civilian fashion of the day, top hat and blue tunic tails,[114] and they carried no more than a truncheon to protect themselves against the criminal underworld of the metropolis. Within 8 months the initial intake of 1000 men[115] had risen to more than 3000.[116] The new police force was led by two commissioners, both of Irish descent, one a lawyer, Richard Mayne[117] and the other a former military officer, Lt. Col. Charles Rowan.[118] Despite initial criticism of Peel and his influential supporter the Duke of Wellington, London's "Raw Lobsters"[119] slowly turned the hearts and minds of its skeptics and the more endearing terms *Peelers* and *Bobby*[120] began to enter the "new policing" language. As one commentator noted, "And yet a couple of years later these same vestries agreed the unfavourable impression and jealousy formerly existing against the new police is rapidly diminishing ... and it has fully answered the purpose for which it was formed...."[121] Every recruit to the new London Metropolitan Police was issued with a handbook of *General Instructions* compiled by Sir Robert Peel. It stated that "It should be understood at the outset that the object to be attained is the prevention of crime.... The absence of crime will be considered the best proof of the complete efficiency of the police,"[122] These words have endured and are still viewed as the fundamental basis for policing in many parts of the world today. By 1856, the County and Borough Police Act required every county and borough in England and Wales to establish a police force.[123] The following year similar legislation was passed in Scotland.

One of the dilemmas Peel faced was whether to establish a uniformed or plainclothed police force. Either way he was likely to be criticized.[124] If uniformed, they would be a *Gendarmerie* and if plainclothed, they would be Paris police "spies."[125] As we know he opted for uniforms. A detective unit was not established in London until 1842. During the interim period Principal Officers[126] from the disbanded Bow Street Police Office served as a detective agency available for hire to individuals as well as the Metropolitan Police. In France, a significant detective police department, much maligned by the English as "sinister," had been operational for more than 100 years. Then under Fouche this unit gained greater notoriety and the name *brigade de sûreté*. But it was not until the arrival of a former criminal, Eugène Vidocq, in 1812 that the *sûreté* became synonymous with sleuths and undercover work associated with contemporary police detection.[127] Vidocq, variously described as, "A lower type of man, yet still a great name in the history of French police ... who began his career as a thief"[128] and "From unpromising origins as a two-bit thief, army deserter, grafter and convict, he rose in fame to become the celebrated chief of the Paris Sûreté police and an internationally renowned private detective."[129] The "poacher turned gamekeeper"[130] Vidocq was apparently a larger-than-life character who captured the friendship and imagination of Dumas and Balzac. He was "Known to embellish his tales, and historians have difficulty separating fact from fiction in his accounts."[131] Regardless of the criticism and colorful nature of his character, Vidocq was a pioneer in detective techniques. Not only did he utilize handwriting, paper, and ink analyses to solve cases, but also foresaw the day when fingerprints would be used to identify suspects.[132] After his departure, the *sûreté* continued to rise in stature as the preeminent detective police agency until the arrival of "Scotland Yard." Notwithstanding the rise of the "Yard" Vidocq's impact traversed the Atlantic and he is credited with inspiring Allan Pinkerton[133] and J. Edgar Hoover.[134] The quality and effectiveness of the *sûreté* did not go unnoticed in London either and a number of years after Vidocq's[135] resignation, a London Metropolitan Police officer implemented a version of his model. There are two dates associated with the introduction of plain-clothed detectives in London, 1842 and then 1878.[136] The first attempts to run an effective detective unit were plagued by allegations of corruption and scandal[137] culminating in the "Trial of the Detectives" in 1877.[138] The following year, Charles H. Vincent,[139] a lawyer, police officer, and politician was given the opportunity to reorganize the detective branch and form the modern Criminal Investigation Department (CID). Over time, Scotland Yard detectives became synonymous with criminal investigation excellence[140] and surpassed the *sûreté* in stature.

Between 1605 and 1905, policing in America was influenced by a multitude of European forces. There is a collective agreement among a number of authors[141] that early policing methods were drawn from the established roles of the sheriffs, constables,[142] Hue and Cry, night watchmen, vigilantes, and "watch and ward," and the wide and varied assortment of criminal justice law enforcement officials that had developed over the previous 1600 years, mostly from England.[143] Attractive as this simplistic and often very brief approach may be these accounts rarely, if ever, pay any attention to the role of France and the influences that were made on English policing by the French. In reality much of the old world systems were either irrelevant or rejected by the new settlers, and the utilization of an established system of policing was adopted due to familiarity until a better system was created that would be uniquely American. For the time that colonies were forced to operate under the English crown adoption of English law, and its policing style, was inevitable. But once the opportunity arose to forge a new body of policing and laws, the colonists moved forward swiftly; modifying the familiar and substituting the irrelevant.[144]

Although few formal policing systems were in place in the seventeenth century, America's[145] informal, ancient and familiar vestiges of a manorial system were prevalent, especially in the Northern states. In England, bring-ing a prosecution for a criminal matter was still an individual affair. The pri-vate citizen bore the entire cost of the prosecution until legislation partially relieved this burden in 1752. In an effort to encourage the participation of the public in curbing the eighteenth-century crime wave, the crown offered increasingly large rewards[146] to those who gave evidence against felons.[147] Due to the high cost of taking a case before the courts, it became common practice for merchants, farmers, and civic groups to form associations to help defray the cost of bringing a criminal prosecution.[148] A version of the English societies manifest as a more forceful "crime-control vigilantism"[149] was the preferred adoption in America, where a relationship between the sheriff and posse, of which a number grew into vigilantes, was not an uncommon feature of the American frontier.[150] A crucial distinction should be drawn, however, the English societies never operated outside of the law, whereas the American development into vigilante groups[151] frequently did.[152] Nevertheless the sim-ilarities are clear; both developments were in response to inadequacies in established policing provision and failures of the criminal justice system to protect the interests of the individual. The corollary between the extra-legal methods employed by the American frontier vigilantes and the emergence of private policing groups that used strong arm tactics on behalf of railroad and mining companies should not be understated.[153]

By the close of the eighteenth century, much as England was struggling to make sense of its own crime problems, especially those in the capital, America too needed to apply a diversity[154] of police responses to the wide variety of challenges facing southern business entrepreneurs, northern bibli-cal refugees, and westward bound migrants. Critics of this view may seek to take refuge in terminology and explain the history of individual entities such as sheriffs as being distinctly different from those of the police. Yet we have seen that the term *police* was unfamiliar in England during much of the colonial years and once adopted had a broad and varied application. Narrowing the parameters of the word to Peel's application may indeed have been a way of circumventing something overtly French, for the English, but the early role of the police constable in America carried a very broad port-folio of responsibilities far more closely resembling a *sergeant de ville* than a "Bobby." As Inciardi reminds us, "But while the powers of the English sheriff diminished over time, those of the American sheriff expanded to include not only the apprehension of criminals, but also the conducting of elections, the collection of taxes, and the custody of public funds."[155]

Alongside appointed local and municipal law enforcement officials, America also adopted private policing.[156] This was due in part to the slow development of city and statewide policing responses and also due to the expansion of railroads, industry, and commerce that sought to protect its own interests often in the face of worker unrest and labor disputes. Familiar names such as Wells Fargo,[157] Brinks,[158] The Pinkerton Agency,[159] and The Burns Detective Agency[160] identified a lacuna in the protection of goods and property, which public entities were unable to fill. At the same time population growth, industrialization, and the development of cities drew much of American society closer to contemporary European standards. Consequently, the policing needs of the burgeoning east coast cities were very different from the needs of the rural communities and the pioneers. Social unrest, unemployment, and vagrancy needed a policing response in accord with contemporary European models. Pioneers attempting to conquer "the Elephant"[161] made do with self-help, vigilantes, posses, and the sheriff.[162] There is mixed evidence with regard to the proactive nature of these "self-help" organizations, but it is clear that these groups were "…appendages to the institutionalized legal system with intention to circumvent it."[163]

By the end of the nineteenth century, Alan Pinkerton, "The Vidocq of the West,"[164] and other private police agencies found it opportune to transition from personal protection to property protection. The declining employment market in America; by the close of the nineteenth century, unemployment was at 20%, 600 banks had closed and Unions had become a significant force in U.S. employment,[165] meant that American industry increasingly needed to have a body of "Cossacks"[166] or hoodlums to break strikes.[167] In 1902, the Great Anthracite Coal Strike devastated Pennsylvania. Coal prices soared[168] and the national and state governments were at a loss as to how to deal with the private labor dispute. Municipal police officers were either incapable or unprepared to arrest striking miners and the private police responses provided by the Coal and Iron Police[169] under the supervision of Pinkerton's Detective Agency were heavy handed and frequently accused of brutality by the miners.[170] It was clear to many observers that these groups "…owed a duty to no one but their employers, and these in turn hired for their private police force the most irresponsible toughs and rough-necks obtainable."[171]

In 1905, the Pennsylvania state governor, Samuel Pennypacker, signed Senate Bill 278 into law. This legislation created the first statewide police agency in America, The Pennsylvania State Constabulary. Capt. John Groome,[172] formerly of the Philadelphia City Cavalry, was tasked with creating and supervising a working statewide police force. During a subsequent Congressional investigation[173] into alleged reprisals against striking miners by the new force, Maj. Groome stated, "Of course there were no rules, no regulations, and nothing to go by; and these men were divided into four troops.[174] They were sent to barracks. I designed the uniforms, decided how they should be armed, and decided that it would be necessary for each man to be mounted; and purchased the horses and drilled men and gave them as much instruction."[175] When questioned about the inspiration for the force he replied, "…I got the Italians, The Germans and Royal Northwestern police, and the Irish police; and from going over their reports I came to the conclusion that the conditions in Ireland were more similar to those in Pennsylvania, so far as the industrial and agricultural conditions and the character of the population were concerned."[176] He then reported to the committee that he had paid a 3-week visit to the Royal Irish Constabulary to fully investigate its organization and operations.[177] Advocates and opponents of the Pennsylvania State Police[178] are agreed; the statewide force copied the Royal Irish Constabulary.[179]

By 1845, New York had abandoned its previous system of watchmen and adopted a London-style municipal police force. It was the first outside of the British Empire.[180] The new force appeared very different from the London model. Officers did not wear a uniform;[181] simply a copper badge and very soon they exchanged truncheons for firearms.[182] But it was not the external appearance of the officers that denoted fundamental differences; it was the exercise of power.[183] The London force had been created to be politically neutral and institutionally controlled.[184] The New York officer's authority was limited by the ballot box.[185] Interestingly, in New York there was a general concern that the London Bobby was too centralized and accountable to the government and yet the London force was considered within England to be decentralized and independent. By 1857,[186] the municipal force was abolished and a metropolitan force was created that would be commanded by state-appointed commissioners.[187] The New York police,[188] although allegedly modeled on the English police were soon undertaking a range of tasks far closer in practice to the Paris police than their London brothers. For example, New York officers provided babysitting services at the police station, helped people find employment, fought fires, fed the homeless, and provided basic medical care.[189] They "...returned lost children by the thousands, shot stray dogs, enforced sanitation laws, inspected boilers, took annual censuses, and performed myriad other small tasks."[190] "Arrests were of little importance, the primary mission of the police was to provide services to citizens and garner votes for politicians."[191] In Paris, the police were tasked with controlling begging, issuing licenses to wine shops and food stores, firefighting and flood control, providing care for abandoned children and pursuing unfaithful wives, inspecting the jails, and they had oversight of the public drainage system and sewers.[192] The London Bobby was maintaining the peace and preventing and detecting crime. Not only was there a remarkably different political and social setting for policing New York, but also there was a remarkably different job specification.[193] In reality, adapting the London police model to New York meant discarding political neutrality and increasing individual discretion.[194] This looks very much like a different force altogether, one that more closely resembles the French police who like America, they too were born out of political instability resulting in a broad palate of responsibilities. As Monkkonen noted, "At best, one could say that the creation of the police force reflected a growing intolerance for riots and disorder, rather than a response to an increase in crime."[195] It was not until after the impact of initial formation settled that the city forces of America became practitioners of the narrow term *police*[196] and "urban reformers took over the welfare functions of the police."[197]

Sheriffs from Anglo-Saxon England whose powers were enhanced by a Frenchman, Hue and Cry vigilantes[198] in "rural areas and small towns across the nation,"[199] uniformed officers patrolling Paris in the seventeenth century, and military police policing civilians in rural France and Ireland,[200] a convict turned sleuth who inspired the establishment of private policing in America, and city police officers responsible for political policing and the provision of welfare services. We have credited Sir Robert Peel with being the "father" of American policing. Perhaps it is time to adopt a contemporary view of this and consider him more of a "significant other" rather than the exclusive patriarch.

Acknowledgment

I would like to thank Zach Richardson, graduate assistant, for his help in locating articles and reference materials.

Endnotes

1. It is believed that there are in the region of 20,000 assorted law enforcement agencies in the United States. Many of these are very small in size and composed of as few as five or six sworn officers. For the purposes of this chapter, my discussion will focus on the development of state and local forces. The large number of federal agencies in the United States has each produced a version of their history that can be viewed on the agency website. Also c.f. the following article that discusses the history of the reorganization of federal agencies: Carl, G. (1979). The reorganization of Federal Agencies Administration & Society. 10, 437–464, doi:10.1177/009539977901000403. cf. Radzinowicz, L. A. *History of the English Criminal Law and Its Administration.* 5 Volumes (Vol 4) London, Stevens & Sons. 1968. cf. Maitland, W. A. *History of English Law before the time of Edward I.* 2 Volumes. Cambridge, Cambridge University Press, 1968 (re-issue).
2. Comprehensive coverage of the entire period is contained within the influential works of, *inter alia,* William Maitland's *History of the English Law,* William Holdsworth's *History of English Law,* and more recently Leon Radzinowicz's *A History of the English Criminal Law.* These works are voluminous and remarkable reading.
3. Morris, W. (1916). The office of sheriff in the Anglo-Saxon period. *The English Historical Review, 31*(121), 20–40 at p. 20.
4. Late O.E. scirgerefa "representative of royal authority in a shire," from scir (see shire) + gerefa "chief, official, reeve" (see reeve). In Anglo-Saxon England, the representative of royal authority in a shire. As an American county official, attested from 1662; sheriff's sale first recorded 1798. http://www.etymonline .com/index.php?term=sheriff.

5. First recorded usage is in the twelfth century to denote the deputy count or holder of a shire. Shire having replaced the Anglo-Saxon term scir. cf. http://www.etymonline.com/index.php?search=count&searchmode=none.

6. For a thorough discussion see: Gladwin, I. (1984). *The sheriff: The man and his office*. London: McCartney.

7. King of Wessex 688–726. Known for formulation of legal codes, Ines laws, 694 and later subsumed into the legal code of Alfred the Great. Ine abdicated in 726 to pilgrimage to Rome.

8. Supra, Morris, p. 20.

9. During the later part of the Anglo-Saxon period the alderman was the chief judicial officer within the shire and the sheriff served as the second.

10. Alfred the Great reigned from 849 to 899. He was responsible for the division of lands into boroughs and a number of boroughs together were designated as a shire. Consequently, many cities in Britain are named as boroughs such as Edinburgh, Peterborough, and Welling borough and numerous counties are shires, for example, Cambridgeshire, Worcestershire, and Leicestershire. In the late 880s or perhaps early 890s, Alfred issued his legal codes known as the *domboc*.

11. Supra, Morris, p. 21 and footnote 5.

12. We take the term from the third century Roman firewatchers, Vigiles. The term has commonly come to mean legal, or extra-legal, citizen participation in law enforcement.

13. The first king of England. Ruled from 924 to 939.

14. Supra, Morris, pp. 21–22, citing 5. Athelstan, 1.5 and 6; Athelstan, 10.

15. His mother never married his father hence he was referred to as "William the Bastard," invaded and conquered England in 1066. He already held the title William of Normandy from 1035.

16. William also retained the services of a number of Englishmen sheriffs such as Marloswein, Freeman, Robert fitzWymarc, Round, Touid, Davis, Edric, Edwin, and Elfwine. Source supra, Morris, p. 26 and footnote 52.

17. Supra, Morris, p. 30.

18. Harding, A. (1960). The origins and early history of the keeper of the peace. *Transaction of the Royal Historical Society (Fifth Series), 10*, 85–109 at p. 87. "…for the preservation of the peace of the kingdom and against foreign invaders or against others acting against the peace of the realm."

19. Clause 1. Referring to the harboring of robbers, murderers. and thieves, "And the Justices shall make this inquest by themselves, and the sheriffs by themselves." Cited in Henderson, E. (1896). *Select historical documents of the Middle Ages* (p. 16). London: George Bell and Sons. (Taken from Stubbs "Charters" p. 142.)

20. Ibid. p. 17.

21. Op. cit. Henderson. p. 147.

22. Henry III of England 1207–1272.

23. Supra, Harding, cites an example form the Public Record Office J.I. 1/734 where in Shropshire 1256 there were … one hundred and eighty six cases of homicide presented, but only nineteen felons executed…. Crime after crime was presented as committed by *malefactores ignoti* [persons unknown]. The system was incapable of dealing with the hardened criminal who wandered from shire to shire." At p. 86

24. Supra, Harding, p. 89.

25. Bailiwick is an interesting term that is a combination of French and English, *balli* a French administrative official and *wick* an Anglo-Saxon village. The Oxford English Dictionary Second Edition apparently implies that the term originates from the fifteenth century. Supra, Harding, p. 92 has sourced this term to the thirteenth century with his specific reference p. 92 note 5 to C.P.R. 1258—1266 at p. 283. cf. http://www.wordorigins.org/index.php/bailiwick/.

26. For example, Fitzpeter, Clifford, Lestrange, Nevill, Gesemuth, Montalt, and Eustace de Balliol. Source supra, Harding, p. 92 and note 6.

27. Perhaps an early example of auxiliary policing, to support the local police in cases of civil disobedience, is found within the supra, Harding, p. 99 where "Edmund of Cornwall was appointed general 'keeper of the peace' in the English counties with power to appoint deputies to deal with improper assemblies beyond the sheriffs' control" citing Calendar of chancery rolls, Various, pp. 271–218 and footnote 5.

28. For example, in 1236 we see the sheriff continuing to have responsibility for forming a jury. C.P.R. 1232-1247, p. 65 cited in supra, Harding, p. 103 at note. 9. This function remained with the sheriff until 1857. (In 1856 all policing functions were transferred to local police constabularies and all prison functions were transferred, in 1857, to the prison service.) The other previous primary role, tax collection, had already been handed to the Exchequer under Henry, I. For further discussion see: Carpenter, D. A. (1976). The decline of the curial sheriff in England 1194-1258. *The English Historical Review, 91*(358), 1–32.

29. The Lord Lieutenant is the monarch's personal representative in a county.

30. The High Sheriff is the sovereign's judicial representative in a county.

31. Moley, R. (1929). The sheriff and the constable. *The annals of the American Academy of Political and Social Science, 146*, 27–33 at p. 27.

32. Op. cit. Buffardi, H. C. (1998). The history of the office of sheriff, Schenedachy County sheriff, not paginated. The appointment was soon followed by numerous other counties and states across colonial America and the sheriff became the *de facto* ranking police officer and chief tax collector for many counties. In 1679, the sheriff of Middlesex county appointed a jailer to run the county prison. Ibid. "Accomac [sic] County Records" 1640-1645, p. 150 in Karracker, C. H. (1930). *The seventeenth century sheriff.* Chapel Hill, NC: University of North Carolina Press.

33. *Posse comitatus* meaning "the power of the county" was the legal basis for sheriffs to recruit assistance from any male over the age of 15 years to assist in the pursuit and capture of felons.

34. Infra.

35. This *connetablie*, or military unit was directed by a Constable of France.

36. In association with his legal colleague Guillame de Lamoigen, Colbert drafted more than 150 pieces of legislation including the 1670 ordinance on Criminal Law and Criminal Procedure.

37. The office was first held by Nicholas Gabriel de la Reynie.

38. Jones, M., & Johnstone, P. (2011). *History of criminal justice* (5th ed., pp. 220–221). Boston: Anderson.

39. For example, supervising markets, repairing municipal drains, inspecting food and wine, surveillance of foreigners, arresting sorcerers, and directing firefighting. cf. Supra, Jones, p. 219.

40. Supra, Jones, p. 220.
41. Ibid.
42. Ibid.
43. By 1716, the police wore a blue uniform, walked a defined beta, and were the only citizens of Paris permitted to carry a firearm. Supra, Jones, p. 221.
44. Ibid.
45. Germinal 28, Year VI of the French Revolution. April 17, 1798.
46. Supra, Jones, p. 222.
47. Typically in brigades of six to ten men. Preference was for single men, but married men were permitted to serve. It was intentional that the officers were recruited from an area different from where they would be policing, however, the Gendarmerie was eventually close to the people and held in higher regard than the despised Administrative Police of Fouche. Notwithstanding this the period between 1789 and 1799 placed France under enormous internal conflict and upheaval and the Gendarmerie was often interpreted as a pro-revolutionary faction that was caught between supporters of the old regime and those who were forging a new. cf. Supra, Broers, p. 28.
48. Broers, M. (1999). The Napoleonic police and their legacy. *History Today*, 49(5), 27–33 at p. 27.
49. Minister of Police 1799–1810 and 1815–1816.
50. Gen. Anne Jean Marie Rene Savary. *Aid-de-camp* to Napoléon and then succeeded Joseph Fouche as Minister of Police until Napoléon's abdication.
51. Supra, Broers, p. 29.
52. Infra.
53. For a comprehensive discussion see: Denys, C. (2010). The development of police forces in urban Europe in the 18th century. *Journal of Urban History*, 36(3), 332–344.
54. The *sergents* were designated specific beats or areas of a town to patrol rather than replicate the previous model of walking around without specific purpose. The result of which rarely led to arrest and supplied ample material for ridicule.
55. For example, *Little Dorrit, Oliver Twist, The Old Curiosity Shop*, and *The Detective Police*.
56. Believed to be based on the real life criminal-turned police detective Eugene Francois Vidocq. Infra.
57. Supra, Broers, p. 33.
58. cf. Emsley, C. (2009). *The Great British Bobby: A history of British policing from the 18th century to the present century*. London: Quercus. Radzinowicz refers to the influence of Henry Fielding in bringing the term *policing* into popular use. He cites Maitlands definition as "such part of social organisation as is concerned immediately with the maintenance of good order, or the prevention or detection of offences." Supra, Radzinowicz, p. 4 and footnote 18.
59. Radzinowicz, L. (1956). *A history of the English criminal law* (Vol. 3, p. 1). London: Stevens.
60. Cited by Radzinowicz, supra, p. 1.
61. Supra, Jones, chapter 10.
62. Supra, p. 227.

63. Blinded at the age of 19 years Sir John Fielding could recognize criminals by their voices. It is reputed, he knew 3000 London criminals by their voice alone.
64. Henry Fielding was well known for his work of fiction *A History of Tom Jones*, he also authored 15 plays, a novel based on the life of London criminal Jonathan Wild and he wrote the weekly law digest the *Covent Garden Journal* as well as the *Police Gazette* (which remains in publication today as a source of information for serving police officers).
65. Contrary to some incorrect reports (a "Google" search of this term shows five incorrect entries on the first page) this group did not wear uniforms and were never referred to as "Robin Redbreasts." They did, however, carry a truncheon as a weapon and this instrument frequently bore a crown or other insignia denoting authority. Dodsworth, F. (2004). "Civic" police and the condition of liberty: The rationality of governance in eighteenth century England. *Social History*, *29*(2), 199–216 at p. 212.
66. For a full account of the establishment of the Bow Street Runners see: Cox, D. (2010). *A certain share of low cunning: An analysis of the work of Bow Street principal officers 1792–1839*. London: Whillan. The somewhat disparaging term *Runners* may have been first used during a criminal trial at The Old Bailey in 1755. Cited by Emsley, supra, in Cox at pp. 2–3.
67. Six were initially appointed. This grew to eight by the early nineteenth century. All were "sworn constables" of the City of Westminster.
68. Supra, Radzinowicz, p. 263; cited in Jones, supra, p. 229.
69. In 1792, policing for London was divided into seven districts.
70. Supra, Emsley, p. 22.
71. This later group wore blue trousers and red waistcoats. They were soon dubbed the "Robin Redbreasts" cf. The police of London. *London Quarterly Review, 129*, 50, 1870.
72. The Middlesex Justices Act 1972.
73. He established himself at Worship Street and then moved to Queen Square where he remained until 1818. Source Radzinowicz, supra. p. 212.
74. Supra, Jones, p. 229.
75. "In his opinion the French police were worthy of careful and impartial consideration" supra, Radzinowicz, p. 249.
76. For further discussion about the impact of Colquhoun see: Barrie, D. (2008). Patrick Colquhoun, the Scottish enlightenment and police reform in Glasgow in the late eighteenth century. *Crime History and Society*, *12*(2), 57–79.
77. His *Treatise* appeared in French in 1807. Supra, Radzinowicz, p. 221 and note 3.
78. He was alone in attempting to introduce legislation. William Pitt introduced a Police Bill in 1785 and four Police Bills were introduced in 1799. All were defeated.
79. Colquhoun was closely associated with the Thames Marine Police and at one time held an official position with the office as its receiver.
80. Patterson, D. *The Thames police history*. Article compiled by PC 128A Richard Paterson 1974–2001 Thames Division, available at Thames River Police Museum, Wapping, London. pp. 1–8 at p. 2. For a comprehensive discussion see: Radzinowicz, L. (1957). *A history of the English criminal law and its administration from 1750* (Vol. 2, part IV new departures chapters 12 and 13). London: Macmillan.
81. By the end of the eighteenth century nearly four-fifths of all imports into England came through the Port of London. Source supra, Radzinowicz, vol. 2, p. 350.

82. Located at No. 259 Wapping New Stairs. Source supra, Radzinowicz, vol. 2, p. 363 and supra, Patterson, p. 4.

83. The force had written "General Instructions" pertaining to roles, responsibilities, conduct, rates of pay, and the entire range of standing orders that are associated with a police force. Supra, Radzinowicz, vol. 2, p. 365. In addition to the 80 permanent staff a further 1120 were available and utilized as needed on a part-time basis. Supra, Radzinowicz, vol. 2, p. 372.

84. Quoted in Patterson, supra, p. 5.

85. It was also in 1800 that Colquhoun authored *Treatise on the Commerce and Police of the River Thames London, Baldwin, 1800* a work that included specific costs associated with the level of crime being committed on the river estimated by Colquhoun to be at least £232,000 in 1798.

86. The final version was significantly different from the previous draft supplied by Colquhoun and Bentham. The Bill passed into law on July 28, 1800. 39&40 Geo 3. C. 87.

87. Master mariner and friend of Colquhoun's who later served with Colquhoun in the Wapping Police Office. John Harroit was himself a justice of the peace and is credited with being the author of the first written plan for the river police. "I have lost no time in transmitting your very sensible paper to Mr. Dundas, which contains a very excellent plan for the protection of shipping in the River Thames..." cited in Radzinowicz, supra, vol. 2, p. 373 and note 65. Reprinted in Harriot's memoirs *Struggles Through Life, Exemplified in the various Travels and Adventures in Europe, Asia, Africa, and America* (3rd ed. 1815) 3 vols. Vol. 3, pp. 112–113. Radzinowicz also supplies evidence of Harriot having first submitted his plan to the Duke of Portland in 1797; supra, Radzinowicz, vol. 2, p. 373 and at footnote 66.

88. By this time Colquhoun was already deeply involved with the Marine Police Establishment as noted in the *Lloyd's Evening Post and British Chronicle* June 27–29, 1978 "A new Office sitting at Wapping New Stairs, to be under the direction of Patrick Colquhoun, Esq..." cited in Radzinowicz, supra, vol. 2, pp. 371–372.

89. In an earlier version of the attempts to gain support for the establishment of a government funded river, police Colquhoun, May 1, 1799, refers to assistance from "...a friend of great legal knowledge." This legal friend was Jeremy Bentham. Supra, Radzinowicz, p. 385 and note 19. Bentham later reports on this involvement in his own memoirs works "Memoirs ... including Autobiographical Conversations and Correspondence" (Bowring's ed. 1843) vol. 10, pp. 330–333. Ibid.

90. Supra, Radzinowicz, vol. 2, p. 389.

91. Emsley, C. (2002). The English police: A unique development? In A. Bottoms, & M. Tonry, *Ideology, crime and criminal justice: A symposium in honour of Sir Leon Radzinowicz* (chapter 4, p. 75). Cullompton, United Kingdom: Whillan.

92. Critchley, T. A. (1967). *A history of the police in England and Wales 900–1966* London: Constable; cited by Neocleous, M. (1998). Policing and pin making: Adam Smith, police and the state of prosperity. *Policing and Society, 8*, 425–449 at p. 426.

93. Supra, Jones, p. 231 and also, in particular, the Ratcliffe Murders of 1811. Reported variously, for example, supra, Radzinowicz, p. 315.

94. The new Police science. Supra, Neocleous, p. 440.

95. For example, the MacDonald Bill had failed in 1785 for these reasons and little had changed as the fervor of war and jingoism increased at the end of this century. See: supra, Neocleous, p. 209.
96. Supra, Jones, p. 230.
97. Robert Peel served as British Prime Minister from December 10, 1834 to April 8, 1835 and again August 30, 1841 to June 29, 1846. He went to Harrow boys school and then read classics, physics, and mathematics at Christ College Oxford where he took a double first. He trained as a lawyer, Lincoln's Inn, and then entered politics in 1809. He made his maiden speech in the Commons in January 1810. Throughout his career Peel was supported by the Duke of Wellington.
98. Act, 54 George III, c.131, July 25, 1814. "To provide for the better execution of the Laws in Ireland, by appointing Superintending magistrates and additional Constables in Counties in certain cases" Herlihy, infra, p. 29. This act created a permanent police force for rural Ireland. It did not include policing for the city of Dublin that had established a city force under the Dublin Police Act 1786 comprising 10 officers, a chief constable, and a night watch. The force wore a uniform dress and carried muskets. Herlihy, J. (1997). *The Royal Irish Constabulary: A short history and Genealogical Guide* (p. 27), Dublin, Ireland: Four Courts press. The force was short-lived. It was abolished in 1795. Dublin maintained a separate force until merger in 1836 when one combined constabulary was established for all of Ireland.
99. Brewer, J. (1989). Max Weber and the Royal Irish Constabulary: A note on class and status, *The British Journal of Sociology*, 40(1), 82–96 at p. 82.
100. Bestowment of the title "Royal" on a police force was unique at the time. "...a circumstance unparalleled and unprecedented in any police force in the world." Brophy, M. (1886). *Sketches of the Royal Irish Constabulary* (p. 17), London: Burns and Oates.
101. Broeker, G. (1961). Robert Peel and the peace preservation force, *The Journal of Modern History*, XXXIII(4), 363–373 at p. 363.
102. Supra, Barrie, p. 5 citing Critchley, T. A. (1967). *A history of police in England and Wales 900–1966*, London: Constable.
103. Supra, Herlihy, p. 31. Shortly after this statement there were intense disturbances in Ireland and the army was called in to assist the new force in establishing order.
104. Fifty seven Irish protestants in the House of Commons signed a petition requesting he not leave.
105. Supra, Brophy, p. 3. "One could almost believe that Sir Robert Peel, inspired by Mr. Drummond, seeing the pitiable condition of Ireland, and feeling that the powerful sister-country had a hand in bringing that condition about, determined on making some small restitution by creating employment of some useful kind, one branch of which assumed the shape of a police force twelve thousand strong." Ibid. There is some degree of support for this if consideration is given to the number of Irish aristocracy who joined the R.I.C. "Serving in the ranks are to be found the sons and heirs of the embarrassed or utterly ruined landed gentry" ibid.
106. Supra, Brophy, p. 14.
107. For comprehensive discussion see: Reynolds, E. (1998). *Before the Bobbies: The Night Watch and Police Reform in Metropolitan London 1720-1830*. London: Macmillan.
108. Supra, Jones, p. 231.

109. The Royal Irish Constabulary required all officers to wear uniform but have available a suit of civilian clothing to perform duties that required a civilian presence. Supra, Brophy, p. 18. This was likely to be interpreted as far too similar to the Paris police "spies" in London, and therefore the metropolis did not have a detective plain clothes presence until 1842. Supra, Jones, p. 232. Initial detective work was provided for by the Bow Street Principal Officers. Cox, supra.

110. "Even had the City authorities been anxious to co-operate with the metropolitan force, either in action or in the exchange of information, their very multiplicity would have made it impracticable." Supra, Radzinowicz, vol. 4, p. 171.

111. The "Square Mile" established its own police force under the City of London Police Act 1839. Daniel Whittle Harvey was the first commissioner of a force of 500 men. The City of London Police continues to operate today across the Square Mile, there are currently 850 officers and 450 support staff of London Police were formed. For further comprehensive discussion see: Harris, A. (1968). *Policing the city: Crime and legal authority in London, 1780–1840.* Columbus. OH: The Ohio State University Press.

112. Ten years later, the 1839 Metropolitan Police Act extended the initial 10 mile zone from Charing Cross to 15 miles. This Act also increased the force size to 4300 officers.

113. Officers were required to walk a beat at a regular and steady pace. Initially set at 3 miles per hour this was soon reduced to two and a half miles per hour. Infra, Emsley.

114. For those opposed to a full-time police presence even the uniform was criticized as "The chief offence of the new police in the eyes of these patriots was the similarity of their dress to that of French gendarmes. Any coats would have been forgiven but blue coats." Hayden, B. R. (1897). *Correspondence and table-talk* (Vol. 2, p. 340), London: Chatto and Windus.

115. Eight Superintendents, Twenty Inspectors, Eighty-Eight Sergeants and nearly nine hundred constables. Radzinowicz, L. (1968). *A history of the English criminal law "grappling for control"*(Vol. 4, p. 161), London: Stevens.

116. Emsley, C. (2009). *The Great British Bobby: A history of British policing from the 18th century to the present* (p. 39). London: Quercus.

117. Mayne was born in Dublin and after attending Trinity College was called to the bar at Lincoln's Inn. He served as the first joint commissioner and then second joint commissioner after the retirement of Colonel Rowan. Mayne finally became sole the first sole commissioner of the force in 1855. And remained in this post until his death in 1868. He served a total of 39 years with the London Metropolitan Police and remains the longest serving commissioner to date.

118. One source of criticism even suggested that, "The appointment of a military officer, Colonel Rowan, of the Irish Constabulary, betrayed the intention of creating a 'veritable gendarmerie.'" Maj. Griffiths, A. (1899). *Mysteries of police and crime: A general survey of wrongdoing and its pursuit* (Vol. 1, p. 85). London: Casell and Co. Charles Rowan served in the British army and then as a magistrate in Ireland, his country of birth, before accepting the position as commissioner of the London Metropolitan Police in 1829. Rowan was not Peel's first choice, which was Colonel James Shaw, he refused and Rowan was offered the position.

119. Ibid.

120. Numerous sources trace the introduction of the term *Peeler* to describe a "new" police officer. It is specifically mentioned in the press: "The 'Peelers' withstand riots in London." *The Guardian*, Friday, November 12, 1830.
121. Supra, Griffiths, p. 87.
122. Charles, R. (1948). *A short history of the British Police* (p. 62). London: Oxford University Press. Also cited by Radzinowicz, supra, vol. 4, p. 163. There are a number of variations on the actual number of "Principles" that peel developed. Some sources cite 9 others 12. For example, Reith, ibid and Jones, supra.
123. This Act established the system of HM inspectors of Constabulary who conducted inspections of each force annually. Every force need to achieve an "efficient" grade if they were to receive one quarter of their budget from the Treasury.
124. Radzinowicz makes numerous references to the obstacles facing Peel especially, supra, vol. 3. His treatment of the subject is discussed by Emsley in *Ideology, Crime and Criminal Justice*, supra. There is also discussion of these matters in Stead, P. (1985). *The police of Britain*. New York: Macmillan and Monkkonen, E. (1981). *Police in urban America, 1860–1920*. New York: Cambridge University Press. An overview of these contributions is available in Miller, W. R. (1986). Police and the state: A comparative perspective (Review Essay). *American Bar Foundation Research Journal*, *11*(2), 339–348 at p. 343.
125. A discussion about the concern over police spies and the Popay affair, infra, is to be found in Emsley, supra, *The Great British Bobby*, pp. 56–64.
126. The principal officer was disbanded in 1839 after 90 years of service. It was replaced by the Metropolitan Police Detective Branch in 1842. Supra, Jones, pp. 232–233.
127. For a colorful description of policing from the eyes of an early twentieth century magazine see: Kemp, R. (April–September 1910 at July 1910). The evolution of the Police. *Munseys Magazine*, *XLIII*(4) 439–450.
128. Supra, Kemp, p. 446.
129. Walz, R. (2003). Vidocq, Rogue Cop. In F. E. Vidocq, *Memoirs of Vidocq: Master of Crime* (p. xi). London: AK Press.
130. Supra, Emsley, p. 89.
131. Supra, Jones, p. 223.
132. Ibid.
133. Op. cit. supra, Morris and Vila, pp. 40–42.
134. Supra, Memoirs, V., p. ix.
135. 1829. He opened a paper mill. Lost all his assets and returned to working for the police but after a scandal involving theft he was dismissed. Francois E. Vidocq dies in Brussels in 1857. As was stated about him, "He has two valid claims for inclusion in the rolls of fame-as the Legendary Detective and as The Father of the Detective Story." Translators notes form the 1935 original edition of Vidocq, supra, 1935 edition translated by Edwin G. Rich, p. 367.
136. Another plausible reason for the delay in establishing the detective unit is that Richard Mayne "distrusted" the existing detective police and therefore was not motivated to increase the size or sphere of its responsibility. Supra, Miller, p. 92.
137. The Sergeant Popay affair of 1833, the Mazzini mail scandal of 1844, both cited by Emsley, supra, p. 90.

138. Also known as the Turf Fraud Scandal was prosecuted at The Central Criminal Court (The Old Bailey), October 22, 1877. R v Clarke and Others. The case involved a horse racing fraud perpetrated by a number of senior Metropolitan Police detectives; Inspector Meiklejohn, and Chief Inspectors Clarke, Druscovich, and Palmer, all stood trial for corruption. D.C.I. Clarke was acquitted; the other three were convicted and given 2-year terms of imprisonment.

139. He was placed in an unusual situation in this role in that he reported not to the commissioner of the Metropolitan Police but directly to the home secretary. His rank was equivalent to assistant commissioner but he never held the formal title. His familiarity with the French *surete* came about during his time studying law at the *Faculte de Droit*, Paris (now Pantheon-Assas II). He resigned from the force to enter politics in 1884. His title in the police was Director of the Criminal Investigation Department (CID).

140. "The detective branch of the (French) civil police, aided by broad powers in investigation and evidence gathering arising from the state's concern for security developed a reputation for being the best in the world during the nineteenth century" supra, Miller, p. 344.

141. For example, Fuller, J. (2006). *Criminal justice: Mainstream and cross currents* (pp. 146–152). New Jersey: Pearson, Bohm, R., & Haley, K. (2008). *Introduction to criminal justice* (5th ed., pp. 139–142). Boston: McGrawHill, Inciardi, J. (1996). *Criminal justice* (5th ed., pp. 163–167). New York: Harcourt Brace, Roberg, R. et al. (2012). *Police and society* (5th ed., pp. 30-36). New York: Oxford University Press, Scaramella, G. et al. (2011). *Introduction to policing* (pp. 6–7). Los Angeles: Sage, Peak, K. (2012). *Policing America: Challenges and best practices* (7th ed., pp. 4–18). Boston: Prentice Hall.

142. Also referred to as "Schouts" in the Dutch settlements. See: Vila, B., & Morris, C. (1999). *The role of police in American society: A documentary history* (p. 8). Westport, CT: Greenwood Press.

143. For example, supra, Fuller, Bohm, and Haley "Every cunstable … hath, by virtue of his office, full powr to make, signe, & put forth pursuits, or hues and cries, after murthrers, manslayrs, peace breaks…" Taken from Massachusetts statute 1646 reprinted in Inciardi, supra, p. 167.

144. Supra, Jones, pp. 112–132.

145. Boston introduced paid night watchmen in 1648 and the Dutch copied this model for New York in 1663, but the expense of running these systems proved too great and both were disbanded due to cost. Supra, Jones, p. 233. See also "The Boston night watch" supra, Vila and Morris, pp. 6–8.

146. Of course the reward concept has never left either the United Kingdom or the United States, where it operates nationally and internationally today. One manifestation of the "reward" that is enshrined in legendary views is that of the reward for the capture of a frontier outlaw. See further: "One feature of the early police system in England that was generally accepted and profoundly affected American law enforcement practices in the eighteenth and nineteenth century was the offer of a reward for the return of stolen property and the arrest and conviction of criminals." Traub, S. H. (1988). Bounty hunting, and criminal justice in the West: 1865–1900. *The Western Historical Quarterly, 19*(3), 287–301 at p. 288.

147. For example, 5 Anne, c. 31 (1706) that created a reward of £40 for prosecuting burglars. For comprehensive discussion see; Beattie, J. M. (2004). *Policing and punishment in London 1660-1750*, Oxford, United Kingdom: Oxford University Press and also McLynn, F. (1989). *Crime and punishment in eighteenth century England*. London: Routledge.

148. "Emerging evidence suggest that 'associations' found in this region (Halifax, Yorkshire) are very similar to the numerous others that spread throughout the rest of the country during this period." Little, C. B., & Sheffield, C. (1983). Frontiers and criminal justice: English private prosecution societies and American vigilantism in the eighteenth and nineteenth centuries. *American Sociological Review*, 48(6), 796–808 at p. 798. At least 450 associations were formed between 1744 and 1846. Ibid.

149. Ibid.

150. As Little and Sheffield comment though, "It would be wrong to infer that vigilantism arose on the American frontier solely in response to a tidal wave of lawlessness. To the contrary, in many cases the *lack* (original emphasis) of crime posed no need of a regular, full-time system of law enforcement..." supra, p. 804, note 18.

151. See further: Rister, C. C. (1933). Outlaws and vigilantes of the Southern plains, 1865–1885. *The Mississippi Valley historical review*, 9(4), 537–554, Smurr, J. W. (1958). Afterthoughts on the vigilantes. *The Magazine of Western History*, 8(2), 8–20, published by the *Montana Historical Society*.

152. A limited number of English style societies did exist in America. In particular anti-horse theft societies, some of which were incorporated into state law and achieved constabulary powers. Ibid.

153. "The big 'establishment' security companies, Pinkerton and Burns, abandoned labor espionage and union-busting services completely by the 1930s in favor of the burgeoning areas of industrial espionage and counterespionage, corporate embezzlement and fraud, and residential and commercial security policing" Weiss, R. P. (2007–2008). From cowboy detectives to soldiers of fortune: Private security contracting and its contradictions on the new frontiers of capitalist expansion. *Social Justice*, 34(3–4), 1–19 at p. 6.

154. Boston had a "warden" as early as 1749 and day watches were prevalent in most major cities; Philadelphia 1833, Boston 1838, New York 1844, San Francisco 1850, Los Angeles 1851, by the middle of the century. By the end of the decade, these cities had combined the day constables with the night watch to provide comprehensive municipal police cover.

155. Supra, Inciardi, p. 168. In some states, the sheriff had authority to direct and control the police, and in some cases, order the call out of the state constabulary. Milton, C. (1921). Legislative notes and reviews. (Edited by W. F. Wood) *The American Political Science Review*, 15(1), 82–93.

156. England was very familiar with private policing as this had been the model within the City of London for 700 years. The Bow Street Runners, though publically funded also provided private policing services and the principal officers of the Bow Street police office hired out their services to private and public entities. Supra.

157. Established in Buffalo, New York, March 18, 1852 by Henry Wells and William G. Fargo.

158. Established as a parcel company by Washington Perry Brink in Chicago, 1859.

159. Famous for allegedly providing personal security to President Abraham Lincoln, the agency was started by a Scotsman, Allan Pinkerton and a Chicago lawyer, Edward Rucker. Originally named the North-Western Police Agency they changed the name to The Pinkerton National Detective Agency in part to secure federal contracts. By 1871, the newly formed Department of Justice had hired Pinkerton's to detect and prosecute those committing federal crimes. The relationship lasted until enactment of the Anti-Pinkerton Act of 1893, which no longer allowed private agencies to be employed by the government.

160. This agency was established by William J. Burns in 1909. Before starting the William J. Burns national detective Agency, he had worked as a secret service agent. He returned to federal employment in 1921 to become head of the Justice Department Bureau of Investigation, which on retirement he handed over to J. Edgar Hoover as Director of the FBI.

161. Op. cit. Reid, J. (1977). Dividing the elephant: The separation of mess and joint stock property on the overland trail. *Hastings Law Journal, 28*(3). Jones, supra. The continent was sometimes referred to as the elephant by pioneers.

162. Written in 1922, Frederic F. Van de Water, author of *Grey Riders: The Story of the New York State Troopers*, New York, Putnam's sons, 1922. p 16 stated, "In America to-day, the countryside for the most part still turns for protection against marauders to the constable and the sheriff's posse that came into being under English law in 1295, as part of the militia system. These no longer carry the long bow or go about jingling in chain mail. Otherwise there is little to distinguish them from the keepers of the King's law in Merrie England of the Thirteenth century." The American militia system that Van de Water refers to "...grew out of the English Assize of Arms which, dating from the reign of Henry II, required all free men to provide arms and submit to training." Reinders, R. (1977). Militia and public order in nineteenth-century America. *Journal of American Studies, 11*(1), 81–101 at p. 82.

163. Supra, Little and Sheffield, p. 806.

164. Supra, Jones, p. 245.

165. Ibid.

166. Ray, G. W. (1995). From Cossack to Trooper: Manliness, police reform, and the State. *Journal of Social History, 28*(3), 565–586. Weiss, R. P. (1986). Private detective agencies and labour discipline in the United States 1855–1946. *The Historical Journal, 29*(1), 87–107.

167. The replies to representative Maurer's questions reveal distressing conditions in nearly every locality where the Cossacks were located. Madison (Darrah P.O.), Pa., February 22, 1911. Hon. James H. Maurer, House of Representatives, Harrisburg, Pa. 1911. It appears that the terms, *Cossacks, Yellow Dogs,* and *Hoodlums* were in use against the Coal and Iron police as well as the Pennsylvania State Constabulary.

168. $20 per ton. The equivalent of paying $12 per gallon for gasoline today.

169. "It was a grime joke. The Coal and Iron Police were actually the mercenaries of the great industries." Supra, Van de Water, p. 24.

170. For example, the Lattimer Massacre that occurred near Hazelton, PA. September 10, 1897.

171. *A history of the Michigan State constabulary* (chapter 2, p. 31). Detroit, MI: Michigan State Constabulary Association, 1919.

172. Capt. Groome is apparently promoted to the rank of Major once he takes responsibility for the Pennsylvania State Constabulary. There are also a number of later references to Groome as superintendent and also Commander Groome. The congressional hearing, supra, consistently refers to him as Maj. Groome.

173. May 6, 1915. The commission on industrial relations created by the act of congress on August 23, 1912, held at the Shoreham Hotel, Washington, DC.

174. Groome took responsibility for a broad range of functions associated with the new force including setting standards for recruits. During the Industrial Relations Committee Hearings, James Maurer, president of the Pennsylvania State Federation of Labor was asked, "From what forces are the State constabulary recruited" to which he replied, "The men are recruited from the ranks of ex-United States soldiers, and again many of them are recruited from the ranks or from the degenerate descendants of the middle classes, young men who are educated, but never amount to anything and no good for anything and generally hunt a job in the State police force." *Final report and testimony submitted to congress by the commission on industrial relations.* May 6, 1915, vol. XI, document no. 415, p. 10932.

175. Williams, D. (1921). State police and the Irish "Black and Tans." *The Bridgemen's Magazine, XXI*(1), 77.

176. Ibid.

177. An interesting lack of geographical knowledge is displayed by Chairman Walsh who at one point asked "Does the constabulary in Ireland have authority in the large cities like Glasgow and Dublin." Williams, supra, p. 78. A more pertinent question followed, "You spent, you say, three weeks at the barracks?" Maj. Groome. "Yes, and got their ideas and their rules and regulations." Ibid.

178. It is variously described as the Pennsylvania State Police and the Pennsylvania State Constabulary. Williams, supra, *Munsey's Magazine*, supra, Van de Water, supra.

179. Describing the officers employed by the new constabulary Maj. Groome stated, "My instruction to each trooper leaves a great deal to his discretion. If he starts out to get his man, he must get him, even if he has to butt into the middle of a mob to find him. The troopers are advised not to use their guns unless they have to." *Munsey's Magazine*, supra, p. 448. This makes an interesting contrast with Peel's policing principles.

180. Supra, Jones, p. 234.

181. When introduced the police were mocked. See supra, Monkkonen, p. 551.

182. See further: supra, Vila and Morris, pp. 36–39.

183. Supra, Miller, pp. 345–347.

184. Miller, W. R. (1975). Police authority in London and New York City 1830–1870. *Journal of Social History, 8*(2). 81–101 posits that the fundamental difference between the two jobs is that the authority each officer possessed was different. The London "Bobby" had impersonal authority and the New York "Cop" had far greater discretion he cites the example of carrying firearms and how the American officer took to taking a firearm to work and as such became a more powerful presence than his London colleague.

185. "Throughout most of the 19th and into the 20th century, the basic qualification for becoming a police officer was a political connection, rather than demonstrated ability." Supra, Scaramella, p. 9.

186. This relationship lasted until 1870 when a second municipal force was created. In the same year, 1857 Boston, having rejected a London police model in 1832, decided to move forward with the creation of an amalgamation of night watch and day police to form a full-time police force.

187. Supra, Jones, pp. 234–235.

188. Op. cit. supra, Vila and Morris, pp. 35–37.

189. Supra, Scaramella, p. 9.

190. Supra, Monkkonen, p. 554.

191. Ibid.

192. Supra, Jones, pp. 108, 219.

193. It can be further suggested that the London police were a centralized force due to the sole reporting line directly to the home secretary. This is true also of the Paris police, but not so the New York police who were decentralized by the Municipal Police Act. It is recognized that local town policing in England became decentralized by the formation of countrywide forces in the 1856 Act, supra.

194. Supra, Monkkonen. Notes for important innovative features of the new police in the Unites States. The second of these is that the U.S. police located the police under the executive rather than the judicial branch. This differed from London where the police ran courts for many years. "This shift also sent the American police down a different developmental path from the English police, who long remained much more active and involved in preparing and prosecuting criminal cases than did their American counterparts." p. 550.

195. Supra, Monkkonen, p. 553.

196. By the early 1900s, most major cities in America had established police forces that prioritized crime fighting as a primary role. The issue of political influence remained prevalent, however, until the 1920s. Commentary on this and the impact of August Volmer as a voice in establishing policing priorities supra, note 134.

197. Supra, Miller, p. 347.

198. Cf. Roberg et al, pp. 36–37and supra, Jones, pp. 242–243.

199. Supra, Fuller, pp. 151–152.

200. Brophy, supra, relates a fascinating event when two R.I.C. officers were on vacation in Paris at a military parade. They both wore their green R.I.C. uniforms at the time. Apparently, Napoléon III saw the officers and questioned their origins. He then invited them to join in the parade and later referred to them as "*Officers de la gendarmerie Irlandaise*" pp. 22–23.

Burying Community-Based Policing to Protect Democratic Law Enforcement

4

STEPHEN B. PERROTT

Contents

Introduction

Community-based policing (CBP) emerged in the 1980s and continues as the philosophical umbrella, or zeitgeist, under which police forces in Western nations identify and export to developing countries, transitional societies, and failed states (Brogden & Nijhar, 2005; Perrott, 2012a,b). One might expect that the tenets and practice of such a broadly embraced approach would be clearly understood. However, CBP has been a particularly tortured concept from the outset (Leighton, 1991) and, 30 years after implementation, can morph into whatever is wished for by policy makers or police administrators. Furthermore, although major policing innovations have emerged subsequent to CBP, most notably Compstat (Magers, 2004), homeland policing in the United States (Oliver, 2006), and intelligence-led policing (ILP) (Ratcliffe, 2003, 2008), most view these as add-ons or as otherwise complementary to CBP (Brogden & Nijhar, 2005).

In this chapter, it is argued that CBP, even if understood most broadly as an approach based "on community consent ... [and] appear[ing] to reflect local community needs" (Brogden & Nijhar, 2005, p. 2), has ceased to exist in any meaningful way; it is further contended that homeland policing and ILP more broadly not only fail to be complementary but are actually antithetical to the central tenets of CBP. To support this argument, the ways in which these changes in policing have been closely linked to the terror attacks of 9/11, a new form of public dissent involving black bloc tactics, and a more general shift toward the neoliberal state are outlined. The central thesis of this chapter is that although the death of CBP need not necessarily equate to the end of a democratic and open style of policing, the continued denial that this era has ended *does* pose a real threat to democratically-based policing.

Attacks of 9/11 and the Growth of Intelligence-Led Policing

The terrorist attacks of 9/11 changed the world view of all in western democracies and profoundly challenged the CBP tenet that effective policing could be based on open, reciprocal partnerships within a geographically limited community. The new focus on globalized terrorist networks, a reduction in transparent practice, and exceptions to what had hitherto been considered due process (backed by the U.S. Patriot Act and analogous legislation elsewhere), revealed a populace willing to trade certain rights for perceived safety (Etzioni, 2005; Paul, 2003). The result for American security forces was the emergence of homeland policing (Lee, 2010; Oliver, 2006) which, although perhaps viewed as an exceptional and limited-time response following the World Trade Center attacks, proved a good fit with the new ILP style of policing taking form in the United Kingdom (National Criminal Intelligence Service, United Kingdom, 2000).

ILP places emphasis on "the *criminal* and not the *crime* as the focal point for intelligence" (Ratcliffe, 2003, p. 4, emphases in original), is managed in a top–down format, relies on informants and surveillance techniques for the collection of intelligence, and is proactive in approach particularly as this pertains to focusing on high-risk criminal targets (Ratcliffe & Guidetti, 2008). Although germinating in England some years before the World Trade Center attacks (about the same time as Compstat in the United States) (Jackson & Brown, 2007), ILP now occupies the preeminent position in western policing and is inextricably linked to our post 9/11 era of terrorism (McGarrell, Freilich, & Chermak, 2007).

Similar to CBP, ILP entered the policing vernacular with such hype and *buzz* that it, too, has come to mean different things to different people. As noted, many see it is an add-on, or complementary, to CBP (Carter & Carter, 2009). In support of this view, Clark (2006) equates ILP with proactive policing, which he connects, logically enough, to CBP. Rather than seeing ILP and the policies of budgetary restraint currently being imposed on police forces as symptoms of an emerging neoliberal agenda, he argues cutbacks are simply part of a new economic reality requiring the police to be *smarter* or more intelligence driven.

Others contest this "evolution-as-complementary" perspective and view ILP as the antithesis of everything for which CBP stands. Murphy (2007), for example, agrees that although ILP has advanced a proactive component, it does so in a way that is inconsistent with CBP. In his view, we are witnessing a move toward a *securitized* approach to policing and away from the public, consent-based style that is so central to CBP. In slightly different terms, de Guzman (2002) equates this shift in the relationship between police and the public to a *fortification* (de Lint, Virta, & Deukmedjian, 2007; Deukmedjian & de Lint, 2007).

Still others have argued that we now live with a hybrid model (de Lint, 2005; de Lint & Hall, 2009) where service-oriented policing (therefore, CBP) coexists with control-oriented policing. From this perspective, ILP is not complementary to CBP, but does not necessarily contradict it either; rather, the police can shift between a largely consent-based approach and a more coercive one as evolving circumstances dictate. Although de Lint (2005) argues for the workability of such a hybrid model of policing, he acknowledges that the growth of ILP-type approaches, requiring equilibrium to be maintained between consent and control, generates tensions and presents a challenge to current notions of public order policing.

As there is little empirical evidence supporting the efficacy of CBP in general (Alpert, Dunham, & Stroshine, 2006), it is not surprising that there is little empirically-based research that addresses the CBP/ILP compatibility/incompatibility question. An exception is Lee's (2010) survey results from across 281 municipal police departments, which provides some evidence for compatibility insofar as officers reported that the implementation of homeland security measures did not impact negatively on the number of community-based initiatives undertaken. These results are consistent with the conclusion that these departments endorse the desirability and workability of a hybrid model. However, as Lee (2010) concedes, his findings should be interpreted cautiously on several grounds including the possibility that these self-reports were simply the "politically expedient thing to say" (p. 358). After all, with all of the money spent, and all of the *feel good* associations created, just which municipal police department is prepared to dissociate itself from the central tenets of CBP?

A note on Compstat, the top–down management model initiated by the New York City Police Department, is in order at this juncture. Although hardly synonymous with ILP in scope or purpose, it is consistent insofar that it is crime-control focused and seen by some as moving away from the tenets of CBP in its rigid, authoritarian style and in alienating the street cop from the community (Eterno & Silverman, 2005). In interests of brevity, unless otherwise specified, Compstat (as well as homeland policing) is imperfectly included here under the ILP umbrella.

Battle of Seattle and the Emergence of Intelligent Control

Although not of equal significance to the attacks of 9/11, the antiglobalization-focused Battle of Seattle 2 years earlier (Levi & Olsen, 2000) marked a sea change in the type of challenges police face when coping with dissent in democratic nations. Although so-called black bloc tactics had been previously used, it was in Seattle where they were placed on the world stage in a way that indicated that it was no longer "business as usual" for policing dissent. This new style of protest manifested across the United Kingdom in the summer of 2011 (Toronto Star, 2011) and in the ongoing, and seemingly absurd, student tuition protests in the Canadian Province of Quebec, where students already enjoy the lowest tuition anywhere in Canada or in the United States (Patriquin, 2012); it is also a mainstay of all G-8 and G-20 gatherings (Perrott & MacNeill, 2012) and plays out, albeit in a somewhat different form, across the Occupy movement (Coyne, 2011).

Managing dissent through the latter parts of the twentieth century had been based on a liaison style negotiation-focused model where the police bargained with protestors to achieve win–win outcomes in nonzero-sum situations (de Lint & Hall, 2009). Compared to the *skull bashing* oppressive tactics used through most of the twentieth century, this negotiation-based approach was one of the inclusions, fitting well within the collaborative and consent-based philosophical confines of CBP (de Lint & Hall, 2009). However, the negotiation-based approach is predicated on the assumption that the police have something that can be offered or traded off to protestors. As argued elsewhere (Perrott & MacNeill, in press), in the case of many antiglobalization protestors who employ *black bloc* tactics, the sole goal is the destruction of private property (or, in less cynical terms, the renouncement of the capitalist state). Under circumstances that prevailed during the 2010 G8-linked riots in Toronto, a collaborative police–protestor approach was bound to fail (Perrott & MacNeill, 2012).

The developmental shift that this new breed of protestor has stimulated has been dubbed *intelligent control* (or intelligent public order policing) by de Lint and Hall (2009); it is a shift that remains incomplete or only partially acknowledged and this, as argued here, is the basis of significant problems for proportional response and community relations in instances of dissent (Perrott & MacNeill, in press). In many ways the development of intelligent control parallels the growth of ILP or perhaps, more accurately, implicitly encompasses that component of ILP that involves the policing of public dissent. At the end of their thoughtful analysis, de Lint and Hall advocate for a hybrid approach to policing public protest that is clearly different from the "soft hat–hard hat" sequential steps already contemplated by CBP. Rather, their prescription, as it is for policing at a more macro level, is for a service focused (i.e., CBP-consistent) approach where analysis (i.e., a priori intelligence) suggests it likely to be effective but a more coercive, paramilitary-type response where intelligence gathering indicates the need.

Concerns about Privatization and Militarization

The increasing privatization and alleged militarization of the police generates concerns about ceding state functions to the private sector, not obviously beholden to the public interest, and to spheres not specialized for providing civilian police services. Regarding privatization, a variety of *policing* functions have long been carried out by agents from for-profit private security firms. However, before the late 1980s much of this activity was restricted to the protection of private property. By the 1990s, a sea change in the locus of responsibility for security between the state and the corporate sector was taking place, such that nonstate interests were increasingly paying for more-and-more *private policing of public space* (Wakefield, 2003). This shift was initially resisted with considerable vigor by the public police (Wakefield, 2003), but as police-security partnership models have grown antipathy from the police seems to be diminishing, public confidence growing, and the reality of the private sector being responsible for policing large swaths of public space increasingly seen as normative (Sarre, 2012, on the Australian experience).

What are the implications for CBP, or for any sort of state-sponsored policing, when policing is carried out for profit in a partnership model or especially when ceded entirely to private security officers? Consider the separate histories and competing principles between public and private policing (Sarre, 2012): public policing, for example, is taxpayer-funded, explicitly in the business of providing public, equally focused service, whereas private policing is profit-driven, beholden to the interests of particular clients, and selective in focus. Regarding selective service provision, it is noteworthy that policing has traditionally been an enterprise that has, to differing degrees throughout history, supported and protected the powerful *haves* from the threat presented from the restless *have nots*. CBP, more than any time previous, saw state-funded police forces shift sharply toward a more inclusive and egalitarian model of service provision (albeit not a gain recognized by critical criminologists). Western police forces even allowed for some degree of what might be referred to as *social context training* (National Judicial Institute, 2009), where the nature of social inequities and power differentials are considered, and have then taken these techniques abroad in their consultations with police forces in developing nations (Perrott, 2012c).

Finally, even in instances where the private sector works in partnership with, or under the supervision of, state-sponsored police, there is a rationale to view the activity as a challenge to a service-based approach. Public–private partnerships have become particularly focused on the fight against world-wide terrorism and, when considered with the "security hardware sector of private policing" (Wakefield, 2003, p. xxi), fits well into an ILP framework. This concern, of course, only has currency with those who view ILP as being in direct opposition to CBP.

Kraska (1999, 2007) is arguably the strongest proponent of the notion that the police have become increasingly militarized through the 1990s and into the post 9/11 period. His argument rests on the premises that (1) in our eagerness to embrace CBP and the service model we too easily dismissed the natural and historic linkages and parallels between the police and the military that continue to exist, (2) there has been a rapid escalation of the number of paramilitary units in the police, along with an expansion in their responsibilities, beginning in the 1970s and really taking off through the 1990s (and provides data to support this contention) (Kraska & Cubellis, 1997; Kraska & Kappeler, 1997), (3) the expansion of these paramilitary units and their attendant cultures have impacted all police units such that the institution as a whole has grown more militaristic, and (4) these changes have taken place in a manner, temporally and otherwise, that a more militaristic policing institution has become normative. Of course, the extent to which he is right signifies a shift that fits well with the ascendance of homeland policing, ILP, and the *War on Terror.*

den Heyer (2014) points out that Kraska's arguments rely too heavily on just two empirical studies (Kraska & Cubellis, 1997; Kraska & Kappeler, 1997) that, in some regard, could be considered as one and that much of the subsequent argument by others joining Kraska's cause continues to make much *hay* out of these two reports. den Heyer's central argument, however, is that the civilian policing institution, at least in Western democracies, simply has not become more militarized. Rather, den Heyer views the growth in paramilitary (or special weapons and tactics [SWAT]) units and growing number of deployments as a natural evolution of, and adaptation to, a more challenging and much changed policing terrain.

After providing some leeway by oversimplifying the respective arguments, Kraska and den Heyer seem not so much at odds about the reality or the specifics of the changes insomuch as they differ on why these changes have occurred, what they should be called, and what are the likely implications. Kraska argues that growing militarization promotes a culture that feeds into further militarization and more of a tendency to think of citizens as enemies (not unlike Skolnick's—1996—notion of the *symbolic assailant*). He sees government as complicit in fostering this change as a means of acquiring more social control as part of the emergent neoliberal state. In contrast, den Heyer views the changes as attributable, indeed necessary, to adaptive civilian police forces coming to terms with hitherto unanticipated challenges.

Neoliberalism, A Changed Policing Milieu, or Both?

Although there are differences about genesis, implications, and relative desirability, it is hard to deny the growth of neoliberalism in Western nations over the last two decades (Ferguson, 2004) and Kraska is not the only police scholar to acknowledge how this agenda has affected the criminal justice system generally (Perrott & Dechman, 2012) or the policing institution more specifically (de Lint & Hall, 2009). To the extent that this sociopolitical milieu is the backdrop against which all of the changes in policing have taken place, it is hard not to be concerned about the viability of CBP or consent-based policing. For a variety of reasons, neoliberalism is not a world view that is particularly amenable to the optimism conveyed by, or the allocation of resources needed to support, CBP programs.

At the same time it is difficult to bicker with den Heyer's (2014) contention that the policing landscape has changed dramatically. A neoliberal agenda did not create hallucinations where we all imagined international terrorist networks, protestors using black bloc tactics bent on destroying property (and throwing feces at police officers), or a young man in Aurora, Colorado who declared war on a theatre full of innocents. If a CBP approach was ever sufficient to go up against the darker elements of our society (and it may never have been), it certainly is not, at least as currently conceptualized, up to the challenge now. On this point of a changed landscape, den Heyer finds common ground with police doyen Jerome Skolnick (2005).

An editorial segue is in order at this juncture. Police scholarship generally finds itself falling into one of two polarized camps. For one camp, often linked to the critical criminology tradition, all police actions are seen as government-police conspiracies designed to control and oppress all the time: consider, for example, those who decried the implementation of CBP in the 1980s as simply another way for the state to gain social control, this time by co-optation (Gordon, 1984). This group is not defined by their view of the police as agents of state control per se because this is undeniably true. Rather, this group is distinguished by the rigid view that the police can never serve the interests of the disadvantaged nor, for that matter, broad-based swaths of the general population. The other camp, often, though not always, has had direct experience as, or with, practitioners, and tend to find the arguments of the first group biased, tedious, and predictable. This second group is arguably inclined to too quickly discount everything coming from the reflexive critics' camp; their scholarship may edge, in some instances at least, toward police advocacy (Matthews, 2009).

The first camp is predisposed to see the changes in policing over the last 20 years as emanating from a neoliberal agenda, whereas the other camp attributes them to the reality of a tougher policing landscape. These, of course, are not mutually exclusive positions. Scholars from both camps undoubtedly recognize this at an intellectual level, but the nature and politics of the polarization is such that there is a resistance to cede any middle ground. Furthermore although the pursuit and identification of causal links is undoubtedly important in understanding how policing got to where it is today (i.e., were changing circumstances, such as occasioned by 9/11 and the Battle in Seattle, primarily responsible for changes in policing or was it really a change in the sociopolitical landscape of Western nations?), it can also be limiting insofar as it tends to discount the reality of interactive effects, keeps us locked into ideological positions, and contributes to a resistance to taking a realistic look at how policing has changed since the 1980s.

Why the Stubborn Grip to the Community Policing Zeitgeist?

So, why produce this backdrop? After all, no new data are presented here and most of the points presented are a remix of what has already been debated in the literature. First, with certain exceptions (Kappeler & Gaines, 2011) much of the literature involves scholars taking on the potential meaning of the various changes (e.g., Compstat, ILP) in considerably more detail but on an issue-by-issue (or innovation-by-innovation) basis. This more holistic analysis is intended to help determine how various changes in policy and sociopolitical milieu have converged to produce a larger change in policing than might be predicted on the basis of any one considered in isolation. Second, a novel interpretation of why this happened, and how we might begin to move forward, is offered.

It is striking just how resistant the policing institution and many police scholars have been to move away from the CBP zeitgeist despite observing the significant changes that have occurred and despite the relevant scholarly contributions that are available for consideration. For example, at the 2010 CBP-focused International Police Executive Symposium (IPES) that the author attended in the Indian State of Kerala, the possibility that the CBP model of policing was under question was simply not contemplated. Furthermore, with one notable exception (Perrott, 2012b), reports about how well CBP was working in the developing world were generally rosy and out-of-synch with what is offered via journalistic reports coming from the mainstream media (this impression appears to be supported by the just published edited collection coming out of the conclave) (Verma, Das, & Abraham, 2012). Two years later, at the 2012 IPES meeting in New York City, where an oral version of *this* chapter was presented, little seemed to have changed. Police administrators continued to herald the success of their CBP programs (in conjunction, of course, with their Compstat and ILP initiatives) without acknowledging any potential inconsistencies or contradictions in stuffing everything together in their CBP grocery bags.

It is important to emphasize that it is not just police administrators, but also police academics, who continue to reinforce the CBP mantra (excepting, of course, those critical criminologists who have never accepted the purported goals of CBP in the first place and others, such as this author, who have specifically addressed the question). As Gaines and Kappeler (2011) point out, "police academicians have mostly played the role of community policing advocates" (p. 483) and that "the phrase has become an umbrella term for almost any innovation in policing" (p. 484). What is the reason for this adamant grip to the CBP zeitgeist? Magers (2014) captures the conundrum pretty well, in this author's view, when saying that "community policing is the politically safe model to embrace ... (whereas Compstat) is more controversial in political circles because it appears to be a less so-called kinder and gentler style of policing than community policing, a more media-friendly model" (p. 72). Homeland policing and ILP might be added to Magers' Compstat-specific analysis.

Some might explain the continuing grip to the *feel-good* appeal of CBP by arguing that the police are moving in a more sinister direction (along with the neoliberal state) and are motivated to trumpet an allegiance to CBP as a public relations exercise designed to mask what is actually happening. I reject this overly simplistic hypothesis of purposeful dissimulation and contend that police administrators, rank-and-file police officers, and even some scholars (as well as politicians and the general public) so much want policing to remain under the CBP umbrella that they simply believe it to be so. If police forces continue to promote CBP in word, whereas escaping it in action, it is not because of a phony public relations strategy so much as it is a case of the institution coming to believe its own press.

In support of my position, I note there is precedence for police officers (and those who study the police) to buy into police mythology despite living a different experience. Consider, for example, the police stress hypothesis that became especially prominent in the late 1980s. Although undoubtedly stressful, policing has never been close to the most stressful of all occupations and data were always available to demonstrate this reality. However, police officers ultimately bought into this erroneous proposition propagated by certain scholars (who perhaps were not so scholarly) because it, too, had a self-serving or feel-good quality; mythology ultimately overtook reality (Perrott & Taylor, 1994; Perrott & Kelloway, 2006).

In a similar way, CBP seems to have become a central pillar in policing mythology. It continues to be advertised as the way that business is done, not as a politically expedient public relations gesture, but because it remains unthinkable that it could be otherwise. It may be that acknowledging the death of CBP is threatening because the only plausible alternative is seen to be a regression to a darker and truly more repressive era that existed before the steady move for progress and professionalization that began a half century ago.

Rethinking Where Policing Is Before Thinking a Way Forward

It seems inconsistent to argue that the era of CBP has ended after first asserting that there has never been agreement about what it meant in the first place. Still, whatever it may or may not have been originally "the spirit of community policing was something quite specific, not nearly the catchall phrase it has become today" (Gaines & Kappeler, 2011, p. 484). As noted above, the challenges of recent years have meant a shift away from geographic communities to *hot spots* and global networks. The notion of the constable/patrol officer generalist has gone by the wayside and replaced by specialists and specialized units (perhaps now more than ever before). Furthermore, increasing hierarchical, top–down management, and centralized command styles (especially as seen in Compstat) stand in contrast to the *flattened* and decentralized management style typically seen as integral to CBP (Gaines & Kappeler, 2011).

Some might argue that these changes amount to *tinkering* rather than the toppling of primary tenets and, thus, can be incorporated within a new, revised CBP template. However, the challenges to initial conceptualizations of CBP do not end here. As indicated earlier, there are also concerns about the effects of privatization on how well all constituencies of society can be served by profit companies and the impact of the growing use of SWAT and Emergency Response Teams on the public face of policing (even if one believes the deployments to be necessary and not a form of militarization). Do all these changes, when considered cumulatively, allow for a firm conclusion that CBP is dead or can they still be accommodated within an ever-stretching CBP tent?

If, even with all these changes, one remains unconvinced that CBP has been mortally wounded there is still the *tour de force* of challenges to consider: the increased securitization of the state, especially as stimulated by the fallout of 9/11 and as nurtured by the growth of neoliberalism (Deukmedjian & de Lint, 2007; Murphy, 2007). Although perhaps more nebulous to measure in objective terms, this security *creep* seems to especially fly in the face of the image of the community-based police officer. Surely, when all of these breaks from the CBP are considered in totality, adherence to the belief that CBP continues to be the primary engine driving western policing begins to defy rational thought.

Importantly, the end of CBP, as we have understood it, does not necessarily mean an end to progressive forms of policing based on accountability, transparency, and community responsiveness, that is, those characteristics most of us consider essential for the policing of open democratic societies. What *may* be a threat to open progressive policing, however, is to have one ideological foot stuck in a framework that is no longer effective (if it ever was) and the other foot in an operational world that often works contrary to the CBP zeitgeist. This world of mixed messages is surely a recipe for role confusion and cognitive dissonance for police administrators, supervisors, and especially the frontline officer (Schaible & Gecas, 2010).

Consider, as an example of this role confusion, the response of the Integrated Security Unit to the violent antiglobalization protestors employing black bloc tactics during the 2010 G-8 meetings in Toronto (Perrott & MacNeill, 2012). On Day 1 the security forces appeared to come out in negotiation-focused (and CBP consistent) mode and promptly lost control of the city. Despite the available intelligence that there was a large cohort of protestors who had no interest in anything the police might have to trade (an integral component of a negotiation-focused model), Day 1 was characterized by a *soft*, largely ineffectual approach. As a result, Toronto suffered many millions of dollars in damage, the police appeared to have taken a trouncing at the hands of the protestors, and the Canadian public wondered why. The CBP-consistent response on Day 1 led to a huge pendulum swing on Day 2, to a full coercion, and perhaps even *payback*, mode. Although this shift in tactics was more successful in regaining control, it was accompanied by excessive force and many obvious breeches of due process. The widespread support the police enjoyed slowly but steadily dissipated as a series of investigations revealed significant malfeasance on the part of a significant minority of police officers.

Perrott and MacNeill (2012) argue that this was the result of shifting expectations coming from the public but even more so from the police command structure and the line officers themselves. Although not entirely naive to the challenges they were up against, the Day 1 mindset seemed to remain stuck in a policing philosophy and response protocol no longer adequate for a changed world. However, the Day 2 recovery from the initial under-response was an over-response. It, too, was not adequate for a changed world, at least not a world driven by democratic principles.

An official company line that professes one ideology (i.e., CBP) accompanied by practice that contradicts it is likely to be especially dissonance producing for the young people entering the policing profession. Although the world encountered on the street has never matched with what is represented in police academies, the divide of recent years is so incongruent as to be seemingly irreconcilable. Deukmedjian and de Lint (2007) trace the internal and more public machinations of Royal Canadian Mounted Police administrators in attempting, ultimately with limited success, to bridge this divide. Ultimately, the attendant dissonance appears to have provided a recipe for a loss of social identity and common purpose in a way likely to underscore growing confusion, resentment and, ultimately, actions that are both regressive and unacceptably coercive (Perrott & Kelloway, 2011).

Skolnick (2005) notes that we could not have anticipated our post 9/11 world when the template for CBP was laid out in the 1980s; importantly, he points out that the recognition that CBP is simply not viable and need not equate to a surrender of the foundational principles necessary for an open, democrat style of policing. To the extent he is correct, it seems well past time that we honestly examine where Western policing really sits free of self-delusion about the presence, or necessity, of CBP. Whether the questions we ask lead us to view a hybrid model (such as proposed by de Lint, 2005; de Lint & Hall, 2009) as optimal or instead to a completely new formulation can but remain unknown until such time as there is a recognition that what is currently professed is widely out of synch with what is practiced. It is time to let go of the confusing contradictions of CBP, and the inevitable uneven patterns of performance that follow, to allow for a more clear-headed examination of where policing should go next.

References

Alpert, G. P., Dunham, R. G., & Stroshine, M. S. (2006). *Policing: Continuity and change*. Long Grove, IL: Waveland Press.

Brogden, M., & Nijhar, P. (2005). *Community policing: National and international models and approaches*. Portland, OR: Willan Publishing.

Carter, D. L., & Carter, J. G. (2009). Intelligence-led policing: Conceptual and functional considerations for public policy. *Criminal Justice Policy Review, 20*, 310–325.

Clark, C. (2006). Proactive policing: Standing on the shoulders of community-based policing. *Police Practice and Research: An International Journal, 7*, 3–17.

Coyne, A. (2011, October 31). A phony class war. *MacLeans, 124*(42), 24–26.

de Guzman, M. C. (2002, September/October). The changing roles and strategies of the police in the time of terror. *ACJS Today, 27*(3), 8–13.

de Lint, W. (2005). Public order policing: A tough act to follow? *International Journal of the Sociology of Law, 33*, 177–189.

de Lint, W., & Hall, A. (2009). *Intelligent control: Developments in public order policing in Canada*. Toronto, ON: University of Toronto Press.

de Lint, W., Virta, S., & Deukmedjian, J. E. (2007). The simulation of crime control: A shift in policing? *American Behavioral Scientist, 50*, 1631–1647.

den Heyer, G. (2014). Mayberry revisited: A review of the influence of police paramilitary units on policing. *Policing and Society, 24*, 346–361.

Deukmedjian, J. E., & de Lint, W. (2007). Community into intelligence: Resolving information uptake in the RCMP. *Policing and Society, 17*, 239–256.

Eterno, J. A., & Silverman, E. B. (2005). The New York City Police Department's Compstat: Dream or nightmare? *International Journal of Police Science and Management*, 8, 218–231.

Etzioni, A. (2005). How patriotic is the Patriot Act? Freedom versus security in the age of terrorism. New York: Routledge.

Ferguson, I. (2004). Neoliberalism, the third way and social work: The UK experience. *Social Work and Society*, 2, 1–9.

Gordon, P. (1984). Community policing: Towards the local police state? *Critical Social, Policy*, 4, 39–58.

Jackson, A. L., & Brown, M. (2007). Ensuring efficiency, interagency cooperation, and protection of civil liberties: Shifting from a traditional model of policing to an Intelligence-Led Policing (ILP) paradigm. *Criminal Justice Studies*, 20, 11–129.

Kappeler, V. E., & Gaines, L. K. (2011). Community policing: A contemporary perspective (6th ed.). New York: Elsevier.

Kraska, P. B. (1999). Questioning the militarization of U.S. police: Critical versus advocacy scholarship. *Policing and Society*, 1, 141–155.

Kraska, P. B. (2007). Militarization and policing—Its relevance to 21st century police. *Policing*, 1, 501–513.

Kraska, P. B., & Cubellis, L. (1997). Militarizing Mayberry and beyond: Making sense of American paramilitary policing. *Justice Quarterly*, 14, 607–629.

Kraska, P. B., & Kappeler, V. (1997). Militarizing American police: The rise and normalization of paramilitary units. *Social Problems*, 44, 1–18.

Lee, J. V. (2010). Policing after 9/11: Community policing in an age of homeland security. *Police Quarterly*, 13, 347–366.

Leighton, B. N. (1991). Visions of community policing: Rhetoric and reality in Canada. *Canadian Journal of Criminology*, 33, 485–522.

Levi, M., & Olson, D. (2000). The battles in Seattle. *Politics and Society*, 28, 309–329.

Magers, J. S. (2004). Compstat: A new paradigm for policing or a repudiation of community policing? *Journal of Contemporary Criminal Justice*, 20, 70–79.

Matthews, R. (2009). Beyond 'so what?' criminology: Rediscovering realism. *Theoretical Criminology*, 13, 341–362.

McGarrell, E. F., Freilich, J. D., & Chermak, S. (2007). Intelligence-led policing as a framework for responding to terrorism. *Journal of Contemporary Criminal Justice*, 23, 142–158.

Murphy, C. (2007). "Securitizing" Canadian policing: A new policing paradigm for the post 9/11 security state? *Canadian Journal of Sociology*, 32, 449–475.

National Criminal Intelligence Service, United Kingdom (2000). *The National Intelligence Model*. London: National Criminal Intelligence Service.

National Judicial Institute. (2009). *Social context education: Integration protocol for social context*. Ottawa, ON: National Judicial Institute. http://njca.anu.edu.au/IOJT%20Conference/social%20context%20session.pdf. Retrieved on July 13, 2014.

Oliver, W. M. (2006). The fourth era of policing: Homeland security. *International Review of Law, Computers, and Technology*, 20, 49–62.

Patriquin, M. (2012, June 4). Quebec's new ruling class. *MacLeans*, 125(21), 16–20.

Paul, R. (2003). Trading freedom for security: Drifting toward a police state. *Mediterranean Quarterly*, 14, 6–24.

Perrott, S. B. (2012a). Community policing in The Gambia: A case study in democratic strategies and best intentions being turned upside down. In A. Saine, E. Ceesay, & E. Sall (Eds.), *State and society in the Gambia since independence* (pp. 211–229). Trenton, NJ: Africa World Press.

Perrott, S. B. (2012b). Predatory leadership as a foil to community policing partnerships: A West African case study. In A. Verma, D. K. Das, & M. Abraham (Eds.), *Global community policing: Problems and challenges*. Boca Raton, FL: CRC Press.

Perrott, S. B. (2012c). Reforming the policing of sex tourism in The Philippines and The Gambia. In C. Taylor, D. Torpy, & D. Das (Eds.), *Policing Global Movement: Tourism, Migration, Human Trafficking, and Terrorism* (pp. 3–20). Boca Raton, FL: CRC Press.

Perrott, S. B., & Dechman, M. K. (2012). The role of the police in administering juvenile justice in Canada: Balancing criminal justice and social welfare concerns in a risk society. In P. Kratcoski, *Juvenile justice administration*. Boca Raton, FL: CRC Press.

Perrott, S. B., & Kelloway, E. K. (2006). Workplace violence in the police. In J. Barling & K. Kelloway (Eds.), *Handbook of workplace violence* (pp. 211–229). Thousand Oaks, CA: Sage.

Perrott, S. B., & Kelloway, E. K. (2011). Scandals, sagging morale, and role ambiguity in the royal Canadian mounted police: The end of a Canadian institution as we know it? *Police Practice and Research: An International Journal, 12*, 120–135.

Perrott, S. B., & MacNeill, S. (2012). Policing protesters 'without a cause': Toronto's G20 Summit. In C. Taylor, D. Torpy, & D. Das (Eds.), *Policing Global Movement: Tourism, Migration, Human Trafficking, and Terrorism* (pp. 41–54). Boca Raton, FL: CRC Press.

Perrott, S. B., & Taylor, D. M. (1994). Authoritarianism, ethnocentrism, and occupational stress in the police: Challenging stereotypes and re-conceptualizing ingroup identification. *Journal of Applied Social Psychology, 24*, 1640–1664.

Ratcliffe, J. H. (2003). Intelligence-led policing. *Trends and Issues in Crime and Criminal Justice, 248*, 1–6.

Ratcliffe, J. H. (2008). *Intelligence-led policing*. Portland, OR: Willan Publishing.

Ratcliffe, J. H., & Guidetti, R. (2008). State police investigate structure and the adoption of intelligence-led policing. *Policing, 31*, 109–128.

Sarre, R. (2012). Public-police cooperation in policing crime and terrorism in Australia. In C. Taylor, D. Torpy, & D. Das (Eds.), *Policing Global Movement: Tourism, Migration, Human Trafficking, and Terrorism* (pp. 75–90). Boca Raton, FL: CRC Press.

Schaible, L. M., & Gecas, V. (2010). Emotional labor and value dissonance on burnout among police officers. *Police Quarterly, 13*, 316–341.

Skolnick, J. (1966). *Justice without trial*. New York: Wiley & Sons.

Skolnick, J. (2005). Democratic policing confronts terror and protest. *Syracuse Journal of International Law and Commerce, 33*, 191–212.

Toronto Star (2011, August 10). Rebels without a cause: Nihilism, not idealism, is sending disenchanted youth onto the streets, say British activists, A6.

Verma, A., Das, D. K., & Abraham, M. (Eds.). (2012). *Global Community Policing: Problems and Challenges*. Boca Raton, FL: CRC Press.

Wakefield, A. (2003). Selling *security: The private policing of public space*. Cullompton, United Kingdom: Willan Publishing.

Pre-Charge Restorative Justice and Its Effect on Repeat and Adult Offenders

5

KEITH ROBINSON, DARRYL PLECAS,
COLETTE SQUIRES, AND KIM MCLANDRESS

Contents

Introduction

Restorative justice processes are growing in importance as an alternative justice measure in Canada, and in many other countries around the world. While some advocates would argue that they ought to be used more extensively than they are at the present time, others remain skeptical that restorative justice can be considered as a significant component of a comprehensive criminal justice system. Although restorative justice programs exist in many Canadian communities and elsewhere, some would argue that there is still only limited acceptance of this alternative response to crime (Bliss & Crocker 2008). One of the reasons for this may be the failure to appreciate how much more effective restorative justice can be in reducing further offending, in comparison to traditional approaches for certain types of offenders.

    With the above in mind, the authors conducted a preliminary study to examine recidivism rates from a restorative justice program operating in a community in British Columbia, Canada. Specifically, that study, which is the focus of this chapter, sought to determine whether offenders (in this case shoplifters) who completed a community-based restorative justice program were any less likely to commit further offences following completion of a restorative justice program than offenders who were dealt with through the traditional criminal charge process. The study is an important one given the need for further empirical evidence regarding the recidivism rates of offenders who received a restorative justice intervention in comparison to those who did not. It is important to note that restorative justice groups are designed to handle many types of crimes in addition to shoplifting; however, in this case, studying exclusively shoplifting files presented the opportunity to compare various groups of offenders in ways that are often not possible with other case types.

Clearly, a study on this issue is more complex than simply comparing one group to another. Specifically, not all shoplifting cases referred to the specific program considered are accepted, certain offenders are transferred to other alternative measures, and, even when offenders are accepted, some fail to complete the program. At the same time, some shoplifters are simply warned on the spot with no further action taken by police. Some shoplifters (i.e., repeat offenders) may not be referred to the program, even if that retailer regularly uses the program for first-time offenders, but may be handed over to police for consideration of charges. At the end of the day, how shoplifters are responded to and whether or not they are referred (i.e., selected) to a restorative justice program or any particular system response is a function of numerous factors, which need to be considered in any fair cross-group comparison. With this in mind, and recognizing that the authors attempt to address the issue with attention to at least some offender characteristics, the study results provide some good indications of the relative impact of community-based restorative justice on groups of offenders often excluded from such programs—as an alternative to traditional criminal justice methods of responding to them.

Background on Restorative Justice

Restorative Justice is growing as an international movement toward participatory, transformative justice that focuses on the repair of harm and the restoration of damaged relationships between people and within communities. Unlike retributive justice models, which focus on the breaking of laws and the use of state power for retribution and punishment to denounce and deter wrongdoers, restorative justice is an inclusive approach that supports the law while also keeping victims and other affected parties in a central place within the justice process. There is no one right definition of restorative justice, but a working definition by Tony F. Marshall (as cited in Latimer, Dowden, & Muise, 2005, p. 128) proves useful: "Restorative justice is a process whereby all the parties with a stake in a particular offence come together to resolve collectively how to deal with the aftermath of the offence and its implications for the future." The United Nations handbook on restorative justice programs defines a restorative process as "any process in which the victim and the offender, and, where appropriate, any other individuals or community members affected by a crime, participate together actively in the resolution of matters arising from the crime, generally with the help of a facilitator" (Dandurand & Griffiths, 2006, p. 7).

The values of restorative justice support the needs of crime victims, and are based on principles of responsibility and accountability to others for one's actions, and the need to repair the harm when a crime or conflict occurs (Zehr, 2002; Sharpe, 1998; Umbreit & Greenwood, n.d.). As explained by Zehr (2002), and Sharpe (1998), the primary beliefs of restorative justice include the following:

> Crime is not the breaking of laws: it is harms committed against people, relationships, and community.
> Harm creates obligations: it is up to the offender to make things right.
> Community and victims of crime have a legitimate place in the resolution process when a crime occurs.
> Victim needs are central to the process of resolution.
> Every person is worthy of dignity, respect, and has a right to a voice in processes that affect them.
> Outcomes need to be agreed upon in a way that is collaborative and non-coercive, with an emphasis on fair, proportionate, and balanced agreements that repair the harm done.

Restorative justice can be applied to a criminal incident at a number of points along the traditional criminal justice process. Latimer et al. (2005) identified five points in the process where an offender might be referred to a restorative justice program. These include pre-charge, by way of police referral; post-charge, by way of crown prosecutor referral; pre-sentence, by way of court referral; post-sentence, by way of corrections referral; and pre-revocation, by way of parole officer referral (Latimer et al., 2005, p. 129). Other points in the process have been identified, such as during the period before an offender is released on parole, statutory release, or sentence expiry (pre-release) and at a time during an interpersonal dispute before an offence has even occurred (pre-offence) (Canada Department of Justice 2000). Programs that function prior to charges being laid, such as the program under study in this chapter, are the most common restorative justice programs in Canada, but it would be misleading to suggest that restorative justice only exists apart from the traditional criminal justice system.

Restorative justice has been growing across Canada as a form of social justice parallel to the criminal justice system since the 1970s. The first recognized case of restorative justice was documented in Elmira, Ontario, Canada, in 1974 (Centre for Restorative Justice, n.d.). After two young offenders vandalized 22 properties in a small Ontario town, the assigned probation officer and a Mennonite prison support worker asked the judge for permission to arrange for the two offenders to meet with the victims of the vandalism to see if reparations could be made. This early experiment captured the idea that justice should include compensation and restitution directly to those affected by the criminal act—an idea that has since become strongly linked with most restorative justice processes. It also provided an opportunity for the young offenders to meet directly with their victims to discuss the offence together, with the hopes of developing an agreement that would be fair and satisfactory to all parties. This historic case led to the establishment of the Victim Offender Reconciliation Program in Kitchener, Ontario, now recognized as one of the first and oldest restorative justice programs in Canada ("Community Justice Initiatives: About us," 2012).

During subsequent years, restorative justice has developed internationally, influenced by a variety of countries and cultures, and in a variety of forms. According to a history provided by Van Ness and Strong (2002), Victim Offender Mediation emerged in the late 1970s, involving the directly affected parties with a process guided by a trained mediator. This model is still used today in various places throughout the United States and Canada, and has also been implemented in England and Europe. Simultaneous with this, the Maori-influenced family group conference developed in New Zealand, involving family members and community representatives as well as the primarily affected parties of victim and offender (Van Ness & Strong, 2002; Wachtel, 1997). The New Zealand model evolved to become an intervention for youth offenders, and was typically facilitated by social workers (Wachtel, 1997). It subsequently spread to Australia, championed by Police Sergeant Terry O'Connell, who devised the group conference to be led by a police officer using a script of questions to ensure consistency in the process (Wachtel, 1997). Further developed by Ted Wachtel in the United States as "Real Justice," this scripted model of the family group conference spread from the United States to Canada, where the Royal Canadian Mounted Police (RCMP), Canada's national police force, adapted it to become the Community Justice Forum, most commonly used by community restorative justice organizations in British Columbia to handle pre-charge referrals sent to them by their local RCMP detachment.

In addition to Victim Offender Mediation, Family Group Conferencing, and Community Justice Forums, the international practices of restorative justice have also included the Canadian aboriginal traditions of healing circles, sentencing circles, and other circle processes that include an even wider group of community leaders, elders, and participants than the family group conference which originated from the Maori aboriginal tradition (Van Ness & Strong, 2002). Canada's Aboriginal Justice Strategy reflects this approach, in which criminal matters are often resolved directly within the aboriginal community where support and accountability is offered instead of incarceration. These processes involve community members as well as criminal justice professionals, and are designed to reflect and include the aboriginal rituals and traditions of the community (Department of Justice Canada Evaluation Division, 2007; Department of Justice Canada, 2011). Circle processes have now been adapted for use in schools and other non-aboriginal settings in Canada (Van Ness & Strong 2002).

Despite the variety of forms and expressions of restorative justice, all these models share the belief that justice needs to include the direct participation of those harmed by crime. These models incorporate some form of encounter between the victim and the offender, with additional support often provided by family or community members. They also promote community involvement, whether through direct participation in the resolution process or through support for the affected parties afterward. Reflecting the belief that those affected know what is needed to make things right again, opportunities are provided for the creation of a reparation agreement that may include restitution, compensation, or some other form of amends, frequently including a component to build the capacities of the offender to prevent future harms, and to address the underlying factors that may have influenced the criminal behavior. These underlying beliefs have been eloquently defined by a number of international leaders in the field including Howard Zehr (2002), one of the first articulators of restorative justice theory. Zehr's work has been expanded by numerous other writers and contributors, and papers, books, and journal articles are now in abundance.

Restorative Justice in British Columbia, Canada

In British Columbia, Canada, there are numerous restorative justice programs sponsored by a variety of community agencies and organizations—some functioning within larger organizations such as the John Howard Society or the Boys and Girls Clubs, and others delivered through not-for-profit organizations designed expressly to deliver restorative justice programming. Program models include community group conferences, circles, victim–offender mediation, and school-based programs. Although there are a few notable exceptions, most restorative justice organizations are small, with one or two staff members, supported by community volunteers. The Government of British Columbia promotes the use of restorative justice through the British Columbia Ministry of Justice's Community Accountability Program (2013). This provides a $2500 annual grant to approximately 50 restorative justice programs across the province. Some programs were able to get a $5000 start-up grant to establish themselves within the community. In addition, British Columbia has a variety of community justice programs delivered with federal government funding through the aboriginal justice strategy. This wealth of programs throughout the province reflects a growing belief in the effectiveness of restorative justice as an alternative justice measure that is often more effective in reducing offending behavior than traditional ways of dealing with offenders.

Many of the community-based restorative justice programs currently functioning in British Columbia are in relationship with the RCMP, the major service provider of police services in the province. According to a survey conducted by Curtis (2008), the majority of the community programs operating in British Columbia use the RCMP's Community Justice Forum model. The RCMP has played a leadership role in supporting restorative justice as an effective strategy for responding to first-time youth offenders involved in lower levels of crime, and has created numerous successful partnerships with community organizations to deliver restorative justice programming. The RCMP provides training in the Community Justice Forums model, the Canadian version of the family group conference that developed in New Zealand and Australia, now the primary model of restorative justice endorsed by the RCMP. This model includes the offender, the offender's supporters, the victim, the victim's supporters, and may also include others affected by the incident as well as the investigating police officer. These processes are guided by a trained facilitator, who is often a community volunteer.

The RCMP has also encouraged the use of Community Accountability Panels (CAPs), allowing for a community-based response to crime from a restorative justice perspective, even when the crime victim is not available or willing to partake in the process. This shift toward involving community volunteers as victim representatives or "surrogate victims" has raised questions amongst some researchers (Latimer et al., 2005; Woolford, 2009), as to the degree to which a process can be considered truly restorative justice if the victim is not included. Despite this philosophical concern, the use of community volunteers trained in restorative justice to represent the interests of an absent victim or the wider community has developed primarily as a way of providing a restorative process for young people involved in crimes against retail stores and other businesses when the corporate victim is not available to participate.

The Chilliwack Restorative Justice and Youth Advocacy Association (CRJYAA) program, the program of focus for the study of focus for this chapter, is one example of a community program that has delivered restorative justice through Community Justice Forums as well as Community Panels.

The Chilliwack Restorative Justice and Youth Advocacy Association Program

Established in 1998, the CRJYAA is one of the more well-established restorative justice associations in British Columbia, having served in excess of 3500 people primarily affected or involved with incidents of shoplifting, arson, assault, theft, break and enter, vandalism, or mischief. Their offices are located inside the Chilliwack Community Policing Office, in close proximity to the patrol officers. When the incident involves individuals personally and directly affected by the offence, a Community Justice Forum is used to provide a group conference setting in which to directly resolve the matter between the victim, the offender, and other affected parties. This captures the philosophical perspective in which victim voice and involvement are considered vital to the integrity of restorative justice.

In cases involving shoplifting, the CRJYAA program uses CAPs, but with innovative program enhancements. Their program features a direct referral process from the loss prevention officer to the restorative justice program, increasing efficiency and reducing the need for police to attend for every shoplifting case. This protects the RCMP's ability to respond to more serious incidents occurring elsewhere in the community at that time, and avoids the necessity of leaving offenders to wait for several hours in a room in the back of the store under the supervision of a loss prevention officer or other staff member until police to arrive, occupying staff time during that waiting period. The direct referral process has worked well for compliant shoplifters who have not resisted arrest. In situations of violence, resistance, or if the arrested person denies the offence, the RCMP are still called to attend the scene.

Using the direct referral process, the loss prevention officer calls the RCMP Dispatcher to give the name and date of birth of the arrested shoplifter. The information is used to conduct a background check to determine if there is an outstanding warrant for arrest, and to check the individual's previous history. If there is no reason precluding the use of restorative justice, a police file number is issued, and the referral is sent directly to the CRJYAA office by the loss prevention officer. The shoplifter is then released.

Previous to the development of the direct referral process, CRJYAA staff observed that it was common for apprehended individuals to be held for 4 hours or more before a police officer was able to attend. The direct referral process has created a more efficient and timely response for all involved, producing benefits for the business as well as the RCMP. Now the loss prevention officers and store employees are able to return to their duties more quickly, relieved of the obligation to supervise the apprehended shoplifter for several hours while waiting for police response. This creates potential for a rapid response for the restorative justice organization as well; the CRJYAA staff can be in touch with the referred shoplifter within a day or two, and often within hours of the offence.

When the CRJYAA program coordinator receives the referral, they conduct a second review of the referred individual's file on PRIME, the RCMP database currently in use in British Columbia, to ensure the referral is appropriate. If there is an extensive criminal history or if the shoplifter has already been through a restorative justice process, it is less likely the offender will be allowed to enter the program. An adult with a criminal history will often be denied access to the program, because the program is intended primarily as a crime prevention strategy for first-time offenders to deter future recidivism. CRJYAA's community volunteers are not specifically trained to respond to the criminogenic and other risk factors that relate to repeat offenders. While youth with a history of negative police contact may be accepted into the program, youth with a history of convictions are less likely to be accepted for the same reasons as those for adults. The CRJYAA program mandate was established at its inception, designed to respond primarily to first-time offenders, recognizing that there are other mechanisms within the court and probation processes to provide restorative measures for repeat offenders if and when that is appropriate. However, as demonstrated here, their program actually had greater success in reducing recidivism among repeat offenders and adult offenders than with the first-time offender group.

In addition to screening for a criminal history, the CRJYAA also screen for voluntary participation, admission of responsibility for the offence, parental support for the referral of youth offenders, and the support of the store for the referral. Following the screening process, initial contact is established by telephone. CRJYAA staff explain the CAP program first to the parent or guardian, and then to the youth. Adult shoplifters are contacted directly. Once agreement to the referral and voluntary participation is assured, an initial meeting is conducted with the person responsible for the offence, plus family or support people as relevant. This initial meeting prepares the client for the CAP process in a variety of ways. First, the staff member describes what will happen at the CAP, and the types of questions that will be asked. They will also explore the offence with the client, to hear what happened and to get the offender's input on what they might be able to do to repair the harm done. The client is encouraged to consider who else has been affected, and what those effects have been. In the case of young offenders, parents and family members are encouraged to share how they have been affected. CRJYAA staff members also inquire about the client's daily life, so that an agreement can be created that will harmonize well with the dynamics and rhythms of the family, to help ensure that the client will be able to fulfill the agreement.

CRJYAA's program is strength-based, so this initial meeting also explores the capacities of the offender. What positive activities are they currently involved in? For youth offenders, are they still in school? Are they involved in extracurricular activities? What are their hobbies and interests? What are they good at? What strengths or protective factors are evident in their life? To whom are they strongly attached, if anyone? That person could then be invited into the process, as appropriate. The information gathered at the initial meeting is brought to the CAP, to help create an agreement that will not only provide an opportunity for reparation and amends, but will also build on the strengths and capacities of the offender.

In general practice in British Columbia, the CAP process is very often used as a way to provide an adapted restorative justice process when a corporate victim does not want to participate. According to CRJYAA staff, often these corporate victims prefer the traditional court process and do not want to release staff to participate in a community-based restorative justice process that may be perceived as taking even more company time and resources. However, that response denies an offender the opportunity to receive the support, learning, and accountability that a restorative process can provide, as well as the benefit of avoiding a criminal conviction. In contrast, a community-based restorative justice option can provide an offender with a timely, meaningful, nonpunitive response to their misdemeanor that will still promote socially responsible and crime-free future behavior.

To address this challenge, the CRJYAA has built strong relationships with several department stores and retail outlets in the Chilliwack community to increase the engagement of the corporate victim. The loss prevention officers and store managers readily refer to the program, asking only for restitution for damaged goods that cannot be re-sold, and a letter of apology. They trust the program volunteers to create the capacity-building, preventative nature of the agreement that will mitigate recidivism. They also know that the CRJYAA program provides a mentor for the offender, to ensure encouragement and support while the agreement is being fulfilled. In some communities, the CAP process would be an end in itself, but in Chilliwack, it serves as a second step of preparation after the initial meeting, as a prelude to a meeting between the offender and the store manager.

The CAP is facilitated by three volunteers. The process begins with introductions, to begin to establish relationship and rapport. The program is explained, along with the role of the volunteers, how confidentiality is handled, a review of the offender's rights, and an additional check to ensure the offender is participating voluntarily. After some preliminary, informal conversation, the facilitators will ask the offender to describe what happened. The facilitators may ask clarifying questions, and may probe for greater detail or deeper reflection on what happened and why. Then the supporters are invited to give input on how they found out about the incident, how it affected them, and what they think about it. Facilitators will often ask what has happened since, and whether there were consequences within the family. The offender is then asked to reflect on and respond to what they have heard from their own family. After this, the facilitators will share what they have learned from the store manager and loss prevention officer in terms of the impacts and effects of shoplifting, if those have not been raised or addressed by the offender. This prompts a group discussion of the effects of shoplifting, and the implications for a criminal record when a person is convicted of theft under $5000, even if the item stolen was very small and inexpensive. This provides an opportunity to educate the offender on the related charge, and how it might be handled through a traditional court process.

When the facilitators feel it is appropriate, they guide the creation of the resolution agreement. Harms have now been discussed, and if the stolen item was damaged or could not be re-sold, then the store will have already asked for restitution and an apology letter at the time of the referral. The CRJYAA staff reported that their history of program success over many years has fostered goodwill, trust, and confidence, such that most store managers and loss prevention officers now trust the program volunteers to help create an agreement that promotes prosocial community activity, volunteerism, and positive involvement with other community organizations. This becomes the restorative component of the agreement that supports the offender in redirecting their activities, restoring their reputation, and creating a more positive identity. The session closes with final remarks, and the facilitators check with the offender and the offender's supporters to ensure everyone agrees that the agreement is fair, achievable, practical, and proportionate to the offence. To maintain program integrity, the facilitators strive to ensure relevance, and a reasonable, restorative approach.

In terms of making an agreement restorative, CRJYAA strives to build agreements tailored to the offender's strengths, and that will frequently enhance their future opportunities. Often it will build their personal assets and capacities through community partnerships with other agencies that will take these offenders as volunteers. The agreements may also include referrals to personal counseling, or other external assistance to help address problematic family dynamics or troubled relationships. Reintegration is an important theme in restorative justice, and this is achieved in the CRJYAA program through helping the offender develop connections with caring community members who will support them while also helping to hold them accountable. Each offender is assigned a community volunteer who becomes their mentor and supporter as the offender carries out his or her agreement.

The program also strives to connect clients with other community members and organizations that will facilitate positive activity and friendships with positive, prosocial people. The CRJYAA program encourages relationship-building and healthy attachments through helping offenders to engage with their community in different, more positive ways. Often this can be achieved by providing a positive outlet for their interests and passions, thereby helping them create a more positive sense of self-esteem and personal identity. Resolving their criminal offence through prosocial activity also helps offenders restore their reputation, and resolve the feelings of embarrassment and shame that may have surfaced when they were first arrested. The facilitators and mentors help the offenders and their families to see that the offence was a mistake and a poor choice, but that they have the opportunity to redeem that mistake through taking responsibility and engaging in better choices and activities in the future.

In addition to the agreement process described above, the CRJYAA program provides for a face-to-face meeting with the offender and the store manager. Although this meeting is usually only 20–30 minutes long, this is an important program component that ensures the importance of victim engagement and participation, and encourages direct responsibility and accountability from the offender. It typically occurs within 2 weeks of the first CAP meeting when the resolution agreement was first created, providing an opportunity for the offender to deliver the letter of apology and any funds required for restitution directly to the store manager, and to engage in a dialogue with the store manager about the offence. The offender's mentor is the facilitator of this "mini-conference," and he or she will have prepared the offender in advance by reviewing the apology letter together to ensure it reflects the offender's understanding of why the act was wrong, and the negative implications and effects that have resulted. The store manager is able to share firsthand the negative effects of shoplifting, and the offender is able to share the details of the resolution agreement so the store manager will know how restoration and reintegration is taking place.

CRJYAA staff reported that offenders typically find this the most difficult but effective part of the program, and it has become an important component of program success. It addresses the corporate victim's need for time efficiency by creating the agreement in advance of this meeting, but maintains the personal encounter between victim and offender that gives restorative justice its unique value. This also helps to address the concerns raised by researchers such as Latimer et al. (2005) and Woolford (2009), who questioned the degree to which a CAP can be truly restorative if the victim is not included. Program staff reported that this meeting plays a significant role in the formation of empathy and concern for the harmed party, and strengthens the offender's desire to make amends. The written and verbal apology becomes much more meaningful when delivered in this personal way.

To ensure program integrity, the CRJYAA has observed that the store managers also need to be prepared for this process to have a meaningful conversation with the offender. This has required further education and relationship building with the participating stores. In the CRJYAA experience, offenders, and in particular, youth offenders are typically scared and remorseful when they attend this meeting. Some store managers have just accepted the apology letter, refused to engage in a meeting, and banned the offender from further shopping at their store, leaving the offender disheartened and upset. Learning from these experiences has caused the CRJYAA staff to work together with the stores to ensure that they provide a store representative who will take the time to meet the offender, and who will be able to acknowledge the offender's apology and desire to make things right.

The CRJYAA affirmed that this is the most significant step in the program because it allows offenders to finally meet the person they have harmed, and to demonstrate how they are taking steps to make direct amends. For the offenders, it represents an opportunity to articulate verbally and on paper what they did, why they did it, and that they are sorry.

After the encounter with the store manager, the mentor supports and assists the client to fulfill the rest of the agreement. By this point, the mentor has already been the sounding board and first reviewer of the apology letter ensuring that the letter addressed all necessary information. The mentor also becomes a liaison between the offender and community partners for the community service component. The mentor plays an important role in helping the offender meet deadlines and to address the barriers and logistical challenges that may thwart success. For young offenders, mentors communicate with parents and guardians to keep them apprised of the process, and to maintain positive relationships and open communication. Mentors provide important support to the family; they can be reached any day of the week, beyond office hours. Mentors provide a friendship component and build positive rapport. It is their role to help ensure the agreement is completed on time, and to provide a positive role model.

When the agreement is fulfilled, a letter is sent from the CRJYAA program to the store reporting on the final outcome of the case. The process concludes when the offender and mentor are invited to a final panel meeting to review the agreement and the offender's experience with the program. The offender receives a letter of completion, and all participants in the process are invited to provide feedback as part of an ongoing evaluation of the program.

Evaluating Restorative Justice

Evaluating restorative justice programs is no easy task, due to a variety of factors. As explained in the United Nations handbook on restorative justice programs (Dandurand & Griffiths, 2006) there is the difficulty of securing adequate control groups of crime victims and offenders who participated in the conventional criminal justice system to provide a comparison with those experiencing a restorative process. Second, programs differ from place to place, with varying goals and objectives. Third, competence and training of facilitators is not consistent between programs. Fourth, performance indicators vary from place to place. Finally, it is also very difficult to measure a process that is highly subjective, personal and interactive, leaving researchers puzzling over how to quantify restorative values such as victim empowerment, offender remorse, and whether growth of empathy and learning did or did not take place.

While some of the goals of restorative justice approaches include a variety of concepts that may be difficult to measure quantitatively, researchers have tried to determine whether or not these programs "work." To do this, programs have been evaluated by comparing the outcomes of the process to those of the traditional criminal justice system. Efforts to evaluate restorative justice programs around the world have generally focused on outcomes related to three general measures: recidivism rates on the part of participating offenders; rates of compliance with restorative justice agreements; and participant satisfaction with the process. The question of whether or not restorative justice can reduce recidivism is most relevant to the purpose of this chapter. While it may be arguable whether reducing future offending is indeed a true intended goal of restorative justice, it is a measure that is often of concern for the general public, policy makers, and other non-restorative justice practitioners in the criminal justice system, and thus they may carry greater weight in influencing skeptics about the promise of restorative justice approaches (Gabbay, 2005).

Due to the lack of adequate control groups for comparison, measuring recidivism is a challenge, and empirical research data on this question is limited. What is known is that the best predictors of re-offending for offenders who go through restorative justice processes seem to be the factors most commonly associated with offenders generally: age, age at first offence, gender (males more than females), and prior offending (Dandurand & Griffiths, 2006). When young people begin offending at an early age, recidivism is more likely. However, there are factors in restorative justice that reduce the likelihood of re-offending: when the one causing harm is remorseful, and sorry for their offending behavior; when they meet and apologize to victims; when conference agreements are decided by genuine consensus; when the offender is not stigmatized or shamed; when they are involved in decision-making; when they comply with the conference agreement; and when they feel they have righted the wrongs done (Dandurand & Griffiths, 2006).

Dandurand and Griffiths (2006) reviewed the data on restorative justice programs around the world, and concluded that "restorative processes have a greater potential than the standard justice process operating alone to effectively resolve conflict, secure offender accountability and meet the needs of victims" (p. 86). When they reported the following general findings emerging from the evaluation studies to date, they noted that restorative justice has proven to be effective in a significant number of ways, including having a positive effect in reducing the frequency and the severity of re-offending. They also noted that there appear to be no inherent limitations in the types of cases that can be referred to restorative processes.

Latimer et al. (2005) also provided evidence for positive outcomes from restorative justice in their meta-analysis examining victim and offender satisfaction, restitution compliance, and recidivism. Despite the methodological difficulties of many studies, their examination of a number of different programs versus control groups determined that restorative justice programs were significantly more effective in the four areas of victim and offender satisfaction, restitution compliance, and recidivism. They acknowledged, however, that restorative processes are not positioned to address factors that influence criminal behavior such as antisocial peers, substance abuse, and criminogenic communities. In addition, they suggested that offenders with high risk and criminogenic factors would benefit more from offender treatment programs as an additional intervention to the restorative process, as a complementary enhancement. In that sense, restorative justice works well as a complement to rehabilitative treatment programs.

The RCMP's Community Justice Forums Model used by the CRJYAA has been evaluated in the past (Chatterjee, 1999). Programs included in the evaluation were from all across Canada. Unfortunately, this evaluation did not address recidivism, an issue that was noted in a later article by Chatterjee and Elliot (2003), but it did demonstrate that the programs using this model achieved very high levels of satisfaction and perceived fairness for victims and offenders (Chatterjee, 1999). Additional, recent evaluations of this commonly used model for restorative justice programs in British Columbia that include measures of recidivism would be a great benefit to understanding the effects of restorative justice practices in the province.

Finally, it is important to qualify that research on restorative justice, such as the large meta-analysis by Latimer et al. (2005), often only includes programs that are voluntary, community-based responses that bring together the victim, the offender, and the community. Therefore, there is little research exploring other types of programs that have restorative elements such as restitution or community service but do not include the party directly harmed by the criminal act, such as the CAPs and the use of "surrogate" victims. Some commentators such as Heather Strang (2002) maintain that victim involvement is a crucial element that makes restorative processes frequently far more meaningful for victims than what the formal criminal justice system often provides. Therefore, there is also a need for research to evaluate the use of restorative justice practices that do not involve direct victims, to compare their effectiveness for offenders if no victim is present.

The CRJYAA program importantly, as the program from which the data upon which the current study is based, meets the criteria established by Latimer et al. (2005), as a voluntary, community-based response to criminal behavior that attempts to bring together the victim, the offender, and the community, in an effort to address the harm caused by the criminal behavior. Unlike other CAP programs in which there is no victim involvement, the CRJYAA program uses the panel as a preparatory step before a direct meeting between the offender and the corporate victim. The research on the CRJYAA program is also significant because there is the presence of a control group, composed of shoplifting offenders at non-participating stores who pursued charges and a traditional court process.

This research project also prepares the way for future research to compare the long-term effects on the offender if they encounter the victim directly in a conference or mediation, or if they experience a process without a direct encounter with the crime victim. For this reason, this research is significant, especially in a field in which program evaluations are still developmental and the empirical data on outcomes is still slim.

Methodology for the Current Study

The methodology for the current study was generally quite straight forward. Specifically, it began with CRJYAA compiling a list of all shoplifters who had been referred to its program from six major retail stores in Chilliwack over the 3-year period from January 1, 2007 to December 31, 2009. At the same time, and using the same timeframe, the local RCMP created another list of shoplifters who had not been referred to the program, but instead, had been processed in the traditional way. This included individuals who were charged with shoplifting from the six major retail stores in Chilliwack, which commonly refer offenders to CRJYAA, and it also included offenders who were caught shoplifting from three major retail stores that almost never refer offenders to CRJYAA. Drawing again on cases from all nine of those major retail stores, the RCMP also included all individuals who came to the attention of police for shoplifting and were considered suspect chargeable (but ultimately were not charged). Collectively, all cases considered provided a sample of 308 cases for study, including 113 shoplifters who successfully completed the CRJYAA restorative justice program, 92 shoplifters who were instead charged, and 103 shoplifters who were suspect chargeable. Not included in the sample, because of the small numbers involved (8), were those offenders who were referred to CRJYAA and not accepted into the program and those who were referred to the program but did not complete it successfully. Also not included were 91 shoplifters who were referred to an alternative measures program for aboriginal offenders (and for whom the authors were unable to know whether or not offenders referred there actually completed the program). Finally, also excluded were the shoplifters (an unknown number) that the retail stores involved simply released with a warning.

With the list constructed, the next task involved searching PRIME, the British Columbia police information system, to determine the number of times (if any) those individuals within the sample were subsequently determined to be either suspect chargeable, charged, or convicted of any criminal offence at any time within a 2-year follow-up period. In this regard, the authors were interested in knowing whether or not the offender was caught shoplifting in that 2-year follow-up period, and whether or not they came to the attention of police for any other criminal offences. At the same time, the authors were mindful of the fact that the three groups being considered were not properly comparable without some matching of shoplifter background characteristics. This is, of course, because the shoplifters were not randomly assigned to whatever group they were in—they were in effect "selected." Accordingly, information on each shoplifter's gender, age, and prior history of offending was recorded. Admittedly, this is not an ideal matching of cases (a more sophisticated matching using other characteristics as well would have been ideal), but more detailed information on each offender was not readily available and the situation was complicated yet further by the fact that the sample size was relatively small. Unfortunately, that sample size could not have been larger because PRIME was not fully up and running in Chilliwack before 2007. If it had been up and running, more cases (i.e., cases from 2002 forward) could have been included. In any case, the breakdown of the resulting sample with background characteristics considered is shown by Table 5.1.

Importantly, to protect the identities of the offenders involved, the creation of the shoplifter list and associated database was all done in-house at the RCMP detachment and under the supervision of the RCMP and CRJYAA and in a manner to ensure that the database to be accessed and used for analysis was anonymized.

Results

The results of the analysis clearly show that shoplifters who completed the CRJYAA restorative justice program are, when compared to shoplifters who are charged or chargeable and not charged, less likely within a 2-year follow-up period to be apprehended for shoplifting again. Moreover, as Tables 5.2

Table 5.1   Group Breakdown of Number of Shoplifters Included in Study Sample

Group	Youths		Adults		Total
	First-Time Offenders (No.)	With Prior History (No.)	First-Time Offenders (No.)	With Prior History (No.)	Shoplifters (No.)
Successfully Completed RJ Program	55	12	37	9	113
Chargeable, but not Charged	22	5	36	40	103
Charged	4	4	21	63	92
Total	81	21	94	112	308

Note: $n = 308$.

Table 5.2   Percent of Males Caught Shoplifting within 2-Year Follow-Up Period

Group	Youths		Adults		Total
	First-Time Offenders (%)	With Prior History (%)	First-Time Offenders (%)	With Prior History (%)	Shoplifters (%)
Successfully Completed RJ Program	25	0	14	0	19
Chargeable, but not Charged	13	67	18	23	22
Charged	0	33	8	48	36
Total	19	43	14	37	28

Note: $n = 138$. All percentages rounded.

Table 5.3   Percent of Females Caught Shoplifting within 2-Year Follow-Up Period

Group	Youths		Adults		Total
	First-Time Offenders (%)	With Prior History (%)	First-Time Offenders (%)	With Prior History (%)	Shoplifters (%)
Successfully Completed RJ Program	3	0	0	27	3
Chargeable, but not Charged	7	100	3	43	20
Charged	0	100	22	65	53
Total	4	21	5	53	18

Note: $n = 170$. All percentages rounded.

and 5.3 show, this is true for both male and female shoplifters. Interesting, however, while that pattern generally still holds true when looking at specific subgroups of shoplifters, it is not true for male or female first-time youth offenders. Specifically, first-time youth offenders who have completed the CRJYAA restorative justice program are no less likely to re-offend with a 2-year follow-up period than offenders who are treated as chargeable or charged. This is interesting, of course, because first-time youth offenders are the offender group typically seen as most suitable for restorative justice programs. Looking at it another way, the results suggest that the recidivism rate is not likely to be lowered for first-time male youth offenders who successfully complete a restorative justice process (Table 5.2). Nor is it likely to be lowered for first-time female youth shoplifters who are likely to have a relatively low rate of subsequent shoplifting, regardless of how they are responded to by the criminal justice system (Table 5.3).

Perhaps more importantly, the results suggest that restorative justice works relatively well for repeat offenders. As Table 5.2 shows, while a substantial percentage of both youth and adult male offenders with prior criminal histories shoplifted within the 2-year follow-up period, none of the repeat offenders who went through the CRJYAA restorative justice program were subsequently apprehended for shoplifting within this period. Further, as Table 5.3, shows, the same pattern is apparent with respect to youth and adult female offenders with prior criminal histories. That is, those shoplifters from this group of offenders who successfully completed the CRJYAA restorative justice program had a substantially lower rate of subsequent shoplifting than did offenders who were charged or regarded as chargeable and not charged.

As suggestive as the results respecting subsequent shoplifting are, the results with respect to general recidivism among the shoplifters studied are more compelling. Specifically, as Tables 5.4 and 5.5 show, the percentage of shoplifters successfully completing the CRJYAA restorative justice program and recidivating within a 2-year follow-up period is substantially lower than it is for shoplifters who are charged or chargeable and not charged. Further, this is true again for every subgroup of shoplifters considered except first-time youth offenders. For example, as Table 5.4 shows, 50% of adult males with criminal histories who successfully completed the CRJYAA restorative justice program recidivated within 2 years, whereas 69% of chargeable (but not charged) shoplifters and 88% of charged shoplifters recidivated. Likewise, as Table 5.5 shows, 29% of adult females with criminal histories who successfully completed the CRJYAA restorative justice program recidivated within

Table 5.4   Percent of Male Shoplifters Recidivating within 2-Year Follow-Up Period

Group	Youths		Adults		Total
	First-Time Offenders (%)	With Prior History (%)	First-Time Offenders (%)	With Prior History (%)	Shoplifters (%)
Successfully Completed RJ Program	38	0	14	50	31
Chargeable, but not Charged	25	100	35	69	54
Charged	67	67	50	88	77
Total	37	71	36	79	59

Note: n = 138. All percentages rounded. Recidivism refers to re-offending involving any crime.

2 years, whereas 71% of chargeable (but not charged) adult female shoplifters with criminal histories and 70% of charged adult female shoplifters with criminal histories recidivated.

Two other issues considered in the analysis included the matter of how much time had passed before a re-offending shoplifter recidivated, and for those who did, the matter of how many times they were apprehended for a crime over the 2-year follow-up period. And here again, the results were strongly suggestive of the benefit of restorative justice over charging a shoplifter or dealing with the offender as chargeable, but not laying charges. Specifically, as Table 5.6 shows, males who successfully completed the CRJYAA restorative justice program and recidivated lasted 13 months before reoffending, while shoplifters who were chargeable or charged lasted only 4 months. Moreover, as

Table 5.5 Percent of Female Shoplifters Recidivating within 2-Year Follow-Up Period

Group	Youths		Adults		Total
	First-Time Offenders (%)	With Prior History (%)	First-Time Offenders (%)	With Prior History (%)	Shoplifters (%)
Successfully Completed RJ Program	10	46	10	29	16
Chargeable, but not Charged	29	100	21	71	41
Charged	0	100	11	70	53
Total	15	57	14	64	31

Note: $n = 170$. All percentages rounded. Recidivism refers to re-offending involving any crime.

Table 5.6 Average Number of Offences within 24-Month Follow-Up Period and Number of Months to First Recidivism among Sampled Shoplifters

Group	Males		Females	
	Months to First Recidivism	Offences in 24 Months (No.)	Months to First Recidivism	Offences in 24 Months (No.)
Successfully Completed RJ Program	13	2	7	2
Chargeable, but not Charged	4	5	7	6
Charged	4	8	3	7
Total	5	6	5	5

Note: $n = 308$. All percentages rounded. Recidivism refers to re-offending involving any crime.

per Table 5.6, males who successfully completed the CRJYAA restorative justice program only committed two offences over the 2-year follow-up period,
as compared to those who were chargeable, who committed five offences,
and those who were charged, who subsequently committed eight offences
within the 2-year follow-up period. Notably, a similar pattern is apparent with
respect to female shoplifters. Those who successfully completed the CRJYAA
restorative justice program and recidivated lasted 7 months before reoffending, shoplifters who were chargeable lasted 7 months, and those who were
charged lasted only 3. As well, female shoplifters who successfully completed
the CRJYAA restorative justice program only committed two offences over
the 2-year follow-up period, as compared to those who were chargeable, who
committed six offences, and those who were charged, who subsequently committed seven offences within the 2-year follow-up period.

Unfortunately, the sample size being as small as it is precludes the
authors from adequately comparing means in terms of months and number
of offences between first-time and repeat offenders. Still, the results shown by
Table 5.6 are stark enough to suggest that restorative justice programs may
be more influential in impacting on a broader range of offenders than they
have generally been given credit for. In any case, the results overall, as told
by all of the tables collectively, call attention to the high rates of re-offending
among shoplifters who are either charged or chargeable (but not charged).
Further, Tables 5.2 through 5.5, also call attention to the generally high levels
of re-offending among offenders who have a history of offending, including
those shoplifters who successfully completed the CRJYAA restorative justice
program. However, at the end of the day, recidivism remains notably lower
for shoplifters who have successfully completed the CRJYAA restorative justice program.

Discussion and Conclusion

As reported by Dandurand and Griffiths (2006), restorative justice processes
have demonstrated success and positive outcomes in a multiplicity of ways:
higher rates of compliance with agreements, a perception of greater fairness
and satisfaction for both victims and offenders, increased sense of closure
and wellbeing for crime victims, and reduced costs and greater efficiencies in
responding to crime. In Canada, there is growing concern regarding a justice
system that is increasing in its inability to process cases in a timely way and
to provide effective results. At the time of writing, the Province of British
Columbia is conducting a large-scale review of its justice system, noting that
"inputs into the system such as the rate of crime and the number of new
cases are down [b]ut the length of time spent by people remanded in custody
or on bail awaiting trial is increasing, as is the total number of people being

managed by the Corrections system. Costs, too, are increasing in real terms" (Modernizing British Columbia's Justice System, 2012, p. 2). These challenges speak of the need to consider practical, effective alternatives. And yet, restorative justice initiatives are primarily engaged for first-time young offenders in British Columbia, and further applications of the process for more serious crime and adult offenders is still quite limited. The British Columbia Ministry of Justice only provides $2500 per year per approved program, with no provision of assistance to community groups to help them develop the evaluation mechanisms they need to demonstrate evidence-based results (Ministry of Justice, n.d.). Sustainability continues to be a primary challenge.

Restorative justice programs are one way to make a positive contribution to the present criminal justice system. This research demonstrates the effectiveness of restorative justice for shoplifting cases, in contrast to those processed through the courts. Given these research outcomes it would be advisable for police, Crown, and the public to consider restorative justice as a first option for shoplifting, to reduce court costs, court delays, and to improve recidivism rates. This aligns with the recommendations in the British Columbia Government's green paper on justice reform, *Modernizing British Columbia's Justice System,* in which it is noted that

> [C]riminal law provides for lower-risk accused persons to be diverted to other options short of a criminal trial ("alternative measures"). These provisions appear to remain under-used. Meanwhile, there is significant growth in charges regarding violations of court-ordered conditions. The result appears to be a system attempting to control accused persons' behaviour by court order when many lower-risk individuals might have been diverted earlier from the courts to more effective measures that protect public safety and reduce recidivism... Increasing the number of lower-risk alternative measures referrals would create additional capacity for all aspects of the justice sector, while not negatively impacting public safety in a meaningful way (2012, p. 25).

Beyond shoplifting, research conducted by Dandurand and Griffiths (2006) has already indicated that there is no limit to the types of cases that can be referred to restorative justice, so a further application is worthy of consideration. This will require meaningful funding and support from government, ongoing commitment to best practices by service providers, and a greater commitment to educate the public and primary stakeholders as to the benefits that restorative justice can provide. The CRJYAA has demonstrated through its shoplifting program that restorative justice can provide significant success in reducing recidivism rates. Reduced recidivism provides economic and social benefits to communities and reduces strain on an ailing justice system. This should encourage serious consideration of restorative justice as an integral part of the Canadian criminal justice system, especially in the area of effective alternative measures.

Admittedly, given the relatively small sample size used by the authors, additional research involving much larger sample sizes is needed to provide greater confidence in the kind of results reported here. As well, additional research should involve looking at a broader range of offence types. In the meantime, those leading restorative justice programs may want to consider accepting referrals for a broader range of shoplifters. There is no doubt that doing so will negatively impact on program completion and subsequent success rates; however, given the recidivism rates of shoplifters who are dealt with outside of restorative justice programs, that negative impact would surely be far outweighed by the impact restorative justice programs could potentially have on those recidivism rates. The bonus, of course, as noted in this chapter and often by others, is that restorative justice brings a range of benefits to the table of criminal justice intervention that our court system simply has not been able to provide.

In addition, the results of this chapter should be seriously considered by management of all retail stores concerned about shoplifting. No doubt, many among them think they are taking the best action by having a significant percentage of offenders handled through the criminal charge process. The results of this chapter would suggest that it is hardly the best action—either for their stores or for community safety at large. At the same time, many among them, no doubt, think that they are doing enough by simply letting off many shoplifters with a warning. Such action, though, is in effect the same outcome as happens to a shoplifter who ends up being treated as chargeable, but not charged. To the extent that those given a warning and those who are chargeable are similar, we should expect a better result from referring those offenders to a restorative justice program instead.

Finally, the results of this chapter should provide the impetus for police and government to consider the wider implementation of restorative justice programs for repeat and adult offenders, and for a wider array of offences. Clearly, it would be important to address issues of consistency, training, and program efficacy from community to community to determine those that would be able to address the criminogenic needs of these two groups, but there is enough evidence from this research to suggest that a well-organized, well-trained community group should have the capacity to address more serious offences and a broader array of offence types than has been previously suggested. Program expansion along these lines would benefit from additional evaluation mechanisms to help determine when, how, and why the restorative justice process triggered positive changes in attitudes and behaviors, resulting in these reduced recidivism rates, as that cannot be determined from this current research study.

What can be determined, though, is that in this case the restorative justice process had a greater impact on repeat offenders and adult offenders than expected, even surpassing the benefits of restorative justice traditionally assigned to first-time young offenders. The CRJYAA was originally established with a mandate targeting first-time young offenders only, with the belief that the volunteer-based program did not have the capacity to handle adult files or repeat offenders. These results demonstrate that the development and maturation of this program has equipped them to handle shoplifting cases involving repeat and adult offenders, so it is reasonable to consider that they may have the capacity to formally expand their mandate.

Timely, affordable, and effective processes of justice remain a priority for most jurisdictions today. This is especially true when considering how to reduce the recidivism rates of repeat offenders, and those who have continued to offend in their adult years. The successes of Chilliwack's restorative justice program suggests that it is worthwhile to consider more widespread implementation of well-designed, effective restorative justice programs to address not just low-level crime by first-time young offenders, but also repeat and adult offenders as well.

References

Bliss, K., & Crocker, D. (2008). Fact sheet on literature reviewed for the public opinion project. Nova Scotia Restorative Justice Community University Research Alliance. Retrieved from http://www.nsrj-cura.ca/nsrj-cura/mediabank/File/PUBLIC_OPINION_literature_fact_sheet_2008-04-14.pdf.

British Columbia Ministry of Justice. (2013). *Community accountability programs.* Retrieved from http://www.pssg.gov.bc.ca/crimeprevention/justice/index.htm#cap.

Centre for Restorative Justice. (n.d.) *Stories of reconciliation: Russ Kelly.* Burnaby, BC: Simon Fraser University. Retrieved from http://www.sfu.ca/crj/kelly.html.

Chatterjee, J. (1999). *A report on the evaluation of RCMP restorative justice initiative: Community Justice Forum as seen by participants.* Ottawa: Research and Evaluation Branch, Community, Contract and Aboriginal Policing Services.

Chatterjee, J., & Elliot, L. (2003). Restorative policing in Canada: The Royal Canadian Mounted Police, Community Justice Forums, and the Youth Criminal Justice Act. *Police Practice and Research, 4*:4, 347–359.

Community Justice Initiatives: About us. (2012). Kitchener, ON: Community Justice Initiatives. Retrieved from http://www.cjiwr.com/about-us-2.htm.

Curtis, B. (2008). *Community-based restorative justice in BC: The state of the field, a survey of Community Accountability Programs.* Victoria, BC: Ministry of Public Safety and Solicitor General.

Dandurand, Y., & Griffiths, C. T. (2006). *Handbook on restorative justice programmes.* New York: United Nations.

Department of Justice Canada. (2011). *Aboriginal Justice Strategy.* Retrieved from http://www.justice.gc.ca/eng/pi/ajs-sja/#cap.

Department of Justice Canada Evaluation Division. (2007). *Aboriginal justice strategy summative evaluation: final report.* Ottawa, ON: Department of Justice Canada. Retrieved from http://www.justice.gc.ca/eng/pi/eval/rep-rap/07/ajs-sja/ajs.pdf.

Gabbay, Z. D. (2005). Justifying restorative justice: A theoretical justification for the use of restorative justice practices. *Journal of Dispute Resolution, 2*:349–397.

Latimer, J., Dowden, C., & Muise, D. (2005). The effectiveness of restorative justice practices: A meta-analysis. *The Prison Journal, 85*:2, 127–144.

Modernizing British Columbia's justice system. (2012). British Columbia, Canada: Minister of Justice and Attorney General. Retrieved from http://www.ag.gov .bc.ca/public/JusticeSystemReviewGreenPaper.pdf.

Sharpe, S. (1998). *Restorative justice: a vision for healing and change.* Edmonton, Alberta: Edmonton Victim Offender Mediation Society.

Strang, H. (2002). *Repair or revenge: victims and restorative justice.* Oxford: Clarendon Press.

Umbreit, M., & Greenwood, J. (n.d.) *Guidelines for victim-sensitive victim-offender mediation: Restorative justice through dialogue.* St. Paul Minnesota: Center for Restorative Justice & Peacemaking, School of Social Work, University of Minnesota.

Van Ness, D. W. & Heetderks Strong, K. (2002). *Restoring justice.* Cincinnati, OH: Anderson Publishing.

Wachtel, T. (1997). *Real Justice: How to Revolutionize our Response to Wrongdoing.* Pipersville, PA: Piper's Press.

Woolford, A. (2009). The *politics of restorative justice.* Winnipeg, Manitoba: Fernwood, Publishing.

Zehr, H. (2002). *The little book of restorative justice.* Intercourse, Pennsylvania: Good Books.

White-Collar Cybercrimes
Cyberespionage

6

JAMES LEWIS

Contents

Introduction

As technology becomes more integrated into society, criminal activity in cyberspace has become more complex in regard to technique, methods of concealment, and types of targets. The techniques used to commit and conceal cybercrimes have become significantly more multifaceted and difficult to detect. While intruders from outside the organization use more readily detectable methods to gain access and acquire internal information, insiders to the organization, whether willingly or unknowingly, often use different techniques. Once unauthorized access to internal databases has been accomplished and the intellectual property has been breached or stolen, egress of it is much more multifaceted. This chapter includes a focus on the methods used to conceal the theft of intellectual property used to commit electronic-based espionage.

Espionage involves illegal acts designed to obtain secret information sensitive to corporate, military, or political entities. Espionage has traditionally been seen as conventional and targeted mainly toward the theft of government secrets that would have an impact on national security. Covert acts involving surveillance and reconnaissance have often been antecedent to the actual acts of espionage. This includes both conventional and a relatively new type known as cyberespionage. Cyberespionage is defined as the intentional use of computers or digital communications activities in an effort to gain access to sensitive information about an adversary or competitor for the purpose of gaining an advantage or selling the sensitive information for monetary reward (Alperovitch, 2011). The intentional and unauthorized electronic copying of corporate intellectual property, trade, or national secrets, when done so to provide to a third party is cyberespionage. Some estimates place the losses from cyberespionage at more than $1.5 trillion annually (Alperovitch, 2011).

Objective

The objective of this research is to demonstrate if first year college students can, with limited technical guidance, devise, create, and execute circumstances where unauthorized and undetected access to a computer network can be established in preparation for performing an act of cyberespionage. This information is then compared to and extrapolated to actual cases where cyberespionage has been successfully conducted. Thumb drive and wireless technology are commonplace in most organizations, including corporate and public businesses. For this reason, these technologies are the focus of this report.

Challenges in Reporting

Much of the emphasis in the news media involving cybercrimes appears to be focused on network penetration from outside sources; however, types of cybercrimes vary significantly and are in no means limited to external threats. One of the challenges in determining how many cybercrimes have been committed and the percentage rates of such is due to the fact that most go unreported. The reasons for underreporting vary, however, as it is a common practice in industry to not expose organizational or network weaknesses to the public. This brings scrutiny against the organization and invites future attacks against the electronic infrastructure presenting it as an easy target. According to the 2012 Cybersecurity Watch Survey (Table 6.1), 72% of cybercrimes go unreported, while 42% of known cases involved copying information to a mobile device such as a Universal Serial Bus (USB) drive (U.S. Secret Service, Software Engineering Institute, CERT and Deloitte [USSS CERT & Deloitte], 2010). This presents a challenge in the acquisition of information for research. The types of thefts reported in this survey include the following:

1. Theft of other (proprietary) info including customer records, financial records, and so on
2. Theft of intellectual property
3. Theft of personally identifiable information

Egress of information is not the only concern when addressing cyberespionage. A study conducted of 10,470 companies in Europe and North and South America revealed that 25% of the newly circulated worms in 2010 were claimed to be able to spread via USB device (USSS CERT & Deloitte, 2010).

Challenges in Research and Demonstration

Although it is not a technical challenge to demonstrate the tools and techniques used in this type of research, it is a challenge to perform these techniques in open society and unannounced on corporate or government

Table 6.1   2012 Cybersecurity Watch Survey

Handled internally without involving legal action or law enforcement	72%
Handled internally with legal action	13%
Handled externally by notifying law enforcement	10%
Handled externally by filing a civil action	5%
Copied information to a mobile device (USB drive, iPod, etc.)	42%
Root kit or hacking tools	9%
Concerns that competitors would use incident to their advantage	5%

Source: U.S. Secret Service, Software Engineering Institute, CERT and Deloitte, 2010. *Cybersecurity watch survey—Survey resuts.* Retrieved May 1, 2012, from Software Engineering Institute: http://www.sei.cmu.edu/newsitems/cyber_sec_watch_2010_release.cfm.

networks. This is due to state, local, and federal laws prohibiting such actions when it comes to unauthorized network access and interception. All laws were followed in the research presented here and duplicate technical environments were created for actual testing of malicious software. This was accomplished by using preconfigured laboratories and the results extrapolated to everyday life situations, particularly when involving wireless eavesdropping, wireless interception, egress of stolen information, and network hacking.

Simple Aspects of Research and Demonstration

There were no challenges in acquiring, configuring, or demonstrating the technical aspects of this research. The tools for conducting and modeling acts of cyberespionage were easily obtainable and configurable while readily available, and willing college students volunteered their time and effort to learn while conducting research in this subject.

Because of limited public information regarding specific cybercrime and cyberespionage cases, it is not possible to be absolute in determining the specific means of a specific compromise. However, it is reasonable to assume that if a first year college student can accomplish a similar feat, so can a technologically astute cybercriminal. Portable storage devices known as USB thumb drives were used in this research. These devices have been reportedly used in several network compromise and security breach situations.

Reported Cases of Intrusion without Immediate Detection

In October 2006, a drug-related investigation at a private residence revealed a thumb drive that contained classified documents from the Los Alamos National Laboratory. The residence was that of a former subcontractor to the laboratory (U.S. Department of Energy, 2006).

In 2008, a USB device was inserted into a Pentagon network computer that was connected to a military network in the Middle East. The USB device was infected with malicious software that spread to numerous internal networks to where it was understood to have gained access to parts of the network that were classified as secret (USSS CERT & Deloitte, 2010).

In 2009, a military contractor had detected programs of a questionable nature in their computer network. Further investigation discovered that the computer networks of the military contractor "had been infiltrated by an unknown malware, classified as a Remote-Access Tool or RAT." The RAT provided hacker's unauthorized access to critical information stored on the network (Coleman, 2008).

Another case of cyberespionage that has been reported as being the world's largest was reported by the Threat Research department of McAfee, a U.S.-based security firm. A report from McAfee titled "Revealed: Operation Shady RAT, an investigation of targeted intrusions into more than 70 global companies, governments, and non-profit organizations during the last five years" (Alperovitch, 2011). This report indicated that "virtually everyone is falling prey to these intrusions, regardless of whether they are the United Nations, a multinational Fortune 100 company, a small, non-profit think tank, a national Olympic team, or even an unfortunate computer security firm" (Alperovitch, 2011).

Simple Vector Attacks

One of the simplest and perhaps one of the most common methods of covert egress of internal information is by the use of what is known as a USB thumb drive. Thumb drives are small electronic, solid-state storage devices that currently have capacities from 4 to 32 GB. These capacities may contain many millions of pages of text, drawings, or software. Thumb drives may be altered in physical appearance to conceal their appearance for purposes of egress of sensitive information or they may be adapted for use in ingress of malicious software. Thumb drives have been identified as having been altered to appear as jewelry, integrated into watches, pens, children's toys, and other commonly used devices, thus making them hidden in plain sight and often overlooked. Thumb drives are one type of attack vector for compromising computer networks from inside and are known to be successful in bypassing network firewalls from outside intrusion. Preknowledge to this research project obtained from an on-site tour of one of the Federal Bureau of Investigation's Regional Computer Forensic Laboratories and training facilities revealed that the average discovery of a search by local law enforcement personnel in cyber forensic training on preconfigured manikins equipped with an unknown number of hidden storage devices yielded approximately 35% discovery by the searching officer. Storage devices were concealed, modified, and hidden in clothing, electronic devices, and various other parts of the body, while officers in training searched them for evidence of hidden storage devices.

College Students' Objectives

Several college students were presented the objective of acquiring information from an internal college network and exporting it to the outside using both the Internet and the thumb drives. In addition, they were tasked with the objective to compromise an internal network using limited technical skills so that it can be accessed from the outside. They were provided several thumb drives and asked to conceal them in a manner that once they accomplished their goals they could transport the information outside of the building. The methods they discovered and demonstrated involved removing the USB storage stick from its native cosmetic casing, thus reducing its size and appearance, and strategically inserting it into a variety of devices, including pens, cell phones, children's toys, packs of chewing gum, printer ink cartridges, caps, the hems of articles of clothing, the soles of shoes, and deodorant sticks, to name a few.

The students were then asked to try to acquire information from five targeted systems in plain sight, without being visually or audibly detected and in less than 30 seconds. One of the systems was a database server; the other four were office systems with their users present. The results were successful in all four demonstrations. In addition, one student was given the objective of establishing a covert channel to the Internet where they could download malicious software for compromising the internal network without being detected.

Methods Demonstrated

One method was to trick an unsuspecting victim within an educational institution into becoming the means for gaining external access as preparation to steal information internal to the network. This was accomplished by an unknown individual handing an office worker inside the organization a compromised thumb drive and asking them to connect it to their system with a request to print a particular type of file for another employee within the organization. This involved some minor social engineering on the part of the student, claiming a false reason for the request. Once the thumb drive was inserted, one of two actions was taken based on the type of operating system used on the target system. If the victim's computer utilized the Windows XP operating system, a covert program would have auto-loaded and installed a remote monitoring tool on the victim's computer. If the victim's computer utilized the Windows 7 operating system, the perpetrating actor asked the victim to print a file that in reality executed a covert program to launch a backdoor access to the system.

Because of U.S. state and federal laws, the actual program used when handed to the unsuspecting office worker was benign. This was accomplished by decommissioning the malicious effect created for this purpose. However, the original malicious file created specifically for this purpose was successfully tested on another less critical network. The actual program allowed free access not only to the targeted computer but also to other locally connected systems as well as from outside the office. Wireless laptop computers were then used to access the newly compromised computer on the isolated network from a remote location outside the building. The approach of getting an employee to insert the benign version of the covert program was attempted four times within one organization with each attempt being successful.

Another method involved having a person of unknown origin enter a server room of a community college and insert the same thumb drive into an operations server without being stopped or detected. The attempt was made and the device was inserted successfully and in plain sight of two individuals working in that room. The weakness in demonstration of this approach was that the room that contained the targeted server often had visitors and student traffic, thus possibly desensitizing the workers in the room from being more sensitive to their environment. This does not negate the overall effect that in an actual cyberespionage attempt a distraction for the employees would seem a reasonable course of action.

The technical objective of this specific demonstration was to demonstrate the elevation of access from end-user computer systems to one that provides more critical services to the internal network. Unauthorized access to a network server provides deeper penetration into the electronic infrastructure of an organization.

Egress of Stolen Information

Another demonstration was to conceal stolen information within the thumb drive itself prior to physical transport outside of the building. This was accomplished by using what is known as steganography. Steganography is the ability to hide information within a file. Many steganographic programs are available freely on the Internet and the one used for this demonstration is known as MP3Stego. This application allows the user to hide information inside of MP3 audio files without corrupting the host file. A targeted file representing confidential information was acquired from the compromised test network mentioned previously. The acquired file was quickly embedded and hidden in the MP3 file using the MP3Stego program and stored on a hidden thumb drive and concealed inside of a bouncing ball. The college student exited the technology building of the college campus bouncing the ball, entered his vehicle, and left the premises, all in plain sight. For the purposes of obfuscation of the intent of the thumb drive, should it be discovered, multiple MP3 audio and various other types of files without intellectual value to the organization were included on the drive.

Previous Field Research

Previous field research conducted by the author was significantly successful when the objective was public reconnaissance. This method involved inserting a thumb drive into hotel or other public computers and using a scripted program known as a batch file. The batch file contained a list of user issuable commands that would display various aspects of information about the system it was inserted into. None of the commands issued violated any security mechanisms or firewall rules but rather read what was allowed and available by the user credentials for that system. The main difference in this approach and someone doing it manually is that insertion of the thumb drive acquired the information in less than 1 minute where it would take a user several hours to accomplish the same objective. The information would then be collected into a text file and stored on the flash drive before being removed.

The amount of information recovered ranged between 12 and 36 MB of specific system information and included a list of every file on the disk, logged on user name, history of user activity including websites visited, Internet chat log data, current connections to the target computer, specific hardware data, and security information. This information takes less than 60 seconds to acquire in most situations and is invaluable in pre-espionage reconnaissance.

Wireless Attack Vector Using USB Connected Devices

Although it is a common understanding in society that computer networks can be compromised or hacked via wireless devices, what is not so common is the understanding how it is done and the simplicity of doing it. To demonstrate this approach, two college students were provided with common tools that can be acquired and purchased from off the Internet for less than $20. One device is an external ALFA 802.11 wireless USB adapter with a long-range high-gain antenna that connects to the local system via a traditional USB port. This connection when mounted to the BackTrack 5* software will allow pass-through of all information from the victim to the internal network. The other component is a downloadable operating system known as BackTrack 5. This software is free and is well known in cybersecurity circles for scanning and assessing the vulnerabilities in computer systems and networks. It contains powerful hacking and monitoring programs commonly used in this profession.

The BackTrack 5 program was installed on a laptop computer equipped with the external high-gain antenna. The use of this particular adapter was optional, but was used to compensate for potentially weak signal strength within the building. The antenna connects to the same interface that is

---

* BackTrack is a distribution based on the Debian GNU/Linux distribution aimed at digital forensics and penetration testing use.

used for thumb drive insertion. This configuration provides the user of this arrangement the ability to monitor and access the precompromised system on the test network, and the ability to hijack wireless sessions from other mobile devices that may connect to this same network.

The students were then tasked with executing the monitoring and interception of the precompromised system on the test network from a remote location. The target system was compromised before using the USB attack method previously demonstrated, however, this target system on this particular network was exposed to the actual covert software and not the benign example used in the social engineering demonstrations.

Within 10 minutes, the mobile monitoring and interception aspect of this project was configured and in operation. Within 5 minutes of operation, the target victim system was compromised and information acquired from it without detection by the user.

In a further field demonstration of this technique and using this same equipment, an authorized laptop computer attempted to connect to a network server connected to this same network via wireless access. The test subject connected and began their authorized access of internal data files while all of their traffic was monitored and recorded on the unauthorized middle device laptop using BackTrack 5 and the high-gain antenna. Once it was determined by the attacker that enough information regarding the specifics of the network connection, including authentication credentials and network addresses were obtained, the test subject was disconnected by the middle device while communications with the victim computer were maintained. This approach is commonly known as a man-in-the-middle attack. In effect, it was easily demonstrated that someone connecting to an open wireless network can have their transmission hijacked.

Wired Attack Vector Using Dark Network Technology

An experiment within an internal test network using what is known as dark network technology was conducted by connecting it to a college network consisting of several thousand systems, servers, and network appliances. The belief that data communications can be concealed from the hosting networks monitoring systems without requiring advanced technical skills by the user was demonstrated. The technique involved using a thumb drive equipped with a free non-Windows-based operating system known as Debian,* and what is known as a TOR Browser. The TOR Browser is a special browser designed to hide any type of information from

---

* Debian is a computer operating system composed of software packages released as free and open-source software primarily under the GNU General Public License along with other free software licenses.

internal network monitoring and sensors. Two computer systems utilizing the Windows 7 operating system were connected to an internal college network that is known to have firewall, malware detection and eradication systems, and monitors all network traffic. The test system downloaded and installed a TOR Browser. TOR is an acronym for The Onion Router and is so named as an analogy that the data that passes through it has layers of protection, including encryption. It is able to connect to specific Internet relay sites that provide anonymity and covert traffic between the two. From the relay sites, traditional search engines such as Google and others can be accessed, as well as those that are part of the TOR network. The technique of this method is that all traffic traveling to and from the test system was indecipherable.

The bootable Debian-based thumb drive was used to provide an operating system environment that would not interact with the host operating system of the attack system, thus eliminating any possibility of traceability to the hard drives of that system. The TOR browser/relay connection also provided what is known as IP (Internet Protocol) spoofing capability between the test system and the rest of the Internet. This provided an additional layer of anonymity for the test system from monitoring and detection from outside of the college network.

The configuration was tested by downloading several files that normally would have been detected and restricted from being downloaded and installed on the test system. In addition to the network monitoring of traffic through the system, all data were viewed at the test system end of the network connection by the use of a switch and data monitoring and filtering program known as Wireshark.* The TOR browser was connected to the TOR network on the Internet while various files were downloaded, including specifically identified software that would normally be prevented from such by the internal host network. All traffic from and to the test systems were undecipherable to the monitoring system and bypassed the safety systems designed to prevent such from happening. This demonstration showed ingress of malicious software into an otherwise well-monitored network.

Challenges in Compromising Systems

Success regarding the use of thumb drive incursion into a network required different coding and configurations designed specifically for the target

---

* Wireshark is a free and open-source packet analyzer. It is used for network troubleshooting, analysis, software and communications protocol development, and education.

operating system. Attacks that worked well on a Windows XP operating system had to be reconfigured to work on a newer version operating system such as Windows 7. The newer versions were found to be somewhat more of a challenge. Whereas the Windows XP operating system only required the insertion of the USB device, the Windows 7 version had a higher level of inherent security that required tricking the user into executing the covert program.

Results

In each case, if physical access was allowed to the room where the targeted computer was located, each system was successfully compromised. In addition, this study begs the question that if college students can compromise an internal network without being detected, and with limited technical skill, then how deep into a corporate network could these same college students penetrate with some advanced training and a financial incentive.

Discussion

It is common knowledge in society that computer networks can be hacked, just as banks can be robbed and homes are invaded. However, it is not a question of if a computer network can be compromised, but how it is done and how often, which, according to the research indicating weaknesses in reporting is almost impossible to tell. In addition, this research has raised questions if employees of educational institutions and private citizens working in positions with access to sensitive and confidential information are properly trained in detecting corporate espionage.

The question is just how much training and exposure does local and state law enforcement personnel have to be able to detect hidden storage devices on a person, in a vehicle, or in a residence during a search and seizure. A lateral research study on this is desired by placing multiple hidden USB and other types of storage devices in luggage and on a person for local law enforcement training purposes.

Acknowledgments

The author would like to acknowledge the assistance of Robert Fisher, Rachel Rumberger, Douglas Redman, Philip Kerek, and Jacob Brabbs.

References

Alperovitch, D. (2011). *Revealed: Operation shady RAT*. Retrieved April 2012 from McAfee: http://www.mcafee.com/us/resources/white-papers/wp-operation-shady-rat.pdf.

Coleman, K. G. (2008). *Cyber espionage targets sensitive data*. Retrieved from SIP Trunking.

U.S. Department of Energy. (2006, November 27). *Energy.gov*. Retrieved April 2012 from Energy.gov: http://energy.gov/sites/prod/files/igprod/documents/SI-11-27.pdf.

U.S. Secret Service, Software Engineering Institute, CERT Program at Carnegie Mellon University and Deloitte (USSS CERT & Deloitte). (2010, January 25). *2010 Cybersecurity watch survey—Survey resuts*. Retrieved May 1, 2012, from Software Engineering Institute: http://www.sei.cmu.edu/newsitems/cyber_sec _watch_2010_release.cfm.

Death by a Thousand Cuts
The Abbotsford Police Department's Multidimensional Program for Gang Suppression

7

COLETTE SQUIRES AND
DARRYL PLECAS

Contents

Introduction

Beginning in the late 1990s, there was a serious increase in violent, illegal gang activity and organized crime in the province of British Columbia, Canada, which was linked to the highly lucrative production and trade of marijuana for weapons, cocaine, and other illegal commodities. From 2005, gang wars triggered unprecedented rates of gun violence and homicides throughout Vancouver, the British Columbia Lower Mainland, and the Fraser Valley. Even though the homicide rates were lower compared to the gang violence that escalated in many large American cities in the 1990s, it nevertheless created an alarming situation in which public safety was seriously at risk and innocent people were losing their lives.

The city of Abbotsford, located in the heart of the Fraser Valley and an hour east of Vancouver, was especially afflicted. A predominantly middle-class city of approximately 135,000 people, and historically known as "the buckle of the Bible belt," Abbotsford was also home to the notorious Bacon Brothers, leaders of the Red Scorpions gang. Fighting for control of the drug trade, the Red Scorpions and the United Nations gang brought their battle for economic control to the streets of Abbotsford, with disastrous results. After Abbotsford was dubbed the "murder capital of Canada" in 2008 and 2009, the Abbotsford Police responded with a highly successful gang suppression response that brought the homicide rate to zero by 2011. Their strategies were influenced by a variety of practices now associated with focused deterrence initiatives and problem-oriented policing, with a strong emphasis on the development of community partnerships.

What made the work of the Abbotsford Police Department (APD) so successful? To explore this question fully, several lengthy interviews were conducted with members of the APD, accompanied by a review of data regarding their targets for homicide reduction.* This provided detailed information and perspective on the department's challenges and successes during this time period, providing valuable information for other communities and jurisdictions that are struggling with gang and gun violence. Abbotsford's experiences also demonstrate the merits of creative thinking and focused deterrence strategies, with similarities—albeit unintentional—to the successful homicide reduction tactics used in many cities in the United States during the 1990s. Nicknamed by the department as "Death by a Thousand Cuts," what the Abbotsford police accomplished can now be considered a comprehensive, multidimensional "what works" initiative, with great potential for cross application to other cities across North America and elsewhere in the world.

Although problem-oriented policing is not a new concept, it is important to recognize that the Abbotsford police exceeded what many other communities had been able to accomplish. Preferring the term "solution-oriented policing," their work provides an important lesson in implementing this proactive approach in a comprehensive and multifaceted way to produce excellence in results. This chapter describes in detail how this was accomplished

---

* Deputy Chief Rick Lucy, Sergeant Mike Novakowski, and Public Information Officer Constable Ian McDonald provided 8 hours of interviews, generating a wealth of information on how and why the APD's gang suppression strategies developed as they did. Their time and generosity is gratefully acknowledged, as is their dedication to their work and the community they serve.

and the positive outcomes that ensued, to provide a toolkit of ideas and examples for other jurisdictions to adapt and use as well. This adds to the currently limited research on Canadian examples of successful gang suppression and expands the analysis of Canadian gang culture in British Columbia in the first decade of the twenty-first century.

Learning from American Gang Violence and Homicides

Before exploring the Abbotsford gang problem in detail, it is helpful to review the research of what was learned in the United States regarding gang violence and homicides. Many large cities in the United States experienced a spike in homicides and gun violence during the 1990s, caused in great measure by chronic, repeat offenders involved in gangs and gun violence (Kennedy & Braga, 1998; Braga, Kennedy, Waring, & Piehl, 2001; Braga, Pierce, McDevitt, Bond, & Cronin, 2008). Traditional policing maintained that there was little that police could do to prevent homicides (Kennedy & Braga, 1998; White, Fyfe, Campbell, & Goldkamp, 2003), whereas new ways of thinking, such as problem-oriented policing and focused deterrence, provided a new paradigm for responding to crime, violence, and disorder.

Problem-oriented policing employs innovative and nontraditional enforcement tactics, focusing first on why things are going wrong through a process of problem identification, analysis, response, evaluation, and adjustment of response (Kennedy & Braga, 1998; Braga et al., 2001; Braga et al., 2008; Corsaro & McGarrell, 2009; Telep & Weisburd, 2012). Focused deterrence posits that crime cycles can be broken when offenders perceive that the costs of committing crime exceed the gains and benefits (Tillyer, Engel, & Lovins, 2012; Braga & Weisburd, 2012). Swift, certain, and severe punishment immediately following an infraction has been historically viewed as both specific and general deterrence, affecting not only those intent on committing crimes but also a wider audience who learns by observation (Braga & Weisburd, 2012). Focused deterrence for gang suppression is grounded in a clear rejection of violence by community and other stakeholders, which is demonstrated by mobilizing law enforcement to "pull every lever" legally available to create predictable and negative consequences for groups or gangs involved in gang violence, and to use a wide range of legal sanctions to do so (Braga et al., 2008; Corsaro & McGarrell, 2009; Tillyer et al., 2012; Braga & Weisburd, 2012). This is typically operationalized as a coordinated law enforcement effort among multiple agencies that have made gangs or violent groups their priority. Second, focused deterrence includes an offer of help for those who want to opt out of the violent gang lifestyle (Corsaro & McGarrell, 2009; Tillyer et al., 2012; Braga & Weisburd, 2012).

Focused deterrence, by its very name, implies that it is designed for a specific target group: in this case, it is for chronic, violent, and gang-involved offenders, not the general population of those in conflict with the law. "Pulling levers" is a strategy that has enabled enforcement agencies to increase the pressure on violent, gang-involved offenders, making it more and more difficult for them to operate freely. Boston's Gun Project and Operation Ceasefire is one of the earliest and most famous examples of this strategy, resulting in significant reductions in youth homicides, shots-fired calls for service, and gun assault incidents (Braga et al., 2001; Chermak & McGarrell, 2004; Braga et al., 2008; Makarios & Pratt, 2012; Braga & Weisburd, 2012). The pulling levers strategy was designed to influence the behavior, and the environment, of the target population of Boston's chronic offenders, gang-involved youths who were the most responsible for Boston's youth violence problems (Braga et al., 2001; Chermak & McGarrell, 2004). One of the distinctive characteristics of pulling levers is direct communication with the target group (Corsaro & McGarrell, 2009); in Operation Ceasefire, this was achieved through meetings with offenders to let them know of the intent of the police to crack down on gang violence in every way possible. A coordinated, criminal justice response involving a variety of legal levers was able to disrupt street drug activity, give focused attention to public drinking and trespassing, serve outstanding warrants, cultivate confidential informants to aid in investigations of gang activities, enforce probation and parole conditions, conduct curfew checks, seize drug proceeds and other assets, ensure stiffer plea bargains and stronger attention to prosecution, ensure stronger bail terms with greater enforcement of bail conditions, and focused investigation and prosecution of gang-related drug activity (Braga et al., 2001; Makarios & Pratt, 2012).

The success in Boston resulted in the implementation of focused deterrence and problem-oriented policing programs in numerous other cities in the United States throughout the 1990s. Well-known examples include Minneapolis, Minnesota, where social services and community interventions were combined with enforcement strategies (Kennedy & Braga, 1998); Lowell, Massachusetts, where police targeted illegal gambling as a pulling levers strategy to reduce gun violence (Braga, McDevitt, & Pierce, 2006; Braga et al., 2008; Telep & Weisburd, 2012); Indianapolis, Indiana, where social services were used for responsive youth offenders, and incarceration was used to limit the influence of those youths who were particularly dangerous and unlikely to accept a social services approach (Chermak & McGarrell, 2004; Corsaro & McGarrell, 2009; Tillyer et al., 2012); and Chicago, Illinois, where increased prosecutions and sentencing were combined with a focused deterrence message delivered through offender notification meetings, letters, school programs, and community and media outreach (Braga et al., 2008; Tillyer et al., 2012). Offenders in Chicago were also offered various social services supports for employment and educational opportunities (Tillyer et al., 2012). In Richmond, California, problem-oriented policing efforts extensively involved prevention and intervention along with investigation and enforcement and capitalized on a partnership with the school district to identify truant youths who were at risk of more delinquent behavior and to develop positive relationships between police and youth (White et al., 2003). Research conducted on the Cincinnati Initiative to Reduce Violence (CIRV) revealed that all of these initiatives yielded timely and significant reductions in homicides and gang-related violence, with later challenges for sustained positive change (Tillyer et al., 2012). Many of these types of initiatives, used in so many differ ent cities across the United States, also appeared in the APD's Death by a Thousand Cuts program. The question of how to implement and then sustain these focused deterrence efforts over longer periods is an appropriate consideration when developing new and similar programs, which will be considered in the discussion on APD's gang suppression strategies.

Rise of Gangs in British Columbia: A Closer Look

Traditionally, gang culture has often been defined by the American experience, in which rivaling gangs are identified by ethnicity or the geographic areas in which gang members live. In this context, a gang is turf based and will fight enemy gang members who enter its turf (Adamson, 1998; Sánchez-Jankowski, 2003). More recently, gangs have been viewed differently; their violent behaviors have been linked with the illegal drug trade and attempts to control illegal commodities as a way of creating wealth, establishing power, and asserting dominance (Adamson, 1998; Sánchez-Jankowski, 2003). This would certainly be the case in British Columbia, where the gang wars in Vancouver and throughout the Fraser Valley that began in 2000 and escalated to their peak in 2009 were fuelled by competition to control the illegal drug trade. Boundaries were defined by drug supply lines, business methods, and allegiances and were geographically fluid. However, there was still a sense of territory, and gang violence resulted when rival gangs began to penetrate the business area and customer groups of another gang. This competition was seen as a threat to an extremely lucrative business, involving local marijuana grow-ops; drug sales; and cross-border shipments of marijuana, weapons, cocaine, and other drugs, amounting to revenues in millions of dollars ("B.C. Gangster," 2012). Violence was used to create deterrence, get information, or send a message that infringing on the gang's business territory would not be tolerated. To accomplish this, attacks resulted against rival gang members in the form of intimidation, assaults, extortion, forcible confinements, home invasions, marijuana grow-rips,* drive-by shootings of homes and vehicles, torture, and murder. One of the most sensational of these events was the slaying of the "Surrey Six" in October 2007, which resulted in the murders of two innocent people, as well as four known gang members and drug dealers ("Two Men," 2007; "Karbovanec Sentenced," 2009).

From 2007 through 2009, gang violence escalated as gangs teetered and shifted to assert control. In 2009, the Vancouver police publicly acknowledged that a gang war was underway ("Vancouver Police," 2009). By this time, the United Nations gang and the Red Scorpions, associated with the notorious Abbotsford-based Bacon Brothers, were fighting for control in the Fraser Valley, and in Abbotsford.

The Abbotsford police reported that in British Columbia the illegal drug business has been a complex network controlled by organized crime members at the upper levels of the operation who worked with local gang members to help accomplish their business on the street. Grow-ops to produce marijuana (BC Bud) were already well established by the year 2000, and side businesses developed to ship product across the border. There was extensive money to be made, but now all those who had previously worked independently as growers or sellers were ultimately forced to join a gang or cooperate with organized crime who had taken complete control of the market. This market control allowed them to engage in massive shipments of drugs and weapons between Canada, the United States, and Mexico. At lower levels, gangs assisted movement of product and controlled drug trafficking through sales on the street and through dial-a-dope operations, allowing customers to arrange drug delivery by telephone. The business structure of the illegal drug trade was a complex hierarchy controlled by organized crime at the top to lower level participants, often teenagers or young adults, who sold drugs to friends, on the street, at local schools, and through dial-a-dope arrangements. Guarding the drug supply line was essential to ensure ongoing revenues. Any threat to business could not be tolerated.

Abbotsford Context

Throughout 2008 and 2009, gang-related gun violence rapidly escalated in Vancouver and neighboring communities of Coquitlam, Surrey, Maple Ridge, Langley, Richmond, and Burnaby. The three Bacon Brothers, now identified as leaders within the Red Scorpions, had grown up in Abbotsford. In January 2009, Jamie Bacon's car was shot at while he was driving through Abbotsford in the afternoon, causing him to flee the vehicle while it was still running

---

* Grow-rip refers to an attack by a rival gang on another gang's marijuana-growing site, known as a grow-op.

("Victim Shot," 2009). It then crashed into the front steps of a popular local restaurant during business hours. This event triggered significant concerns for public safety, helping to shift thinking from a previously held view that gangsters primarily targeted one another and the public was not usually at risk. At the end of March 2009, Sean Murphy (aged 21) and Ryan Richards (aged 19) were murdered ("Two Men," 2009). Although they identified with the gang culture, they were not seen by local police as leaders within the gang structure. In the beginning of May 2009, high school students Joseph Randay (18) and Dilsher Singh Gill (17) were abducted and then fatally shot ("Police Identify," 2009). Their bodies were discovered on the perimeter of the city, in an abandoned SUV. This latter event was the tipping point that triggered the beginning of what is now recognized as the APD's gang suppression program.

What was it about the murder of these two young men that mobilized a different police response, a different approach to enforcement? According to Constable Ian McDonald, public information officer, the APD recognized that gang behavior was shifting; previously, there had been a gang "code" in place that gang members would not target children, families, or youth. Now the Abbotsford police recognized that rapidly shifting alliances within gangs were destabilizing the structure, and it was harder for gangs to target rival members higher in the ranks. Loyalties and memberships were changing so rapidly that young people who had been recruited as low-level gang workers often did not know who they were working for, and when allegiances changed rapidly they often would not know that either. Gang leaders still wanted to demonstrate power, create fear, and mark their territory, and many of these individuals were drug-addicted themselves. Their decision making was influenced by fear of betrayal and paranoia.

According to the Abbotsford police, those fears were justified. The gang wars reached their height when former friends within the gangs began to betray one another. Trust was diminished and suspicion abounded: the trusted foot soldier could quickly feel that he had been sold out, or others could look at him suspecting that he had taken more than his share of the profit. Members switched gangs, loyalties were bought and sold, and there was constant movement of people from one gang to another. Pressure intensified as rival gangs competed for the same customers within the same city. In this environment, paranoia flourished and the only value was financial gain. Gang leaders were left wondering who they could trust and questioned the loyalty of all those around them. They were recruiting from other gangs, so they knew that other gangs were recruiting from within their ranks as well. In this environment, the youngest and most peripheral members and the general public became targets in ways that had never been seen before.

The murders of Randay and Gill, local high school students, deeply affected the community. The previously held belief in public safety and immunity was gone, and it was a critical turning point for the leadership within the city. Chief Constable Bob Rich held a news conference and town hall meeting on May 14, 2009, communicating that the problem was escalating out of control and that the community, city, and police needed to work together to protect their young people and reestablish public safety. A 24-hour help line was immediately established to provide assistance to youth, concerned parents, or anyone involved in a gang. For those who were involved in gangs and were willing to cooperate, the police helped them develop an exit strategy.

In the months immediately following, the APD grappled with how to most effectively tackle the problem. Meanwhile, homicides continued to mount, again giving Abbotsford the dubious distinction of being the murder capital of Canada in 2009 (Hopes, 2012; Statistics Canada, 2012b). The department had never had a gang squad before, and it became a question of how to most effectively allocate resources. This was new and unexplored territory for the department, and the entire region was struggling to create an effective police response for a situation that was unprecedented.

What emerged during the following year was a multidimensional approach that channeled every possible resource into gang suppression. Abbotsford Chief Constable Bob Rich and his team recognized that the problem had become so serious and pervasive that only a multifaceted, aggressive, and innovative assault on the problem would be sufficient to restore public safety. Given how many people had died already, they felt they could not risk anything less.

Strategy One: Education and Awareness for Gang Suppression

While APD members were developing their gang suppression enforcement tactics, the first visible dimension of the APD gang suppression strategy was community education and awareness. There were two primary goals: decrease youth involvement with drug dealing and local gangs and increase community support and participation in gang suppression activities. This process began with the press conference and community town hall meeting of May 2009, which was followed by a comprehensive messaging initiative.

When considering community education for gang suppression, it is helpful to consider that the "community" is actually a mosaic of subgroups and neighborhoods that together create the larger social fabric of a town or city. The APD's gang suppression program targeted various subgroups to first cultivate specific partnerships and relationships, and with help from the media and their own website the police were eventually able to reach the much wider audience of Abbotsford's general public who were less directly involved but still needed to be kept informed. As observers on the periphery, the rest of the community was seen by the police to be largely supportive and no longer willing to tolerate rampant gang violence. This goodwill endures to the present, as revealed in a 2012 survey of Abbotsford residents who indicated overwhelming support for the Abbotsford police (Plecas, Cohen, Armstrong, & Burk, 2013).

The first target for "gang suppression through education" was the student population, which was followed by parents and then the wider community. Simultaneously, the Abbotsford police were building partnerships with community agencies that could provide follow-up support to at-risk youth. The business community was a second target group. The police provided information on gang activity and encouraged the business community to stop providing services to known gang members, leading to the implementation of Bar Watch and other similar strategies. Neighbors living in gang hot spots were another community group who were approached by the police, to encourage a cooperative dialogue regarding the suppression of gang violence and criminal activity around their homes. In particular, the neighbors whose houses surrounded the family home of the three gangsters the Bacon Brothers were invited to an informational meeting before surveillance cameras were installed on their street. Community and civic leaders were also encouraged to work together with the police to assist in gang suppression. Previously, there had been pressure to not talk openly about gang problems; it was seen as being bad for business, property values, and tourism. Now the approach was to talk openly about the problem and create as much public awareness as possible, dispel the myths, and warn young people and others of the danger to their lives if they associated with members of a gang. Civic leaders, parents, community members, and business owners also needed to understand the risks to public safety when gang members operated freely.

Of all of these strategies, the school-based gang suppression program was the most comprehensive. The brainchild of Mike Novakowski, sergeant of community policing, it comprised almost a dozen different educational approaches designed to change the thinking of students and their parents.* Unlike the economically marginalized street gangs of the United States, the gangs in the Lower Mainland of British Columbia largely comprised middle-class youths and young adults, who were recruited through the promise of material gain; a sense of belonging; and the "coolness factor" of being part of a violent, powerful group such as they would see in video games or in popular films. The police noted that gang-recruited youth believed that "you're cooler if you have money and it doesn't matter where you get it." This attitude has been verified by Sánchez-Jankowski's (2003) research on gangs, in

---

* Sergeant Novakowski received the Kenneth M. Lemckert Community Policing Award in 2011 from the British Columbia Ministry of Public Safety, solicitor general, and BC Crime Prevention Association for this work in school-based gang prevention. Information was retrieved from http://www.pssg.gov.bc.ca/crimeprevention/awards /docs/award-winners2011.pdf.

which he concluded that "it is money, and the social 'respect' that money can buy, that is the primary motivation for young people to join gangs, and not simply status" (p. 194). Additionally, research* was conducted in 2009 by the Search Institute on 5384 students from the Abbotsford School District with some startling results: only 25% percent of them felt they had parents or other adults who were a positive role model, and only 38% reported that their parents monitored their whereabouts and provided clear family rules and consequences. A mere 18% said that their parents were involved in helping them succeed in school. Whereas only 30% reported that they knew how to plan ahead and make good choices, only 29% indicated that they could communicate positively with their parents and would seek their counsel.

Knowing this, the rationale behind the school-based program was less about gangs and more about encouraging youth to make good choices. The police department perspective was that early, small choices influenced young people in terms of their longer term life direction. Therefore, if young people could receive appropriate guidance to stay on the right path during childhood and early adolescence, then they would be less likely to become problematic or criminally involved when they were older. This view is expanded on the APD website, which states as follows:

> Crime prevention starts at home. Preventative efforts should not be limited to schools and educational institutions where the focus is only on young people. Parents and other caregivers play a crucial role in public safety, and crime prevention should start at an early age.[†]

Once children and youth begin to engage in delinquency, police-reported rates of offending reveal a rapid escalation from 12 to 18 years of age, with high levels being noted between the ages of 16 and 21 before a measurable decline is noted in subsequent years (Statistics Canada, 2012a). Crime prevention, therefore, needed to provide children and youth with the right impetus to remain crime free and off this criminal trajectory before those critical ages were reached. The police were also concerned that early onset of criminal activity is often a predictor of later, more serious, and sustained criminal behavior.

To stop the recruitment of youth into gangs and the local drug culture, it became obvious that the police needed a multifaceted approach that would reach students of all levels and also their parents. High school students were targeted first as the group most highly at risk, especially as so many of them

---

* Search Institute survey statistics were posted by the APD on its website, http://www .abbypd.ca, drawn from Developmental Assets: A profile of Your Youth Executive Summary Results, from the Search Institute survey, *Profiles of Student Life: Attitudes and Behaviours*. School District #34, Abbotsford, British Columbia, August 2009, pp. 1–3.
† Retrieved from http://www.abbypd.ca/Operation-Lodestar.

had indicated that they lacked appropriate supervision and had difficulty in making good choices. Following this, younger children and parents would be reached through subsequent programming.

In September 2009, Operation Tarnish was launched as a full media poster campaign, with new posters being released every 3 weeks throughout the fall of 2009. These images appeared everywhere, first in high schools and then they were distributed through the media to the general public. They could be seen at bus stops, on billboards, in the newspapers, on police bumper stickers, and featured at local hockey games. The Abbotsford police also posted them in the prison booking area, and on jail cell ceilings, to be seen when an apprehended person was lying on a bunk.

The posters were provocative, startling, and edgy and designed to "tarnish the gleam" of gangster behavior through graphic images that would catch a young person's attention and make them think. Police were aware that successful gang recruitment appealed to self-interest and greed through the promise of money, access to drugs and weapons, and the prestige of gang involvement. The aggressive but positive message of Operation Tarnish to choose a crime-free lifestyle also appealed to self-interest: the young person's desire to remain alive, out of jail, and with hope for a better future.

Operation Tarnish was supported by Operation Impact, an hour-long presentation delivered to 6500 students at all of Abbotsford's high schools. The aim was to warn, inform, and encourage. Together with the poster campaign, these presentations sent a relevant message with local examples to ensure that it would make sense for local youth. The Abbotsford police felt it was vital to remove the sense of immunity and naïveté that caused many young people to dismiss the seriousness of drug dealing and gang involvement. Every poster, image, and presentation was designed to send a real, relevant, and powerful message that each young person controlled the decisions that they made and it was essential for the preservation of their lives that they made good decisions. It is significant that the chief of police spoke at every session, informing the students of the current situation and the recruiting strategies that were being used to draw youth into gangs and prevent them from exiting. Even low-level drug dealing had become dangerous, as exemplified by the murders earlier that year. Many of the students knew the young people who had been killed, requiring sensitivity along with a clear message.

Operation Impact included a 15-minute talk from a former gang member whose criminal involvement had been influenced by his upbringing and his struggle for popularity and belonging. Sergeant Novakowski concluded each presentation by sharing some of his own life story, followed by a message of encouragement that most of them were making wise choices, could use that as positive peer pressure to influence their friends, and should take a stand against what was happening. The overall message related to their decision making, communicating that a series of small decisions and steps could ultimately lead to bigger, worse decisions that could ultimately draw them into situations that would be impossible to exit. Knowing that a number of the students came from unhealthy homes and dire situations, the police felt it was important to provide inspiration and hope and to let the students know that support was there for them, especially for those feeling helpless and discouraged. At the same time, the many accomplishments and achievements of each school and its students were celebrated and the police affirmed that they had the power to make good choices. This sense of celebrating good choices, achievements, and positive behavior as a strength-based approach was also emphasized in later presentations for elementary and middle schools. It also mirrors the approach of many other focused deterrence programs, in which building relationships, providing support, and the offer of help balance enforcement tactics (Makarios & Pratt, 2012).

This first thrust into Abbotsford's schools was completed with Operation Veritas in 2010, a series of short antigang videos that were displayed on viewing screens in Abbotsford's high schools and public buildings, in the Abbotsford police website, and on YouTube. Together, Operations Tarnish, Impact, and Veritas created a saturation of the antigang message. It was an educational, broadly based "spray and pray" approach designed to reach every young person in the community, mimicking commercial marketing strategies that air an advertisement repeatedly to create growing awareness and desire for a product. There was a sense of urgency and concern in the community, creating the vital ingredient of public support and acceptance to help spread the word.

In 2010, the police released Operation Impact 2 for 5500 middle school students, emphasizing the dangers of drug and gang involvement and bullying and how to build inner strength to enhance self-respect and positive decision making. Student achievements, charitable efforts, and accomplishments were recognized to increase a sense of belonging and collective school pride. Again, the chief of police was present and, together with Sergeant Novakowski, delivered a positive, activity-filled "fun for kids" experience that demonstrated the differences between inner and outer strengths and how to make the right choices and decisions even when it would be hard to do so.

As stated earlier, parents also needed to hear the antigang message and know what they could do to keep their children safe and crime free. Operation Lodestar was designed specifically for this target group. A total of 13 presentations were delivered: 2 for the general public and 11 for parents associated with local public and private secondary schools. Of the 13 presentations, 3 were delivered in Punjabi to ensure accessibility for local members of Abbotsford's Indo-Canadian community. The chief of police and the mayor of Abbotsford invited parents and caregivers of all school-aged children to attend. In these presentations, it was important to denormalize negative youth behavior that many parents had been accepting as unavoidable, widespread, acceptable, or typical. Operation Lodestar provided five key points for parents that represent protective factors in a child's life: the importance of setting a good example, knowing the child's whereabouts and activities, valuing the child's education and the importance of school, the need for parental rules with clear limits and expectations, and parental involvement in a way that promotes the child's best interests. In 2012, the police released a *Parenting Matters* video on their website as an additional component of Operation Lodestar, which featured local specialists in parenting, youth, and families, supplemented by additional reading material and fact sheets.

Five additional initiatives followed Operation Lodestar in 2011 and 2012. Operation Acorn was presented to 8800 elementary-school children, communicating a positive message about making good choices. Using team-building games and other fun activities, the police encouraged the students to care for themselves, each other, and the environment. Operation Congratulation stressed the protective factors of school completion and academic achievement. Police visited high schools again with Operation Vector presentations in 2011, providing follow-up encouragement to students to adopt a positive life direction. Police provided current information on progress made against local gangs, with references to several new tragedies that had occurred since 2009. The Operation series concluded with Project Prime, outlining a series of six positive character traits developed by the City of Abbotsford's "Communities of Character" initiative: courage, empathy, integrity, respect, responsibility, and service. The police believed that negative labeling could increase negative behavior; so, Project Prime was strength based, encouraging the formation of prosocial, positive behaviors through a series of small posters defining each of these six character traits in child-friendly language. These were posted on school buses and, based on the ridership numbers provided by the Abbotsford School District, the police estimated that they likely received 1.3 million views over the school year.

As their work began to garner interest outside Abbotsford, the police were questioned regarding the costs related to delivering such comprehensive school-based programming. The police were pleased to report how inexpensive the entire initiative had been: all the posters and videos were made by the department, featuring local citizens rather than paid actors. Staff time and photocopying costs were the primary expense for the poster campaign; a grant supplied additional revenue for Project Prime. The police department had also received a Hummer through the provincial government's Civil Forfeiture Program, another free benefit that allowed them to create a "rolling billboard" covered with antigang slogans and images to increase the diversity of their messaging and extend their program reach. Overall, the chief expense of implementing the prevention program was an investment of staff time, energy, and creativity.

To summarize, the first strategy of the APD's multidimensional approach to gang suppression was the comprehensive Operation series for education and crime prevention. It was cost-effective and was based on relevant content drawn from local examples with positive messaging rather than a "scared straight" approach. The initiative emphasized positive choices, good decisions, and effective parenting, and it featured key leadership within the police department with additional support from community and civic leaders. The first goal was to increase safety for youth through decreased involvement in drug dealing and gangs, with two additional goals of increased community understanding of the public safety threat posed by local gangs and increased understanding among parents of their role in gang suppression through increased support and supervision of their children.

Strategy Two: Inform and Mobilize the Community

Following the public announcements and media coverage provided in 2009, the Abbotsford police knew that community engagement would support gang suppression. Prior to this, there had been a mistaken community belief that targeted kills were primarily gangster against gangster, without realizing the public safety implications of overt gang warfare. Media exposure and a town hall meeting provided a means for the Abbotsford police to clearly communicate a pointed message to the business community and other members of the public that there was real reason for worry, gang violence knew no boundaries, and gang members had little concern for the safety of the public. The risk for collateral damage was high. The police stressed that the community needed to take ownership of their role in turning the situation around, especially as an investment in their children and youth. By this point in time, gang violence was occurring carelessly in busy public locations during business hours. Gang members had started wearing body armor, driving armored vehicles, and going into restaurants in groups with their armor on. As awareness grew, members of the public rightly concluded that they had a choice to make whether they would go to certain restaurants frequented by known gang members or to wear clothes that suggested they might be gang affiliated, thereby increasing their chances of becoming a victim.

As it became apparent that gang members were vulnerable to attack wherever they were, the business community worked with the police to institute Bar Watch in local restaurants, made possible by a local city bylaw that allowed police and bar operators to ask gang members to leave, or to prevent the entry of those who posed a public safety risk. To facilitate this, the police made a presentation to local bar owners about Vancouver's Bar Watch program, adapting it for Abbotsford as a shared information strategy that functioned between establishments and between bars, restaurants, and the police. First, information was shared among business owners and with the police about undesirable customers who had caused problems. Then, restaurant and bar owners began to screen their guests at the door, to prevent undesirables from entering. If a gang member or group had already entered unnoticed, then the owner would call the police to remove them to avoid a confrontation or a threat to their own safety. According to the police, there were a few arguments from angry customers who were removed; but, on the whole, there was surprisingly little negative feedback from restaurant guests, owners, or the public. The police only removed guests who were recognized or could be validated as being involved with gangs, and the normal response was appreciation from the remaining guests. Abbotsford Bar Watch was a police-supported but owner-led initiative that fostered good community relations and reduced the threat of violence in public establishments.

The strategies involved with Bar Watch spread to other commercial establishments, as other businesses began to realize the need to refuse service to known gangsters. This meant that gang members were finding it harder and harder to live and do their business in Abbotsford, as a whole variety of commercial services, stores, restaurants, and bars began to deny them entry.

In summary, a cooperative school district and city hall working with a mobilized business community meant that prevention, education for awareness, and intervention tactics such as Bar Watch could occur simultaneously in schools, in commercial areas, and throughout the community. This directly reduced the likelihood of gang violence occurring in public places.

Strategy Three: Intervention to Create Change

While the public education stream of the antigang strategy was developing through the Community Policing Branch of the APD, leaders within the department recognized that partnering with community agencies would be an important component of addressing youth violence and gang involvement. In 2007, the Abbotsford Community Assessment and Action Network (CAAN) was formed to address youth gang trends that were developing in the community. In the summer of 2009, the Abbotsford Police Youth Squad identified 20 high school youths, 95% of whom were South Asian, who were involved with two opposing youth gangs. A Punjabi-speaking youth worker from CAAN's youth gang prevention project worked with the police to bring together the parents of these youths, interpreting and translating the police department's concerns about the potential for these young people to become seriously involved in and affected by violence and other gang-related activities.

Following the parents' meeting, the youths participated in a mediated dialogue facilitated by a registered clinical counselor, at Abbotsford Community Services' South Asian Community Resource Office (SACRO). This mediated session was intended to allow these two groups of high school males to reconcile with each other, with the goal of resolving the conflict that had been characterized by physical fights, which then escalated to damaging each others' cars and homes, followed by higher levels of violence and assaults, and then serious assaults involving weapons. Even though these youth had not yet formed the business base of a gang, it was assuming a form resembling the rival neighborhood groups seen in the American gang model. The Abbotsford police felt that there was a real possibility that these young men would become engaged in serious criminal activity and involvement with gangs with a criminal purpose if an intervention for them and their parents did not interrupt the escalating cycle of violence and retaliation.* Overall, the intervention was considered a success, although some continued to need help. To ensure ongoing intervention and support, police and school district staff referred 25 South Asian youth from 2009 through 2012 to the SACRO antigang youth support program. As stated earlier, a 24-hour help line was established by the police as another means of providing help to gang-involved youth, their parents, and others who needed information and resources.

Direct and proactive intervention became an important hallmark of the APD gang suppression strategy. In the case of the South Asian youths, the police went directly to them and their families to talk about the problems that were developing and provided a mediated session to help resolve the conflict underlying the violence. The police also employed this approach of proactive dialogue as a tactic to confront known gangsters, engaging them in a conversation first, followed by overt and covert enforcement tactics if the gangster did not leave or desist from further gang activity. Working with the focused deterrence principle that people tend not to change their negative behavior until the unpleasant consequences of their negative behavior are greater than the potential reward, the police determined to make life so uncomfortable for gangsters in Abbotsford that they would become persuaded to either get out of the business or leave the area, if they had not been arrested or killed first. This is explained more fully in Strategy Four, as outlined in the following section.

Strategy Four: Enforcement-Oriented Prevention

One of the innovative aspects of the APD's approach was enforcement-oriented prevention. This refers to a proactive policing approach rather than

---

* APD Youth Squad Constables Davin Turner and Mark Zawadsky received the 2011 Wael T. Audi Youth Policing Award from the British Columbia Ministry of Public Safety, Solicitor General, and BC Crime Prevention Association for spearheading this intervention to dissolve the rivalry between these two groups. Retrieved from http://www.pssg.gov.bc.ca/crimeprevention/awards/docs/award-winners2011.pdf.

waiting for new crimes to occur and has similarities to the problem-oriented policing strategies and pulling levers tactics used in the American gang suppression models discussed earlier. As mentioned, the police directly confronted gangsters to encourage them to stop their criminal activities or leave town. This was followed by a series of overt and covert strategies and tactics to lead to an arrest. These strategies were part of a larger, comprehensive web of tactics that evolved from an intelligence-led, solution-oriented approach, which slowly emerged and developed throughout 2009 and 2010 as the Abbotsford police created what is now known as Death by a Thousand Cuts. Together, all of these tactics and strategies worked together to generate relentless pressure on gang members, reducing the desirability of doing their business within Abbotsford. To better understand the evolution and development of this enforcement component, it is helpful to examine an overview of what was involved and how it developed.

In Deputy Chief Lucy's view, the enforcement aspect of the APD gang suppression strategy had the greatest impact on gang activity during the critical years of 2009–2011. While the education and prevention initiatives reduced the stream of new youth recruits into local gangs, the enforcement component combated gang activity directly. In 2009 the major crime and drug enforcement units led the way, and the APD Strategic Plan of 2009 identified gang suppression as their primary goal for public safety. The key performance indicators would be a reduction in gang-related shootings and homicides.

To achieve this, the APD redistributed and reprioritized their resources. In April 2010, a 15-person gang suppression unit was created and combined with the drug enforcement unit. Members, resources, and assets were drawn from patrol, the major crime unit, and the drug squads to make this possible. In total, they recruited 29 officers and a crime analyst to focus specifically on gang crime, which was considered a significant investment of resources and personnel for a department of their size. Meanwhile, other officers were seconded to the provincial Integrated Gang Task Force dedicated to regional gang suppression.

To gain a completely accurate picture of the gang situation within Abbotsford, the analyst was tasked with determining who was involved, with whom they were operating, where they were operating, and what they were doing. The goal was to focus completely on Abbotsford, with the most comprehensive and detailed list of who was involved in gang activity, either by living in Abbotsford or doing business within the city. Although the police had been aware of the main players and prominent gang members, they needed the expertise of the crime analyst to surface the identities of the rest. This created a much larger list than anticipated; at one point, there were 180 individuals involved. However, gang membership was becoming very fluid and at times it was difficult to identify how people were connected. Gang members would switch allegiances; others would assume a role between the gangs, supplying firearms and other resources to both groups.

To interrupt gang activity, they needed the crime analyst to measure a wide number of variables, allowing the police to attack the problem and pull levers from every possible direction with prevention, intervention, and enforcement strategies. Their approach avoided large, time-consuming, and sophisticated investigations, preferring the flexible, nimble approach later dubbed Death by a Thousand Cuts. Their daily actions were guided by a simple question: what is the biggest public safety risk? Employing Bar Watch, enforcing the new legislation banning body armor and armored vehicles, and publicizing their arrests of high profile gangsters all helped to turn the tide.

Deputy Chief Rick Lucy noted that enforcement and suppression worked together to achieve results. First, they began to follow and watch Jamey Bacon of the Red Scorpions, who was a significant public safety threat. They employed overt strategies such as setting up surveillance cameras on his street, with a police vehicle parked at the adjacent intersection, making it impossible for other gang members to do business with Jamey Bacon at his house. They issued public warnings, informing restaurants, gyms, taxi companies, and food delivery companies that there was significant risk in providing service to gang members. They ensured that the public were aware that innocent people were being injured and killed, caught in the cross fire of gang warfare. Worse yet, gang members could start a shoot-out at a wrong address, using incorrect information to target the wrong people, with no control over where the rounds of ammunition were going.

Suppression and enforcement meant flipping traditional thinking that these unfortunate community members who had been murdered had just been "in the wrong place at the wrong time." In actuality, those innocent members of the public had been exactly where they had a right to be, carrying out the day-to-day business of their lives. Now, the police needed to enforce that the gang members themselves were in the wrong place at the wrong time and there would be no place of refuge for them within the City of Abbotsford.

To achieve maximum effect in the APD gang suppression strategy, every part of the organization needed to be mobilized with gang suppression as their primary priority. This caused the Abbotsford police to do a number of things differently: they set measurable targets and began to track relevant activities in a detailed and deliberate manner, such as numbers of shots fired, home invasions, and grow-rips, making note of what happened, who was involved, whether it was gang or drug related, who were the victims and what were their allegiances and affiliations, and who was attacking them.

Additionally, there were criminal freelancers who were opportunistic, working both sides to gain personal advantage, such as conducting a grow-rip and then giving the stolen property to a competitor. Weapons and drugs were the commodities to sell, and the willingness to commit violence created criminal opportunities that needed to be tracked for frequency rates to determine if activity was increasing or decreasing. As assaults, intimidation, extortion, and enforceable confinements were committed by gang members to get information, or to create deterrence, the APD used the analyst to track, analyze, and assess the situation to determine the most timely and strategic response.

Once the Gang Suppression Unit was initiated and the entire department was engaged in various gang suppression activities, they began strategy meetings every 2 weeks. Each department sent a representative to look at the most recent intelligence and data on all the categories of offences that had recently occurred, with a detailed report of recent activity. Together, they strategized across the organization regarding what they believed would be the best next step. Intelligence-led policing undergirded and guided the APD antigang strategy of intervention, prevention, and enforcement. The tone of these strategy meetings was designed to be creative and positive, generating new ideas and avoiding criticisms of how certain investigations were going. The emphasis was on teamwork, with all members privy to the same conversations.

The Abbotsford police had already adopted this approach to target other categories of crime in the past, so they were confident it would work well in this new situation. It was communicated throughout the department that every member, no matter what their role in the department, needed to work together with the rest to address this significant threat to the people of Abbotsford. Everyone needed to be committed to this larger goal. Looking back, APD leadership has noted that as police members began to see the positive changes occurring they became even more motivated, understanding that their efforts were really making a measurable difference.

The Abbotsford police have reflected that all their strategies were employed at the same time, creating layers of response. This multidimensional approach involved prevention approaches in schools and business and community involvement simultaneous with police-generated gang suppression tactics in the community. All facets needed to work together. As leaders, the police chief and senior management recognized that they needed to foster an environment that was very focused, with a willingness to try anything and everything that made sense, tweaking and adjusting later or abandoning an ineffective strategy in favor of another. This willingness to experiment and take risks supported their need to create gang suppression from every possible direction, as they felt the problem was far too serious and pervasive to employ only one means of response. In the department's view, the risk was too great to do anything but respond in the fullest possible manner. Doing nothing was not an option; they were open to all options and ideas that might make a difference.

With a goal to suppress, enforce, and disrupt gang activity, they began to use a variety of tactics: partnerships with community members, paid informants, relentless attention using CompStat,* and warrant executions and seizures prioritized by which would have the most impact. Types of warrants varied: some were to search and seize drugs and weapons, knowing that every firearm off the street would increase safety and reduce potential violence. Other warrants were designed to arrest traffickers, with a goal of reaching others higher in the criminal structure. A successful warrant execution would result in the arrests of one or more people, strategically creating maximum disruption, with the aim of dismantling different pieces of criminal operations. Every warrant and arrest was intended to ultimately reach those who were most involved and who presented the most serious public safety risk.

Throughout this period, the police became more and more aware of the important role that marijuana growing played in the whole gang picture. The dangers associated with marijuana grow-ops were also becoming a regional concern for fire departments, and BC Hydro implemented "smart meters" to locate grow-ops and track stolen electricity. Various communities were creating bylaws to help reduce home-based marijuana production. Medicinal marijuana growing through Health Canada began to penetrate the illegal marijuana industry, the federal government implemented mandatory minimum sentencing for drug-related crimes, and provincial civil forfeiture legislation was enacted to allow seizure of goods and property acquired through drug-related criminal activity. These external factors positively influenced the success of APD's gang suppression strategies by increasing pressure from different directions on gang activities, thereby reducing the ease with which gang business had been previously conducted. The civil forfeiture legislation was especially helpful because it targeted what mattered most to gangsters: their money and assets. Police used this strategically: when requirements were met for the civil forfeiture process and they could establish the link between a criminal activity and an asset such as a house used for a grow-op, they would turn over the file to the civil forfeiture office that could then seize the asset.

The APD's greatest commitment was to set and reach their targets. Through Census Metropolitan Area data, Abbotsford had been identified as the murder capital of Canada in 2008 and again in 2009, with even higher

---

* CompStat was originally developed in New York City and is a multilayered approach to crime reduction that involves, among other things, crime mapping, problem identification, strategizing, and use of computer-generated statistics.

numbers of gang-related deaths* (Statistics Canada, 2012b). By the beginning of 2010, the antigang unit was established; the Abbotsford police now had a full inventory of gang members, creating an accurate picture of who was living or doing business within the community. The first target for 2010 was to reduce the numbers of active gang associates in Abbotsford by 15%. The second target was a 75% reduction in drug- or gang-related homicides, bringing it down from eight to two. In all other crime categories, the target was a 20% reduction of violent gang crime. To achieve this, they used the Gang Suppression Unit, the crime analyst, the biweekly strategy meetings, and communication with officers in provincially based gang suppression units, working together with neighboring communities and regions while intensely focusing on the local situation. In the end, while recognizing that it was part of a bigger, regional response,† the strategy was primarily dedicated to improving public safety and suppressing gang crime right within the community of Abbotsford. This has remained the single most important priority to this day.

Once their strategies and approaches were in place, they began to track and follow their targets. Interestingly, in 2010 their list of local gang associates grew in numbers. Now, the Abbotsford police were much better able to know who was doing what; so this growing list was divided into their top 20 offenders, followed by the minor players. Measuring criminal activity had become much more refined, enabling them to know which criminal and violent acts were linked to gangs and which were not. Tracking homicides was the most obvious.

The Abbotsford police noted that others felt it was not possible to reduce the homicide rate by 75% in a single year, but they exactly met their homicide target in 2010. This was made possible by the focused deterrence tactic of confronting gangsters directly, combining creative intervention with

---

* Statistics Canada reported 8 and 9 homicides for 2008 and 2009, respectively, whereas the Abbotsford police reported 11 homicides in 2009. The additional two deaths were the teenagers Randay and Gill, who had been abducted in Abbotsford and likely killed there. Their bodies were later found a short distance outside the city limits, abandoned on aboriginal reserve land policed by the Royal Canadian Mounted Police. Even though it increased the numbers, the police felt it was important to see those murders as part of Abbotsford gang violence and included them in their numbers and messaging. See Table 7.2 for further information on gang-related homicides compared to total homicides.

† The Abbotsford police acknowledged the importance of the regional Integrated Gang Task Force that was part of the Combined Forces Special Enforcement Unit (CFSEU). APD members were seconded to assist the CFSEU, and the APD was assisted by the Integrated Gang Task Force to achieve timely, important arrests of key players and gang leaders operating throughout Vancouver and the Fraser Valley, including Abbotsford. This cooperation and collaboration between various police departments is another noteworthy achievement that contributed to gang suppression throughout the region. Part of the APD strategy was to be embedded in and connected to these larger regional combined units, which also included the Integrated Homicide Investigation Team.

enforcement, as mentioned in Strategy Three, in the preceding section. Through the work of the crime analyst, the Abbotsford police now knew who the gang members were, but they did not have enough evidence to arrest them. First, they announced they were going to create a gangster "Top Ten" list, based on a complete inventory of gangsters in the community. The message went nationwide. They anticipated 100 on the list; but, as stated earlier, 180 individuals were revealed to be gang involved. The police then shifted from a Top Ten gangsters list to a Top Twenty-Five Public Safety List. These individuals were not ranked by status or money; they were determined to be the gangsters who posed the most serious public safety threat at that time. For example, if a gangster came to town to eradicate his competitors and was attempting to obtain firearms or other criminal assets, then that individual would move to the top of the list and the police would directly intervene. By May 2010, they had made their first arrest.

They also employed a communication strategy with other gang members, confronting them in their homes, on the street, or pulling them over when their vehicles appeared in the city. The message was straightforward and direct: "We're not here to arrest you, we're here to talk. We are warning you that if you don't leave town we will arrest you and you'll end up in jail, or your rivals will kill you. We are not going to allow you to ply your trade here and we will hound you relentlessly until you get out, are killed, or arrested." The police reasoned that they needed to tell the gangster underworld that Abbotsford would become a hostile place for gangsters or those who wanted to become one. They sent a unified, consistent message from every department of the Abbotsford police to every gangster they could contact and followed through on their word to ensure that the criminal element would take them seriously. This enforcement-oriented prevention strategy was effective and increased police credibility as they were able to demonstrate their ability to hamper gangs from operating freely. As demonstrated in similar gang suppression programs in the United States, sending a message and following through with enforcement is an essential component of a successful focused deterrence program.

In addition to this direct communication followed by warrant executions and arrests, the Gang Suppression Unit engaged in preemptive strikes: if they knew from informants or investigative leads that a gangster had come to town for retribution and was rumored to be preparing to kill someone, the police went to him first and told him that they were watching and he would be followed. This information was passed to the patrol members who followed them and parked outside their houses, making it difficult for the gangsters to operate. This aggressive, proactive approach created a sense among gang members that the police knew exactly what was going on and would stop at nothing to prevent further gang activity from occurring. They facilitated this approach by a department-wide understanding that any relevant information from informants or leads gleaned by any member would be forwarded to the full-time crime analyst, who was dedicated solely to gangs. A second analyst focused on property crime, and both were supported by an assistant. This style of intelligence-led policing defined and supported their proactive enforcement strategy.

Another proactive aspect of Death by a Thousand Cuts was checking the court conditions of all known gangsters. By reviewing their curfews and other restrictions, the police were able to determine if they were breaching their conditions. They kept them accountable to their court conditions and communicated directly with them that any criminal activity would be attended to immediately. Police presence was increased in the neighborhoods where they lived, and parking police cars in front of their houses was a common event.

When arrests were made, the Abbotsford police again departed from conventional police practice by letting the public know about the arrests and, whenever possible, named the gangs involved. Others in the policing field opposed this, concerned that this publicity would give credibility to a gang and give information to other gangs. However, the Abbotsford police had asked the community to become involved and this communication strategy sustained public interest and support, helping to maintain community engagement. The idea was to shine a bright light on the problem, keep telling the story, and make the names public.

Gang members began to see that the police priority was stopping the violence and criminal activity, with a simple message, "Stop, leave, or get dealt with." Police members encouraged gang members to exit the gang lifestyle and provided what help they could to make that happen, which is another aspect of focused deterrence. The priority was not to relocate gang activity to another vulnerable community, although many gangsters did leave the area to do business elsewhere. The priority was to stop the criminal activity altogether, whenever possible.

Now, the police department had two well-functioning prongs of attack against gangs: community education and engagement through the community policing Operation program and Bar Watch and enforcement through the Gang Suppression Unit. The prevention campaign was building and was well received within the community as well as outside the community and across North America. Other communities, police departments, and organizations were asking for the Operation Tarnish posters and other resources to use in their own cities and towns. This helped establish a reputation that the APD was a department that was willing to tackle the problem.

As previously stated, the Census Metropolitan Area of Abbotsford-Mission had been identified as the murder capital of Canada in 2008 and 2009, with 8 and 9 homicides, respectively, although the Abbotsford police reported the 2009 homicide number as 11, because Randay and Gill were Abbotsford citizens who were most likely killed in the city. Their bodies were later found a short distance outside the city boundaries on aboriginal reserve land policed by the Royal Canadian Mounted Police. In 2010, however, only four homicides occurred. This was the first serious statistical indicator that their gang suppression program was working. However, due to the unpredictability of gang activity, there was cautious optimism. In 2009, 8 of the 11 homicides were gang related. In 2010, only two of the four homicides were gang related and two to three homicides per year were the norm for the community prior to the escalation of gang activity. In 2011, there were no gang-related homicides at all (see Table 7.1). This represented an extraordinary success, demonstrating how their focused, serious dedication to gang suppression had paid off. Public Information Office Constable Ian McDonald reflected, "It was a huge year for the department and the community. That's why we did what we did: we were serious about changing the way things were."

Lessons Learned

Compared to neighboring communities in British Columbia who were also afflicted with problems of gang violence, Abbotsford was exemplary as a community in which gang activity had been successfully suppressed. Problem-oriented policing strategies involve evaluation to determine which strategies work and which are less effective, with follow-up adjustment to increase and sustain ongoing success. In this regard, it is helpful to summarize what the three interviewees reported as their "lessons learned" from implementing Death by a Thousand Cuts.

1. Pay attention to early warning signs:
   As the gang suppression strategy began to work, the Abbotsford police were able to look back and reflect on the early stages of gang growth and the markers that were evident, although no one at that time was anticipating what was ahead. It had been slowly building toward an eruption, and the warning signs had been there, unattended. Specifically, there were key individuals, such as the Bacon Brothers and their associates, who had demonstrated behaviors earlier in their lives that were later understood to be precursors to their involvement in gangs and organized crime. If that had been more clearly understood, it might have been possible to intervene in ways that would have changed the future course of many of the young people who later became involved in a gang lifestyle, redirecting them from violence and crime toward something more desirable and safe. For the police, a critical opportunity had been missed. This was why the Operation program and the mediated intervention with South Asian youth were so important to the Abbotsford police: it

represented their commitment to learn from this oversight and to act swiftly to try to protect and guide others who were at risk. The police felt it was necessary to create significant exposure of the problem and ask others to help address it. They also felt it was necessary to reach out to young people in ways that were caring, anchored in good values, with positive messaging geared toward the specific age groups they were targeting.

2. Set targets that are tough to meet:

As stated earlier, the Abbotsford police shifted to a unified, department-wide focus with specific, measurable, and aggressive targets. The police chief boldly stated that their goal was to make Abbotsford "the safest city in BC" with a long-range goal to get crime rates to zero. Even though others in the field predicted it could not be done, they were able to reach and exceed their short-term targets of reducing gang-related homicides, violence, and criminal activity. They have now shifted to target other dimensions of criminal activity, to continue to reduce crime rates overall.

3. Lead with courage:

Tackling the Abbotsford crime problem required the police to publicly acknowledge that gang violence was now out of control. This required a combination of courage and humility without denial or minimization of the problem, and with the recognition that this admission could put the department's reputation at risk. However, this combination of courage and openness enabled them to connect with significant numbers of community members in ways that would not have been possible otherwise, and the community responded positively and with shared engagement. It is interesting to note that courage and humility in identifying the problem, followed by aggressive, strategic action to deal with the problem, ultimately led them to their successes and increased esteem in the eyes of the public. This was verified by a community survey in 2012 indicating overwhelming community support for the Abbotsford police (Plecas et al., 2013).

4. Be innovative and optimistic:

In 2009, when the department was first grappling with the gang problem and trying to determine how to best respond, they adopted an approach that encouraged brainstorming for good ideas, creativity, innovation, and support for those who were experimenting with strategies that might work. The chief and senior management team felt that it was essential to avoid negativity, to ensure that every good idea or approach could surface. This reflects the belief that negative thinking and nay-saying will inhibit creativity and growth. Encouraging creative, innovative thinking is especially essential from the leaders within a police department, who become the champions for all of those who are working for them, celebrating their successes and giving credit where it is due.

Problem-oriented policing is grounded in this positive attitude toward innovation and experimentation, which is why solution-oriented policing may be a better term. Each community must determine which tactics to try and which levers to pull according to the unique needs of their situation. However, innovation and experimentation are very difficult without strong leadership from the top, as noted by White et al. (2003).

"Successful implementation of a new philosophy is dependent on the formal and informal policies of the police leadership. In other words, if the new strategy is perceived as being nothing more than rhetoric intended to assuage the community, the rank and file of the department will not buy in to the philosophy and will not change the way they conduct their business. Importantly, the central theme of the problem-oriented philosophy involves changing the way patrol officers do their jobs. Thus, the police leadership must be able to inspire change at all levels of the department for the philosophy to take hold" (White et al., 2003, p. 219).

5. Take action and go for it:

Great ideas without action lead nowhere. Stimulating creative thought and innovation had to be followed by strategic choices and plans. If those plans failed or were less successful than hoped, they were tweaked or discarded. The important component was the action flowing from ideas, avoiding the paralysis that can come from too much discussion without creating a plan. Action then translated into measurable goals and targets, which could be evaluated.

6. Take a comprehensive, multidimensional approach:

As already noted, the successes in Abbotsford were derived from a comprehensive, multidimensional set of strategies that were implemented simultaneously. It is doubtful that similar results could have been achieved without this thorough approach.

In retrospect, Sergeant Mike Novakowski observed that they could have strengthened their schools program even further with a teachers' package for follow-up after the presentations, to ensure sustained and ongoing messaging. In a culture that is saturated with violent media and video games, it seems appropriate to ensure that the positive messaging regarding choosing a nonviolent crime-free life is repeated from many sources and in many different ways.

It is also noteworthy that the school- and community-based prevention program involved 11 different programs and strategies, not just 1. These initiatives were released successively over time, in many different settings, and for many different groups. This is another example of a multidimensional, comprehensive approach.

Similarly, the enforcement tactics were comprehensive, generated from intelligence and involving a wide variety of overt and covert tactics to respond to gang activity in ways that were preemptive, proactive, responsive, and ranging from small to large, thereby producing the nickname Death by a Thousand Cuts.

For future work in Abbotsford and for other communities as well, the Abbotsford experience suggests the benefits of a multidimensional strategy for gang suppression and crime prevention that combines the efforts of police enforcement with social service and school system supports, with strategies that improve parenting skills for the early years as well as adolescence, while also building the positive capacities and attitudes of youth to assist them in making prosocial choices. This becomes an important complement to the enforcement strategies that actively inhibit and suppress gang activity and helps to reduce recruitment into gangs over the longer term. This is validated by research that indicates that comprehensive, multidimensional programs are most effective, especially those that combine community-oriented strategies with community partnerships for prevention with at-risk youth, while capitalizing on the strengths of multiple law enforcement strategies (Makarios & Pratt, 2012).

7. Be relevant:
The education and awareness components were relevant, involving local examples and referencing the violent murders of teenagers and young adults that many local students and citizens knew personally. The message needed to be very real and relevant to penetrate the naïveté of young people who felt they were omnipotent and immune to harm. Sergeant Novakowski advised that any other community or police department wanting to use Abbotsford's materials or resources should adapt them to suit their own context, using their own local examples and stories.

8. Create public support, starting first with community leadership:
The success of the APD gang suppression strategies was significantly strengthened by support from police leadership, the mayor's office, and community leaders. This gave more weight, importance, and credibility to what the police were trying to do. With high-level support behind them, the police were able to work effectively with the rest of the public.

In retrospect, the Abbotsford police feel that they could have benefitted from even more parent participation, supported by more proactive effort on the part of school personnel to reach out and invite parents to attend meetings. Although some schools did this very effectively, the result was mixed in other locations. Again, the support of senior leadership at the school and district levels will greatly enhance the success of the outreach and awareness components of the program.

9. Create community partnerships:
   The Operation series of initiatives required cooperation and participation from the Abbotsford School District. Bar Watch required support and engagement from the business community. The intervention with South Asian youth was made possible through partnering with SACRO. More can be accomplished when silos are reduced and collaborative partnerships are formed.

10. Find the right personnel:
   An effective public information officer was a critical part of the APD's approach to tackling gang crime. Fostering regular contact and positive relationships with the media helps to get the message out.

   When delivering prevention programming in schools, it is essential to find presenters who are engaging, passionate, and creative and relate well to children and youth. They need to be able to create awareness and send a positive message in a way that makes sense to young people. This was especially important for younger children with limited attention, who responded really well to high-level activities in a tightly scripted, rapid pace format that kept them on edge and gave them opportunities to get involved. Young children want to please and respond well to praise: the Abbotsford police worked with that to affirm and engage them. The teenagers also responded well to the personal stories of the former gang member and Sergeant Mike Novakowski, both of whom used personal experiences to create relevant and important messages that young people could understand and accept.

11. Follow-up with ongoing support and resources:
   One of the dangers of success is the risk of complacency. For as long as organized crime and gang activity continues in Canada, the Abbotsford police will need to sustain their efforts to discourage gangsters from entering the community, swiftly apprehend those who break the law, and continue their prevention messaging. New, unanticipated threats may arise, which is a reason to maintain the nimble approach to ensure rapid response. In 2011, a number of Abbotsford teenagers were experimenting with tainted Ecstasy and two teenagers died. As drug sales to youth are controlled by organized crime and gangs, the police once more responded with media messaging, producing Operation X: The Straight Goods on

"E," * a short documentary featuring the family and friends of the two deceased youths, with a graphic, personal, and relevant message about the dangers of using Ecstasy and other street drugs. All of these resources are now available on the APD website, to ensure easy accessibility.
12. Ensure ongoing sustainability:
The concern about ongoing sustainability is a valid one, given the research by Tillyer et al. (2012) that indicates that many of these focused deterrence programs were highly successful for a few years but could not be sustained. They observed that institutionalizing the program with ongoing positions rather than linking the program to particular people is an important step. It is also likely that complacency may affect ongoing efforts, as homicide rates come down.

Looking to the Future

Although the successes of Abbotsford's gang suppression strategy is commendable and has significantly reduced loss of life, the benefits of this program are still in the early stages. It is premature to determine what will happen when recently incarcerated gangsters are released and what new alliances are currently being formed within the prison environment that will affect gang life on the outside. This is a rising concern in the United States and Canada as more and more gangsters are incarcerated with an emphasis on longer sentences, resulting in prison gangs that are asserting more and more control over youth gangs inside and outside the prison environment (Sánchez-Jankowski, 2003; Parry, 2006). How effectively criminal justice agencies in British Columbia are responding to this rising threat is still to be evaluated. In the United States, higher incarceration rates have created the unintended effect of prison gang alliances, enabling them to create greater control over street gangs, especially as gang members go in and out of prison. These alliances have become necessary for survival, and the end result has unified the drug markets. The unification of street gangs and prison gangs means that the resulting collective organizations are even more organized and have greater resources to sustain themselves (Sánchez-Jankowski, 2003).

However, the ongoing vigilance of the Abbotsford police to maintain focused deterrence with its prolific violent offender target group, while also fostering strong community engagement, support, and participation in active crime prevention, will prove to be helpful if it is sustained over the long term. These efforts must be supported by social policy and support for addressing

---

* Available at http://www.youtube.com/watch?v=rl9jS8oPtEc.

Table 7.1   Homicide Survey, Number, and Rates (per 100,000 Population) of Homicide Victims

Geography	Homicides	2005	2006	2007	2008	2009	2010	2011
Canada	Number of homicide victims	663	606	594	611	610	554	598
	Homicide rates per 100,000 population	2.06	1.86	1.80	1.83	1.81	1.62	1.73
Abbotsford-Mission, British Columbia	Number of homicide victims	4	3	2	8	9	4	1
	Homicide rates per 100,000 population	2.45	1.83	1.20	4.71	5.21	2.28	0.56

Source: Statistics Canada. *Table 253-0004. Homicide survey, number and rates (per 100,000 population) of homicide victims, by Census Metropolitan Area (CMA), annual.* CANSIM (database). Retrieved from http://www5.statcan.gc.ca/cansim/a26?lang= eng&retrLang=eng&id=2530004&pattern=homicide+rates&tabMode=dataTable& srchLan=-1&p1=1&p2=1.

Table 7.2   Abbotsford Police Department Statistics for Gang-Related Homicides in Abbotsford

	2005	2006	2007	2008	2009	2010	2011	2012
Total homicides	2	3	1	6	11	4	0	3
Gang-related homicides	2	2	0	3	8	2	0	1

Source: Abbotsford Police Department Crime Statistics. Retrieved on August 13, 2014 from http://www.abbypd.ca/Crime-Statistics.

Note: Statistics Canada reported one homicide for the Abbotsford-Mission Census Metropolitan Area in 2011, but this represented an in-custody death in a correctional facility in Mission. The Abbotsford police did not include it as it did not relate to homicides and gang violence in Abbotsford.

poverty and social disadvantage; the challenges of an immigrant population to find meaningful work and integrate into society so that their children will be less tempted by the lure of ill-gotten gains; and assistance to parents generally in raising their children to be prosocial, contributing members of society. These larger social issues have been observed in American cities, with gangs thriving where young people have disdain for the low-paying, menial jobs of their parents, with little hope for themselves to find more lucrative means of employment without engaging in crime (Adamson, 1998). Whereas this has traditionally afflicted poorer neighborhoods, in Abbotsford it manifested itself with certain middle-class youth looking at the hard work of their parents and wanting the easy wealth of drug dealing instead. Indeed, the profits of the drug trade were so extreme that youth had the capacity to earn vast amounts of money in relatively short periods of time, greatly exceeding what they (or their parents) could earn through legitimate employment.

This suggests that multidimensional gang suppression approaches should also tackle the antisocial attitudes, low moral reasoning, and antisocial behaviors that allow gang members to engage in callous acts of violence to assert their power and protect their economic assets. Much of gang behavior is driven by a capitalistic desire to control an economic market, but without the laws and regulatory bodies in place to provide oversight, restraints, and reasonable limits (Sánchez-Jankowski, 2003). In reviewing the CIRV for focused deterrence, Tillyer et al. (2012) observed that the program would have benefitted from using principles of effective intervention that come from correctional, rehabilitative programs, providing cognitive behavioral treatment to tackle the inherent problems of low moral judgment and antisocial, aggressive attitudes. Although it helps to restore safety on the streets to incarcerate chronic violent offenders, it is a short-term fix if the necessary rehabilitation does not occur to prevent further relapses into violence when they leave the prison setting. For violent youths, incarceration may only worsen their criminal associations and deepen their gang affiliations, raising the possibility that traditional incarceration practices may yield poor results.

Conclusion

Abbotsford police's Death by a Thousand Cuts is a comprehensive multidimensional program of gang suppression involving intelligence-led, solution-oriented policing, with an emphasis on focused deterrence strategies. These involved enforcement tactics to disrupt gang activity; community engagement to limit gangster access to services, restaurants, and retail outlets; prevention programs to limit recruitment of youths into gangs; and parent support programming in partnership with community agencies, proactive interventions, and extensive public awareness with ongoing media support. The results of these efforts enabled the Abbotsford police to reach its targets of reducing homicide, with the significant achievement of no homicides within 2 years of program implementation.

Quite unintentionally, the Abbotsford police adopted practices similar to those associated with focused deterrence programs used in the United States, implementing them at a very high level specifically designed for the Abbotsford context. The department was unified in its goal to make Abbotsford "the safest city in British Columbia" with strong support from the chief of police and the senior management team, ensuring that all members of the department are committed to implementing the new philosophy.

Although questions remain regarding the next stages of the program's implementation and sustainability, it is reasonable to conclude that the practices associated with Death by a Thousand Cuts have served the community well, increasing police legitimacy and support while also increasing public safety and the preservation of life.

References

Abbotsford Police Department Crime Statistics. Retrieved on August 13, 2014 from http://www.abbypd.ca/Crime-Statistics.

Adamson, C. (1998). Tribute, turf, honor and the American street gang: Patterns of continuity and change since 1820. Theoretical Criminology, 2(1), 57–84.

B. C. gangster Jarrod Bacon gets 12 years on cocaine charge. (2012, May 4). CBC News: British Columbia. Retrieved from http://www.cbc.ca/news/canada/british-columbia/story/2012/05/04/bc-jarrod-bacon-sentence.html.

Braga, A., Kennedy, D., Waring, E., & Piehl, A. (2001). Problem-oriented policing, deterrence, and youth violence: An evaluation of Boston's Operation Ceasefire. Journal of Research in Crime and Delinquency, 38(3), 195–225.

Braga, A., McDevitt, J., & Pierce, G. (2006). Understanding and preventing gang violence: Problem analysis and response development in Lowell, Massachusetts. Police Quarterly, 9(1), 20–46.

Braga, A. A., Pierce, G.L., McDevitt, J., Bond, B. J., & Cronin, S. (2008). The strategic prevention of gun violence among gang-involved offenders. Justice Quarterly, 25(1), 132–162.

Braga, A., & Weisburd, D. (2012). The effects of focused deterrence strategies on crime: A systematic review and meta-analysis of the empirical evidence. Journal of Research in Crime and Delinquency, 49(3), 323–358.

Chermak, S., & McGarrell, E. (2004). Problem-solving approaches to homicide: An evaluation of the Indianapolis violence reduction partnership. Justice Policy Review, 15(2), 161–192.

Corsaro, N., & McGarrell, E. F. (2009). Testing a promising homicide reduction strategy: Re-assessing the impact of the Indianapolis "pulling levers" intervention. Journal of Experimental Criminology, 5(1), 63–82.

Hopes, V. (2012, January 3). Abbotsford records no murders in 2011. Abbotsford News. Retrieved from http://www.abbynews.com/news/136593913.html.

Karbovanec sentenced to life in Surrey slayings. (2009, April 9). CBC News: British Columbia. Retrieved from http://www.cbc.ca/news/canada/british-columbia/story/2009/04/09/bc-surrey-six-sentence.html.

Kennedy, D. M., & Braga, A. A. (1998). Homicide in Minneapolis: Research for problem solving. Homicide Studies, 2(3), 264–290.

Makarios, M., & Pratt, T. (2012). The effectiveness of policies and programs that attempt to reduce firearm violence: A meta-analysis. Crime & Delinquency, 58(2), 222–244. Retrieved from http://cad.sagepub.com.proxy.ufv.ca:2048/content/58/2/222.full.pdf+html.

Parry, B. (2006). Intelligence: The key to gang suppression. Corrections Today, 68(2), 42–45. Retrieved from http://ehis.ebscohost.com.proxy.ufv.ca:2048/ehost/pdfviewer/pdfviewer?vid=10&sid=3c96ef79-e994-4a80-9afe-f1edb862f6d7%40sessionmgr111&hid=101.

Plecas, D., Cohen, I., Armstrong, J., & Burk, K. (2013). Abbotsford Public Safety Survey. Abbotsford, Canada: University of the Fraser Valley, Centre for Public Safety and Criminal Justice Research.

Police identify teens found dead in Abbotsford. (2009, May 2). CBC News: British Columbia. Retrieved from http://www.cbc.ca/news/canada/british-columbia/story/2009/05/02/bc-abbotsford-bodies-identified.html.

Sánchez-Jankowski, M. (2003). Gangs and social change. Theoretical Criminology, 7(2), 191–216.

Statistics Canada. (2012a). Police-reported crime statistics in Canada: Chart 15 Table Data. Retrieved from http://www.statcan.gc.ca/pub/85-002-x/2012001 /article/11692/c-g/desc/desc15-eng.html.

Statistics Canada. (2012b). Table 253-0004. Homicide survey, number and rates (per 100,000 population) of homicide victims, by Census Metropolitan Area (CMA), annual. Retrieved from http://www5.statcan.gc.ca/cansim /a26?lang=eng&retrLang=eng&id=2530004&pattern=homicide+rates&tabMod e=dataTable&srchLan=-1&p1=1&p2=1.

Telep, C., & Weisburd, D. (2012). What is known about the effectiveness of police practices in reducing crime and disorder? Police Quarterly, 15(4), 331–357.

Tillyer, M., Engel, R., & Lovins, B. (2012). Beyond Boston: Applying theory to understand and address sustainability issues in focused deterrence initiatives for violence reduction. Crime and Delinquency, 58(6), 973–997.

Two men found dead in Abbotsford. (2009, March 31). CBC News: British Columbia. Retrieved from http://www.cbc.ca/news/canada/british-columbia /story/2009/03/31/bc-abbotsford-shooting-bateman-road.html.

Two men 'in the wrong place at the wrong time' in Surrey slayings: Police. (2007, October 23). CBC News: British Columbia. Retrieved from http://www.cbc.ca /news/canada/british-columbia/story/2007/10/23/bc-homicides.html.

Vancouver police change tactics in gang war. (2009, March 6). CBC News: British Columbia. Retrieved from http://www.cbc.ca/news/canada/british-columbia /story/2009/03/06/bc-vancouver-gang-arrests-sanghera.html.

Victim shot, beaten and bound at Abbotsford grow-op robbery. (2009, January 22). CBC News: British Columbia. Retrieved from http://www.cbc.ca/news/canada /british-columbia/story/2009/01/22/bc-abbotsford-shooting.html.

White, M., Fyfe, J., Campbell, S., & Goldkamp, J. (2003). The police role in preventing homicide: Considering the impact of problem-oriented policing on the prevalence of murder. Journal of Research in Crime and Delinquency, 40(2), 194–225.

Traditions in Basic Police Training Programs

8

An Interview Study among Swedish Police Students

JONAS HANSSON

Contents

Introduction

Police students have assumptions about what kind of knowledge they need to learn during basic training to function well in their future job. These assumptions, which are based on their past experiences, are not always what the police academy provides. Consequently, tensions arise among the police students' expectations of what police work requires, what the police academy provides, and what police work actually entails (Bäck, 2010; Haarr, 2005; Heslop, 2011; Karp & Stenmark, 2011). In this chapter, it is argued that these tensions affect police students' training and learning during basic training.

Although basic police training is a type of vocational education, it has started to become more similar to academia and to develop partnerships with institutions of higher education. Paterson (2011), for example, discusses the trend in the United States, Australia, and parts of Europe in which traditional police training is approaching and interacting with academia. The rationale is that this fusion advances basic police training to enhance, for example, critical thinking among the students. Scholars such as Lee and Punch (2007) and Nikolou-Walker (2010) have emphasized the importance of critical thinking, in addition to the acquisition of knowledge and skills, in vocational education. A further rationale is that police students should receive a schooling that prepares them to continue in an academic career if they so desire. Signs of tensions also exist between the academic nature of higher education and the more practical aspects of police work and training (Alemika, 2009; Bayley & Bittner, 1984; Knutsson, 2010; MacDonald, 1987; Paterson, 2011).

Many, if not all, police forces around the globe have an apprenticeship culture that stresses on-the-job training and instruction for new recruits (Ekman, 1999). It has been argued that this type of learning reproduces existing knowledge, because senior police officers operate within a given framework of culture, which inhibits the learning process of their more junior colleagues (Stenmark, 2005). However, Nikolou-Walker (2010) argues that collaboration between the university and the police authorities as employers results in a level of education that offers flexibility and encourages lifelong learning. Learning new knowledge is emphasized rather than reproduction of existing knowledge. In addition, Holgersson's (2005) research yields a complex view of the various skills required of a police officer. On the other hand, Granér (2004) declares that police culture demands that police action be short, clearly defined, and firm. Therefore, a conclusion to be drawn is that police work is complex and that the need exists for both specific professional skills and a broader, more general knowledge acquired through higher education.

The tensions among the police students' expectations of what police work requires, what the police academy provides, and what police work actually entails and the tension between the academic nature of higher education and practical police work complicate police training. Research has tended to concentrate on teaching rather than learning. Apart from Heslop (2011) and Werth (2011), researchers have paid little attention to the police students' view of learning. This chapter focuses on the situation in one European country, Sweden, where a recent government report (SOU 2008:39, 2008) stipulates that police training should emulate and interact with academia. The purpose of this chapter is to analyze Swedish police students' opinions about the teaching and the lessons that they receive during basic training. This chapter aims to contribute new knowledge about teaching and learning in police training. Kolb's (1984) concept of learning styles—the view that previous experience, as well as interactions with others, is important for the acquisition of new knowledge—is used as a theoretical foundation for this chapter.

Methodology

The main evidence in this chapter was gleaned from narrative interviews. Eight semistructured interviews were conducted with police students at the end of their final semester in the 2-year-long Basic Training Program for Police Officers in Umeå, Sweden. The sampling was based on the participating students' learning style, using a Swedish version of Kolb's Learning Style Inventory (Marke & Cesarec, 2007); thus, two students from each of four learning styles were interviewed, three women and five men. All eight students agreed to participate, and the interviews lasted approximately 1 hour.

The purpose of the analysis was to reach the interviewees' life worlds, using a hermeneutical method inspired by Lindseth and Norberg (2004). This interpretation method was performed in three steps: naive understanding, thematic structural analysis, and comprehensive understanding. Within a few weeks, the recorded interviews were transcribed and the transcriptions were then interpreted in a naive understanding developed from an initial reading. An overall interpretation was made from this initial reading. First, each interview was interpreted separately and then summarized into one naive understanding. Second, keeping in mind the naive understanding, the transcriptions were divided into meaning units consisting of a part of the text that conveys a single meaning. The meaning units associated with learning were condensed into subthemes, which were then divided among main themes. In parallel with this thematic structural analysis, the naive understanding was revised. Finally, the transcriptions were read again in light of the naive understanding, main themes, and subthemes. A summary and reflection were conducted according to the purpose of this chapter. This summary was associated with relevant literature, yielding a comprehensive understanding. Further, this analysis was made with imagination and an open mind to discover new possibilities. The comprehensive understanding is the interviewees' life world, first configured in the interviews; then refigured in the researcher's interpretation; and, finally, interpreted by the reader.

Background

Police training in Umeå, where the empirical data for this chapter were collected, is a 2-year contract training program at the Umeå University in northern Sweden that leads to 6 months of work placement at one of the country's police authorities. The training program is also conducted at the Police College in Sörentorp, Stockholm, and at Linnaeus University, Växjö.

Theoretical Framework for This Chapter

The term experiential learning theory (ELT) (Kolb, 1984), first coined in the early 1970s, defines learning as "the process whereby knowledge is created through the transformation of experience" (p. 38). This approach to learning dates from Aristotle (350 B.C.E.), who wrote, "For the things we have to learn before we can do them, we learn by doing them" (Book 2, p. 1). Inspired by the educational giants John Dewey, Jean Piaget, and Kurt Lewin, Kolb developed four elements in the experiential learning process: concrete experience; reflective observation, when the experience is processed through reflection; abstract conceptualization, when conceptions and theories are assimilated and distilled; and, finally, active experimentation, which tests these conceptions and theories.

While experiential learning is a process of constructing knowledge that involves these phases, these phases also coexist as learning modes. The ELT model demonstrates that knowledge results from a combination of grasping and transforming experience. Grasping is a dialectically related mode between concrete experience and abstract conceptualization, whereas transformation is a dialectically related mode between reflective observation and active experimentation. However, all four elements are present in the process, building a learning cycle, or spiral. In other words, experiencing, reflecting, thinking, and acting provide a learning spiral, with experiencing as the foundation.

Results

What Makes the Teaching Meaningful?

The results show that students experience teaching as meaningful when it concerns matters directly related to their profession. To become motivated to learn, students must feel that the knowledge is useful for them, either because it relates to what they believe is important for police officers to know or because it simply arouses their interest. The instruction might be experiences from field studies, a concrete exercise that provides insight, or a committed teacher who explains what might be in store for them and shares pictures during a lecture. Students experience a sense of meaningfulness when they can see the whole picture and understand the connections between its parts. They gain understanding of why things should be done in a certain way through a learning process that combines theory and practice in exercises, discussions with teachers and fellow students, seminars, and tests.

Throughout the interviews, students reiterated the importance of the instruction's relevance to and usefulness in the police profession:

> We will work with the legal medical officer. It is relevant, and we will work with that. He connected it to our job in a good way (5).

They were aware that they lacked the knowledge to judge what is relevant and that they often used their own feelings to decide what was relevant:

S: Not all of it was relevant, and we did not understand how to use it. We understood better how to use the law.

I: How can you know what is relevant?

S: Well, one doesn't know, really. It's what one got a feeling of, really (7).

Students' feeling of professional relevance was connected to what they thought would be important for doing their job in the future.

If it feels as if it is of relevance or importance for me to do a good job or for the job (2).

Students also gave examples of training that they did not feel was relevant:

I: What features of the training do you think have been the least fun?

S: Difficult question! (Thinks aloud and long) It was probably criminology. It was the first time we started working with something related to police work, but it didn't feel relevant. It was about a lot of statistics of crime and old theories of crime patterns that one doesn't know if they work. It was not relevant somehow.

I: What makes it irrelevant?

S: It's too complicated. It's nothing we can use at work. I remember some of the simpler theories. They probably make sense in some way, but I can hardly remember the names of some of them, and they cannot be used when you are out working. It's probably that, I think.

I: What is the reason why you don't think it's useful for you as a police officer to know why people commit crimes?

S: It's not to do with why people commit crimes? It's statistics. We learned a lot that didn't have to do with why people commit crimes, and besides, they have never been proven to be true. They are old and are like a historical retrospect. Statistics are important in themselves, but the important thing there was how to generate statistics. It's not relevant if you don't work with crime prevention. All police officers do that, I suppose, but not directly (5).

Along with the feelings they developed in field studies and exercises, what police instructors told students influenced their conceptions of what is relevant to the profession. Concrete and clear examples providing a picture of what to expect in practical police work gave students an understanding of what the profession requires. The students identified elements in the training that were not sufficiently concrete to be conceived of as being relevant to the profession. Students understood intellectually that these elements had a connection to the profession, but the connection was too abstract to be thought of as important.

What Is Required for the Students to Understand That the Teaching Is Relevant to the Profession?

The students revealed that they learn best when they understand the purpose of the instruction and, thus, become interested in it. Their interest is strong when the lesson contains a concrete element.

> After an exercise that one failed to manage, interest is aroused in learning. One understands why and what one has to read and learn to cope with the job out there (3).

An emotionally affective exercise or lesson can create interest.

> He raised a question! Now we get to the core. A question I want an answer to: "Why is it like this?" That's it! A question I want an answer to. Interest is aroused. The lecturer gives me a purpose for being interested (6).

In some cases, a police instructor who describes a concrete situation makes the lesson meaningful and interesting. Skilled and committed teachers can also arouse students' interest.

> It's the enthusiasm, commitment, and interest in knowing one's subject and the will to communicate what they should do (8).

Narratives that create a clear picture of what the students can expect as professionals keep their interest.

> I've never been at a school where I've learned so much. It's because it was interesting, and we've taken it in and done our best. The teachers were high quality, and they tried to arouse interest. Many of them have been police officers and can give concrete examples, and then one feels the importance of learning (7).

The students' own interests and expectations influence their willingness to learn. "The basic interest made it fun," and when the instruction is fun the students find that they learn a lot (1).

> You sift on the basis of what you imagine. What is important and unimportant? Then it's also got a lot to do with your interest. I would like to work as a point duty police officer, which makes me more interested and focused on that. The interest makes it easier to learn (5).

Discussion

Expectations

This chapter explains a relationship between students' expectations of police training and what police training actually offers. In a parallel relationship between students' expectations of what they need to be professional police officers and how they learn to practice the profession, the students' expectations lead to feelings about what is relevant for them to learn. In a study of police students, Lauritz (2009) describes how the students create an identity in different social groupings until their identity gradually becomes "I am a police officer." The police students' search for a professional identity might create their need to find professional relevance in their education. Karp and Stenmark (2011) think that police students tend to prefer listening to a teacher with a police background than to a teacher without this background. Although the findings of this chapter are certainly true, the students' preference is created by their sense that a lesson is meaningful to becoming a police officer. The results show that they like listening to both police officers and civilian professionals connected to the police, such as a lawyer who has worked as a prosecutor or a medicolegal expert who discusses what a police officer might face. It is difficult to say whether this sense of meaning is created by the authority of a police officer, prosecutor, or medicolegal expert or by the concrete examples they give. The surveyed students repeatedly stated that instruction has to be concrete to be meaningful.

Meaningfulness

The question arises whether meaningfulness is simply a matter of understanding all the situations one confronts. As stated earlier, Kolb (1984) thinks, "Learning is the process whereby knowledge is created through the transformation of experience" (p. 38). In other words, to learn people use their previous experience to create new knowledge. Therefore, police students use their previous experiences in their endeavor to learn the profession. Their experience, or preunderstanding, gives them a feeling of what is meaningful in learning to be a police officer. My interpretation is that the meaningfulness derives from the students' way of understanding and interpreting their world. In addition, Johnson, Young, Foster, and Shamblen (2006) found that usefulness is the single most important factor in learning, even if other factors are influential. I interpret the circular process, which, according to Kolb's theory of experiential learning (1984), consists of concrete experience, reflecting observation, abstract theory formation, and active experimentation, as the whole picture that the students describe as essential for learning.

Granberg and Ohlsson (2009) describe a loop instead of a circle; this symbolism points to the fact that the learner does not return to the same point. New knowledge is created in this process, which constantly goes on in and out of formal educational settings.

The whole of effective learning described by students consists of both theoretical and practical elements, and in both types of learning students stress the need for something concrete to relate to in discussions, theoretical knowledge, and exercises. Kolb and Kolb (2005) think that while knowledge is created out of experiences, not all experiences create knowledge. Drawing on the work of Dewey, the authors postulate that context also influences learning. They describe nine learning spaces that are productive in the creation of learning, including basing the teaching on the learner's experience of the subject even if the student has no prior knowledge of the subject. The crucial lesson from this theory is that teachers cannot erase students' preconceptions with only persuasive explanation.

The students in this chapter related that they learned from both concrete examples and teaching that appealed to their prior experience of the subject. On the one hand, they discussed bad examples of lessons they felt were irrelevant and, on the other hand, they described examples of good teaching, such as an instructor who sparked and maintained their interest in a subject. It is difficult to discern whether this interest was related to the students' previous experiences or a concrete example. Zimbardo (2005) thinks that, among other things, teaching should be memorable and relevant. Students experience that the teaching is relevant to them on a personal level, which creates interest. A student remembers what is interesting, which, in turn, makes the teaching memorable.

> Education is not preparation for life; education is life itself (Dewey, 1897/2003).

Dewey (1916/1999) thinks that to be meaningful education needs to relate to the larger society outside school, and combined with social activity meaningful education enables the individual to handle both freedom and responsibility. Kolb and Kolb emphasize that learning proceeds from internal motivations and the learner's own interests; accordingly, several participants in this chapter described their own interests as an important factor in learning. Jang, Reeve, and Deci (2010) show that teachers can positively influence students' commitment by both supporting autonomy and providing structure. In this vein, one survey participant described the teachers' follow-up of their work as a good learning tool. A negative finding of this chapter revealed that students' commitment tended to decrease during this period of education. Toward the end of the program, discussions were not as lively and did not reflect as many different perspectives as in the beginning. These phenomena might indicate that the learning environment's support of autonomy and structure adversely influences students' motivation to learn. Another explanation is that the students are being influenced by a strong, male-dominated police culture. According to Stenmark (2005), learning within a police force often reproduces the existing culture because of the apprentice model and teachers who work within the given framework of the culture.

It is impossible to say if this group of study participants is in any way representative of police students. Although they represented all four learning styles, police students seem to be characterized mainly as accommodating, meaning that they learn primarily through acting and feeling. This distorted sample could be resolved with more theoretical and reflective interviewees, which might require additional interviews to be conducted to further validate the findings.

Implications

The results show that the most important factors that influence learning are concrete examples and a sense of professional relevance. These elements guide students to the larger picture through concrete experience, reflective observation, abstract conceptualization, and active experimentation that combines practical and theoretical elements. This process results in an understanding of why the knowledge is important. The challenge in police training and higher education is to create a sense of professional relevance while expanding students' knowledge.

Acknowledgments

This chapter has been supported by the Director of the Basic Training Program for Police Officers at Umeå University Dr. Lars-Erik Lauritz. The author also appreciates the support and tutorial from Associate Professor Kent Lofgren and Lecturer Mats Klingvall. Most importantly, the author extends his sincere appreciation to the police students who so truthfully and generously gave accounts of their experience.

References

Alemika, E. E. O. (2009). Police practice and police research in Africa. *Police Practice and Research: An International Journal, 10*(5–6), 483–502.

Aristotle. (350 B.C.E.). *Nicomachean Ethics.* Book 2, p. 1. Retrieved July 30, 2014 from http://classics.mit.edu/Aristotle/nicomachaen.html.

Bäck, T. (2010). *Från student till yrkesverksam polis—mental träning i polisutbildningen och polisyrket: Polisstudenters och yrkesverksamma polisers upplevda kompetens i mental träning.* [From student to professional police—mental training in police training and police work: police students and professionals policemen perceived competence in mental training. Unpublished licentiate dissertation.] Umea, Sweden: Umeå University, Department of Education.

Bayley, D. H., & Bittner, E. (1984). Discretion in law enforcement. *Law and Contemporary Problems, 47*(4), 35–59.

Dewey, J. (1897/2003). My pedagogic creed. In T. Kroksmark (Ed.), *Den tidlösa pedagogiken.* [The timeless pedagogy.] Lund, Sweden: Studentlitteratur.

Dewey, J. (1916/1999). *Demokrati och utbildning.* [Democracy and Education.] Gothenburg, Sweden: Daidalos.

Ekman, G. (1999). *Från text till batong: Om poliser, busar och svennar.* [From text to baton: Police officers, crooks, and the layman. Unpublished doctoral dissertation.] Stockholm, Sweden: Stockholm School of Economics.

Granberg, O., & Ohlsson, J. (2009). *Från lärandets loopar till lärande organisationer.* [From learning loops into learning organizations.] Lund, Sweden: Studentlitteratur.

Granér, R. (2004). *Patrullerande polisers yrkeskultur.* [Patrolling police officers professional culture Unpublished doctoral dissertation.] Lund, Sweden: Lund School of Social Work.

Haarr, R. N. (2005). Factors affecting the decision of police recruits to "drop out" of police work. *Police Quarterly, 8*(4), 431–453.

Heslop, R. (2011). Reproducing police culture in a British university: Findings from an exploratory case study of police foundation degrees. *Police Practice and Research: An International Journal, 12*(4), 298–312.

Holgersson, S. (2005). *Yrke: Polis.* (en omarbetad populärutgåva av doktorsavhandlingen med samma namn). [Profession: Police. (A revised popular edition of the doctoral dissertation with the same name).] Stockholm, Sweden: GLM Reklam.

Jang, H., Reeve, J., & Deci, E. L. (2010). Engaging students in learning activities: It is not autonomy support or structure but autonomy support and structure. *Journal of Educational Psychology, 102*(3), 588–600.

Johnson, K., Young, L., Foster, J. P., & Shamblen, S. R. (2006). Law enforcement training in Southeast Asia: A theory-driven evaluation. *Police Practice and Research: An International Journal, 7*(3), 195–215.

Karp, S, & Stenmark, H. (2011). Learning to be a police officer. Tradition and change in the training and professional lives of police officers. *Police Practice and Research, 12*(1), 4–15.

Knutsson, J. (2010). Nordic reflections on the dialogue of the deaf. *Police Practice and Research: An International Journal, 11*(2), 132–134.

Kolb, A. Y., & Kolb D. A. (2005). Learning styles and learning spaces: Enhancing experiential learning in higher education. *Academy of Management Learning & Education, 4*(2), 193–212.

Kolb, D. A. (1984). *Experiential learning: Experience as the source of learning and development.* New Jersey: Prentice Hall.

Lauritz, L. E. (2009). *Spirande polisidentiteter: En studie av polisstudenters och nya polisers professionella identitet.* [Growing police identities: A study of police students and new police officers, professional identities. Unpublished doctoral dissertation.] Umeå, Sweden: Umea School of Business and Economics.

Lee, M., & Punch, M. (2007). Policing by degrees—police officers' experience of university education. *Policing and Society, 14*(3), 233–249.

Lindseth, A., & Norberg, A. (2004). A phenomenological hermeneutical method for researching lived experience. *Scandinavian Journal of Caring Science, 18*(2), 145–153.

Marke, S., & Cesarec, Z. (2007). *Erfarenhetsinlärning och lärstilar.* [An analysis and standardization of Kolb's learning style inventory from a Swedish perspective, with an English summary.] Stockholm, Sweden: SIS.

MacDonald, B. (1987). *Research and action in the context of policing—an analysis of the problem and a programme proposal.* Norwich, England: Police Foundation. Retrieved October 10, 2011 from https://ueaeprints.uea.ac.uk/26812/.

Nikolou-Walker, E. (2010). Vocational training in higher education: A case study of work based learning within the Police Service of Northern Ireland (PSNI). *Research in Post Compulsory Education, 12*(3), 357–376.

Paterson, C. (2011). Adding value? A review of the international literature on the role of higher education in police training and education. *Police Practice and Research: An International Journal, 12*(1), 286–297.

SOU 2008:39. (2008). *Future police training: Official report of the Swedish government.* Stockholm, Sweden: Department of Justice.

Stenmark, H. (2005). *Polisens organisationskultur: En explorativ studie.* [The organizational culture in the Swedish police: An explorative study. Unpublished doctoral dissertation.] Umea, Sweden: Umeå University, Department of Education.

Werth, E. P. (2011). Scenario training in police academies: Developing students' higher-level thinking skills. *Police Practice and Research: An International Journal, 12*(4), 325–340.

Zimbardo, P. G. (2005). Optimizing the power and magic of teaching. *Journal of Social and Clinical Psychology, 24*(1), 11–21.

Opportunities and Challenges of Research Collaboration between Police Authorities and University Organizations

9

JOHAN BERTILSSON, PETER FREDRIKSSON,
LARS-FOLKE PILEDAHL, MANS MAGNUSSON,
AND PER-ANDERS FRANSSON

Contents

Background

In a recent poll performed in 2011 by 15 European countries as well as the United States, Brazil, Colombia, and India, the Swedish police was ranked number 1 in public trust with 89% satisfaction (GfK Trust Index, 2011). However, when the question in a Swedish poll was rephrased to asking about whether Swedish citizens associate certain professions with high competence, then the police profession was associated with high competence by only 62% of the population (Holmberg & Weibull, 2012). In comparison, 79% of the public associate physicians with high competence and 74% associate researchers in general with high competence (Holmberg & Weibull, 2012). Hence, there seems to be a discrepancy between trust in the police officers and in the competence of the policing work done. This is troublesome from the perspective that being trusted by the society, both as an organization and for providing competent work, is essential for the police authorities' ability to function, for example, by making people inclined to report crimes and testify.

Furthermore, the present technical development if applied wrongly may pose new risks to distance the police from the society. For example, if the presence of police patrols (on foot and in vehicles) on the streets are replaced with modern more cost-efficient camera surveillance, the police may seem to have abandoned the area and the role of policing henceforth to have changed from crime prevention to a reactive role of acting first when a crime has been committed (Alemika, 2009). Thus, one way of increasing public trust and rationalizing new policing techniques to the public might be through information displaying that changes implemented are systematically based on scientific research, similar to how the medical health care system is expected to continuously improve their performance and competence to treat health issues through research.

However, one problem is that the efficiency of policing, in the view of the public, may not be properly reflected by official crime statistics and quantitative measures of interventions, such as by the number of speeding tickets issued or by the number of road-side alcohol tests performed. Effective policing is also about ensuring public confidence and security at home, at work, and when driving through unknown neighborhoods. Thus, an essential but difficult task is to determine the most effective policy to distribute, often strictly, limited resources between crime prevention and law enforcement. However, it is not a simple task to document the effectiveness of the policing performed in all its aspects and to transform this information into a format that can be used to motivate within the organization as well as to politicians and journalists that allocated resources has been appropriately used. Moreover, the public may still feel unsafe even if the real risks are small (Eberhard, 2006). Here, scientific research studies might give the objective support to pursue policing projects with long-term goals, which concomitantly increase the trust among the public.

Challenges for Establishing Research Cooperation between Police Authorities and the University System

Collaboration between police authorities and universities can provide a base for mutual exchange of recent scientific discoveries and instigate new research projects within the areas of special relevance for law enforcement and society. Concomitantly, such cooperation provides opportunities for law enforcement personnel to gain experience in general scientific methods and procedures. This is of increasing importance in a knowledge-based society. For example, based on firsthand experience, the police are particularly well suited to define problems that need attention from different scientific, social, and legal perspectives. Universities, on the other hand, are experienced in effectuating research projects aimed to create the solutions required, training new students in the process. Scientific research training will also educate police officers in how to perform evaluations when presented with reports and novel scientific studies, and thus, how to detect possible flaws and shortcomings before implementation. However, the awareness that this opportunity for productive collaboration exists might be low within both organizations.

A precondition for a research cooperation between police authorities and the university system is that police authorities may have limited opportunities to perform changes and update methods because "...policing is an institution fundamentally framed by the law" (Thacher, 2001; Neyroud, 2009, p. 30) and directives from the national government and "...therefore, there is a need to build the 'legal knowledge' of policing as well as develop the social science research base" (Thacher, 2001; Neyroud, 2009, p. 30). Hence, the definition of good policing and law enforcement is strongly associated with how we define the society that we would like to live in.

Establishing Research Collaboration between People from Different Educational Backgrounds and Expertise

A review of the literature reveals that police–academic relationships often have been affected by mutual misunderstandings that have had negative effects on the attempts to establish research collaborations. From the police authorities' side, part of this mistrust might come from publications made by academic researchers acknowledging the "critical research traditions" as superior, which "...prides itself on its detachment and independence from the police as subject matter, and, almost always, manages to find fault with rather than celebrate the role and activities of the public police" (Bradley & Nixon, 2009, p. 13). On the other hand, some academics fear that research from close collaborations might not be objective. Some critics have even suggested that the approach "evidence-based policy"—" ... has, instead, tended to work the

other way around—'policy-based evidence-making' or creating the supporting case after the policy has already been determined" (Neyroud, 2009, p. 29).

Another major obstacle can be that when groups with different kinds of
education, background, and knowledge are to collaborate, there needs to be
an exchange of knowledge between all parties involved before a collaborative
research project can be properly designed. Thus, one must acknowledge that in
collaborations, different people contribute with different pieces in the knowledge
puzzle. In the literature, one has especially acknowledged that the practitioner's
knowledge and experience has not been rated as highly as it should be to ensure
successful scientific research. A new approach has therefore been advocated that
"...recognizes that practitioners, through engagement with their everyday world,
learn solutions to the problems they face, and build up tactic knowledge, based
on deep learning involving many cases. If evidence-based research is to help
improve practices, the nature of those practices must be understood from the
point of view of practitioners themselves" (Bradley & Nixon, 2009, p. 22). Hence,
one should respect knowledge gained from years of experience of multicomplex
situations and recognize that such knowledge sometimes cannot be easily, or at
all, transferred into simplified statistical form (Gladwell, 2005).

Relevancy of the Research

The knowledge about what kind of topics that merit scientific research studies and why changes of the present policies and procedures might enhance
productivity and cost-efficiency is often restricted to the group of people
working with the tasks (Hackman & Oldham, 1980). Thus, one challenge
for establishing fruitful research collaborations is to find relevant research
projects and the people within the organization that have the required expert
knowledge. Another challenge can be the process of exchanging knowledge
between collaborative partners through a mutual learning process, acknowledging and considering the collaborative partner's expertise in their respective areas. Only thereafter can one design the research project with its steps
of setting relevant aims, design how to carry out the research using the correct procedures, determine the required objective information to collect, and
determine how to draw the correct conclusions from the findings.

Occasionally, information presented as research is actually a description of
how things already work in practice. To describe how other police forces around
the world work is an essential task. However, equally important is that those
who write such reports already from the start have in mind the target group for
whom the report is written, for example, other academics, police administrator,
or practitioners, so the presentation and relevance are kept clear for the target
readership. Moreover, the label "research" should be used with caution and only
be denoted on information obtained from a valid scientific research process,

that is, one should make a clear difference between papers that are opinions and normative from papers that contain substantiated and descriptive knowledge (Wong, 2009). Moreover, research papers should also contain novel information of relevance about the research subject and contribute with a relevant advancement in knowledge compared with prior publications (Wong, 2009).

Complexity of the Research Subjects

Scientific research requires that a number of conditions are fulfilled. For example,

- One needs to have access to all data parameters required for accurately describing the process (e.g., efficiency of the policing).
- The research data must be accurate and objective.
- The evaluation process of the data should be neither limited to nor require certain sets of findings to be made.
- The reports presenting the research findings should be an objective and unbiased transcription of all findings made, including both findings regarded as negative and positive. Research evidencing that policies are working fine is equally important as research evidencing that policies do not work properly or as intended.

All these requirements may be difficult to fulfill for police research and especially so for large-scale studies of the effectiveness of policing policies to reduce and prevent criminality. This may be one reason why formal scientific research has played a smaller role in policing and criminal justice, "…since this is an area of social science study in which it is more difficult, than in medicine, to draw tight conclusions and provide 'hard evidence'…" (Neyroud, 2009, p. 30).

One major problem is that the policing work done is very difficult to define and assess, even if one knows how many police officers were assigned to the area and know what they were scheduled to do (Manning, 2009). A number of factors, from individual police officer level to local and government organization level, influence the policing done, for example, police education, experience, motivation, patrolling on foot or in a car, legal framework, and judicial system (Holgersson, 2005). The police organization may itself provide incentives influencing efficiency through positive or negative feedback. Positive feedback can be to notice and commend efforts, chance for promotion or increased salary, increased respect among colleagues, and offer a chance to join elite units. Negative feedback can include compulsory duties to do extensive paper work after each policing action (Holgersson, 2005).

Another major problem for scientific studies is to objectively define and determine the criminality in the region investigated. For example, there might be large discrepancies between the number of crimes done and the number reported to the police. Moreover, when describing and rating the criminality, one may have to consider if all kinds of crimes should be rated as of the same severity for the society or if some kind of severity ranking system should be applied. Furthermore, there might be large international discrepancies between what is regarded as a crime.

After the official crime rate statistics have been collected, a difficult task is to determine how to correctly interpret the data. For example, do a low number of reported crimes mean that the policing are efficient or that the policing are so poor so that the citizens no longer care to report crimes to the police? Hence, poor specificity, objectivity, and accuracy in what reported crime rates actually represent can be a major issue when evaluating crime statistics and, thus, effectiveness of police organization and used policing policies. Moreover, proactive policing, such as surveillance of the area by foot patrolling, might be difficult to motivate to administrators if it does not add any documented value in the official crime statistics in the same way as reactive policing actions. Hence, to properly interpret official crime statistics, one may need to add complementing parameters and use more advanced analysis methods, so the data is analyzed in its correct context. Here, collaborations with university institutions, skilled in advanced statistical and mathematical analyses, might present new opportunities to study the more complex aspects of using different organizational structures and different policing policies, for example, effect of duration of applied policy.

Funding Opportunities

The last two decades, the police have received increasing academic attention in the United States, the United Kingdom, and Australia. However, it is important that the governments, donors of grant, and research institutions are aware of the nature of this research, for example, that a new policing policy may have to be applied for many years before its true effectiveness can be determined through scientific studies. Hence, for studies of the more difficult issues of policing, such as the long-term effects of applying different policing policies, the funds need to match the research tasks given, both in size and in sustainability. Moreover, some of the most interesting developments and challenges of applying different policing policies can presently be studied in various African and Latin American countries (Alemika, 2009; Fruhling, 2009). Thus, it can be advocated that international funding should more frequently be made available to study policing wherever in the world it may be scientifically motivated to do so.

Police Policy Changes Due to Research Findings

Despite the already large volumes of policing research and the police openness to research policies, strategies, and tactics, police research has had difficulties leading to widespread operational changes even when the research finding has been accepted as true (Bayley, 1998; Knutsson, 2004). Thus, to diffuse research findings into policing policy changes, it may not be sufficient to evidence relevant enhancements from an academic perspective. The research findings and its beneficial effects if applied may also have to be expressed using practical application and relevance as a descriptive framework, for example, enhanced cost-efficiency, less paperwork, and better safety for the police and the public (Roman et al., 2008). Thus, the presentation should be made so that all levels in the police organization, from practitioners and senior officers to police leaders, can see a positive value from their own perspective of applying a proposed change.

Research reports can often be summarized into a list of conclusions, essentially expressing—"This works"/"This does not work." However, a research report with its final conclusions only represents a fraction of the knowledge actually obtained during a research process. Hence, of major relevance is also to pass on interrelated knowledge obtained from the research process itself so that one can give scientific support to answer follow-up questions normal to ask, such as "why"/"why not." Hence, for knowledge to survive the scrutiny of decision makers, practitioners, politicians, and media resulting in the application of new policing policies, it may be beneficial if the motivations for "why" one wants to apply a change from a scientific research perspective are generally known within the organization.

Benefits from Establishing Research Cooperation

Technical Equipment Development

The police authorities and university researchers may have common interests to promote development of new technical devices, assessment and analysis techniques, which both have applications within law enforcement and as a vehicle to enhance scientific studies. Two of the new technologies that have found a wide array of applications within both agencies are DNA testing and better chemical classification of substance composition. Furthermore, new software applications have been developed for existing techniques so that it can be applied for policing and as an evidence provider, such as Global Positioning System (GPS) or transmission area position tracking of mobile phones and mobile data systems for frontline officers. In addition, better cameras, hardware, and software for graphical analyses have led to techniques such as automatic fingerprint reading, face recognition tools, and automatic number plate reading. However, research validating the cost-efficiency and investigating the best policies how to apply these new techniques is often lacking. For example, the effectiveness of using DNA testing in criminal investigations has not been subjected to proper scientific evaluation other than in the United States (Roman et al., 2008).

One example from our research group of how a device developed for policing can be used for medical research is our application of the portable alcohol breath analyzer system Evidenzer™ (Nanopuls AB, Uppsala, Sweden). The Scandinavian countries have one of the toughest regulations in the world regarding drinking and driving, and breath analyzers have for many years been used as a roadside screening tool by law enforcers around the world. However, none of the common commercially available breath analyzer systems up to now are exact enough to provide admissible evidence of alcohol intoxication. To address this and other problems, the portable Evidenzer system was developed. The analysis methodology used by the equipment is based on a new infrared light (IR) technique where the ethanol level is determined from the absorption of IR at several wavelengths (Fransson et al., 2005). The analysis results from the system are regarded as admissible evidence of alcohol intoxication of the same reliability as blood sample analyses by Swedish courts.

However, the Evidenzer system has also found applications as a vehicle enhancing scientific medical research. For clinical and scientific reasons, including determining valid legislation limits for drunk driving, it is vital to objectively determine how human physiological and psychological responses are affected by alcohol intoxication at various blood alcohol concentration (BAC) levels. However, a large limitation in older research studies has been that true BAC levels at that time could only be determined exactly in retrospect by laboratory analyses of blood samples. The magnitude of this problem has been illustrated by Nieschalk et al. (1999), showing that when 30 subjects were given the same amount of alcohol, the BAC ranged in the test group from 0.022% to 0.159% 30 minutes after the alcohol consumption. The development of the Evidenzer system means that the BAC level now can be monitored in real time, ensuring that all subjects in research groups are submitted to scientific investigations exactly at intended BAC levels. Hence, the physiological and psychological effects of alcohol intoxication at different BAC levels can be determined scientifically much more accurately and objectively, because new equipment allows stricter study designs (Fransson et al., 2010; Modig et al., 2012).

In addition, new technologies suitable for roadside testing of drug abuse while driving using breath analysis techniques are also under development. Presently, a breath analyzer system is under development in Sweden, which is able to detect substances such as amphetamine, methamphetamine, cannabis, cocaine, methadone, 6-acetylmorphine, and benzodiazepines in exhaled air (Beck et al., 2010).

Evaluation of Policing Policies and Police Organization

An efficient police service is a vital part of upholding a civilized society. A sudden loss of effective policing in larger communities may cause the society to deteriorate fast into political and economic disarray with subsequent fear and poor life quality among the citizens. The same is true when criminal constellations overtake local areas. However, can the police become too effective and powerful? This may be a more common fear in nondemocratic countries and in countries who just recently returned to a democratic rule, where the police policies previously gave higher priority to protect the government of nondemocratic rulers than to protect the country's citizens from criminality and violations of human rights (Alemika, 2009; Fruhling, 2009). One way to prevent this might be to make sure that the police officers have a firm personal motivation to uphold proper policing under mutual respectful cooperation with the citizens in the area they are responsible for. Another approach encompasses structural reorganization of the police agencies through regional decentralization into largely sovereign police authorities, individually responsible to act within the regulations set by the national legislation (Fruhling, 2009), thus, if breaches from legal protocol are made by the central command or by a regional police authority, then this may not necessarily affect the nation's entire police organization but can be contained. Other reforms undertaken by Latin American police forces are demilitarization of the police and strengthening of internal accountability mechanisms, which play a key role in preventing and controlling abuse (Fruhling, 2009).

However, there are also risks with letting the police become too weak/ineffective, allowing criminal structures to take over turf and scare local residents into silence. At first, in the official crime rate statistics, this may appear as though the area has reduced criminality (Holgersson, 2005). Subsequently, policing activity may be reduced for economic reasons or redirected to enforce other districts elsewhere with more apparent problems. In the absence of a present and active police, criminal gangs and organizations might silently establish or grow stronger. First when rivaling gangs start to fight openly for control over the area or the criminality spreads into new areas might the true magnitude of the problems be revealed to outside officials. This kind of weak policing spots might also be present in countries with generally good policing, but where there exist "hot spot" areas with weaker police presence or where the police forces available or policing efficiency does not match the criminality. That official crime rate statistics may not give proper reflection of the criminality in an area is a substantial problem for policing administrators and researchers, especially for those working at the national level without direct access to other firsthand information sources such as the local police and social workers working at the local level (Manning, 2009). For example, 61% of the assault victims that attended the emergency department at the Stockholm South General Hospital (Södersjukhuset), Sweden, during 2007 did not intend to report the assault to the police, compared to 40% in 2000 (Carlsson-Sanz, 2000, 2008). Hence, one possible collaborative research area might be to investigate the limitations of officially reported crime statistics and whether crime statistics in combination with information from other governmental and community sources, such as the health-care sector and the local social service sector, might better reflect the requirements of specific policing services in the respective areas.

Security and safety is one of our human basic needs to be able to prosper and we will look for it wherever we can find it. If the local police are too weak, the security gap may be filled with something else. Thus, young people living in socially disadvantaged areas may join criminal gangs just in a mere search for safety, if the local police are not strong and efficient enough as well as helpful, reliable, and supportive. In some African countries, especially in Nigeria, South Africa, Uganda, Tanzania, and Kenya, this problem has been addressed by forming informal community-based policing structures (Alemika, 2009). Many of these groups enjoy community support as well as financial assistance from the state and local governments (Alemika, 2009). Although there are several strengths with this approach, there are also severe weaknesses in that these informal structures may themselves evolve into criminal organizations or become political instruments used for oppressing opponents (Alemika, 2009). Thus, a healthy society needs not only a strong sovereign police authority but also a democratic political control system that ensures that the nation's laws, police, and other legal authorities share the majority of the citizens ethical outlook on the world and that they protect their citizens from unlawful treatment from criminals and of course from the upholders of the law itself.

The long-term stability of any community or state demand that the citizens to a large degree feel that the police are on their side and are effective in executing tasks within a law that the citizens, including the police (Granér, 2004), also agree are fair and just. Such trust for the police must be earned. However, with wearing a uniform comes that trust largely is earned—and lost—as a group. The individuality is lost and replaced with one single identity—a police officer, that is, "he did it" is replaced by "the police did it." Thus, it is of outmost importance that corruption and abuse among the police and in the legal system is addressed fast, before it is allowed to spread further in the police and governmental organizations. Hence, it is of outmost importance that a nation have a firm internal accountability mechanisms with moral strength, sovereignty, and legal power enough to control and prevent abuse at whichever level it may arise within the police, politics, and governmental institutions (Fruhling, 2009). A firm sovereign internal accountability mechanism might also be needed within the police organization, for example, striving to develop an efficient and supporting administration.

Research-Supported Development of Police Tactics

Even without the effects of a sympathetic stress response, we have physiological limitations including minimum time to perceive, locate, identify, define, decide, and react to different possible problems or threats. Observations made by mainly police officers and military all over the world for more than the last century repeatedly confirms that our perception, cognitive and motor skill abilities are affected and changed depending on the strength of the sympathetic stress response. To some extent the research within the field, analyzing in detail real-life incidents, has been performed out of a general scientific interest in how human skills and behavior can change under extreme circumstances. Another important driving factor has been that repeatedly, in history and at various places around the world, police officers and others have been forced to handle extensive amounts of threatening and violent incidents (Fairbairn & Sykes, 1942; Grossman, 1995). This has initiated research in new police tactics and methods of training to prepare people for these situations. In Shanghai's international settlement in the early twentieth century, with about 2000 police officers and 1 million inhabitants, there were several police officers killed every year (nine were killed in 1919). Therefore, in 1910, the police officer and instructor W. E. Fairbairn started groundbreaking work to address this problem. He participated in as many dangerous assignments as possible, made forensic analyses of scenes of shootings, and interviewed the survivors thoroughly.

When he was questioned by his superiors about what was wrong with their officers after the large losses of police officers in 1919, he was able to show that it was the education of the police officers that was flawed. He was then allowed to change the education and police tactics according to the hard-earned experiences many police officers made during terrible conditions for several years. Soon after, the losses of police officer lives were reduced by more than 50%. Fairbairn's work displays how one can map the effects of police tactics by determining patterns in the actions made in real-life incidents. He was also able to show large differences between how the police officers were expected to react to specific threatening situations and how they actually did react in the real-life incidents (Fairbairn & Sykes, 1942; Cassidy, 1993; Siddle, 1995). Fairbairn and Sykes research procedures, of starting with systematic gathering of vital information and then based on this information propose changes, resemble the processes used for developing the health care and life sciences during the twentieth century.

However, when the firsthand experiences from real-life situations becomes scarce after long period of peace and low crime rates, speculations and myths can replace the knowledge obtained from firsthand experiences. Instead, experiences made from sports and competitions incorporating fighting activities start to influence choices of techniques and tactics used by police and military. Movies have also problematically directly or indirectly influenced the choice of equipment, tactics, and techniques (Grossman, 1995; Grossman & Christensen, 2004). These problems are best countered by continuous, systematic, scientific in-detail investigations and research documentation of hard-earned real-life experiences, which show what actually takes place and objectively display how well different police tactics and techniques actually work in real-life situations. Scientific methods and interdisciplinary screening contribute further in that they give much better understanding about how and why situations and human reactions and behaviors appear to be what they are. The greater our knowledge and understanding of underlying factors, such as the basic functions, strengths, and limitations of our human neurology and physiology, the better we can adapt police tactics, methods of education, training, and equipment for the real-world events, to maintain and enhance the trust given to the police by the community.

Police Training and Police Equipment Development

Occasionally, police officers may be exposed to life-threatening situations as part of their occupation. Often, however, the training of police officers emphasizes the physical and technical aspects, whereas the psychological side is largely neglected (Oudejans, 2008). Although the problems associated with psychological stress are well-known among those working professionally with this issue, it is still a subject surrounded by a large amount of taboo in many professions and feelings of guilt and shame for not performing as well when it really mattered (Paton & Violanti, 2008). Nonetheless, even highly trained athletes, SWAT team members, and experienced soldiers suffer deteriorated performance due to psychological stress if the threat stimulus is sudden, potentially catastrophic, or unfamiliar to them (Meyerhoff et al., 2004; Murray, 2004). Recently published studies have shown that there are a number of opportunities to preemptively address the risk and consequences of psychological stress, which could be valuable in saving lives or preventing serious events from occurring. By using custom-made realistic training, those trained will be allowed to repeatedly sense the feelings of psychological stress and become familiar to its physical and psychological effects. From these experiences, the individual may learn to handle their task more effectively because practicing with anxiety can prevent choking in perceptual motor performance through acclimatization to the specific processes accompanying anxiety (Oudejans & Nieuwenhuys, 2009).

Typically, psychological stress that increases pulse rates above 115 beats per minute (BPM) causes degraded fine motor control (Siddle, 1995; Oudejans, 2008). Furthermore, stronger stress activation to pulse rates above 145 BPM has been shown to cause degraded ability to perform complex motor control (Siddle, 1995). Under very strong stress activation, the cognitive and physical performance degrades, resulting in hypervigilance, freezing, or ability to perform only very simple cognitive tasks and gross motor skills (Siddle, 1995; Grossman & Christensen, 2004; Vonk, 2008). Hence, the performance deficits caused by psychological stress may render people unable to use equipment requiring certain fine motor skills or complex motor control (Oudejans & Nieuwenhuys, 2009).

Our own experience concerning effects of enhanced psychological stress on motor skill and cognitive performance is that already during training can the performance become affected depending on the complexity of the task. Even individuals who are well trained and considered very skilled in handling their equipment suffer from the effects and can perform very poorly. For example, officers trying to use their pepper spray under high stress had severe problems putting their thumb under the protective lid using extension and abduction (fine motor skill). Thus, research projects are motivated to investigate the design of equipment used by professions where psychological stress may occur, so it is suitable for handling under severe psychological stress and under the physical repercussions associated with this state.

Research Cooperation to Define Criminality and Update Legislations

An active research policy within law enforcement institutions may not only be supportive to the work of police authorities but also have an equally important role in keeping the nation's legislation updated with the nation's technical, economic, political, and social development. That laws are a product of the societal conditions and state of technical development at a certain time is "The Locomotive Acts (or Red Flag Acts)" an illustrative example of.

The "Locomotive Acts" were a series of Acts of Parliament in the United Kingdom to control the use of mechanically propelled vehicles on British public highways during the latter part of the nineteenth century. The 1865 act required all road locomotives, which included automobiles, to travel at a maximum of 4 mph (6 km/h) in the country and 2 mph (3 km/h) in towns and have a crew of three—one of whom should carry a red flag walking 60 yd (55 m) ahead of each vehicle.

We may regard such laws as bizarre today. However, more importantly, how would our society have developed if such a law, found appropriate at that time, were still in effect today? What are the risks with having policing and law enforcement policies being guided by court verdicts deemed as of principal importance for future verdicts in that legislative area for decades, because they were at that point of time found reasonable and relevant? With the present fast development of the society, only after a few years, verdicts may no longer be in agreement with new knowledge, scientific research, and the demands set by enhanced complexity of the society. Thus, a successful dynamic development of policing policies that encompass new knowledge, may be strongly intertwined with that modernizations of the legal systems, is not hindered by traditions and bureaucratic procedures. Hence, there should be an understanding and willingness among legislators and politicians to adjust the legal system procedures and laws in line with new knowledge obtained and social, economic, and technical developments of the society.

Continuous cooperation between researchers from various fields, legislators, and politicians might be essential to provide a framework for defining whether actions and/or its consequences oppose the best interest for the country and its citizens. It is equally important that researchers and legislators monitor the long-term effects of applied laws so that they are applied as intended, have the effect intended, and do not prohibit the development and modernization of the society. In many cases, the knowledge required in making relevant and effective legislations for complex technical, economical, and medical issues is restricted to the group of professionals executing these professions or tasks. However, this may also suggest that regular police officers will not have the expert knowledge required to determine whether legal violations have been committed. This puts new emphasis on police organizations and legal institutions having access to a large variety of experts within various fields. Many countries may not be able to afford having such extensive police organizations covering all areas of law enforcements or will not find it cost-effective. However, these specialists may be available within the university system. Hence, cooperation with university institutions and research facilities might offer an opportunity for more effective use of both police resources and university facilities and for providing unique channels for knowledge exchange.

Still, one can advocate the benefits with that the police organization on a national level has a core group with their own independent professional experts educated as physicians, psychologists, engineers, and pharmacologists, to mention some examples. This group of experts may serve multiple roles within the police organization, such as giving support to local police districts with expert knowledge from a legal point of view associated with their respective area of expertise. This core group of experts might also serve as an information hub to other governmental institutions, legislators, courts, and as an initiator of policing research projects associated to their area of expertise.

Medical Considerations and Law Enforcement

The medical and health-care sector presents a wide array of topics where research cooperation between university medical institutions, police authorities, governmental institutions, and legal institutions may be especially essential. Research projects may support defining legislation limits, policing procedures to be applied, and assessment methods to determine criminal violations. For example, for driving, strict limits exist for allowed blood alcohol level and specialized tools have been developed for road-side assessment of alcohol intoxication. However, a large number of other factors may also cause hazardous driving such as intoxication by drugs or proscribed medication, severe sleep deprivation, dementia, and mental illness, to mention a few examples.

Particularly, the issue of how to detect and handle people that might become violent due to mental disorders has received extensive media attention in Sweden due to several tragic incidents. Mental disorders with dormant violent components might be very difficult to diagnose even for psychological experts. Thus, this is a field offering many opportunities for valuable research collaborations between psychological experts, police, and legal authorities, possibly resulting into new practical guidelines for policing policies as well as in new law enforcements policies where the courts cooperate more closely with psychological experts.

Business Establishments and Law Enforcement

Also, the industrial and business sectors present a wide array of topics where research cooperation between university institutions, police authorities, and legal institutions may provide a new knowledge framework to support policing and instigation of new legislation, for example, by rating risks on the environment and on humans from industrial activity. The fast development of internet service has also provided a new large sector allowing criminality to operate independently of national borders. What would be especially valuable is if research collaborations could instigate more preventive policing actions within this area. Also, one way of combating Internet crime is for police organizations to have access to a variety of trained experts to determine legal violations.

Our Own Experiences of Police—University Research Cooperation

One example of how cooperation can be established between the university system and the local police authorities is our own ongoing collaboration between the Skåne County Police Department and the Department of Clinical Sciences at Lund University, Sweden. The foundation of the collaboration was based on a shared interest in learning more about human motor control abilities and how the human central nervous system is able to learn so fast how to handle a vast array of movement control challenges. The physical and mental stress conditions police officers sometimes have to work under offer an intriguing new perspective on what the human central nervous system is able to handle and how advanced the human self-preserving protective systems are. For example, can massive blood loss after physical lesions be prevented by changing the blood vessels throughput of blood—apparently a function developed through natural selection to enhance our likelihood to survive after traumatic incidents.

For police officers, training a motor skill is not sufficient. A key element is the ability to apply the trained skills in real-life situations, perhaps under imminent risk of being harmed or even killed if failing to perform the tasks correctly. One of the objectives with the cooperation between Lund University and Skåne County Police Department is to better describe the acute psychological stress police officers can be exposed to in their daily work. Another objective is to investigate how human central and peripheral motor functions are affected by high physical or psychological strains and to develop a new police training paradigm so that the skills trained also remain largely intact under conditions of high physical and psychological strains. The overall objective of the responsible Commissioner and the Skåne County Police Department, Sweden, is the interest in education and striving to expand science- and experience-based knowledge aimed at enhancing the safety of police officers by improving their skills through better training methods and equipment.

Already from the start of our cooperation, it became clear how important it is that both cooperative parties share the same genuine interest in the research topic and that the collaborative partnership includes the whole process of knowledge generation, validation, diffusion, and use (Bradley & Nixon, 2009). In addition, before effective research can be performed, there needs to be an exchange of knowledge between both parties involved.

Summary

The article, "Ending the 'dialogue of the deaf': evidence and policing policies and practices. An Australian case study" by Bradley and Nixon (2009), summarizes very well our own experiences and recommendations for research collaborations between academics and police. We find it vital that academic researchers and the police meet each other as equal partners in a shared enterprise to gain new knowledge, where both parties are prepared to learn from the collaborative partner's expertise in their respective areas. In addition, it is also essential that the collaborative partnership between academics and their clients includes the whole process of knowledge generation, validation, diffusion, and use (Bradley & Nixon, 2009). Collaborations between universities and police authorities may not only be limited to universities cooperating with police authorities in research projects. The universities might also be able to provide formal educational programs where police officers could pursue an academic career, that is, receiving a degree as specialists within different fields of policing.

References

Alemika, E. E. (2009). Police practice and police research in Africa. *Police Practice and Research, 10*, 483–502.

Bayley, D. (1998). *Policing in America: Assessment and prospects*. Washington, DC: Police Foundation.

Beck, O., Leine, K., Palmskog, G., & Franck, J. (2010). Amphetamines detected in exhaled breath from drug addicts: A new possible method for drugs-of-abuse testing. *Journal of Analytical Toxicology, 34*, 233–237.

Bradley, D., & Nixon, S. (2009). Ending the 'dialogue of the deaf': Evidence and policing policies and practices. An Australian case study. *Police Practice and Research, 10*, 423–435.

Carlsson-Sanz, S. (2000). *Large city violence I* (Swedish title: *Storstadsvåld I*). Stockholm: Stockholm South General Hospital (Swedish: Södersjukhuset).

Carlsson-Sanz, S. (2008). *Large city violence II* (Swedish title: *Storstadsvåld II*). Stockholm: Stockholm South General Hospital (Swedish: Södersjukhuset).

Cassidy, W. L. (1993). *Quick or dead*. Boulder, CO: Paladin Press.

Eberhard, D. (2006). *In the country of the security addicts* (Swedish title: *I trygghetsnarkomanernas land*). Stockholm: Prisma.

Fairbairn, W. E., & Sykes, E. A. (1942). *Shooting to live*. Boulder, CO: Paladin Press.

Fransson, M., Jones, A. W., & Andersson, L. (2005). Laboratory evaluation of a new evidential breath-alcohol analyser designed for mobile testing—The Evidenzer. *Medical Science Law, 45*, 61–70.

Fransson, P. A., Modig, F., Patel, M., Gomez, S., & Magnusson, M. (2010). Oculomotor deficits caused by 0.06% and 0.10% blood alcohol concentrations and relationship to subjective perception of drunkenness. *Clinical Neurophysiology, 121*, 2134–2142.

Fruhling, H. (2009). Research on Latin American police: Where do we go from here? *Police Practice and Research, 10*(5–6): 465–481.

GfK Trust Index. (2011). GfK Trust Index for the spring 2011 GfK Custom Research.

Gladwell, M. (2005). *Blink: The power of thinking without thinking*. New York: Little, Brown and Company.

Granér, R. (2004). Occupational culture among patrolling police officers. *In: School of social work*. Lund, Sweden: Lund University.

Grossman, D. (1995). *On killing: The psychological cost of learning to kill in war and society*. New York: Back Bay Books.

Grossman, D., & Christensen, L. W. (2004). *On combat: The psychology and physiology of deadly conflict in war and peace*. Millstadt, IL: PPCT Research Publications.

Hackman, J. R., & Oldham, G. R. (1980). *Work design in organizational context*. Greenwich, CT: JAI Press.

Holgersson, S. (2005). *Profession: Police* (Swedish title: *Yrke: Polis*). Stockholm: GML Reklam AB.

Holmberg, S., & Weibull, L. (2012). Media Academy Trust Barometer (Swedish title: Medie akademins förtroendebarometer) 2012 TNS SIFO AB.

Knutsson, J. (2004). *Problem-oriented policing: From innovation to mainstream*. Cullompton, United Kingdom: Willan.

Manning, P. K. (2009). Policing as self-audited practice. *Police Practice and Research, 10*, 451–464.

Meyerhoff, J. L., Norris, W., Saviolakis, G., Wollert, T., Burge, B., Atkins, V., & Spielberger, C. (2004). Evaluating performance of law enforcement personnel during a stressful training scenario. *Annals of the New York Academy of Sciences, 1032*, 250–253.

Modig, F., Fransson, P., Magnusson, M., & Patel, M. (2012). Blood alcohol concentration at 0.06 and 0.10% causes a complex multifaceted deterioration of body movement control. *Alcohol, 46*, 75–88.

Murray, K. R. (2004). *Training at the speed of life, vol. 1: The definitive textbook for police and military reality based training.* Gotha, FL: Armiger Publications.

Neyroud, P. (2009). Squaring the circles: Research, evidence, policy–making, and police improvement in England and Wales. *Police Practice and Research, 10*, 437–449.

Nieschalk, M., Ortmann, C., West, A., Schmal, F., Stoll, W., & Fechner, G. (1999). Effects of alcohol on body-sway patterns in human subjects. *International Journal of Legal Medicine, 112*, 253–260.

Oudejans, R. R. (2008). Reality-based practice under pressure improves handgun shooting performance of police officers. *Ergonomics, 51*, 261–273.

Oudejans, R. R., & Nieuwenhuys, A. (2009). Perceiving and moving in sports and other high-pressure contexts. *Progress in Brain Research, 174*, 35–48.

Paton, D., & Violanti, J. (2008). Law enforcement response to terrorism: the role of the resilient police organization. *International Journal of Emergency Mental Health, 10*, 125–135.

Roman, J. K., Reid, S., Reid, J., Chalfin, A., Adams, W., & Knight, C. (2008). *DNA field experiment: Cost-effectiveness analysis of the use of DNA in the investigation of high-volume crimes.* Washington, DC: The Urban Institute. (NCJ 244318).

Siddle, B. K. (1995). *Sharpening the warrior's edge: The psychology & science of training.* Millstadt, IL: PPCT Management Systems.

Thacher, D. (2001). Policing is not a treatment: Alternatives to the medical model of police research. *Journal of Research in Crime and Delinquency, 38*, 387–415.

Vonk, K. D. (2008). *Police performance under stress.* Deerfield, IL: Hendon publishing company.

Wong, C. K. (2009). Police scholarship in China. *Police Practice and Research, 10*, 503–519.

Reforming Policing to Improve Economic and Social Development in Emerging Democracies and New Industrialized Countries

Rule of Law and Justice Administration in Kosovo

10

Evaluating the Challenges in Policing a Postconflict Developing Democracy

JAMES F. ALBRECHT

Contents

History of Kosovo

Kosovo is a region located in the southernmost area of the former People's Republic of Serbia that had previously been under the political control of the former Federal Republic of Yugoslavia. It encompasses around 4,200 mi.^{2} (or 11,000 km^2) with a population of approximately two million, which presently consists of a majority (+90%) ethnic Albanians who had moved into the region during the 500-year Ottoman occupation. Kosovo was originally designated an autonomous province in 1945, but it did not gain actual political autonomy until 1946 (Mertus, 1999). After the fall of Yugoslavia, autonomy came to an end under the direction of Serbian President Slobodan Milosevic in 1989. Milosevic ordered that all government positions could only be filled by ethnic Serbians. The ethnic Albanian population formed a parallel society and declared their independence in 1990. This was not recognized by Serbia, or by other countries, and Milosevic flooded Kosovo with Serbian paramilitary and law enforcement officials. The Albanian population countered by forming the Kosovo Liberation Army (KLA) and engaging in guerilla conflict with the Serbian authorities. Originally, the KLA was designated a terrorist organization by the international community, but the widespread ethnic cleansing perpetrated under Milosevic's guidance later resulted in repeated efforts by the international community to end the armed conflict. Milosevic and Serbian officials repeatedly participated in peace negotiations but refused to sign any treaties. As such, in March 1999 the North Atlantic Treaty Organization (NATO) engaged in an 11-week bombing campaign that crippled Serbia's infrastructure and military operations in Kosovo (Hagan, 1999; Solana, 1999).

In June 1999, NATO and Serbia signed a technical agreement that led to the withdrawal of Serbian troops from Kosovo. In 1999, the United Nations (UN) Security Council also ratified Resolution 1244, which designated the region of Kosovo as a UN-administered territory. As such, the UN took over political control of this area. More than 700,000 ethnic Albanians, who had mainly fled to neighboring Albania and Macedonia during the NATO conflict, quickly returned, but many found their homes, businesses, and neighborhood mosques destroyed by Serbian forces or their ethnic Serbian neighbors (Sklias & Roukanas, 2007). With a power and security vacuum in existence, the KLA leadership took control and advantage, engaging in organized crime to gain financial resources, and also took revenge by killing ethnic Serbs and destroying their homes and by killing other Albanians who either were accused of collaborating with Serbian authorities or were not considered to be in line with KLA endeavors.

United Nations–Administered Kosovo

Once Serbia capitulated at the conclusion of the NATO bombing raids, the UN Security Council adopted Resolution 1244 on June 10, 1999, which established the UN Interim Administration in Kosovo (UNMIK). The first UN officials arrived 3 days later to observe a devastated and destroyed region with a limited population. However, by July 1999, it is estimated that more than 650,000 refugees, predominantly ethnic Albanians, had returned. Initial criminality commonly involved looting and destruction of Serbian residences and intimidation against the Serbian population. The previous law enforcement and judicial system had collapsed, and the majority population took advantage of the crime control vacuum. Criminal gangs, mainly headed by former KLA leaders, engaged in rampant organized crime, which included smuggling and drug and human trafficking among other illicit activities (Strohmeyer, 2001). The suppression of violence, interethnic criminality, and organized crime became the responsibility of the Kosovo Force, which was an international military mission staffed by UN member nations. However, their responsibilities ended after apprehension and detention. The overwhelming challenge involved the creation of a justice system, specifically the hiring and training of prosecutors and judges to move the cases along. However, the task proved to be difficult as the quest for developing a pool of prosecutors and judges from the different ethnic groups often led to intimidation and violence. Quite quickly, a prosecutorial and judicial backlog developed, which exists to this day.

One of the daunting tasks was the development of a legal framework. The majority of the ethnic Albanian population refused to accept legislation that had been imposed by the oppressive Serbian regime, so former Yugoslavian law was instituted. On December 12, 1999, UNMIK promulgated a regulation that the legal framework in place before March 22, 1989 would serve as the provisional legislation within Kosovo. However, this proved to cause difficulties as some of the provisions were in violation of accepted human rights practices (Strohmeyer, 2001). In May 2001, UNMIK implemented the Constitutional Framework for Provisional Self-Government in Kosovo, which resulted in subsequent elections in November 2001 and later the development of provisional legislation for criminal justice administration (Yannis, 2004). Thereafter, local political, government, and criminal justice actors have remained under the supervision and guidance of UN personnel.

As for law enforcement, the primary responsibility fell on the international community under the supervision and coordination of the UN (i.e., the CIVPOL program*). The 1800 international police officers in 1999 rapidly increased to 4450 in 2000. All were professional law enforcement practitioners from UN member countries. Their two primary tasks were to immediately establish law and order and to develop law enforcement capabilities at the local level. While UN CIVPOL rapidly deployed throughout Kosovo, the responsibility of developing, training, and deploying a new Kosovo Police Service (KPS) was predominantly accomplished through the United States Department of Justice International Criminal Investigative Training Assistance Program and through the support of the Organization for Security and Cooperation in Europe (OSCE). The KPS commenced recruitment in

---

* CIVPOL is the designation granted to civilian law enforcement, in contrast to military police, that is deployed to postconflict regions by the UN. The complement is composed of police personnel from contributing UN member states.

June 1999, and the KPS School in Vushtri, Kosovo, became fully operational in March 2000. There were 2516 KPS officers working across Kosovo in 2000, and this increased to 5704 in 2004 (Wilson, 2006) and finally to the present level that exceeds 7000.

In addition to the establishment of rule of law and the development of criminal justice agencies (i.e., police, prosecutors, judges, and correctional system), the UN has also been responsible for the administration and coordination of humanitarian assistance, civil administration, democratization and institution building, and reconstruction and economic development (Wilson, 2006). What this resulted in was the distribution of funds from many donor nations and organizations, which eventually supported the corrupt atmosphere endemic in Kosovo.

Ahtisaari Proposal

In 2007, Secretary General of the UN Ban Ki-moon requested special envoy Martti Ahtisaari to prepare the report *Comprehensive Proposal for the Kosovo Status Settlement*, often called the Ahtisaari Proposal or the Ahtisaari Plan, which outlined requirements for the region of Kosovo to declare its independence under international supervision and eventually to gain its total independence once the provisions outlined within the document were achieved. Elimination of interethnic tension; decentralization of government; a professional and impartial justice system; protection of religious and cultural heritage; protection of property and investigation of missing persons; sustainable economic development; a professional, multiethnic, and democratic security sector comprising the Kosovo Police and the Kosovo Security Force; and the continuation of an international supervisory mechanism that will include NATO, the European Union (EU), and the OSCE are included within these requirements. A new constitution, legislation, and general and local elections were to follow within a 9-month time period (Ki-moon, 2007).

European Union Involvement

As part of the Ahtisaari Plan, there was to be a 120-day transition period allowing transfer from UN administration to supervision under the European Security and Defense Policy (ESDP) program. In April 2006, the EU in conjunction with the United States* and Norway deployed the EU Planning Team in Pristina, Kosovo, to prepare for this development. The ESDP initiative was

---

* The author was the sole American representative on the EU Planning Team from 2007 through 2008.

called the EU Rule of Law Mission in Kosovo (or EULEX–Kosovo). EULEX would be primarily deployed to support the Kosovo institutions responsible for law enforcement, customs, and justice and act in a monitoring, mentoring, and advisory capacity. The EULEX mission would also retain limited executive authority* and be responsible for conducting criminal investigations involving war crimes, corruption, organized crime, and financial crimes. The total complement of EULEX was planned for approximately 1950 international staff, with more than 75% of this cadre dealing with policing and customs control.

"Russian Roadblock"

The 120-day transition from UN administration to supervised independence under the guidance of the EU was to commence on February 17, 2008 with the UN-supported declaration of independence and formation of the new Republic of Kosovo. The plan called for the end of UN administration on April 9, 2008. Only days prior to the declaration of independence and the implementation of that stage of the Ahtisaari Plan, Russia, as a permanent member of the UN Security Council, obstructed the initiation of the process in mid-February 2008. This created chaos and an atmosphere of indecision. In February 2008, the Republic of Kosovo declared her independence, but there was no coinciding transition of control from the UN to the EU. In reality, the last-hour ploy by the Russian government, consistently a Serbian ally, created overwhelming confusion and an abrupt end to international rule of law participation across Kosovo. By then, many UN member states had commenced the withdrawal of personnel and those involved in criminal justice functions that had remained undertook a "wait and see" position, leaving arrests and case prosecutions in limbo. As the EU and the EULEX mission had not been granted executive authority, the staff maintained their planning mode. In the interim, this uncertainty ultimately hampered many UN member states from recognizing Kosovo as an independent country.†

European Union Rule of Law Mission in Kosovo

Even given the ambiguity, the EU and other cooperating nations commenced the large-scale deployment of justice, customs, and law enforcement personnel to Kosovo in the spring of 2008. Eventually, in November 2008 the UN Security Council, with overwhelming pressure from the United States,

---

* The author was the EULEX police chief with executive authority to conduct criminal investigations involving war crimes, corruption, terrorism, organized crime, and other politically sensitive cases from 2008 through 2010.
† To date, no more than 90 UN member states recognize an independent Kosovo, which is not sufficient for UN participation and representation.

Germany, the United Kingdom, France, and other key nations, approved a resolution that called for a 1-day transition of authority from the UN to the EU. The date designated for the application of executive authority to the EULEX mission was December 9, 2008.

Two things compounded the initial ineffectiveness. Although the EULEX mission had sufficient rule of law personnel to undertake their designated responsibilities, the mission headquarters had not arranged logistical support and office accommodation for these resources.* As such, not only did the staff not have adequate office space but they also did not have sufficient transportation means and office equipment. The December commencement had another interesting effect. As soon as the Christmas and New Year holiday season commenced, which was around December 15, 2008, the vast majority of EU personnel went on vacation with most not returning until mid-January 2009 after the date of Orthodox Christmas. In plainer English, even with the confusion of mission commencement the EU opted to unofficially suspend overall operation for more than 1 month so that EU managers and personnel could go home for the holiday season.

Sensing the disarray, Serbian radicals in the northern ethnic Serbian enclave of North Mitrovica engaged in routine attacks on ethnic Albanian residents and businesses. Gunfire, arson, and serious assaults were common throughout December 2008[†] and were only deterred by the eventual presence of NATO forces. In addition, due to the confusion caused by the recent UN Security Council resolution, which reported that concessions had been made to Serbia to commence the EULEX mission, ethnic Albanian radicals reportedly planned an attack likely using explosives at one of the EULEX facilities. The response by EULEX was to close all of their sites. The preemptive action appeared to have prevented the attack, but it left key personnel without the ability to continue mission planning and deployment for a brief period. As a result, the first 2 months of the EULEX mission did not result in notable progress or achievement.

On April 6, 2009, the head of the EULEX mission announced full operational capability. Of course, without functional work accommodations, sufficient vehicles to get to work, and key investigative equipment, the mission was functional only in theory and not in practice.

---

* As the commencement date of the EULEX mission was uncertain and as the UN suspended the transition stage until direction was provided by the UN Security Council, the transfer of work accommodations, vehicles, and equipment did not occur and the EU Planning Team had not requisitioned any supplies.

† The author and a number of other American EULEX mission personnel responded to the sites of all the attacks because most international police officers from EU states were on leave.

European Union Institute for Security
Studies Evaluation of EULEX

One year after the EULEX mission commenced, the EU Institute for Security Studies (EU-ISS) conducted a comprehensive evaluation (European Union Institute for Security Studies, 2009) of this endeavor. The EU-ISS noted that the EULEX mission is the largest of all ESDP deployments and is the only mission with integrated justice, police, and customs mechanisms that are further divided into advisory and executive responsibilities. Although late in implementation, the mission has been recognized for its programmatic approach in which performance indicators with attainable timetables were delineated for the mission and for local criminal justice actors.

On the other hand, the mission was also noted for its overwhelming lack of efficiency and effectiveness. Rule of law reform and institution building can best be described as being negligible to minor. Mission personnel did not deploy across all of Kosovo, most specifically into and throughout the ethnic Serbian enclave of North Mitrovica.* EULEX justice personnel stood idle as ethnic Serbian enclaves continued to honor UNMIK and Yugoslavian law, even after the Kosovo government implemented its own national laws. In addition, EULEX made no effort to recognize Kosovo border and customs laws at the northern borders with Serbia and did not support the local Kosovo Police Border Department and the Kosovo Customs Authority in undertaking their new responsibilities. An unexpected decision was made at EULEX headquarters to permit the Kosovo Police working in ethnic Serbian enclaves to report directly to the head of EULEX police, rather than through the Kosovo Police chain of command. As previously reported, EULEX failed to provide functional work sites and equipment to mission personnel. And EULEX rule of law staffing levels regularly fluctuated between 50% and 80%. Most importantly, the failure of all 27 EU member states† to recognize an independent Kosovo has caused the EULEX mission to operate with the dictum that they are "status neutral" but at the same time supporting "local ownership." Politically, this situation has caused confusion and misunderstanding among both EULEX mission personnel and their local counterparts and has proven to be counterproductive in gaining cooperation with regional

* The EULEX mission had deployed a significant complement of rule of law personnel, mainly international police officers, with the intent of mobilizing them throughout North Mitrovica, but these resources were reassigned to other responsibilities. The mission could have easily flooded the North Mitrovica region to ensure security and restrict smuggling and organized crime activity.
† Spain, Greece, Slovakia, Romania, and Cyprus have yet to recognize the independence and statehood of Kosovo.

governments, authorities, and organizations* (European Union Institute for Security Studies, 2009). The transfer of both police and prosecution cases from UNMIK to EULEX was slow and has led to most cases being dismissed due to legal temporal constraints.[†] New cases at the local level that were to be monitored by EULEX prosecutors and police advisors have not received the mandated attention within courts, which has led to a backlog in excess of 100,000 criminal cases that continue to fail to receive investigative or prosecutorial action. It is interesting to note that similar failures and shortcomings were reported within the EU Police Mission in Bosnia and Herzegovina (Howorth, 2007) and, as a result, the EU has recently opted to conclude its law enforcement advisory capacity there.

Rand Corporation Analysis of European Union Postconflict Involvement

The U.S. Office for the Secretary of Defense in 2009 requested Rand Corporation to conduct a thorough assessment of the EU's capabilities to participate in postconflict environments. As a result, the EULEX mission in Kosovo was examined to determine the extent to which the United States should support or directly participate in future ESDP endeavors. The Rand study concluded that the nonmilitary institution building capacity of the EU was limited and faced a number of challenges. The most notable shortcomings were the failure of the EU to properly staff mission positions, inability to maintain designated staffing levels, and inability to improve the training capabilities of the Kosovo Police (Chivvis, 2010). This analysis reported that the EULEX mission in Kosovo could be considered a success compared to the inadequacy and ineffectiveness of the EU's police training mission in Afghanistan. Ultimately, Rand supported future EU involvement in civilian capacity building in postconflict regions and proposed that the U.S. government consider providing logistical support and personnel resources to those initiatives (Chivvis, 2010). However, the budgetary restraints placed on the U.S. government over recent years have caused the United States to dramatically reconsider, reduce, or withdraw prior commitments, specifically those for the EULEX mission in Kosovo.[‡]

---

* The Interpol, Europol, and SECI would not cooperate in criminal investigation and intelligence sharing with similarly tasked EULEX personnel.
† To continue investigating and prosecuting criminal cases, judicial approval must be obtained within legally designated time frames (e.g., 6 months). Failure to renew the investigation or prosecution before a judge has led to the dismissal of almost all inherited cases.
‡ The CIVPOL staffing by the United States has declined from 220 in 2008 to 80 in 2009 to 30 in 2012.

Criminality and Safety within Kosovo

The development of a relatively professional and effective Kosovo Police agency supported by international advisors and colleagues has resulted in continuing crime reductions since the conflict officially concluded in 1999. Although the rates for most crime categories are relatively low compared to EU and U.S. averages, the most accurate measure of violence affecting the estimated population of two million could be assessed through the analysis of murder incidents. The reported murder rate in Kosovo for 2000 was 12 per 100,000 residents; for 2005, it was 3 per capita (United Nations Office on Drugs and Crime, 2008); and for 2010, it was 2.5 per capita (International Crisis Group, 2010). Murder statistics have disclosed a continuous downward trend that reflects the overall decline in crime recorded within Kosovo Police annual reports from 2000 through 2010.

Kosovo is not noted for overwhelming danger and violence, and most murders and assaults can be said to be the result of property, family, or personal disputes. On the other hand, the UN and other international organizations estimate that there are more than 350,000 unaccounted small arms present throughout Kosovo (United Nations Development Programme, 2010). Given this potential threat, it is quite surprising that firearm-related incidents are limited. However, the greatest safety hazard within Kosovo involves the general lack of traffic safety. In 2007, there were 127 vehicle fatalities and 17,006 vehicle accidents; in 2008, 114 fatalities and 15,939 accidents; in 2009, 176 fatalities and 19,212 accidents; and in 2010, 175 fatalities and 18,030 accidents (Bislimi, 2011). Police traffic enforcement, other than speed control, is negligible. The vast majority of drivers within Kosovo operate defective vehicles,* do not wear seat belts,† and drive in a reckless and haphazard fashion. Traffic accident statistical evaluations were not conducted by the Kosovo Police, and traffic intersection engineering assessments were clearly not supervised by international experts. Quite amazingly, the command staff of the Kosovo Police was repeatedly unresponsive to proposals by international law enforcement experts to enhance vehicular, pedestrian, and traffic safety.‡

---

* Most vehicles are purchased from car dealers in EU countries after the cars can no longer pass safety and inspection standards.
† The author repeatedly surveyed drivers in Kosovo and noted that more than 95% of all drivers failed to wear a seat belt or utilize child safety seats.
‡ The author lived in Kosovo for 3 years and discontinued walking outdoors due to the lack of vehicle-related safety and because most areas had no pedestrian sidewalks; even when sidewalks existed, they were used for residential and business parking, thereby forcing pedestrians to walk on the street.

Organized Crime Activity within Kosovo

Although crime in general is relatively low, Kosovo is a notorious smuggling hub between Asia, Africa, South America, North America, and Europe. Two main smuggling routes are used for smuggling drugs, humans, contraband, and other goods from Asia to the EU. Goods from the east enter Turkey and exit either into Bulgaria, continuing through Romania into Hungary, or into Greece, traveling through Macedonia and ending up in Kosovo. Afghanistan heroin is smuggled in this fashion. Although farmers in Kosovo have been known to grow marijuana,* both cocaine and marijuana normally arrive in Kosovo after arriving at Albanian and Montenegrin ports. Ethnic Albanian crime groups then repackage the material into small parcels for transit to European nations, normally in private vehicles, tour buses, and commercial trucks.

Due to the large number of illegal small arms and explosives still remaining from the conflict, the smuggling of weapons between ethnic Albanian groups in Kosovo to ethnic Albanian communities in southern Serbia and Macedonia is routine. Most of the illegal weapons are under the control of former KLA fighters (or Serbian radicals in North Mitrovica).

Human smuggling mainly takes three forms. A very small number of females are smuggled from Ukraine or Moldova into Kosovo for sex trade purposes, but prostitution routinely involves ethnic Albanian females to avoid the attention of the international community or UN/EU law enforcement. Organized crime groups are active in offering stolen, counterfeit, or duplicate[†] travel documents (i.e., passports and visas) to the local population for them to gain entry into the EU. Finally, due to the presence of the UN and other human rights organizations and due to lax passport and border control, Kosovo has become a location where persons from China, Afghanistan, Iraq, Somalia, Pakistan, Algeria, and other countries enter, request asylum, and then continue on their illegal journey to Europe.[‡]

Both ethnic Serbian and ethnic Albanian organized crime groups are known to engage in regular fuel smuggling to avoid paying related customs fees and taxes. Coffee, tobacco, and other goods routinely enter Kosovo in a similar illegal fashion, normally through unguarded mountainous border areas. In addition, Kosovo is recognized for the open sale of pirated and counterfeit products (United States Department of State, 2011). Finally, due

---

* Kosovo does not have a large consumer drug population.
† Duplicate travel documents include actual passports and visas that are resold to similar looking individuals in an effort to allow them to travel to the United States or EU.
‡ The author noted numerous cases in which these illegal migrants requested asylum, received financial assistance, and then in less than 24 hours entered Serbia illegally through unguarded forest border regions.

to the lack of cooperation and information exchange with other law enforcement agencies, it is common to observe vehicles stolen from the U.S. and UN nations being operated on the streets of Kosovo with their original license plates.*

Corruption within Kosovo

Corruption within southeast Europe normally takes three general forms. Government employees routinely demand bribes from citizens and business persons to engage in official misconduct, thereafter either performing or failing to perform the responsibilities of their job. The second type of corruption involves direct political interference into the justice process. The third version of corruption involves the participation of government representatives overseeing or taking part in organized crime activity. Because these factors are common within Kosovo, Kosovo is often referred to as "Europe's mafia state" (Filiminova, 2010), because government leaders have consistently engaged in all three activities with little to no reaction from the UN, EU, American, and other international supporters. And many of the local criminal justice actors within Kosovo are under the control and influence of key political leaders, so no investigative or enforcement action from their side has occurred or is anticipated.

A survey of the residents of Kosovo has revealed that corruption is a highly perceived occurrence among government actors. Findings revealed that corruption was present in all government sectors, including political party leaders (33.7%), municipal government (28.2%), the judiciary (27.7%), prosecutors (25.2%), Kosovo president (16.4%), parliament (15.6%), and Kosovo government (14.3%), but it was viewed as being limited within the Kosovo Police (9.4%). Almost 39% of Kosovo residents rated corruption as the second most relevant problem facing Kosovo (following unemployment), and 40% of the public believed that all government officials are involved in corrupt practices. Over 16% of all residents report being asked for unofficial cash by a municipal official to deal with an official issue, compared to 10% who were coerced to pay a bribe to a federal government official over the last 12 months (Spector, Winbourne, & Beck, 2003). A more recent survey that has measured the perception of corruption across the globe reported that Kosovo presently ranks at 112 out of the 183 countries and received a score of 2.9 out of 10[†] in corruption perception (Transparency International, 2011) by Kosovo citizens.

---

* Neither the Kosovo Police nor the EULEX Police have access to EU or U.S. vehicle databases.
† It is noted that 10 is perceived as the most legitimate and 0 as the most corrupt.

The political leadership of Kosovo, at the request of the international community, has developed a number of official mechanisms to address the issue of corruption. The Kosovo Anti-Corruption Agency was introduced in 2007, and the Prime Minister established the Task Force against Corruption in 2010. However, both have proved to be ineffective. Both are staffed by relatives or party members from the prime minister's ruling PDK party, who clearly have been appointed to provide warnings to corrupt politicians and other government employees and to obstruct investigations. The head of the Task Force against Corruption was himself arrested in April 2012 for engaging in bribery and for covering up corruption involving prominent government leaders (Karadaku, 2012).

What is likely most disturbing is that the most identifiable corrupt officials in Kosovo are the present prime minister, two former prime ministers, and the most recent minister of transport and telecommunications. The present Prime Minister Hashim Thaci, the leader of the ruling PDK political party, has been recognized as the leader of the Drenica organized crime group (Marty, 2010). Although Thaci cannot account for his questionable financial resources in any credible fashion, the international community has permitted him to remain in power. The former prime minister Ramush Haradinaj, the leader of the AAK party, the ruling party in western Kosovo, is recognized as the leader of the Haradinaj organized crime group functioning throughout the western province of Peja. Haradinaj is presently being detained at the Hague and is awaiting a war crimes trial. The former minister of transport and telecommunications Fatmir Limaj, a top member of the PDK party, stepped down from office due to recurrent allegations that he accepted bribes in return for major government contracts. Former prime minister Agim Ceku, the present minister of security forces and a member of the PDK party, has been reported to be a key coordinator of narcotics trading that has occurred and continues to occur within Kosovo's borders. In addition, it is extremely noteworthy that the aforementioned four former KLA members and "national heroes" are all suspects in serious incidents involving genocide and war crimes that targeted both ethnic Serbian and Albanian populations during and after the Yugoslavian conflict.*

Corruption will remain endemic among the political elites of Kosovo until the international community ensures that corrupt officials are removed from their positions and guarantees that their illicit actions are properly addressed through the criminal justice system. In addition, beyond their involvement in organized crime activities it is imperative that they are held accountable in a court of law, be it at the Hague, in Serbia, or in Kosovo or whether by local, regional, or international prosecutors, for the war crime atrocities that they have been associated with. There is presently sufficient evidence to at the least advocate that they all be removed from their present positions and be barred

---

* These are the four most notable corrupt national officials. The list of all other recognized federal or municipal corrupt officials would be overwhelming.

from active involvement in Kosovo government and politics. Unfortunately, these criminals have moved from one critical government position to the next without much criticism or input from key international players. As such, Kosovo has sincerely earned the title of Europe's mafia state.

Recommendations for Kosovo to Move Forward

A number of recommendations could be proposed to improve the distressing situation in Kosovo and permit the nation and her citizens to move forward. The most critical step is for the international community, most notably the EU, which has supervisory authority over Kosovo, with the support of the United States, a key supporter of Kosovo, to direct the immediate removal of suspects of serious war crime allegations and those with noted affiliations with organized crime groups and bar those individuals from government employment. A fresh start will permit Kosovo to integrate more rapidly into the EU and to earn the cooperation of her regional neighbors. This may sound severe; but until this occurs, Kosovo will deserve the title of mafia state and will continue to be looked on as an illegitimate regional presence, ruled by "thugs" and supported financially by rampant organized crime activity.

In addition, effort should be made to revise Kosovo legislation so as to permit the criminal justice system to evolve into a functional institution. Political influence into the appointment of police commanders and the assignment of Kosovo Police personnel should be eliminated, and more importantly police criminal investigations must remain free of political interference. Overall, justice effectiveness could be instantly and dramatically improved by enacting legislation to switch to a common law system, which would permit independent police investigations and arrests.* This would eliminate the present legal requirement for personal direction by prosecutors and judges to commence and continue criminal investigations. It is also crucial that the legislated mandate to renew a criminal investigation before a judge every 60 days is immediately removed. As the law presently delineates the statue of limitations for each crime, this suffices to ensure that cases are not excessively drawn out. Mandatory court renewal of criminal investigations merely delays the investigatory process and allows corrupt and politically influential judges the opportunity to bring an end to major cases, particularly those involving government officials or members of their families or clans.

Quite honestly, other than a small number of top police chiefs, the Kosovo Police are not noted for being overly corrupt and impressively has been

---

* This is strongly recommended, as the Kosovo Police are likely the most professional and least corrupt of the criminal justice actors; however, the bigger concern deals with political interference into serious police investigations.

recognized as the least corrupt law enforcement agency in southeastern Europe. It is imperative that the upper stratum of the Kosovo Police hierarchy, which includes police directors (i.e., department chiefs) and regional commanders, be revetted to ensure that they have no connection with the present political parties, no war crime associations, and no allegations involving affiliations with organized crime or other criminal groups. The process should be conducted under the direct supervision of the international community to ensure legitimacy. The EU and the EULEX mission failed to take this critical step after the declaration of independence of Kosovo. The Kosovo Police should also be trained and equipped to engage in crime and traffic safety analysis and "hot spot" deployment to further reduce crime rates and traffic accidents.

A workload analysis must be conducted to rectify the overwhelming backlog of criminal cases and eliminate direct political interference or corruption in court cases. Efforts must be made to recruit, properly screen, hire, and train a sufficient number of prosecutors and judges with similar vetting instructions that have been outlined above and have been recommended for the Kosovo Police.

All personnel working in the Kosovo Anti-Corruption Agency and the Task Force against Corruption should be immediately terminated, and international actors should implement a revised vetting and training process to hire new staff to root out political control, influence, and interference.

In lieu of reducing agency staffing levels, EULEX should increase the number of prosecutors within the EULEX Special Prosecutors Office in an effort to deal with the overwhelming criminal caseloads with an emphasis on cases involving government officials, including those operating within the Serbian enclave of North Mitrovica who have repeatedly coordinated and been involved in attacks on international officials, NATO troops, and the Kosovo Police. In particular, war crime, terrorism, and organized crime cases that possess sufficient evidence for arrest should be moved forward.

The predominant international actors present within Kosovo must take or support necessary measures to bring legitimacy to Kosovo. Unfortunately, many countries appear to be more concerned with their own national interests than with the welfare of the people living within Kosovo. Uncomfortable decisions have to be made, and all recommendations to Kosovo government officials to improve the current state of affairs and to eliminate corruption and organized criminal activity must be made with a "stick" and "carrot" mind-set. There is hope for Kosovo but not when the international community continues to exhibit indifference to clear and unacceptable misbehavior and corruption.

Summary and Conclusion

The KLA was a guerilla organization that took up arms against Milosevic's Serbia to obtain self-governance for the former Yugoslavian province of

Kosovo. The freedom and liberty of the predominantly ethnic Albanian population that had lost the possibility of employment and education following the directive of Milosevic to "Serbianize" the entire Kosovo region were at stake. Small-scale guerilla warfare turned into a full-scale confrontation, with most of the regional population fleeing into neighboring countries. Genocide and atrocious war crimes committed by both parties led to the involvement of NATO forces, eventually bringing an end to the conflict in 1999. As part of the peace agreement, the UN took over administration of the Kosovo region. By the start of the new millennium, a locally elected government and a criminal justice mechanism were in place under the supervision of the UN. The Ahtisaari Plan called for the transfer of international management from the UN to the EU. This was to take place in 2008 and coincide with the declaration of independence of Kosovo. Unfortunately, due to the objections of Serbia and the interference of Russia, the timetable and objectives outlined within the Ahtisaari Plan were sent into disarray. Eventually, the EU did take over the supervision of Kosovo, but the deployment of EU and partner nation staff did not occur smoothly.

After the declaration of independence in 2008, Kosovo had the unique opportunity to enact new legislation and elect and appoint new government officials who would move the country forward into a functional democracy with effective and legitimate rule of law practices. Unfortunately, even with the presence and guidance of the international community, nothing has dramatically changed. The government hierarchy is loaded with former KLA commanders who are suspected not only of involvement in serious and horrific war crimes but also for their connection to organized crime groups involved in illicit drug, human, and weapons trafficking. Global leaders, most notably those from the United States and EU, have missed a significant opportunity to guide the people of Kosovo in a positive direction. It would appear that many have looked in the opposite direction, failing to admit that "the king has no clothes," likely in an effort to further national agendas and personal aspirations. There is hope for the people of Kosovo, but until key global actors initiate steps to "clean house," support the replacement of corrupt officials, and assist in developing a legitimate and effective rule of law mechanism, Kosovo will retain the title of being Europe's dysfunctional mafia state.

References

Bislimi, M. (2011). *An Assessment of Road Traffic Safety in Kosova*. Pristina, Kosovo: American University of Kosovo.

Chivvis, C. S. (2010). *EU Civilian Crisis Management: The Record So Far*. Santa Monica, California: Rand Corporation.

European Union Institute for Security Studies. (2009). *European Security and Defence Policy: The First 10 Years (1999–2009)*. Paris, France: EU-ISS.

Filiminova, A. (2010). *Kosovo: Europe's Mafia State and the Rule of Law*. Montreal, Canada: Centre for Research on Globalization.

Howorth, J. (2007). *Security and Defence Policy in the European Union*. Houndmills, England: Palgrave Macmillan Publishers.

Hagan, W. H. (1999). The Balkans' lethal nationalisms. *Foreign Affairs, 78*, 52–64.

International Crisis Group. (2010). *The Rule of Law in Independent Kosovo: Executive Summary and Recommendations*. Washington, DC: International Crisis Group.

Karadaku, L. (2012). Head of anti-corruption task force arrested for corruption. *Southeast European Times*, April 4, 2012, Pristina, Kosovo.

Ki-moon, B. (2007). Letter dated March 26, 2007 from the United States Secretary General to the United Nations Security Council.

Marty, D. (2010). *Inhumane Treatment of People and Illicit Trafficking in Human Organs in Kosovo*. Report to the Parliamentary Assembly of the Council of Europe in Brussels on December 12, 2010.

Mertus, A. J. (1999). *Kosovo: How Myths and Truths Started a War*. California: University of California Press.

Sklias, P., & Roukanas, S. (2007). Development in post-conflict Kosovo. *South-Eastern Europe Journal of Economics, 2*, 267–287.

Solana, J. (1999). NATO's success in Kosovo. *Foreign Affairs, 78*, 114–120.

Spector, B. I., Winbourne, S., & Beck, L. D. (2003). *Corruption in Kosovo: Observations and Implications for USAID*. Washington, DC: Management Systems International.

Strohmeyer, H. (2001). Collapse and reconstruction of a judicial system: The United Nations mission in Kosovo and East Timor. *The American Journal of International Law, 95*(1), 46–63.

Transparency International. (2011). *Corruption Perceptions Index 2011*. Berlin, Germany: Transparency International.

United Nations Development Programme. (2010). *Dogs Join Fight against Weapons in Kosovo*. New York: United Nations.

United Nations Office on Drugs and Crime. (2008). *Crime and Its Impact on the Balkans and Affected Countries*. Vienna, Austria: United Nations.

United States Department of State. (2011). *Money Laundering and Financial Crimes Country Database*. Washington, DC: U.S. DOS Bureau for International Narcotics and Law Enforcement Affairs.

Wilson, J. M. (2006). Law and order in an emerging democracy: Lessons from the reconstruction of Kosovo's police and justice systems. *Annals of the American Academy of Political and Social Science, 605*(1), 152–177.

Yannis, A. (2004). The UN as government in Kosovo. *Global Governance, 10*(1), 67–81.

The Shortcomings of Anticorruption Program in Addressing Public Corruption

11

A Forensic Criminological Case of South Africa

SETLHOMAMARU DINTWE

Contents

Introduction

The dawn of democracy in South Africa experienced the adoption and proliferation of vast economic policies and strategies based on a desire to address the ills of the past and those emergent just before the country's democratization. Similar to the previous regimes, the new democratic government that came to power in 1994 had to contend with a myriad of socioeconomic ills. These ills, such as the HIV-AIDS epidemic, poverty, illiteracy, and corruption, topped the government agenda and policy development. Although it is not insinuated that these problems were not taken seriously during the apartheid era, it is submitted that people were now free to raise their voices and demand government's intervention after the first democratic elections. Corruption, in particular, which forms the crux of this chapter, has been one of the toughest challenges faced by South Africa. Manifestation and prevalence of corruption led to the sending of clear messages everywhere confirming that it erodes the fabric on which South Africa's economy is built and that it needed to be addressed as a matter of urgency. This was not a simple call though, particularly because in the beginning of the 1990s a flood of public corruption hit not only South Africa but also the rest of the world, becoming a global phenomenon (Gildenhuys, 2004, p. 5).

Although public corruption may have existed for many years before 1994, the main purpose of this chapter is to analyze the government's reaction to corruption that the white minority government conceded to democracy. This means that the author will use forensic criminology in attempting to establish the ability and effectiveness of anticorruption programs between 1994 and 2012. For the purposes of this chapter, forensic criminology goes beyond traditionally defined criminology as it is a scientific study of crime and criminals for the purposes of addressing investigative and legal issues (Petherick, Turvey, & Ferguson, 2010, p. xxi). This chapter therefore looks at how corruption manifested itself after democratization, how this affected the country at large, and what the responses of the government are as far as public corruption is concerned. In addition, this chapter looks at the elements that define an effective anticorruption program internationally and whether these elements are present in the current mechanisms employed by the South African government. In each case, the author uses analyzed literature to arrive at conclusions pertinent to the observation of the elements of an anticorruption program. In the final analysis, the author creates erudition around specific actions and statements made by senior government officials and which are not assisting the endeavors to eradicate corruption in South Africa.

Rationale

A lot of research has been conducted on corruption in South Africa. The prevalence thereof is known, and a lot of government strategies on countering public corruption have been analyzed over time. Different theories on how to counter corruption have been in the public domain as well, and the fact that corruption is still prevalent and almost out of control in South Africa confirms that dealing with corruption of any form is a very complex phenomenon normally influenced by internal and external factors. It is also proved that public corruption is a multifaceted phenomenon and as a result of its complexity it is often not easy to rely on a single theory on how to address the problem of corruption. Although there are main theories pertinent to corruption, this chapter briefly articulates around only two theories that are commonly used to understand corruption and react to corruption in the public sector.

The first theory of dealing with corruption is known as the Principal Agent theory, where the employee or managers are incentivized by the owner to exert effort (Shar, 2007, p. 256). It is clear as argued and conceded by the proponents of this theory that it can only be used effectively in trivial cases of corruption. This is because the punishment associated with this theory is also very light and may include steps such as a salary cut or a mere attendance of an improvement program. In fact, this theory is more concerned with the ability of employees to perform optimally rather than dealing with issues of corruption. It is therefore submitted that if an act of corruption is too harmful for any organization this theory may not yield the necessary results. In the same breath, it is likely that if monitoring is not done sufficiently this theory may be manipulated further. The second theory of dealing with corruption is known as the Economics of Crime Theory, which focuses on how potential criminals can be discouraged from committing crimes by severe punishments based on observable and verifiable behavior (Shar, 2007, p. 256).

The main point is that there are various reasons that prompted this analysis. The truth is that many good policies, summits, conferences, and strategies came to the fore over time in South Africa, but the scourge of corruption still remained. This means that there is a problem with the implementation of strategies and the protection of our own policies as well as our own strategies. The ineffectiveness of policies and strategies are sometimes so visible that even senior government officials have expressed their concerns regarding the failures experienced in trying to deal with corruption. This is evident in the following statement made by the former president Thabo Mbeki:

> Only the mentally blind would fail to see that the things that happen in our country everyday point precisely to this: that among many of our fellow citizens, there is no ethical barrier which blocks them from actions that are wrong (Thabo Mbeki, National Anti-Corruption Summit, April 1999).

The second reason that led to this research is premised on the following: if there are clear policies, why is it so difficult to bring the transgressors to book? This chapter will therefore articulate issues of political will and equally the level of interference by senior politicians in anticorruption mechanisms. Different law enforcement agencies were created to exclusively deal with issues of corruption, yet there was never an indication that the level of corruption was decreasing. Such bodies include the Special Investigating Unit (SIU); now defunct Directorate of Special Operations, popularly known as the Scorpions; Independent Police Investigative Directorate; and Public Protector, to mention a few. This state of affairs is among those aspects that prompted the author to look at the universally accepted facets of an anticorruption program common in many countries and attempt to diagnose its ineffectiveness in South Africa.

It is therefore against this background that this chapter attempts to analyze how an anticorruption program should look like in pursuit of incorporating different theories of countering corruption. This emanates from the submission that an effective anticorruption program is one that incorporates all theories dealing with the eradication of corruption. Such a program needs to be balanced and multifaceted as corruption can take place at any level of the government as well as in the business sector. Most importantly, such a program must still exist within the ambit of the constitution and take rule of law and human rights seriously. In the same breath, a good anticorruption program should be achievable and understood by all for it to be seen as fit for purpose. If it cannot be implemented because there are certain internal or external factors hindering such implementation, it means that there is still a lot to be done in realigning such a program and making it more effective. Hypothetically, the main rationale behind this analysis is that there must be an acknowledgment of the problem of corruption, development of remedial measures, and effective implementation of these remedies without fear of prejudice or favor. Once this is achieved, there is a likelihood that the majority of people will obey all laws and regulations of government as well as the simplest unwritten social rules of society, which are the rules of just being decent (Gildenhuys, 2004, p. 36).

Manifestation of Corruption

The first democratic elections and the democratization of South Africa in 1994 were later characterized by an unprecedented transference of the means of production and part of the wealth into the hands of those who were previously marginalized (Randall, 1996, p. 666). In addition, former exiles and those who had been imprisoned by the apartheid regime were appointed to high offices of the public sector. Some of these people, especially the political appointees, did not possess any experience and, on the extreme, any skills, knowledge, or attributes to run the public office. It is therefore this author's argument that, although much of the contemporary corruption may be inherited from the past, the democratization of South Africa made her more vulnerable to public corruption.

The transition of South Africa from an apartheid regime to a more democratic government can be equated to a weakened state. The reason for this analogy is that almost everything that was present and used as policy and regulations was totally irrelevant to the new dispensation and everything suited to the new had to be created almost from nonexistence. Corruption can manifest easily in cases where institutions are poorly developed or poorly enforced, rules are ambiguous, and consequently leaders are not held accountable for their actions. Institutional weakness, as argued by Eicher (2009, p. 8) lead to bribery, nepotism, and other undesirable behaviors. The breaking up of the former Soviet Union is a good example of a weakened formal institution where almost everything such as laws, government agencies, and codes of conduct were wiped out and had to be reinvented (Eicher, 2009, p. 8). It was during this period that new economic graft and rent-seeking opportunities were created. It was also during this period that politicians grabbed an opportunity for directing state resources into their personal portfolios. Manifestation of corruption in South Africa after 1994 cannot be differentiated from the weakened institution's analogy. It must be borne in mind that in 1993 and 1994 a lot of changes took place as a result of the negotiations for a unified government and the first democratic elections. This was also the period that the newly elected government contended with legislative processes such as the enactment of the Constitution of the Republic of South Africa as well as the amendment and repealing of legislation that excluded other population groups from participating in government. This is supported by Southall (2004, p. 314), who argued that democracy had set in motion a rapid mobility whereby propertied and professional sections of the black community gained from advancement and their relative advantage could easily render such elements antiethical to the interests of the poor.

Manifestation of public corruption in South Africa can also be understood simultaneously with the conceptual analysis. According to Mafunisa (2000, p. 11), corruption refers to immoral, deprived, or dishonest practices of persons. Corruption is further understood as a specific cultural attitude regarding loyalty, morality, and usurpation of public good, which summarily means promotion of private gains or selfish interests, against the overall objectives of the government, by whomever is in charge and responsible within the area of work. The elements appearing in the conceptual analysis of the word "corruption" clearly indicate that there is an exchange of value in every corrupt activity. The most worrying character of corruption is that it is perpetrated in collusion by those who are in authority. This is true particularly for public corruption because it mostly involves those who are charged with the responsibility of managing public finances and well-being.

Professor Vil-Nkomo in Gildenhuys (2004, p. 1) contends that corruption and its manifestation when understood in a simplistic way includes acts of bribery, extortion, kickbacks, fraud, forgery, embezzlement, or graft. In short, corruption manifests itself in many ways and at different levels. There is a broad range of corruption manifestation in tax administration, government expenditure programs, and other areas of fiscal policy and management (Martinez-Vazquez, Granado, & Boex, 2007, p. ix). Apart from these formal manifestations, corruption can also take a nonfiscal shape in which public officials abuse their public powers for private gains outside the realm of fiscal processes. Other examples include job reservations for spouses, children, family, siblings, and relatives of parliamentarians and other influential people in government as well as bribery, fraud, theft, extortion, and maladministration.

Degree of Public Corruption in South Africa

The level of corruption in South Africa cannot be easily measured with a claim of accuracy. Some of the reports were taken from perception indexes, which may not provide real statistics of corrupt activities. However, there are reports that can be used to estimate the level and the degree of corruption in South Africa. The following reports can be trusted as at least reflecting this phenomenon:

- In 2013, 47% of South Africans reported to have paid a bribe to one of the public services officials (Global Corruption Barometer 2013, p. 34).
- In 2013, the police in South Africa was regarded as the most corrupt institution in the public sector (Global Corruption Barometer 2013, p. 17).
- According to Corruption Watch Annual Report (2012), the latest Transparency International Corruption Perceptions Index placed South Africa at 69 out of 176 countries with a score of 4.3 out of 10 as far as corruption is concerned.

More clarification in terms of the degree of corruption in South Africa was given by the former auditor general Wronsley (1994, p. 14), who painted a very daunting picture about the losses incurred due to corruption. According to Wronsley, the loss of cash through corruption by the South African government increased from a tiny fraction of 1% in 1990 to more than 15% in 1998. Although there is a concession that the levels of corruption in South Africa are lower than most of the sub-Saharan African countries, its extent is still sufficient to derail service delivery in South Africa. Although difficult, there are a few additional ominous indications that can be used to measure the levels of corruption in South Africa. In 2010, South Africa was rated as the fifty-fourth most corrupt nation out of 178 countries surveyed (Transparency International, 2008, 2010). Comments by senior government officials including ministers and a Public Service Commission (2002, p. 27) report confirmed that bribery, fraud, nepotism, and systemic corruption are prevalent in contemporary South Africa. Other indicators of corruption include the results of different surveys, all of which confirmed the prevalence of corruption in South Africa. For instance, a survey conducted by the Institute for Democracy in South Africa (IDASA) in 1996 showed that 46% of those surveyed felt that most officials were involved in corruption and only 6% believed that there was a clean government (Lodge, 1998, p. 157). In another survey conducted by the World Value Survey (1996, p. 41), 15% of the respondents were certain that all public servants were guilty of bribery and corruption, whereas another 30% thought that most officials were venal.

It is clear that even though it is not easy to provide real statistics of corruption in South Africa, corruption is indeed rampant. It is therefore concluded that public corruption is located within the institutions of government including the legislature, courts, bureaucracies, and other statutory bodies including parastatals and commissions. Further, it is clear that corruption is constituted by transactions or exchanges of public resources and benefits between actors, some or all of whom are officials or public representatives (Lodge, 1998, p. 158).

Character of an Anticorruption Program: A Forensic Criminological Perspective

The approach adopted in this chapter is based on a multi-inter-trans-disciplinarity approach, which means that public corruption is looked at not only within the ambits of public administration but also through the forensic criminological lens. In forensic criminology, the interest does not end with understanding a particular phenomenon but encompasses mechanisms aimed at reacting to a particular phenomenon. In this instance, the main interest is harbored on whether the implementation of existing anticorruption strategies has yielded desired results or not. The aforesaid can be understood better if there is erudition around the character of an anticorruption program and whether the universally accepted elements of an anticorruption program have been observed in South Africa. Experience has shown that in certain instances there are good strategies that are developed but are sometimes badly implemented or compromised by those in power. It will therefore be established whether the South African government observes such elements in letter and in spirit. Even in cases where there is enough progress, the author will seek to clarify some of the events that may adversely affect these elements and generally the government's willingness and ability in dealing with public corruption.

Comprehension of Public Perceptions on Corruption

The first step in developing a successful anticorruption strategy begins with understanding what the citizens think as far as corruption is concerned. This element of an anticorruption program is less concerned with the accurate statistics of corruption but revolves around the feelings of those who live in a particular country. It is imperative that any government should strive to measure the perceptions of citizens about the extent of public corruption in government. A good knowledge is critical in developing strategies aimed at combating corruption.

However, this measurement will not be fruitful if the denial and spin-doctoring of corrupt activities by the government's communicators continues as is the case currently. It is often argued that the government in South Africa is not corrupt but that there are individuals within the ranks of public service who perpetrate acts of corruption. As fair as it may sound, the argument of this chapter is that corruption has elevated itself to a level of a normal feature of official business in South Africa. This means it is high time authorities accept that there is corruption in government and stop regarding the incidents of corruption as being sporadic and excluded. Statistics of corruption from different media have shown that corruption did not cease after the African National Congress (ANC) took over the government in 1994. Although this is the case, there is another school of thought that although corruption still existed after 1994 very little was known about it immediately after democratization. The reason advanced by the advocates of this thought is that after 1994 the people who were mostly affected were very poor and disenfranchised while the rich minority were unlikely to come face to face with public corruption. Most of the government agencies that were financed through government funds were not under strict scrutiny. For instance, out of 648 bodies financed through public funds only 34 reported to parliament while 200 bodies had to submit their records to parliament.

There are no satisfying statistics to conclude that the South African government has done enough in measuring and comprehending public perceptions about corruption. In cases where independent research bodies provided research results regarding these perceptions, the government did not readily accept the results; instead, such results were normally met with great denial by the government. Apart from low-level researches and disintegrated investigations about perceptions of corruption, there are no other clear avenues that the government used to gauge the level of corruption in South Africa. Although the environment to report corruption became favorable after 1994 because of the removal of restrictions of public knowledge about government business and the opposition parties' commitment to expose corruption, the measurement of public perception about corruption still remained sporadic. Some of the agencies, such as the IDASA, Human Sciences Research Council, and Institute for Security Studies (ISS), to mention a few, kept on publishing research results indicating public perception about the prevalence of corruption. The results published by these agencies were not always accepted by the government. In addition, these interventions should have been initiated by the government itself as part and parcel of an anticorruption program. Therefore, the general conclusion is that, apart from sporadic measurements of public perceptions by independent agencies, the government of South Africa cannot be said to have done enough in assessing what the citizens of South Africa think about corruption. This vacuum is bad for any anticorruption program, as repeated exercises of this nature and at repeated intervals, correlated with other indicators of institutional efficiency, can reveal a good picture about corruption and guide the responses appropriate for such.

Public Awareness about Corruption

There is a constant need to teach the public continuously about ethical values, the damages caused by unethical behavior, as well as the benefits of ethics in the public service and in society at large. This kind of education becomes more successful when coupled with mobilization of public interest in dealing with issues of corruption. In many governments, public awareness can be achieved by the utilization of nongovernmental monitoring, anticorruption hotlines, and a general civic participation. It is evident that the creation of an ethical environment can be beneficial to the fight against corruption in the argument of Treisman (2000, p. 401), who submits that the "legal culture" had an impact on the reduction of corruption and that this was more distinct in some of the former British colonies.

This trait has been seen in South Africa, although at a very slow pace. The recent few-months-old Corruption Watch launched by the Congress of South African Trade Unions (COSATU) is an example of such civic and nongovernmental intervention. The fact that some of these bodies are still being formed 18 years after the democratization of South Africa is a clear indication of the snail's pace at which this effort is unfolding. The creation of awareness about corruption seems to be a known factor by the government, but the implementation of such has been mired in troubles. For instance, the Mbeki administration called for a robust education campaign against corruption with the intention of creating "zero tolerance," "total war," and "morale submits," but this never saw a systematic official campaign to educate the public about the nature and consequences of corruption. In the same breath, the 1998 undertaking by the Public Service Commission to mount public campaigns to reinforce the "fear of detection punishment," 1999 resolution of the National Anti-Corruption Summit, and creation of the Anti-Corruption Forum did not bear desirable fruits because there were no clear plans for any state funding and the resources allocated were rather modest (Lodge, 2001, p. 58).

Although there are codes of conduct for public servants and parliamentarians, these remain less publicized and the average citizen has no acumen for understanding these codes. The *Ministerial Handbook* is one such initiative, which to date remains unclear and greatly contested. The greatest drawback in creating awareness is the failure by the government to disclose its disciplinary cases involving corrupt officials and repudiation of nongovernmental interventions. For instance, in November 2000 the then minister of police Steve Tshwete repudiated a proposed private sector agency to monitor police corruption. The actions of the minister further justified the maintenance of a toll-free anticorruption hotline by the South African police and Gauteng government (Lodge, 2001, p. 59). The failure to create public awareness and involvement in anticorruption initiatives is a setback for any anticorruption program.

From a forensic investigation perspective, the independence of bodies charged with monitoring and evaluation is of utmost importance. It is therefore clear from the given example that it would not have been effective for the police to monitor themselves as far as corruption is concerned. There is a need to involve more independent bodies that will monitor corruption and provide impartial reports.

Eradication of Corruption Incentives

Disincentivizing corruption can be seen as a hallmark of many anticorruption programs worldwide. It may involve a good number of mechanisms, which are intended to curb the possibility of benefiting from corruption. In certain countries, this is achieved by improving the payments of political office bearers. In South Africa, this can be achieved by a total review of the tendering process. Most of the services such as the building of road infrastructure, provision of water and cleaning, as well as maintenance of public buildings are often provided by private companies, which apply for tenders from government. Experience has shown that a lot of corruption takes place in this kind of arrangement. Statistics have shown that most of the money lost to corruption happens during tendering and procurement of services. For instance, the SIU claimed that the R10 billion (South African Currency in rands) worth of fraud that it was investigating in 1998 represented only 5% of the total cost of corruption. The very same trend of procurement fraud was also experienced in the delivery of low-cost housing to the extent that this has drawn comments and aroused the concern of the former Minister of Human Settlement Tokyo Sexwale (Rubin, 2011, p. 483).

An effective anticorruption program should be able to identify gaps in the procurement systems and try to disincentivize corruption where it is imminent. In South Africa, this could be achieved by a reduction of outsourced services such as the provision of water, sanitation, health, and housing facilities. There is no doubt that exorbitant amounts of money have been squandered while claiming to pay the service providers. It is therefore argued that if most of the mainstream services were provided by government departments, then there would be fewer incentives associated with corruption. The construction of roads in South Africa and particularly in the North West province has shown that a lot of graft could have been prevented if the government had been in the forefront of rolling out such services. According to Lodge (2001, p. 60), with the government's retreat from the "dirigiste" models of public administration being favored under apartheid, proliferation of privatization, and contracting out of what were exclusively government functions, the government's regulatory functions expanded rapidly, well beyond its administrative capacity.

Consistency and Visibility of Sanctions

Those who are caught committing acts of corruption must be processed effectively through the courts of South Africa. The most important aspect of arresting and convicting corrupt individuals is that the punishment meted out must have a deterring effect. The punishment can only be a deterrent if it is consistently applied to all found guilty and when such a punishment is a visible one. Because the theories of dealing with corruption suggest two alternatives in punishing those guilty of corruption, visible sanctions mean criminalizing some of the activities that are dealt with through internal departmental disciplinary procedures. Different means of punishment such as criminal sanctions, dismissals, and recovery of losses from the corrupt individual's assets must be meted out. The punishment meted out in cases of corruption should not discriminate and should be applied equally, irrespective of whether a particular person is having a political influence or holds an important position in the government or the political party. Visible sanctions are based on the premise that deterrence is accomplished through a variety of efforts associated with internal controls and ethic programs that create a workplace of integrity and encourage employees to report potential wrongdoings (Kranacher, Riley, & Wells, 2011, p. 13).

The South African experience is that there is not much visibility as far as the sanctions for corruption are concerned. The conclusion is that the current state of affairs leaves a lot to be desired. The wheels of justice are grinding at the lowest pace, and most of those accused of corruption escape unscathed due to prolonged criminal justice processes. The following are some examples of how the sanctions imposed on those suspected and accused of corruption may not be visible to the general public:

- Officials remain on the payroll while the prosecution is protracted.
- In Mpumalanga, the scandal involving the testing station was prolonged to such an extent that the person who exposed it, John Muller, was removed from his post before the case could be finalized.
- Organized labor unions such police and the Prison Civil Rights Union (POPCRU), South African Police Union, and others continue to protect their members amid allegations of corruption. For instance, the POPCRU labeled the dismissal of Commissioner Khulekani Sithole as the loss of a most committed and dedicated civil servant, although he was found guilty of corruption.
- Police officials can be dismissed only after they have been found guilty and an imprisonment has been mandated. The affairs and processes that surrounded the case of the former commissioner of police Bheki Cele exemplify this.

Although the government has established a number of agencies and mechanisms that deal with the reporting or investigation of public corruption, such as the protection of whistle-blowers, constitutionally protected offices of the auditor general and public protector, and establishment of the SIU, the problem still lies with whether visible sanctions are being meted out or not. Although these agencies are able to secure conviction on some of the cases that they are investigating, the problem is that such prosecutions are sometimes protracted to such an extent that when the punishment is meted out the public may have forgotten completely about a particular case. This therefore means that the citizens may not even be aware that a particular individual was sanctioned for public corruption. The investigation of arms deal in South Africa is a prominent example of delayed justice processes that can upset the visibility of sanctions.

Reforming Government Bureaucracy

Political appointments, exodus of skilled managers from the public service, affirmative action, and in certain instances employment equity, if not implemented judiciously, can compromise the integrity of the civil service. Due to this compromise and lack of skills in the public service, especially in the times that public service has grown complicated, can lead to serious gaps in management systems, thereby allowing graft to flourish. Although it is envisaged that the South African government may outgrow this problem of political bureaucracy, it is currently known that there are challenges of leadership and skill shortages in the public sector. For instance, the auditor general's reports annually indicate that public funds are not in order and this is frequently attributed to a shortage of accounting skills in the public sector.

Any effective anticorruption program takes the issue of leadership and the deployment of skilled people seriously. It is therefore concluded that due to political appointments in current government structures, the government did not progress adequately in embracing this effort of an anticorruption program. There have been cases where municipal managers were dismissed from one municipality for public corruption only to be recruited by another municipality. This is unfortunate because although the government has tried its best in sourcing necessary skills and reforming different bureaucracies, the number of shortcomings in the anticorruption program in South Africa remain so high that it defeats the good aspects of such a program. There is no clear indication of who is the political leader in government departments. An ideal situation is that public departments are politically led by a minister and a deputy minister while the director general is a skilled person who may not have any political inclinations. This means that policy would be developed at a political level and will be implemented by director generals who are not politicians but skilled practitioners in a particular field. A clear line that separates the political leadership and those who are mere executors can have a very positive influence on how the affairs of a particular government department are run, thus reducing graft and corruption within the echelons of that department.

Political Will

The South African government cannot keep on claiming that they believe in a clean government and are working toward such if there is no clear indication of political will to turn the tide against corruption. The establishment of different agencies and development of policies and strategies aimed at dealing with corruption cannot suffice if senior government officials continue to criticize the decisions of courts and other tribunals when their colleagues in the public service are involved in corruption. This trend has been clear since 1994, and in certain instances the judges are labeled counterrevolutionary if their decisions seem to contradict the aspirations of those in parliament and the upper echelons of government. This effort of an anticorruption program is therefore creating mixed feelings in South Africa because while the government reiterates its willingness to deal with corruption comments by senior government officials undermine the same political will. Unfortunately, all negative moves by the political leadership in criticizing the outcomes of independent bodies overshadow all efforts by the government to succeed in establishing a profound anticorruption program.

Lodge (2001, pp. 62–63) summarizes the actions of government leaders that contradict the political will to deal with corruption:

- In 1999, the Minister of Energy Penuel Maduna lashed out at the auditor general and concluded that that auditor general had grossly misrepresented the accounts of the Strategic Fuel Fund. Although these allegations by the minister were proved to be untrue later, no withdrawal was ever forthcoming from the then minister. Although in other democracies this move by the minister of energy could have tarnished his political vigor, the same minister was appointed as the minister of justice by the Mbeki administration after 1999. One of his other judicial blunders as far as corruption is concerned was his hinting that he might shut down the then Heath Commission, which is now known as the SIU.
- In the same year, South African courts were lambasted by the ruling party through its spokesperson, Smuts Ngonyama, who questioned

the integrity and the level of transformation of these courts. This was after Allan Boesak, the then ANC leader, was found guilty of embezzling the monies of the charity organization that he was heading. Ngonyama alluded that Boesak's main sin was his "lack of accounting skills." As if this was not enough, an attack by senior politicians on corruption-busting mechanisms, Ngonyama went further and accused the Appeals Court of being totally biased after Boesak's conviction was confirmed. Further, senior government officials and members of the ruling party attended in large numbers a church service presided by Allan Boesak after his release from prison in May 2000.

- In 1999, the *Mpumalanga News* (1989) ran an interesting story of the reappointment of the disgraced members of the Executive Council (MECs). These MECs were previously implicated in corruption scandals. Although the then premier of Mpumalanga Ndaweni Mahlangu said that the people he had chosen were "the best team," this was a setback in the fight against corruption. This trend is still continuing, and an example is that of a municipal manager of Mangaung who was deployed to the Ngaka Modiri Molema municipality while he was still being investigated for corruption. All these actions are surely equivalent to a setback in trying to convince the citizens that the government is intolerant of corruption.

- In addition to these acts, which contradict the political will to deal with corruption, the issue of political appointments, secrecy about electioneering funding, and retention of as well as openly praising some of the director generals despite revelations about their involvement in corruption cast a shadow on the political will of the South African government in dealing with public corruption. The director general of home affairs, Albert Mokoena, was praised by Minister Mangusuthu Buthelezi as a "competent and capable person" amid the findings that he unlawfully sponsored his private basketball team using state funds. The same happened with the director general of correctional services, Khulekani Sithole, who was defended by his minister, Ben Skosana.

Although the few examples given thus far may be contradicted by some good moves by the government, the crux of the matter is that the political will in dealing with corruption must be clear and consistent. It must be seen and followed in both letter and spirit. It is unfortunate that although some executive managers and ministers were recently axed, such as Sicelo Shiceka and Gwen Mahlangu-Nkabinde, this happened only after the opposition parties in parliament demanded the action from the President of the republic. It is against this background that it is concluded that political will in dealing with corruption by the government is tainted, skewed, inconsistent, minimal, and less visible.

Conclusion

It is clear from the preceding discussion that the program intended to deal with corruption in South Africa is not totally aligned with the internationally accepted cornerstones. Although the South African anticorruption program is based on the universally accepted elements such as political will, understanding of public perceptions on corruption, bureaucratic reform, and others, it is clear that these elements are mostly compromised. From the literature gathered and analyzed, it can be concluded that the programs adopted after 1994 in South Africa to deal with corruption did not succeed. The author could not detect any mistakes as far as the development of strategies and the programs are concerned, but in each case the implementation of such was challenged by various factors.

It is therefore concluded that the anticorruption strategies adopted by the government fell short of being effective as some of the important facets and elements were compromised, ignored, and not implemented. An anticorruption program is a set of actions that must all be observed equally if any democracy is truly committed to addressing corruption and its repercussions on service delivery, political stability, and well-being of the entire country. It is clear from the preceding discussion that some of the elements were observed while others were left to chance. The events that have been reported in a myriad of media are justifications of this conclusion. The desire of the government to deal with public corruption is characterized by opacity, confusion, and capriciousness, which exacerbate the picture regarding the government's will to thwart corruption and reverse its adverse impact on ordinary citizens.

The analysis is deemed fair and fit as democracy has been practiced in South Africa for a considerable number of years. Even in cognizance of the inheritance of public corruption from the apartheid era, a more willing government would have reduced corruption tremendously as corruption weakens the corporate governance principles desired by any democracy. Although there are positive aspects such as the establishment of several corruption-busting bodies and enactment of anticorruption legislation, such as The Prevention and Combating of Corrupt Activities Act, Act 12, of 2004 and the recently launched nongovernmental Corruption Watch of COSATU, the level of corruption in the country continues to reach epidemic levels.

In conclusion, and in agreement with Lodge (1998, p. 161), the government is still haunted by bureaucratic secrecy, absence of mutual surveillance procedures by government agencies, protracted rule by one political party or an aging one party dominant system, administrative inefficiency, complicated hierarchical decision-making procedures that create lengthy delays, and extensive patterns of political appointment in the civil service. All these are adverse to any anticorruption program and leave marginal opportunity for all corruption-fighting mechanisms to succeed.

References

Corruption Watch Annual Report. (2012). *Turn up the volume*. Retrieved July 17, 2014 from http://corruptionwatch.org.za/content/corruption-watch.

Eicher, S. (2009). *Corruption in International Business: The Challenge of Cultural and Legal Diversity*. Surrey, United Kingdom: Ashgate Publishing Limited.

Gildenhuys, S. H. (2004). *Ethics and Professionalism*. Stellenbosch, South Africa: Sunpress.

Kranacher, M., Riley, R., & Wells, J.T. (2011). *Forensic Accounting and Fraud Examination*. New York: ACFE.

Lodge, T. (1998). Political corruption in South Africa. *Journal of African Affairs*, 97(387), 157–187.

Lodge, T. (2001). *Countering Public Corruption in South Africa*. Retrieved January 15, 2012 from http://archive.lib.msu.edu/DMC/African%20journals/pdfs.

Mafunisa, M. J. (2000). *Public Service Ethics*. Kenwyn, United Kingdom: Juta and Company.

Martinez-Vazquez, J., Granado, J., & Boex, J. (2007). *Fighting Corruption in the Public Sector*. Amsterdam, the Netherlands: Elsevier.

Mpumalanga News. 1999. June 24: 3.

Petherick, W. A., Turvey, B., & Ferguson, C. (2010). *Forensic Criminology*. Amsterdam, the Netherlands: Elsevier.

Public Service Commission. (2002). *A Review of South Africa's National Anti-Corruption Report, Annexure 3*. Pretoria, South Africa: Department of Public Administration.

Randall, D. J. (1996). Prospects for the development of a black business class in South Africa. *The Journal of Modern African Studies*, 34(4), 661–686.

Shar, A. (2007). *Public Sector Governance: Performance Accountability and Combating Corruption*. Washington, DC: The World Bank.

Southall, R. (2004). The ANC and black capitalism in South Africa. *Review of African Political Economy* 31(100), 313–328.

Transparency International. (2008). *Corruption Perception Index*. Retrieved January 15, 2012 from http://www.transparency.org/policy_research/surveys_indices/cpi/2008.

Transparency International. (2010). *Corruption Perception Index*. Retrieved July 17, 2014 from http://www.transparency.org/policy_research/surveys_indices/cpi/2010.

Transparency International. (2013). *Global Corruption Barometer*. Retrieved July 17, 2014 from http://www.transparency.org/policy_research/surveys_indices.

Treisman, D. (2000). The causes of corruption: A cross-national study. *Journal of Public Economics*, 76(3), 399–457.

World Value Survey. (1996). *WVS Wave 3 South Africa*. Retrieved July 17, 2014 from http://www.worldvaluessurvey.org/WVSdocumentationWV3.jsp.

Wronsley, R. P. (1994). Controlling corruption. *SAIPA Journal of Public Administration*, 29(1).

Analysis of South African National Anticorruption Agencies 12

JOHANNA BERNING AND MOSES MONTESH

Contents

Introduction

Concerns about corruption have intensified globally in recent years. Corruption affects all sectors of society adversely. It corrodes national cultures and undermines development by distorting the rule of law, the ethos of democracy, and good governance. It endangers stability and security and threatens social, economic, and political development. Corruption also drains the government of resources and hinders international investments. Although corruption is a universal problem, it is particularly harmful in developing countries. These countries are the hardest hit by economic decline. They are also the most reliant on the provision of public services, and the least capable of absorbing additional costs associated with bribery, fraud, and the misappropriation of economic wealth. Therefore, it is very important that countries should develop effective measures to deal with corruption. Since 1994, South Africa has developed strategies and agencies aimed at combating corruption. However, as of 2012, corruption is still a problem in South Africa. The problems are multifaceted. Some noticeable problems include legislative deficiencies, institutional problems, and enforcement. This chapter is aimed at outlining the problems with our current model and ends with an international benchmarking as well as recommendations.

Methodology

In this study, the researcher has followed a qualitative approach. Literature study was used as a data collection technique. Document research and analysis focused largely on official documents, legislation, and media reports on the subject. Unstructured interviews were conducted with members from the police, Public Service Commission (PSC), and National Prosecuting Authority (NPA).

Aim of This Research

The aim of this research is as follows:

- To outline roles of various anticorruption agencies (ACAs) in South Africa
- To outline the mandates of various ACAs in South Africa
- To look at the effectiveness of various ACAs in South Africa
- To make a comparison with other countries
- To propose a way forward

Research Demarcation

South Africa has a substantial number of agencies whose function among others includes combating corruption. In this case, the selected institutions are the Office of the Auditor General, Office of the Public Protector, PSC, Asset Forfeiture Unit (AFU), Special Investigating Unit (SIU), Directorate of Special Operations (DSO), and Directorate for Priority Crime Investigation (DPCI).

Definition of Corruption

Section 3 of the Prevention and Combating of Corrupt Activities Act 12 of 2004 states that

> any person who directly or indirectly accepts or agrees or offers to accept a gratification from any other person whether for the benefit of himself or herself or for the benefit of another person: or gives or agrees or offers to give to any other person any gratification for the benefit of that other person or for the benefit of another person in order to act personally or by influencing another person so to act in a manner that amounts to the illegal, dishonest, unauthorised, incomplete, or biased: or misuse or selling of information or

material acquired in the course exercise, carrying out or performance of any powers, duties or function arising out of a constitutional or statutory contractual or any other legal obligation that amounts to the abuse of a position of authority; a breach of trust; or the violation of a legal duty or a set of rules; designed to achieve an unjustified result; or that amounts to any other unauthorised or improper inducement to do or not to do anything is guilty of the offence of corruption (p. 10).

In this instance, defining corruption is problematic. One of the most common definitions of corruption is "the use of public office for private gain." This definition needs to be broadened to include the following features: abuse of power and breach of trust; the fact that corruption occurs in the public, private, and nongovernmental sectors; and the fact that private gain is not the only motive for corrupt activity. Therefore, for the purpose of this chapter, corruption can be described as any conduct or behavior in relation to persons entrusted with responsibilities in public office that violates their duties as public officials and that is aimed at obtaining undue gratification of any kind for themselves or for others. This should not be viewed as a legal definition but rather as a working definition for the purposes of simplifying the definition as stipulated in the act.

Extent of Corruption in South Africa

According to the PSC (Public Service Commission, 2011), *Measuring the Effectiveness of the National Anti-Corruption Hotline (NACH) 19/2011*, a total of 1125 cases of alleged corruption have been received with respect to national departments (Table 12.1). These figures exclude cases reported directly to agencies such as the DSO, SIU, Office of the Auditor General, and Office of the Public Protector, just to mention a few.

Table 12.1 Extent of Corruption in South Africa

Name of Department	Number of Cases	Feedback Received
Education	7	7
Social Development	240	1
Health	8	5
Government Communication and Information Service	1	1
Department of Communication	4	1
SAPS	97	21
Department of Home Affairs	181	126
Department of Transport	5	1
Department of Justice and Constitutional Development	42	23

Table 12.1   Extent of Corruption in South Africa (*Continued*)

Name of Department	Number of Cases	Feedback Received
Department of Labour	30	6
Department of Correctional Services	178	41
Department of Land Affairs	12	7
Department of Housing	10	5
South African National Defence Force	18	2
Department of Trade and Industry	54	21
Independent Complaints Directorate	69	47
Department of Science and Technology	3	2
National Treasury	7	5
South African Revenue Services	28	0
NPA	17	15
Department of Public Enterprises	1	1
National Intelligence Agency	2	0
Office of the Public Protector	2	1
Department of Provincial and Local Government	68	2
Department of Water Affairs and Forestry	22	5
Department of Public Works	6	3
Safety and Security	5	5
PSC	3	3
Department of Public Service and Administration	3	1
Department of Environmental Affairs and Tourism	2	1

Note: This table excludes corruption reported in the private sector and in public entities.

Corruption Perceptions Index 2011

Every year, Transparency International publishes the Corruption Perceptions Index, which ranks countries according to their perceived levels of public sector corruption. The 2011 index draws on different assessments and business opinion surveys carried out by independent and reputable institutions. The surveys and assessments used to compile the index include questions relating to bribery of public officials, kickbacks in public procurement, and embezzlement of public funds and questions that probe the strength and effectiveness of public sector anticorruption efforts (Public Service Commission,

2001, p. 23). Perceptions are used because corruption—whether frequent or rare—is to a great extent a hidden activity that is difficult to measure. Over time, perceptions have proved to be a reliable estimate of corruption. Measuring scandals, investigations, or prosecutions, while offering "nonperception" data, reflect less on the prevalence of corruption in a country and more on other factors, such as freedom of the press or efficiency of the judicial system. The Corruption Perceptions Index complements Transparency International's many other tools that measure corruption and integrity in public and private sectors at global, national, and local levels. According to Transparency International (2011), the perceived levels of public sector corruption in 183 countries/territories around the world revealed that South Africa was ranked 64th. This is worrying, especially when you look at the stature and status of the country in Africa.

Causes of Corruption

Incidence of corruption varies among societies, and it can be rare, widespread, or systemic. When it is rare, it is relatively easy to detect, isolate, and punish the perpetrators and to prevent corruption from becoming widespread (South Africa, 2007). When corruption is widespread, it is more difficult to control and deal with. But the worst scenario is when it becomes systemic.

When systemic corruption takes hold of a country, the institutions, rules, and peoples' behavior and attitudes become adapted to the corrupt way of doing things and corruption becomes a way of life. Systemic corruption is very difficult to overcome, and it can have a devastating effect on the economy. According to Ngobeni (2008), the following aspects have a potential of opening gaps for corruption to take place: an ambiguous legal framework, a weak legislative system, greed, a weak judicial system, poor governance, and political instability.

Ambiguous Legal Framework

A lack of clear rules governing the public sector and its procedures creates loopholes for persons or firms to receive a government benefit to which they might not be entitled. In South Africa, the Corruption Act 94 of 1992 was vaguely formulated; hence, it was replaced by the Prevention of Corruption and Related Practices Act 12 of 2004.

Weak Legislative System

A weak legislative system, including parliament and any other institution of the country's criminal justice system, creates an opportunity for corruption to take place (Gbadamosi, 2006, p. 63). This may include lack of recognition of corruption as a morally and socially perverse phenomenon, which may be a very serious fetter to socioeconomic development.

Greed

Naturally, human beings are greedy. The desire to fulfill one's selfish motives and a lack of professional integrity can cause individuals to potentially abuse their positions of authority for private gain. An inability to live within one's regular earnings can also compel an individual to seek irregular ways of meeting the demands of his or her lifestyle (Kyambalesa, 2006, p. 109).

Weak Judicial System

A weak judicial system fosters corruption by not being able to adjudicate fairly, impartially, and professionally in matters relating to corrupt practices by government leaders and civil servants due to inadequate financial resources and lack of independence of the judiciary from the executive branch of a country's government (Gbadamosi, 2006, p. 263).

Poor Governance

If political leaders and top bureaucrats set an example of self-enrichment or ambiguity over public ethics, lower level officials and members of the public might follow suit. If informal rules come to supersede formal ones, even the most stringent legal principles and procedures lose their authority (Kyambalesa, 2006, p. 108). Hence, bribery and corruption may become the norm, even in the face of formal rules intended to support clean governance.

Political Instability

An unstable political setting like Zimbabwe and other countries can create an atmosphere of job insecurity, uncertainty, and anarchy in government institutions. As such, this can tempt government leaders and civil servants to engage in unscrupulous schemes to amass wealth quickly in anticipation of a sudden change in their employment status (Kyambalesa, 2006, p. 108).

Dimensions of Corruption

According to the Country Assessment Report (2003), the following is a list of examples of various manifestations of corruption in South Africa: nepotism, favoritism, insider trading, conflicts of interest, abuse of power, extortion, embezzlement, and bribery.

Nepotism

This involves a public servant ensuring that family members are appointed to public service positions or that family members receive state contracts from state resources. This manifestation is similar to conflict of interest and favoritism.

Favoritism

This involves the provision of services or resources according to personal affiliations of a particular servant. This practice is normally practiced along ethnic, religious, and party political affiliation.

Insider Trading

This involves the use of privileged information and knowledge that a particular public servant possesses as a result of his or her office to provide unfair advantage to another person or entity to obtain a benefit, or to accrue a benefit for himself or herself.

Conflict of Interest

Conflict of interest involves a public servant acting or failing to act on a matter where the public servant has an interest or another person or entity that stands in a relationship with the public servant has an interest.

Abuse of Power

Abuse of power involves a public servant using his or her vested authority to improperly benefit another public servant, person, or entity.

Extortion

This involves coercing a person or entity to provide a benefit to a public servant, another person, or an entity in exchange for acting in a particular manner.

Embezzlement

Embezzlement involves theft of resources by persons entrusted with the authority and control of such resources.

Bribery

Bribery involves the promise, offering, or giving of a benefit that improperly affects the actions or decisions of a public servant. These acts are normally committed by law enforcement officers. This benefit may accrue to the public servant, another person, or an entity.

A variation of this manifestation occurs when a political party or government is offered, promised, or given a benefit that improperly affects the actions or decisions of the political party or government. In South Africa, the Corruption Act 94 of 1992 defined bribery as "the offering of a benefit that improperly affects the decision of an official in a position of authority and the acceptance of such an offer thereof." However, this act has since been repealed by the Prevention and Combating of Corrupt Activities Act 12 of 2004 and this act does not contain the definition of bribery. Therefore, bribery does not exist in the South African statutes. Apart from the aforementioned acts of corruption, the following are also forms of corruption: theft of government property, sexual harassment for employment or promotion favors, fraudulent qualifications and certificates, ghost workers normally committed by the employees of the department of education, white-collar crime/fraud, kickbacks, private use of state vehicles by public officials, lack of transparency in business transactions, tender rigging, and social grant fraud. These acts take place in both private and public sectors.

Indicators of Fraud and Corruption

The behavioral aspects of an individual assist in profiling a typical fraudster, whereas those of organizations typify the risks that make the organizations susceptible to fraud and corruption. According to the Country Corruption Assessment Report (South Africa 2003), the following are regarded as indicators or red flags of the potential existence of corruption and fraud:

- Unusually high personal debts
- Living beyond one's means
- Excessive gambling habits
- Alcohol/drug problems
- Undue family or peer pressure to succeed
- Feeling of being underpaid
- Feeling of insufficient recognition for job performance
- Close association with suppliers
- Wheeler–dealer attitude
- Desire to "beat the system"
- Criminal record
- Not taking vacations
- Not allowing someone access to area of responsibility
- Undisclosed conflict of interest
- Rationalization for conflicting behavioral patterns

Effects of Corruption

Being rated or perceived as a country with a high level of corruption can adversely affect a nation's ability to develop sound bilateral and multilateral relations with other countries. Corruption can have negative consequences on diplomatic and economic relations that a country may seek to pursue with other sovereign states (Kyambalesa, 2006, p. 112). Other effects of corruption may include economic and human rights violations. In South Africa, the case of Jacob Zuma, the African National Congress (ANC) president, may have had an impact on South Africa's relations with the international community (Ngobeni, 2008, p. 4).

Costs of Corruption

Although it is undisputed that corruption has become global in scope, it has particular damaging effects on the domestic environment of countries. It is difficult to quantify the cost of corruption because it comes in many forms, including monetary as well as human. According to the Country Corruption Assessment Report (South Africa, 2003), there are generally four costs of corruption: macro-fiscal, reduction in productive investment and growth, costs to public and the poor in particular, and loss of confidence in public institutions. Corruption deters investment because it is a disincentive to prospective investors, thereby inhibiting economic growth.

The values and norms of people are also distorted as a result of corruption, thus undermining moral standards and promoting charlatans to the detriment of honest endeavors (Kyambalesa, 2006, p. 108).

International and Regional Initiatives to Curb Corruption

United Nations

In December 1996, the United Nations General Assembly adopted two important instruments in the fight against corruption: the Code of Conduct for International Public Officials, which was adopted to provide member states with a tool to guide their efforts against corruption through a set of basic recommendations that national public officials should follow in the performance of their duties, and the Declaration against Corruption and Bribery in International Commercial Transactions. Furthermore, these legal instruments state that each state party "shall, in accordance with the fundamental principles of its legal system, develop and implement or maintain effective, coordinated anticorruption policies that promote the participation of society and reflect the principles of the rule of law, proper management of public affairs and public property, integrity, transparency, and accountability"

(United Nations, 2003). In addition, these legal instruments also suggest that each state party shall endeavor to establish and promote effective practices aimed at the prevention of corruption. South Africa is a signatory to these resolutions; hence, the South African Parliament promulgated the Prevention and Combating of Corrupt Activities Act 12 of 2004 to combat corruption. On November 15, 2000, the General Assembly also adopted the United Nations Convention against Transnational Organized Crime (2000), which includes several provisions related to corruption. In particular, the convention focused on the following:

- The establishment of corruption as a criminal offence for both offenders and accomplices in acts of corruption
- The liability of legal persons corrupting public officials
- The promotion of the integrity of public officials and the provision of sanctions

As a result of these resolutions, member states, including South Africa, were required to tighten the fight against corruption and organized crime. In response to these resolutions, agencies such as the DSO, Asset and Forfeiture Unit, as well as SIU were established in South Africa.

African Union Initiatives

At the first session of the Assembly of the African Union in Durban in July 2002, a declaration relating to the New Partnership for Africa's Development was adopted. This declaration calls for the establishment of a coordinated mechanism to combat corruption effectively. In response to this (and in response to various other decisions and declarations), the African Union Convention on Preventing and Combating Corruption (2003) was adopted by member states as a guiding tool in the fight against corruption. In response to these initiatives, a number of ACAs were established in South Africa with varying mandates.

Southern African Development Community Protocol against Corruption

On August 14, 2001, in a meeting in Blantyre, Malawi, heads of state of the Southern African Development Community (SADC) region adopted the SADC *Protocol against Corruption* (Southern African Development Community, 2001). Three member states, including South Africa, ratified the protocol. However, for the protocol to be effective, it needed to be ratified by nine member states. The SADC protocol followed in the wake of the Inter-American Convention against Corruption of 1996 and the European

Convention on the Fight against Corruption of 1997. The purpose of the SADC protocol is threefold:

1. To promote the development of anticorruption mechanisms at the national level
2. To promote cooperation in the fight against corruption by state parties
3. To harmonize national anticorruption legislation in the region

Article VI of the protocol criminalizes bribery of foreign officials. This is in line with the OECD Convention on Combating Bribery of Foreign Officials in International Business Transactions. The protocol addresses the issue of proceeds of crime by allowing for their seizure and confiscation, thereby making it more difficult to benefit from the proceeds of corruption (South Africa, 2008, p. 29). It makes corruption or any of the offences under it an extraditable offence, thereby removing the "safe haven" for criminals in SADC countries. The protocol can serve as a legal basis for extradition in the absence of a bilateral extradition treaty. The SADC protocol also provides for judicial cooperation and legal assistance among state parties. This is important because corruption often involves more than one country.

Southern African Forum against Corruption

Within the SADC region, the Southern African Forum against Corruption (SAFAC) was established in June 2000. The SAFAC aims to be the designated authority to implement the SADC protocol at the regional level. The forum seeks to enhance cooperation among the anticorruption institutions within SADC countries. The constitution still needs to be adopted and its relationship with SADC defined (South Africa, 2008, p. 45). The SAFAC recognizes that a major shortcoming of all anticorruption campaigns throughout the SADC region is the absence of training facilities and structures focused on the unique range of skills and abilities required of personnel engaged in anticorruption campaigns or employed by anticorruption bodies. According to Country Assessment Report (2008), the SAFAC's key objectives are as follows:

- Strengthen networking among member organizations, and update members on appropriate legislation and relevant international instruments on corruption
- Facilitate the upgrading of skills relevant to fighting corruption through training
- Cooperate and facilitate transboundary investigations and prosecution of corruption cases
- Implement the provisions of the SADC *Protocol against Corruption*

- Identify and share experiences on best practices on combating corruption
- Share relevant information on corruption and intelligence

South African Government's Action against Corruption

In March 1997, South African government ministers responsible for the South African National Crime Prevention Strategy established a program committee to work on corruption. This program resulted in the development of the Public Service Anti-Corruption Strategy (South Africa, 2002), which contained nine considerations that are interrelated and mutually supportive. These are as follows:

1. Review and consolidation of the legislative framework
2. Increased institutional capacity to prevent and combat corruption
3. Improved access to report wrongdoing and protection of whistle-blowers and witnesses
4. Prohibition of corrupt individuals and businesses (blacklisting)
5. Improved management policies and practices
6. Managing professional ethics
7. Partnerships with stakeholders
8. Social analysis, research, and policy advocacy
9. Awareness, training, and education

This was done to satisfy the requirements of the Constitution, Public Service Anti-Corruption Strategy, and recommendations of the National Anti-Corruption Summit. Furthermore, several of the government's policy decisions have also been translated into a number of anticorruption measures, although with unstructured mandates (Department of Public Service and Administration, 2002).

Institutional Capacity to Curb Corruption

Auditor General

The auditor general conducts audits of government departments and other public sector bodies to provide assurance to parliament that these accountable entities have achieved their financial objectives and managed their financial affairs according to sound financial principles and in accordance with the legal framework created by the parliament. In terms of section 188 of the Constitution of the Republic of South Africa Act 108 of 1996, the functions of the auditor general are set out as follows:

> To audit and report on the accounts, financial statements, and financial management of all national and provincial state departments and

administrations; all municipalities; and any other institution or accounting entity required by national or provincial legislation to be audited by the auditor general.

In addition to the duties prescribed in subsection (1), and subject to any legislation, the auditor general may audit and report on the accounts, financial statements, and financial management of any institution funded from the National Revenue Fund, from a Provincial Revenue Fund, or by a municipality or any institution that is authorized in terms of any law to receive money for a public purpose.

The auditor general has been established as a Chapter 9 institution in terms of section 181 of the South African Constitution. The Auditor-General Act 12 of 1995 further sets out the powers and functions of the auditor general in terms of the constitution and other legislations. Following the adoption of the constitution in 1996, the Office of the Auditor-General recognized a need to review the Auditor General Act. A task team was appointed to undertake the review process. The Auditor General Act is currently being reviewed to align it with the constitution and with any other relevant, newly promulgated legislation; improve specific operational provisions; and bring the provision of services in line with the latest trends in international public sector auditing.

Public Service Commission

The PSC is a constitutionally mandated body responsible for investigating, monitoring, and evaluating the organization and practices of the South African public service. The PSC derives its mandate from sections 195 to 196 of the Constitution Act 108 of 1996. Section 195 sets out the values and principles governing public administration that must be promoted by the commission. In terms of section 196(4) of the Constitution of the Republic of South Africa, the main functions and powers of the commission are

- To promote the values and principles of public administration set out in section 195 of the constitution, throughout the public service
- To investigate, monitor, and evaluate the organization and administration and the personnel practices of the public service and, in particular, the adherence to the values and principles set out in section 195
- To advise national and provincial organs of state regarding personnel practices
- To report its finding and recommendations at least once a year to the National Assembly or provincial legislature
- To report issues of immediate operational concern to the relevant executive authority

- To investigate grievances of employees and recommend appropriate remedies
- Propose measures to ensure effective and efficient performance within the public service

The work of the PSC is structured around six key performance areas (KPAs) and two additional focus areas. The six KPAs are professional ethics and risk management, anticorruption investigations, management improvement and service delivery, labor relations monitoring, human resources management, and senior management conditions of service, and the additional focus areas are monitoring and evaluation and institution building.

Asset Forfeiture Unit

The South African National Director of Public Prosecutions established the AFU in May 1999 to focus on the implementation of Chapters 5 and 6 of the Prevention of Organised Crime Act 121 of 1998. Chapter 6 of the act permits the state to forfeit the proceeds and instrumentalities of crime in a civil process that is not dependent on or related to any criminal prosecution or conviction. The Prevention of Organised Crime Act makes provision for property tainted by criminal activity to be forfeited to the state by way of a civil action. Commonly called civil asset forfeiture, this allows the state to confiscate assets from suspected criminals purely through a civil action against the property without the need to obtain a criminal conviction against the owner of the property. The AFU does not have investigative functions but renders services to both the South African Police Service (SAPS) and the (now defunct) Scorpions. The unit was set up to ensure that the powers in the act to seize criminal assets would be used to their maximum effect in the fight against crime, particularly organized crime. The AFU has powers to do the following:

- Seize cash associated with the drug trade
- Seize property used in the drug trade or some other crime
- Investigate corruption
- Investigate white-collar crime
- Target serious criminals
- Investigate violent crime

A further priority has been to deal with corrupt officials. However, this function overlaps with the functions of the SIU.

Special Investigating Unit

The SIU is an independent statutory body established by the South African president, which conducts investigations at his request. It reports directly to the president and parliament on the outcomes of such investigations. The SIU functions in a manner similar to a commission of inquiry in that the president refers cases to it by issuing a proclamation that sets out the scope and ambit of the investigation. Section 2(2) of the Special Investigating Units and Special Tribunals Act 74 of 1996 defines the allegations that the SIU may investigate and for which proclamations may be issued.

Essentially, the SIU investigates fraud, corruption, and maladministration within government departments. It uses civil law to fight corruption, which has important advantages. It is often difficult to prove the crime of corruption because it usually takes place between individuals who are equally guilty and do not want to give evidence. A civil case is easier to prove because the case only has to be proved on a balance of probabilities, and not beyond reasonable doubt, as in a criminal case.

The SIU may investigate any matter set out in section 2 of the Special Investigating Units and Special Tribunals Act 74 of 1996. These include the following:

- Serious maladministration in connection with the affairs of any state institution
- Improper or unlawful conduct by employees of any state institution
- Unlawful appropriation or expenditure of public money or property
- Any unlawful, irregular, or unapproved acquisitive act, transaction, measure, or practice that has a bearing on state property
- Intentional or negligent loss of public money or damage to public property
- Corruption in connection with the affairs of any state institution
- Unlawful or improper conduct by any person who has caused or may cause serious harm to the interest of the public, or any category thereof

The major function of the SIU is to investigate corruption and maladministration, and to take civil legal action to correct any wrongdoing. The focus of the SIU is the public sector, but it also deals with private sector accomplices. It can investigate private sector matters that cause substantial harm to the interests of the public. The SIU does not have powers to arrest, but in instances of criminal wrongdoing it adopts a multidisciplinary approach to law enforcement (Montesh, 2007). The SIU focuses mainly on corruption in small- and medium-sized entities where it is an endemic problem and impacts on service delivery, such as pensions, local government, and housing. Some of the functions of the SIU overlap with those of the PSC and the Office of the Public Protector.

Directorate of Special Operations (the Scorpions)

The DSO, nicknamed the "Scorpions," was launched in September 1999 in Gugulethu near Cape Town, South Africa. After experiencing some problems, the National Assembly amended the National Prosecuting Authority Act 32 of 1998 to establish the DSO as an investigating directorate of the NPA.

This was done in terms of the National Prosecuting Authority Amendment Act 61 of 2000. The DSO used the troika principles of intelligence, investigations, and prosecutions to fight national priority crimes, including corruption. The focus of the DSO was corruption within the criminal justice system as well as high-level corruption crimes of an organized nature. The DSO was established from the merger of the previous investigating directorates of organized crime and serious economic offences and corruption. However, as the Scorpions gained public favor they also exceeded their area of jurisdiction by performing functions that fell outside their mandate, such as intelligence gathering.

Downfall of the Directorate of Special Operations

During the course of the investigation into the arms deal that started in 2001, the DSO uncovered irregularities in the award of tenders by the Department of Defence.

Among those who benefited from these irregular deals was Schabir Shaik, the then deputy president Jacob Zuma's financial adviser and confidante for many years. The DSO investigation led to Shaik being charged on two counts of corruption and one of fraud related to bribes involving Zuma. In *State v. Shaik & Others*, the accused, Schabir Shaik, was found guilty of corruption and fraud and was sentenced to 15 years in jail. The court found that he had contravened the Corruption Act 94 of 1992. The first charge related to 238 payments into the account of a politician holding high political office (i.e., fraud). The second charge related to incorrect journal entries in the financial statements of the accused's companies, and the third charge related to the soliciting of a bribe by the accused. Throughout the trial, which lasted from January 12, 2002 to February 17, 2005, Shaik's relationship with then deputy president Jacob Zuma was in question, yet Zuma was never called to testify either for the state or for the accused. This led to questions being raised in the media about why Zuma was not charged jointly with Shaik (Montesh & Berning, 2012, p. 17).

In 2005, when Shaik was found guilty and was convicted, President Thabo Mbeki dismissed Zuma as deputy president, a move that led to enormous political tensions in the ANC and among its alliance partners, the Congress of South African Trade Unions (COSATU), the ANC Youth League, and others within the ruling party, as Zuma was the preferred successor of Mbeki. The conviction of Shaik did not signal the end of the Scorpions' investigation and, shortly thereafter, on August 18, 2005 the Scorpions raided Shaik's house, this time searching for evidence against Zuma (Ngobeni, 2008, p. 18).

These raids were heavily criticized by the union federation COSATU, who accused the NPA and the judicial system of being manipulated and influenced to take biased political decisions and actions. This case and the DSO's handling of it was arguably the single most important factor leading to its downfall, not least because during the course of the DSO's investigations several mistakes were made. One of these was to violate the principle of attorney/client privilege. Section 14 of the constitution provides for the right of an individual to refuse to disclose admissible evidence. This means that any confidential communication made directly between a client and his or her legal advisor, or made by means of an agent, is privileged and a person cannot be compelled to disclose such communication. Neither is he or she compelled to disclose any communication that was obtained with a view to litigation. In 2006, the DSO had also raided the offices of Zuma's lawyers and seized documents for the purpose of an investigation into the alleged corruption charges. Zuma brought a case against the DSO for violating attorney client privilege, which was upheld by the court (Montesh & Berning, 2012, p. 19). The court ruled that the actions of the DSO were a direct violation of section 201 of the Criminal Procedure Act and section 35 (3) (h) of the constitution. With the DSO having taken on such high-profile political cases so early in its existence it was almost inevitable that it would attract strong criticism, at least from those who saw it as meddling in power broking in the ruling party. Criticism focused on the location and mandate of the directorate; this prompted President Thabo Mbeki in 2005 to establish an independent commission of inquiry to look into these matters, which was headed by Judge Sisi Khampepe. The Khampepe Commission (South Africa, 2006) found that although the DSO as a structure was not unconstitutional, it did not have a legal basis to collect intelligence.

Furthermore, although the DSO was mandated to gather, keep, and analyze information in terms of section 7(1) (a) (ii) of the NPA Act, the evidence adduced before the commission as well as the onsite visits to the DSO tended to show that the DSO had established intelligence-gathering capabilities. As a result, the commission found that this was in serious violation of sections 1, 2, and 3 of the National Strategic Intelligence Act 39 of 1994.

The Khampepe Commission also found that the directorate lacked oversight. Section 43 of the National Prosecuting Authority Act 32 of 1998 made provision for the establishment of a ministerial coordinating committee to develop regulations and standard operating procedures for the members of the DSO. However, the same section did not make provision for the establishment of a structure or institution to oversee the DSO, which the ministerial committee was not expected to do. It is also noted that although the NPA Act made provision for the minister to exercise oversight over the DSO, such provision was not extended to the inspector general of intelligence. Section 7(7) of the Intelligence Services Oversight Act 40 of 1994 makes provision for the establishment of an inspector general for intelligence, whose primary role and functions are to *inter alia* monitor and review the intelligence and counterintelligence activities of any service.

So far it has been shown that mistakes by the Scorpions themselves, the failure of the law and executive to determine appropriate oversight over the unit, as well as intense political pressure as a consequence of pursuing investigations that involved high-level politicians all contributed to the downfall of the DSO.

As a result of these recommendations, in December 2007 the ANC held its 52nd National Policy Conference, where it was resolved that the DSO should be incorporated into the SAPS. The resolution led to the tabling of the General Law Amendment Bill (2008) and the National Prosecuting Authority Amendment Bill (2008) before the parliament. During the second sitting of the parliament in 2008, the National Assembly approved the dissolution of the DSO and its incorporation into the SAPS's DPCI. The dissolution of the unit was decried by the media, organized business, and opposition parties, who argued that the state's ability to investigate and counter corruption had been severely compromised by the closure of the unit.

South African Police Service: Directorate for Priority Crime Investigation

The DPCI, also known as the "Hawks," was established on May 21, 2009, after the South African cabinet approved the appointment of Deputy National Commissioner Anwa Dramat to take charge of this new directorate of the SAPS. This was done in terms of the National Prosecuting Authority Amendment Act 56 of 2008 as well as the South African Police Service Amendment Act 57 of 2008.

The DPCI has been tasked with preventing, combating, and investigating national priority offences as well as other offences or categories of offences referred to the directorate by the national commissioner (Parliamentary Monitor, 2011). The division is composed of the Commercial Crime Unit, Financial Investigation and Assets Forfeiture Unit, Organised Crime Unit, and Priority Crime Management Centre and Support Services.

Hugh Glenister v. President of the Republic of South Africa & Others [CCT 48/10]

In the *Hugh Glenister v. President of the Republic of South Africa & Others [CCT 48/10]*, the key question was whether the national legislation that created the DPCI, and disbanded the DSO, was constitutionally valid. The majority of the court (in a joint judgment by Deputy Chief Justice

Moseneke and Justice Cameron, in which Justice Froneman, Justice Nkabinde, and Justice Skweyiya concurred) found that Chapter 6A of the South African Police Service Act 68 of 1995, as amended, was inconsistent with the constitution and invalid to the extent that it failed to secure an adequate degree of independence for the DPCI. As a result, the court made two key findings.

First, it held that the constitution imposed an obligation on the state to establish and maintain an independent body to combat corruption and organized crime. Although the constitution did not in express terms command that a corruption-fighting unit should be established, its scheme taken as a whole imposed a pressing duty on the state to set up a concrete, effective, and independent mechanism to prevent and root out corruption. This obligation is sourced in the constitution and international law agreements, which are binding on the state.

The court pointed out that corruption undermines the rights in the Bill of Rights and imperils our democracy. Section 7(2) of the constitution imposes a duty on the state to "respect, protect, promote, and fulfill" the rights in the Bill of Rights. Second, the Court found that the DPCI did not meet the constitutional requirement of adequate independence. Consequently, the impugned legislation did not pass constitutional muster. The main reason for this conclusion was that the DPCI is insufficiently insulated from political influence in its structure and functioning. This is because the DPCI's activities must be coordinated by the cabinet—the statute provides that a ministerial committee may determine policy guidelines with respect to the functioning of the DPCI, as well as the selection of national priority offences. This form of oversight makes the unit vulnerable to political interference.

Further, the court held that the safeguards that the provisions create were inadequate to save the DPCI from a significant risk of political influence and interference. Sadly, in February 2012 the South African government published the South African Police Service Amendment Bill of 2012 for comments in response to Glenister's case. After going through the bill, the authors are convinced that South Africa is still far from establishing a single ACA. As it stands, the bill will never pass through the Constitutional Court.

Office of the Public Protector

The public protector has the power to investigate any conduct in state affairs, or in the public administration in any sphere of government, that is alleged or suspected to be improper or to result in any impropriety or prejudice. National legislation regulating the office is found in the Public Protector Act 23 of 1994. The Public Protector Act supports section 182 of the Constitution Act 108 of 1996 by spelling out that maladministration, abuse of power,

improper conduct, undue delay, and an act resulting from improper prejudice to a person may be investigated.

The Public Protector Act broadens the jurisdiction of the public protector to include any institution on which the state is the majority or controlling
shareholder or any public entity as defined in the Public Finance Management
Act 1 of 1999. Such institutions include, for example, the major providers
of electricity, telecommunications, and postal services. In 1998, the Public
Protector Amendment Act 133 of 1998 came into operation to amend the
Public Protector Act to bring it in line with the Constitution of the Republic
of South Africa, 1996, and matters connected, such as providing for the preliminary investigation stage. The public protector is an advocate neither for
the complainant nor for the public authority concerned. The office ascertains
the facts of the case and reaches an impartial and independent conclusion on
the merits of the complaint. The office has the following core functions:

- To undertake investigations within its sphere of jurisdiction.
- To provide administrative support for such investigations.
- "During an investigation, the Public Protector may, if he/she consid-
  ers it appropriate or necessary: (1) Direct any person to appear before
  him/her to give evidence or to produce any document in his/her possession or under his/her control which, in the opinion of the Public
  Protector, has a bearing on the matter being investigated, and may
  examine such person for that purpose; (2) Request any person at any
  level of government, or performing a public function, or otherwise
  subject to his/her jurisdiction, to assist him/her in the performance
  of his/her duties with regard to a specific investigation; (3) and make
  recommendations and take appropriate remedial action."

Discussion

Bribery, fraud, nepotism, and systemic corruption are some of the forms that
corruption takes in contemporary South Africa. A number of state agencies are in place to combat and prevent corruption. To some, the mandates
of some of these agencies overlap, thus creating unnecessary duplication of
functions. It is also clear that the creation of the DSO was in direct competition with the SAPS, resulting in a duplication of functions. According to the
Public Service Commission (2001, p. 34), in 2000 there were 890 cases investigated by both the SAPS and the DSO. This could have been avoided if the
legislative mandate governing the two agencies was clear.

Furthermore, it is worth noting that the core business of both the
AFU and the SIU are similar in that both units aim to recover funds for
the government. The idea of having the AFU is very good. However, the

establishment of the AFU and SIU amounts to a duplication of functions. The SIU functions like a commission of inquiry and virtually does what the AFU does. Both AFU and SIU use civil action to recover and seize assets from criminals. To add to the confusion, both units are accountable to the National Director of Public Prosecutions (NDPP). The AFU's role is to ensure that it takes the profit out of crime by seizing the proceeds of crime. This is also done by the SIU. The author is of the opinion that the AFU and the SIU should not exist as separate entities. It is therefore recommended that the two agencies merge and form one strong asset forfeiture unit under the NPA. Such integration could ease both functional and operational responsibilities.

Way Forward: A Need for a Single Anticorruption Agency

ACAs are specialized agencies established by governments for the specific aim of minimizing corruption in their countries. Heilbrunn (2004) has identified four types of ACAs:

1. The *universal model*, with its investigative, preventive, and communicative functions, is typified by Hong Kong's independent commission against corruption (ICAC).
2. The *investigative model* is characterized by a small and centralized investigative commission, as it operates in Singapore's Corrupt Practices Investigation Bureau (CPIB).
3. The *parliamentary model* includes commissions that report to parliamentary committees and are independent from the executive and judicial branches of the state (e.g., the Australian New South Wales Independent Commission against Corruption).
4. The *multiagency model* includes a number of agencies that are autonomous but together weave a web of agencies to fight corruption.

The U.S. Office of Government Ethics, with its preventive approach, complements the Justice Department's investigative and prosecutorial powers, and together these organizations make a concerted effort to reduce corruption.

Corruption is a major problem in many parts of the world. To combat corruption, a number of governments have created specific bodies tasked with fighting corruption. These ACAs come in a variety of shapes and forms. One particular title for an ACA, which has gained a high degree of global prominence, is "independent commission against corruption." Since the first ICAC was started in Hong Kong in 1974, a number of other ICACs have been created in a range of countries around the world (Chen, 2006). A key point to note is that not all countries have an ACA. Indeed, the general consensus is that not all countries require an ACA (Lee, 2005, p. 45). However, the key rationale for establishing an ACA is that it will increase the effectiveness of anticorruption efforts within a country. In general, an ACA will achieve this by

- Resolving coordination issues among integrity agencies involved in anticorruption work
- Sending a signal by government that corruption is a serious issue
- Centralizing information and intelligence about corrupt activity
- Not being subject to control by vested interests within wider society

A lack of coordination and centralization of anticorruption activities by a country's integrity institutions leading to low levels of success in combating corruption is thus a central reason for establishing an ACA. However, we need to note that the creation of an ACA will not necessarily be able to control all aspects of corruption within a country. A United Nations Development Program report (United Nations, 2005, p. 8) concluded thus: "Several countries have opted for or are currently considering creating an independent commission or agency charged with the overall responsibility of combating corruption. However, the creation of such an institution is not a panacea to the scourge of corruption. There are actually very few examples of successful independent anti-corruption commissions/agencies." The key reason for the lack of success of these organizations is not that ACAs by themselves are not an appropriate option for these countries but rather that they lack political will and proper resourcing in their implementation. But where these factors have been provided, such as in Hong Kong and Singapore, these jurisdictions of ACAs have been extraordinarily successful.

However, in cases where there has been a lack of political will, a shortfall of resources, and/or noncooperation by other institutions in the country's integrity network such as in Botswana's Directorate on Corruption and Economic Crime, the results have been less than spectacular. As such, it is the author's opinion that a full-fledged ICAC body such as that found in Hong Kong or Botswana is a feasible proposition given current South African capacity. The lack of communication, coordination, and cooperation currently found in the system means that a single-agency ACA would be the most appropriate in South Africa.

This proposed single ACA must be committed to fighting corruption through a three-pronged strategy of effective law enforcement, education, and prevention to maintain South Africa as a fair and just society. Further delay in attempting to address the issue of corruption will inevitably lead to a situation where the problem is so grave that public and international confidence will reach such a low level that any measures that could be introduced will have little or no prospect of succeeding. Over and above this, there is a need for an independent oversight capacity to enhance the integrity, accountability, and transparency of the new agency. This can be done by extending the mandate of the current Independent Police Investigative Directorate.

Therefore, to establish a single ACA, South Africa must take into account the following aspects:

1. The ACA must be incorruptible: the ACA must be incorruptible for two reasons. First, if the ACA's personnel are corrupt its legitimacy and public image will be undermined as its officers have broken the law by being corrupt themselves when they are required to enforce the law. Second, corruption among the ACA's staff not only discredits the agency but also prevents them from performing their duties impartially and effectively.

2. The ACA must be independent from the police and from political control: the United Nations Convention against Corruption (Merida Convention) provides an obligation for the countries to establish an independent agency for the prevention of corruption. Each country shall determine the status of its ACAs and decide on the best manner for efficient prevention of corruption and what powers it will entrust to these agencies so that they are independent and autonomous in the performance of their function. The experiences of Singapore and Hong Kong in fighting corruption clearly show the importance of not allowing police to be responsible for corruption control especially when the police are corrupt (Lai, 2001, p. 16). In other words, the police were the biggest obstacle to curbing corruption in Singapore and Hong Kong before the establishment of the CPIB in October 1952 and the ICAC in February 1974, because of the prevalence of police corruption in both the city-states. Accordingly, the success of the CPIB and ICAC in combating corruption has confirmed that the best practice in curbing corruption is as follows: do not let the police handle the task of controlling corruption as this would be like giving candy to a child and expecting him or her not to eat it.

3. There must be comprehensive anticorruption legislation: comprehensive anticorruption legislation is an important prerequisite for combating corruption effectively. More specifically, the anticorruption laws in a country must (1) define explicitly the meaning of corruption and its different forms and (2) specify clearly the powers of the head and/or members of the ACA.

4. The ACA must have adequate staff and funding: as fighting corruption is expensive in terms of skilled personnel, equipment, and financial resources, the incumbent government must demonstrate its political will and support by providing the required personnel and budget needs of the ACA (Quah, 2007, p. 76).

5. The ACA must enforce the anticorruption laws impartially: the anticorruption laws must be impartially enforced by the ACA. The

ACA's credibility will be undermined if it devotes its efforts to petty corruption by convicting "small fish" and ignores grand corruption by the rich and powerful in the country (Rose, 2005, p. 32). If the "big fish" are protected and not prosecuted, the ACA is ineffective and will probably be used by political leaders against their political rivals, as was the case with the DSO in South Africa.

6. Political will is crucial for minimizing corruption: political will is perhaps the most important precondition for the effectiveness of an ACA. The political leaders in a country must be sincerely committed to the eradication of corruption by showing exemplary conduct and adopting a modest lifestyle themselves. This means that those found guilty of corruption must be punished, regardless of their status or position in society (Quah, 2007, p. 74). Political will is absent when the big fish or the rich and famous are protected from prosecution for grand corruption and only the small fish or ordinary people are caught and punished for petty corruption.

7. System of checks and balances: the fourth factor is checks and balances to ensure that the operation of the powerful antigraft agency is accountable. The ICAC is subject to a healthy and effective system of checks and balances. For example, the ICAC, although vested with the power of investigation, does not have the authority to prosecute as prosecution powers have always been vested with the Secretary for Justice. The judiciary is also independent. Some of the legal powers mentioned earlier are subject to the scrutiny of courts to ensure checks and balances (Quah, 2007, p. 78). The ICAC is also subject to probing questions on its funding and performance raised by legislators who may review and amend ICAC's legal powers as circumstances require. In addition, the ICAC's performance is monitored by four advisory committees with members drawn from all sectors of the community. A senior committee looks at the overall policy of the ICAC, whereas each of the three departments is guided by its own advisory committee. These committees meet regularly and closely examine the work of the antigraft agency. Collectively, they have made the ICAC a more open and accountable organization.

8. International cooperation: last but not least, international cooperation from overseas ACAs is also an important factor contributing to any success in the fight against corruption. As the corrupt is quick to exploit divergent laws and bureaucratic systems in various jurisdictions, the ICAC finds it extremely important to establish efficient and effective liaison channels with its counterparts in other parts of the world so as to enable multilateral exchanges of legal and investigative assistance.

Conclusion

It is clear that there is a lack of political leadership in South Africa. The fact that anticorruption agencies and units have established and disbanded on various occasions is a clear indication that there is poor political leadership. Corruption and fraud pose a serious challenge in South Africa. It is clear that the SAPS is not coping in dealing with each crime that is reported. This is the time when South Africa needs to assemble its best resources to fight the scourge of fraud, corruption, and commercial and economic crimes. Therefore, from a strategic and policy point of view South Africa seems to be on the right track, but the application and implementation of those strategies seem to be problematic.

References

African Union. (2003). *Convention on Preventing and Combating Corruption*. Maputo, Mozambique. African Union.

Chen, M. (2006). Liaison officer at the Head Quarters of the Independent Commission against Corruption. Personal interview, 12.11.2006. Hong Kong.

Country Corruption Assessment Report. (2003). United Nations Office on Drugs and Crimes, Department of Public Service and Administration, South Africa.

Country Corruption Assessment Report. (2008). United Nations Office on Drugs and Crimes, Department of Public Service and Administration, South Africa.

Department of Public Service and Administration. (2002). *Public Service National Anti-Corruption Strategy of 2002*. Pretoria, South Africa: Department of Public Service and Administration.

Gbadamosi, A. (2006). *The Effects of Corruption*. Tbilisi, Georgia: International Management Development Association (IMDA) conference proceedings.

Heilbrunn, J. R. (2004). *Anticorruption Commissions: Pancrea or Real Medicine?* Washington, DC: World Bank.

Kyambalesa, G. (2006). Anti-corruption strategies in Africa. *Journal of Contemporary African Studies, 23*(1), 27–50.

Lai, A. N. (2001). Keeping Hong Kong clean: Experiences of fighting corruption post 1997. Harvard Asia Pacific.

Lee, G. B. (2005). *The Synonan Years: Singapore under Japanese Rule 1942–1945*. London, United Kingdom: Routledge.

Montesh, M. (2007). *A Critical Analysis of Crime Investigative System within the South African Criminal Justice System: A Comparative Study*. Submitted in accordance with the requirements for the degree of DLitt et Phil in the subject Police Science. University of South Africa.

Montesh, M., & Berning, J. (2012). Countering corruption in South Africa: The rise and fall of the Scorpions and Hawks. (2012, March 3–12). *South African Crime Quarterly*, no. 39.

Ngobeni, W. (2008). Zuma probe was beginning of the end. (2007, January 27). *City Press*.

Parliamentary Monitor. (2011). *Parliamentary Monitor Group*. Cape Town, South Africa: South African Parliament.

Public Protector Amendment Act 133 of 1998. *Government Gazette, Republic of South Africa*, Vol. 401, no. 19524: 5.

Public Service Commission. (2001). *Public Service Commission Report*. Pretoria, South Africa: Public Service Commission.

Public Service Commission. (2011). *Measuring the Effectiveness of the National Anti-Corruption Hotline (NACH) 19/2011*. Pretoria, South Africa: Public Service Commission.

Quah, J. S. T. (2007). *National Integrity Systems in East and Southeast Asia 2006. Regional Overview Report*. Berlin, Germany: Transparency International.

Rose, R. (2005). *Learning from Comparative Public Policy: A Practical Guide*. Singapore (Lengkok Bahru City): National Archives of Singapore and Epigram.

South Africa (Republic). (1992). Corruption Act, (Act no.94) of 1992. Pretoria, South Africa: Government Printer.

South Africa (Republic). (1994). Public Protector Act, (Act no.23) of 1994. Pretoria, South Africa: Government Printer.

South Africa (Republic). (1994). Intelligence Services Oversight Act 40 of 1994. Pretoria, South Africa: Government Printer.

South Africa (Republic). (1994). Public Protector Amendment Act, (Act no.133) of 1998. Pretoria, South Africa: Government Printer.

South Africa (Republic). (1995). Auditor-General Act 12 of 1995, (Act no.12) of 1995. Pretoria, South Africa: Government Printer.

South Africa (Republic). (1995). South African Police Service Act, (Act no.68) of 1995. Pretoria, South Africa: Government Printer.

South Africa (Republic). (1996). Constitution of the Republic of South Africa Act, (Act no.108) of 1996. Pretoria, South Africa: Government Printer.

South Africa (Republic). (1998). Prevention of Organised Crime Act, (Act no.121) of 1998. Pretoria, South Africa: Government Printer.

South Africa (Republic). (1998). National Prosecuting Authority Act, (Act no.32) of 1998. Pretoria, South Africa: Government Printer.

South Africa (Republic). (1999). Public Finance Management Act, (Act no.1) of 1999 Pretoria, South Africa: Government Printer.

South Africa (Republic). (2000). *Anti-corruption framework*. Pretoria, South Africa: Department of Public Service and Administration.

South Africa (Republic). (2000). National Prosecuting Authority Amendment Act, (Act no.61) of 2000. Pretoria, South Africa: Government Printer.

South Africa (Republic). (2002). *Public service anti-corruption strategy of 2002*. Pretoria, South Africa: Department of Public Service and Administration.

South Africa (Republic). (2003). *Country corruption assessment report*. Pretoria, South Africa: Department of Public Service and Administration.

South Africa (Republic). (2004) Prevention and Combating of Corrupt Activities Act, (Act no.12) of 2004. Pretoria, South Africa: Government Printer.

South Africa (Republic). (2006). *The Khampepe commission of inquiry into the mandate and location of the Directorate of Special Operations*. Final Report, February 2006. Department of Justice and Constitutional Development.

South Africa (Republic). (2007) *National Anti-Corruption Hotline 19/2007*. Pretoria, South Africa: Public Service Commission.

South Africa (Republic). (2008). *General law amendment bill of 2008*. Pretoria, South Africa: Government Printer.

South Africa (Republic). (2008). *National prosecuting authority amendment bill*. Pretoria, South Africa: Government Printer.

South Africa (Republic). (2008). National Prosecuting Authority Amendment Act, (Act no.58) of 2008 Pretoria, South Africa: Government Printer.

South Africa (Republic). (2008). South African Police Service Amendment Act, (Act no.57) of 2008. Pretoria, South Africa: Government Printer.

South Africa (Republic). (1996). Special Investigating Units and Special Tribunals Act, (Act no.74) of 1996. Pretoria, South Africa: Government Printer.

Southern African Development Community. (2001). *Protocol against corruption*. Botswana: SADC Head office.

Transparency International. (2011). *Corruption perceptions index 2011*. Transparency International. Brussels.

United Nations. (2000). *Convention against transnational organized crime*. New York: United Nations.

United Nations. (2003). *United Nations Convention Against Corruption Resolution*. United Nations Office on Drugs and Crime, Vienna.

United Nations. (2005). *United Nations Development Programme (UNDP) report*. Pretoria, South Africa: UNDP South Africa.

Need for a Youth Crime Prevention Strategy for South Africa 13

MOSES MONTESH AND JOHANNA BERNING

Contents

Introduction

The initiative to develop a National Crime Prevention Strategy (NCPS) in South Africa began in early February 1995 in response to former President Mandela's plea to parliament, in which he raised concerns about crime. Part of this response was the development of the South African Police Service (SAPS, 1995) "Community Safety Plan," a package of short-term policing measures aimed at tackling the priority crimes in the country. In May 1995, an interdepartmental strategy team, composed largely of civilian officials, began the process of drafting a long-term Crime Prevention Strategy, which would become known as the NCPS. The intention was that the long-term strategy would tackle the root causes of crime, in parallel to the Police's Community Safety Plan, which would deliver more effective responses to crimes that had already been committed or planned. The NCPS was approved by the cabinet in May 1996, and launched in the final days of the Government of National Unity. Thirteen years later the last review was done in 1998, the NCPS has not been amended or reviewed, whereas various forms of crimes such as automated teller machine bombings, police killings, police brutality, and youth crime have now taken South Africa by storm. This chapter seeks to establish the need to develop a Youth Crime Prevention Strategy that will focus on youth crime. A literature study was used as the baseline to see if there are gaps in the youth crime prevention knowledge. Conclusions reached in this regard show that not much has been done because the NCPS was approved by the cabinet in 1996.

Background

The need to create safer communities drives countries all over the world to search for better ways to understand and prevent crime. It has become more and more evident that traditional responses to crime, especially youth crime are not effective. Putting young people through the courts and locking them up, is expensive for the government. In South Africa, it was through the NCPS (South Africa, 1996) that policy officially embraced a number of fundamental shifts. The first shift was the recognition that policy in relation to crime does not always have to be reactive. At that time former Minister Mufamadi (1995) admitted that being too reactive, the police could be criticized. Furthermore, Maduna (1996) argued that the addition of more proactive tactics such as diagnosing and managing community problems that produce crime as well as fostering closer relations with the community to facilitate the solving of crimes would greatly enhance the crime-control capability of the police. The second shift was the acknowledgment that crime was caused by a range of social, political, economic, and other factors.

According to Burger (2007, p. 11), a clear distinction was made between crime control and crime prevention in the first NCPS of 1996. Furthermore, Burger states that crime control refers to largely reactive measures, whereas crime prevention "... involves a deeper process ... longer term and ... focuses on preventing crime at an early stage." In addition, the NCPS (South Africa, 1996, p. 5) states that "crime prevention involves a deeper process than crime control; it is longer term and focuses on the prevention of crime at an early stage." Research studies have confirmed that the criminal justice system alone cannot succeed in preventing crime (Tshwete, 1999). The minister emphasized that the need for formation of a partnership resulting in the development of integrated Crime Prevention Strategies could not be overemphasized. It was essential that as many people as possible became involved in an effort to prevent crime. Furthermore, the minister also indicated that working hand-in-hand with the community improves service delivery, builds trust between the community and the police, promotes joint problem identification and prioritizes problem solving. It also makes the police be more accountable and transparent. Therefore, it is important to analyze the NCPS to gauge it if its goals and objectives have been achieved. In this instance, it is clear that youth crime prevention is inadequately addressed in the current strategy; hence there is a need for such a strategy.

Current Government Initiatives

National Crime Prevention Strategy of 1996

Preventing crime has been a priority for the government since 1996 when the NCPS of 1996 was launched. This strategy shows that preventing crime—rather than relying on the criminal justice process to arrest and convict offenders—was critical to making our communities safer. The NCPS is based on the idea that the police alone cannot reduce crime. Without the involvement of the community and government departments other than the Department of Safety and Security (police), it will be difficult to reduce crime.

As a result the Departments of Justice, Correctional Services, and Welfare also have primary responsibility for the NCPS, together with the provincial safety and security secretariats. The NCPS has laid the foundation for crime prevention. Local government was identified in the policies of the Department of Safety and Security and the Department of Provincial Affairs and Local government as the partner best able to carry out crime prevention programs. This approach was emphasized because it was argued that crime occurred in specific places and was often related to the conditions experienced in a local context. This strategy did not adequately and specifically address youth crime in South Africa.

White Paper on Safety and Security of 1998–2003

According to the *White Paper on Safety and Security* (South Africa, 1998–2003, p. 20), crime could be reduced through two strategies, law enforcement and social crime prevention. Law enforcement largely only involved the police. Crime prevention needed a much broader participation by government and community members. The involvement of the following different levels of government was regarded as the key to making this happen:

- National government would provide leadership, guidelines, coordination, and, where possible, funding on an incentive basis to ensure effective local implementation.
- Provincial government would coordinate social crime prevention initiatives in the province.
- Local government would actively participate by planning programs and coordinating a range of local actors to ensure that these projects were carried out.

The White Paper implied that crime prevention should be an integral part of good urban management and not something that was added on to existing functions. With this in mind, practical ways for local government to reduce crime included the following:

- Preventing crime in the structures of, and on the property of, the municipality
- Working with local police; aligning internal resources, objectives, and development projects with the principles of crime prevention
- Coordinating crime prevention efforts in the municipal area to avoid duplication
- Enforcing by laws and traffic laws, assisting victims by providing information on services, and initiating targeted crime prevention programs

Again, this White Paper also failed to address youth crime adequately.

White Paper on Local Government of 1998

In terms of the Constitution, local government should promote integrated spatial and socioeconomic development that is socially just and equal for everyone in the community. This implies that crime prevention principles are integrated with other aspects of local development, including economic development.

The *White Paper on Local Government* (South Africa, 1998b, p. 19) also encouraged local governments to form partnerships with organizations in the community, especially where these agencies had expertise that was lacking in local government (such as expertise in crime prevention). This policy is also silent about youth crime in South Africa.

New Crime Fighting Approaches after 1999 Elections

The new ministers in the justice, safety, and security and prison portfolios commenced their terms of office with remarks and policy statements intended to clearly differentiate them from their predecessors. This was made clear by Minister Maduna, the then Minister of Justice and Constitutional Development soon after his appointment. According to Rauch (1999, p. 30), the minister on his inaugural speech stated that

> .... as our country embarks on the second democratic term, we have to reflect on the shortcomings of the previous term and resolve to improve significantly on performance. While over the last five years the Department was able to lay a solid legislative and indeed infra-structural foundation for a strong and responsive justice system, many problems continue to plague our justice system and at times evoking public sentiments that the new democratic order is more sympathetic to human rights concerns of criminals and less sensitive to the plight of victims of crime and the general sense of insecurity that continues to besiege our country (Maduna, 1999).

His colleague, Minister of Safety and Security, S. Tshwete adopted a tough tone from the outset by stating that

> The criminals have obviously declared war against the South African public. ... We are ready, more than ever before, not just to send a message to the criminals out there about our intentions. We are now poised to rise with power and vigour proportional to the enormity and vastness of the aim to be achieved (Tshwete, 1999).

The new ministers infused the NCPS with the rhetoric of "war on crime," distancing themselves from its origins as the "soft," developmental side of government's strategy to deal with crime.

Although, perhaps a perversion of its original intents, this approach permitted the survival of the NCPS, understood now mainly as a mechanism

for government coordination. The new government followed the recommendations of the NCPS Review (South Africa, 1998a, p. 12) in prioritizing the
following issues.

Crime Involving Firearms

The easy availability of firearms was identified as a major contributor to
the prevalence of interpersonal violence and lethal crime in South Africa.
Statistics on offenders and victims in gun killings from the National Victim
Survey and the Department of Health Mortality Survey showed that almost
all offenders and victims were young men from ages 18 to 30 (offenders) and
16 to 35 (victims) (NCPS Review, South Africa, 1998a, p. 16). As a result, the
government recommended that efforts must be made to fight the scourge.

Organized Crime

The recognition by the original NCPS that much of South Africa's crime
problem was organized was largely absent. By tackling organized crime,
government believed it would be able to impact on vehicle crime, drug trafficking, trade in illegal weapons, and endangered species as well as money
laundering and certain forms of commercial crime (*White Paper on Safety
and Security*, South Africa, 1998–2003, p. 45; NCPS Review, South Africa,
1998a, p. 17).

White-Collar Crime

Commercial crime, although often perceived as "victimless crime" robbed
the South African economy of billions of Rands every year, thereby reducing opportunities for economic growth and development. A continued focus
on white-collar crime would ensure that the strategy was balanced to also
include a focus on "white-collar crime."

Intergroup Conflict

According to the NCPS Review (South Africa, 1998a, p. 15), this type of
crime needed to remain a national priority in the light of continuing conflicts in KwaZulu-Natal, the taxi industry, and the Western Cape. This focus
would ensure that the government was able to deal with problems of vigilante
groups, organized gangs, and political conflict. One can deduct from this
explanation that the government was not concerned about youth crime but
had other priorities.

Vehicle Theft and Hijackings

The figures for vehicle crime in South Africa remained unacceptably high
and the violence that had come to be associated with these crimes generated
high levels of fear in the community. The NCPS Review (South Africa, 1998a,
p. 16) suggested that agreements and protocols within the Southern African

Development Community needed to be developed to fight vehicle theft and cross-border crimes. These efforts did not include youth crime.

Corruption within the South African Criminal Justice System

The NCPS Review (South Africa, 1998a, p. 19) conceded that if this problem was not effectively addressed, it would undermine all government efforts in respect of crime prevention. As a result, efforts were made to fight corruption, which included the establishment of agencies such as the Directorate of Special Operations, the Special Investigating Unit, and the Asset Forfeiture Unit.

Interpersonal Violence

This new focus would enable government to prioritize violence against women and children, murder, assault, and aggravated assault, which made up the bulk of South Africa's violent crime problem. A new focus would require social crime prevention to prevent young people from becoming perpetrators of violent crimes, and a range of strategies to prevent certain groups of people from becoming victims, and repeat victims, of these crimes (e.g., women, children, and the elderly) (NCPS Review, South Africa, 1998a, p. 20; *White Paper on Safety and Security*, South Africa, 1998–2003, p. 19). The selection of these priorities showed that some lessons had been learnt from the early years of the NCPS. For example, violent crime needed to be prioritized, as did organized crime. The new approach to the NCPS was strengthened by the emergence of the National Director of Public Prosecutions (Asset Forfeiture Unit and the Scorpions) as major role players in the new "war on crime" (Montesh, 2007, p. 78). With strong direction from the president, interdepartmental coordination improved significantly in the post 1999 period.

These developments were driven by a political leadership that was far more sensitive to the concerns of the citizenry—no longer focused largely on the transformation of the bureaucracy, and more concerned with delivery of services, government began responding to crime with the sense of urgency and toughness that their constituents demanded. However, since then, no efforts have been initiated to review or to evaluate the successes or failures of the NCPS to strengthen it or abandon it. Instead, new strategic plans are drawn every year, which are used to combat crime in South Africa. According to Col. J. Schnetler (personal communication, 2010), a researcher within the South African Police Service Strategic Management, there is no information indicating whether the NCPS has been discarded or is still a policy framework for crime prevention.

Furthermore, Schnetler indicated that the main objectives of the NCPS have been incorporated in the police's Annual Strategic Plan. This has been corroborated by Z. Mnisi (personal communication, 2011), the spokesperson of the Minister of Police. These explanations are not convincing. However, all the annual police plans do not outline the methods and approaches in which youth crime should be prevented. Again this approach also failed to address youth crime in South Africa.

Integrated Social Crime Prevention Strategy of 2011

The concept of social crime prevention is promoted by the NCPS and the *White Paper on Safety and Security* of 1998–2003. The latter states "Crime prevention and, particularly, social crime prevention, not only targets the causes of crime, but in the longer term, does so in the most cost-effective way." It addresses those factors that contribute to the occurrence of crime, and requires a focus on three broad and overlapping target groups or areas:

1. Offender-based strategies—this focuses on those known to be criminals, or thought to be at risk of offending, and aim to ensure positive behavioral change.
2. Victim-based strategies—these focus on support for those who have become victims of crime by providing information aimed at minimizing the likelihood of victimization.
3. Environment-based strategies—these strategies are aimed at altering the social, economic, and other related factors, which contribute to the occurrence of crime.

The *Integrated Social Crime Prevention Strategy* is a policy document from the Department of Social Development (2011). This policy also does not adequately outline youth crime in South Africa.

Council for Scientific and Industrial Research

The Council for Scientific and Industrial Research (CSIR) collaborates extensively with national and state government ministries and with the South Africa Police Service. It has helped many South African government departments, develop crime prevention guides and toolkits, design and implement programs on the ground, supported local municipalities in developing their own prevention strategies, organized conferences to facilitate exchange and good practices, and undertaken training programs for local authority and state government staff. The CSIR even went one step further by developing a document called *A Manual for Community Based Crime Prevention: Making South Africa Safe*, 2000. Surprisingly, the government has failed to develop a youth crime prevention policy using some of the guidelines from this important document.

Safer City Program

The Safer City Programme of UN-HABITAT (United Nations—HABITAT, 1998, p. 12) was established in 1998, at the request of African mayors. Apart from its work in supporting cities to develop comprehensive prevention strategies, it has held a series of international and regional conferences in Africa and Latin America over the past 12 years. These have brought together mayors and other stakeholders to promote exchange, for example, on local government crime prevention, women's safety, youth at risk, and youth participation programs and projects. Ethekwini Municipality (Durban) was used as a case study in South Africa, but so far nothing has come out of the project that informs the national government on how to deal with youth crime.

United Nations Office on Drugs and Crime's South–South Project

United Nations Office on Drugs and Crime's *South-South project on Regional Cooperation for Determining Best Practices for Crime Prevention in the Developing World*, linked policy makers and researchers in Southern African and Caribbean countries to provide technical assistance and to build capacity between regions experiencing very high levels of violence (United Nations [UNODC], 2008). A number of exchanges took place, good practices were identified, and a handbook on best practices was published. Again these proceedings have never been implemented within South Africa, nor nationwide and no policy has been developed to address youth crime.

Initiatives from Other Stakeholders

The National Secretariat for the Police (previously Secretariat for Safety and Security), under the Department of the Police (previously Department for Safety and Security), is tasked with the monitoring of the South African Police Service as well as the implementation of the crime prevention principles as laid out in the NCPS (*Civilian secretariat for the police strategic plan*, 2011, p. 40). In terms of the section 3(1) of the South African Police Service Act 68 of 1995, the Secretariat's mandate is "to monitor the implementation of policy and of directions issued by the Minister, and report to the Minister on these matters; conduct research into any policing matter in accordance with the instructions of the Minister, and report the results to the Minister." So far nothing has come from this department that could be used to address youth crime.

Causes of Youth Crime

There is no single root cause of crime and these differ from country to country. Crime is primarily the outcome of multiple adverse social, economic, cultural, and family conditions. To prevent crime it is important to have an understanding of its causes.

Economic Situation

The major economic factors that contribute to crime are poverty, unemployment, and the political situation. Financial crisis due to poverty causes the person to become involved in criminal activities. Lack of employment opportunities may also lead to criminal activities among the unemployed. An unemployed person needs to run his household by any means and when he does not find any legal opportunity to earn, he may become involved in criminal activities to finance his living. Because of political uncertainty, a sense of insecurity develops in members of a society.

Social Factors

Community social structure mirrors citizens and community's values and how we set priorities. The social environment is needed to be studied with respect to different environmental scenarios. According to Muhammad (2008, p. 3), the core social root causes of youth crime are inequality, lack of support to families and neighborhoods, real or perceived inaccessibility to services, lack of leadership in communities, low value placed on children and individual well-being, as well as the overexposure to television as a means of recreation. The social environment is needed to be studied with respect to different social scenarios.

Furthermore, school environment is another factor that should never overlooked when dealing with social factors. According to the Department of Correctional Service (DCS) Annual Report (2009/2010, p. 120), causes related to the school environment are disruptive behavior of a child and lack of commitment in school. In addition, community environment can also contribute to youth crime. Major causes of crime related to community environment are lack of cohesion in the society, disorganization and neglect especially for youth, and easy availability of drugs and high population turnover (number of children), among others (DCS Annual Report, 2009/2010, p. 121).

Family Structures

According to Muhammad (2008, p. 3), the youth whose family have one or more characteristics listed below, are more likely to be involved in crime. This includes the following: parents who are involved in crime, poor parental supervision, parents who neglect their children, where there is erratic discipline or they are treated harshly, family income is low or they are isolated, family conflict, lack of communication between children and parents, lack of respect and responsibility among family members, abuse and neglect of children, and family violence and family breakups. Muhammad (2008, p. 4) further states that "crime prevention especially youth crime prevention must focus on improvements in all possible areas." To see how societies can

develop and implement crime prevention strategies, societies need to identify the factors that are actually responsible for the crime so that they can be
targeted in the policy framework.

Legacy of Apartheid

According to the DCS Annual Report (2010/2011, p. 198), young "black"
men in South Africa remain the primary victims and perpetrators of crime
and violence in South Africa. The Report further states that very few "black"
youth have escaped unscathed from the effects of apartheid—including family dysfunction, poor-quality education, and lack of safety.

Muhammad (2008, p. 2) and the DCS Annual Report (2009/2010, p. 35),
highlight that marginalization is common in South Africa; and among South
African youth, 27% could be defined as "marginalized" whereas a further
43% of young people could be defined as being "at risk" of engaging in antisocial behavior.

Experience of Victimization

Very little is known about the implications of victimization for young
people's involvement in crime and violence and later in life, about whether
victimized youth become violent themselves and why. Bullying in schools
does seem to be one of the responses that some children and youth adopt in
response to being victims themselves (DCS Annual Report, 2009/2010, p. 35).

Extent of Youth Crime in Youth Africa

According to the South African Police Service (SAPS, 2011) *Crime
Statistics*, murder and nonfatal assaults are one of the main contributors
to the burden of premature death, injury, and disability among young
people in South Africa. The scale of violence in South Africa, particularly
among young people, amounts to a national public health crisis, and warrants urgent preventive and rehabilitative interventions. The perpetrators
of school violence are often learners at school, classmates, and other young
people in the community.

According to the DCS Annual Report (2010/2011, p. 150), statistics on
the numbers of young people in prison provide some indication of the extent
of involvement of youth as perpetrators of crime and violence. The Report
further states that in 2002, 36% of the prison population was below the age of
26 years, and over half of prisoners awaiting trial (53%) were in the same age
group (Palmary & Moat, 2002, p. 32).

The world report on violence and health (World Health Organization,
2002, p. 150) outlines risk factors for youth violence at the individual level (e.g.,

low educational achievement, history of early aggressive behavior); relationship level (e.g., poor supervision and harsh, physical punishment of children by parents, low socioeconomic status of families, associating with delinquent peers); and community, cultural, and societal levels (e.g., presence of gangs, guns, and drugs in the community; low levels of social cohesion, income inequality, poor law enforcement, and normative use of violence to resolve conflict). Various explanations have been offered as to why South African youth are disproportionately involved in crime and violence (Palmary & Moat, 2002, p. 23). Some of these relate to South Africa's past, to the high levels of political and other forms of violence to which children and young people were exposed, and to the disintegration of families and communities under apartheid. The current context of high levels of unemployment and poverty in South Africa also create both the opportunity and incentive for youth involvement in crime and violence.

For example, out-of-school and out-of-work youth find themselves without structured activities to absorb their energies and to give them direction and a sense of self-worth. Such youth spend more time on the streets, where they come into contact with youth gangs and are tempted to compensate for their lack of earnings by resorting to crime. In fact, rapid change in the age structure of a population through a youth bulge, in a context of expanding education and contracting work opportunities, can become a recipe for young people's involvement in crime and violence (Palmary & Moat, 2002, p. 23). According to the DCS Annual Report (2009/2010, p. 36) as of March 31, 2010, South Africa had a total of 1275 children (21 of whom were girls) under the age of 18 years.

In March 2010, the DCS had a youth inmate population between 18 and 25 years of 56,520, against the total offender population of 164,793. Of this total, approximately 58% were sentenced and 42% were unsentenced. The Report further states that the largest number of youth offenders was between the ages of 22 and 25 years and represented approximately 62% of the total number of youth offenders. Currently, the DCS has 15 youth development centers, accommodating both medium and maximum offenders, but housed separately, with programs of formal education; skills development (vocational and entrepreneur training) (DCS Annual Report, 2009/2010, p. 31). From the above analysis, it is clear that youth crime in South Africa is a problem and that there is an urgent need to develop a youth crime prevention strategy.

A Critique of the Current Approach in South Africa

From a policing point of view, the NCPS portrayed an excellent strategy, although some may argue that it was more policy than strategy. It recognized that the police could only contribute to short-term visible policing measures, while much more was needed to address crime in the longer term. In this regard, the government placed a specific focus on those issues that were seen to be associated with the social and developmental factors thought to cause or facilitate crime.

However, 14 years after its launch, few people argue that the NCPS has not lived up to its expectations. On the contrary, at this stage the NCPS can only be regarded as a good strategy on paper, but one that has failed in practice. According to Burger (2011, p. 10), a retired South Africa Police Service assistant police commissioner and now a senior researcher with the Institute for Safety and Security, as well as Rauch (2002, p. 13), a senior consultant on criminal justice issues and formerly a member of the Secretariat for Safety and Security, there are a number of criticisms of the NCPS and the government's approach to dealing with crime as follows:

- The launch of the NCPS in 1996 followed too soon after the launch of the Annual Police Plan of 1996/1997. This was a "public relations blunder," to which the public reaction was that this (the NCPS) was "just another plan." For government, it resulted in a conceptual confusion between the police's short-term "plan" and the long-term goals and objectives of the NCPS. According to Rauch (2002, p. 13), "...it created a conceptual gulf between immediate short-term policing responses to rising crime rates, and the need for a developmental approach aimed at the causes of crime, especially youth crime—a gulf that still exists today."
- The NCPS itself contained very little detail on how the programs it proposed, were to be developed and implemented, especially the youth crime component.
- It was a mistake to assume that cooperation between government departments would arise naturally and spontaneously. This was crucial considering that the

> [s]uccessful implementation of the NCPS was predicated on the assumption that inter-departmental cooperation was achievable, and that government departments and other role-players would be able (and willing) to agree on joint priorities and share information.

- The NCPS did not fully conceptualize or explain the relationship between the four "pillars" or categories of crime prevention and the seven national priority crimes it identified. The result was an implementation approach with a strong focus on the "pillars" and, consequently, the establishment of structures and processes, which had little in common with the content of the crimes, they were supposed to address.
- No government funding was dedicated to the implementation of the NCPS. Instead, government departments were encouraged to rationalize their existing resources to also accommodate the NCPS. This is the opposite of what is practiced in countries such as Canada and the Czechoslovakia Republic.

- Two key recommendations were outlined in 1996, thus the establishment of specialized units to tackle corruption and crimes against women and children. What happened is that the Directorate of Special Operations (Scorpions) was established to fight corruption and organized crime but was mysteriously disbanded in 2008. This has been seen as a step back in the fight against crime in South Africa, especially youth crime.

Recommendations

In terms of *Article 2 of the United Nations General Assembly E/CN.15/2002*, "It is the responsibility of all levels of government to create, maintain and promote a context within which relevant governmental institutions and all segments of civil society, including the corporate sector, can better play their part in preventing crime" (United Nations, 2002a). Their role as a government is to provide leadership, coordination, and adequate funding and resources. Therefore, the authors believe that it is the responsibility of the South African government to ensure that this resolution is properly implemented. In this regard, matters affecting youth crime prevention need to be addressed by means of a Youth Crime Prevention Strategy.

Youth Crime Prevention Strategy

To formulate a Youth Crime Prevention Strategy, South Africa needs to focus on the factors that are leading to the increasing number of crimes. The solutions to the dominant factors that are responsible for such high crime rates can be addressed by focusing on the three forms of crime prevention, namely primary, secondary, and tertiary crime prevention approaches. In this regard, the authors would like to recommend the three approaches as outlined by the *Handbook on the United Nations Crime Prevention Guidelines: Making them work—A guide for implementing the United Nations Crime Prevention Guidelines* (United Nations, 2002b, p. 32).

Primary Prevention   This refers to programs or initiatives aimed at those who have never been involved in the criminal justice system, such as programs to educate or alert the general public or young people about domestic violence or bullying in schools. According to Muhammad (2008, p. 4), initiatives for the primary prevention of juvenile crime include the following:

- Provision of support to young children and families (otherwise known as developmental crime prevention)
- Programs that target children at school to deter and divert them from crime

- Curfews that aim to restrict criminal opportunities by keeping children off the streets at certain times and places
- Situational crime prevention methods, including increased surveillance and design for crime prevention

Secondary Prevention   Secondary prevention refers to programs specifically targeted to children and young people who are identified by the social service, educational, or justice systems as "at risk" of crime. Initiatives for the secondary prevention of youth crime may include some elements that have been listed in Section Primary Prevention, but applied to groups of young people who are considered to be at an elevated risk of involvement in crime (DCS Annual Report, 2010/2011, p. 198). It may also include "scared straight" programs; therapeutic interventions for children who are displaying signs of aggression, antisocial behavior, and/or substance abuse; mentoring; targeted policing of youths; and targeting of areas where youths are known to commit crimes.

Tertiary Prevention   According to Muhammad (2008, p. 13), tertiary prevention refers to programs for those who are in the criminal justice system, and/or returning to the community, with the aim of preventing reoffending. Prevention efforts that are targeted at young people who have already become involved in crime include many of the therapeutic programs listed earlier, and also include "zero tolerance" policing, probation, imprisonment, boot camps, and trying juveniles in adult courts and restorative justice. These approaches have been implemented successfully in countries such as Tanzania, United Kingdom, Czechoslovakia Republic, the Netherlands, and Belgium (Stevens, Kessler, & Gladstone, 2006, p. 21).

Additional Recommendations

Government Leadership
All levels of government should play a leadership role in developing effective and youth crime prevention strategies and in creating and maintaining institutional frameworks for their implementation and review.

Socioeconomic Development and Inclusion
Crime prevention considerations should be integrated into all relevant social and economic policies and programs, including those addressing employment, education, health, housing and urban planning, poverty, social marginalization, and exclusion. Particular emphasis should be placed on communities, families, children, and youth at risk.

Cooperation/Partnerships
Cooperation/partnerships should be an integral part of effective youth crime prevention, given the wide-ranging nature of the causes of crime

and the skills and responsibilities required to address them. This includes partnerships working across ministries and between authorities, community organizations, nongovernmental organizations, the business sector, and private citizens.

Sustainability/Accountability

Youth crime prevention requires adequate resources, including funding for structures and activities, to be sustained. There should be clear accountability for funding, implementation, and evaluation and for the achievement of planned results.

Knowledge Base

Youth crime prevention strategies, policies, programs, and actions should be based on a broad, multidisciplinary foundation of knowledge about crime problems, their multiple causes, and promising and proven practices.

Interdependency

National youth crime prevention diagnoses and strategies should, where appropriate, take account of links between local criminal problems and international organized crime.

Conclusion

Crime prevention has become an increasingly important component of many national strategies on public safety and security. The concept of prevention is grounded in the notion that crime and victimization have many causal or underlying driving factors. They are the result of a wide range of factors and circumstances, which influence the lives of individuals and families as they grow up, and of local environments, and the situations and opportunities, which facilitate victimization and offending. If we are able to determine what factors are associated with different types of crime, then we can develop a set of strategies and programs to change those factors, and prevent or reduce the incidence of those crimes.

References

A manual for community based crime prevention: Making South Africa safe. 2000. Pretoria, South Africa: CSIR.

Burger, J. (2007). *Strategic perspectives on crime and policing in South Africa.* Pretoria, South Africa: Van Schaik Publishers.

Burger, J. (2011). *South Africa in 2020: An internal security perspective.* Pretoria, South Africa: Institute for Security Studies.

Department of Correctional Services (DCS). (2009/2010). *Annual report*. Pretoria, South Africa: Department of Correctional Services.

Department of Correctional Services (DCS). (2010/2011). *Annual report*. Pretoria, South Africa: Department of Correctional Services.

Department of Social Development. (2011). *Integrated social crime prevention strategy*. Pretoria, South Africa: Department of Social Development.

Maduna, P. (1996). *The department of justice and the national crime prevention strategy*. Pretoria, South Africa: Department of Justice.

Maduna, P. (1999). *Statement by the Minister of Justice and Constitutional Development*. Parliamentary Media Briefing, Cape Town, 28 June 1999.

Montesh, M. (2007). *A Critical Analysis of Crime Investigative System within the South African Criminal Justice System: A Comparative Study*. Submitted in accordance with the requirements for the degree of DLitt et Phil in the subject Police Science. University of South Africa.

Mufamadi, F. S. (1995). *Introductory remarks by the Minister for Safety and Security at the first meeting of an inter-departmental committee on the National Crime Prevention Strategy*. May 16, 1995.

Muhammad, A. (2008). *Youth crime: Causes and remedies*. MPRA Paper No. 17223. Pakistan: University of Karachi.

Palmary, I., & Moat, C. (2002). *Preventing criminality among young people*. Braamfontein, South Africa: Centre for the Study of Violence and Reconciliation.

Rauch, J. (1999). *The 1996 national crime prevention strategy*. Braamfontein, South Africa: Centre for the Study of Violence and Reconciliation (CSVR).

Rauch, J. (2002). *Changing step: Crime prevention policy in South Africa*. Pretoria, South Africa: Institute for Security Studies (ISS).

South Africa (Republic). (1995). South African Police Service Act 68 of 1995. Pretoria, South Africa: Government Printer.

South Africa (Republic). (1996). *National crime prevention strategy*. Pretoria, South Africa: Government Printer.

South Africa (Republic). (1998a). *National crime prevention strategy review*. Pretoria, South Africa: Government Printer.

South Africa (Republic). (1998b). *White paper on local government*. Pretoria, South Africa: Government Printer.

South Africa (Republic). (1998–2003). *White paper on safety and security*. Pretoria, South Africa: Government Printer.

South Africa (Republic). (2011). *Civilian secretariat for the police strategic plan*. Pretoria, South Africa: Secretariat for Police.

South African Police Service (SAPS). (2011). *Crime statistics*. Pretoria, South Africa: South African Police Service.

Stevens, A., Kessler, I., & Gladstone, B. (2006). *A review of good practices in preventing juvenile crime in the European Union*. Kent, United Kingdom: EISS University of Kent.

Tshwete, S. (1999). *Statement by the Minister for Safety and Security, Parliamentary media briefing*. June 28, 1999.

United Nations—HABITAT. (1998). *The safer city programme of UN-HABITAT*. Nairobi, Kenya.

United Nations. (2002a). *Article 2 of the United Nations General Assembly E/CN.15/2002*. New York.

United Nations. (2002b). *Handbook on the United Nations crime prevention guidelines: Making them work— A guide for implementing the UN crime prevention guidelines*. Vienna, Austria: United Nations Office on Drugs and Crime.

United Nations (UNODC). (2008). *South-South project on regional cooperation for determining best practices for crime prevention in the developing world*. United Nations.

World Health Organisation. (2002). *World report on violence and health: Summary*. Geneva, Switzerland: WHO.

Policing and Urban Road Traffic Safety in India

14

With Reference to the Hyderabad Metropolis

ADKI SURENDER

Contents

Introduction

With the increasing urbanization, industrialization, and advancement of science and technology, traversing long distances has become the order of the day. Many in urban areas have to travel hundreds of kilometers to reach their place of work. Faster modes of transport are being introduced to minimize traveling time. The automobile industry is in a race to produce vehicles that will be able to cover distances in short period. Most people in urban areas prefer to possess either two- or four-wheel vehicles. Besides, being a necessity, a car has become a status symbol in India. During the past decade, there has been tremendous increase in the production of vehicles, especially of four-wheelers. Although this increase has helped urban dwellers to overcome many of commutation problems, at the same time, it has been creating serious problems of safety on the road. Of all the systems that people have to deal with on a day-to-day basis, road transport is the most complex and the most unsafe mode of transportation.

According to World Health Organization (WHO) reports,* each year nearly 1.2 million people die in India as a result of a road traffic collision or more than 3500 deaths each day. Moreover, worldwide between 20 and 50 million more people sustain nonfatal injuries from collisions each year. These injuries are an important cause of disability worldwide. Ninety percent of road traffic deaths occur in low- and middle-income countries, which claim less than half the world's registered vehicle fleet (48%). India is a leading country in this phenomenon. More than 142,000 persons are killed and around half a million injured in about half a million reported road accidents in the country every year and the social cost of road accidents constitute about 3% of the Gross Domestic Product (GDP).

At a plenary meeting of the United Nations General Assembly on April 14, 2004, a resolution, cosponsored by India, expressed grave concern about the large number of fatalities in road crashes. The WHO also declared 2004 as the Year of Road Safety and launched World Health Day in April 2004 with the slogan "Road safety is no accident." In response to a growing concern about road traffic injuries, the United Nations has launched The Global Plan for the Decade of Action for Road Safety 2011–2020, which began in May 2012, and has the goal of saving 5 million lives. The global plan decade provides a framework for governments, civil society, and the private sector to work together to improve road management; upgrade the safety of roads and vehicles; and educate drivers, passengers, and pedestrians on safe behavior. Despite, road safety receiving international attention and support, the results presented in WHO reports shows that much more is needed to be done especially in developing countries like India.

Focus of the Study

This chapter is designed to analyze the road traffic safety situations in India, and focus on various steps taken by the Indian government to counter the

---

* Global status report on road safety: Time for action. Geneva, World Health Organization, 2009 (www.who.int/violence_injury_prevention/road_safety_status/2009).

threats posed by growing vehicular traffic to public safety and peaceful living. The primary objective of the chapter is to comprehend and evaluate the level of adequacy of the steps taken by the government in harmonizing safety, security, and sustainability in relation to urban transport, with a special focus on metropolitan city of Hyderabad.

The scope of the research is limited to highlighting major issue areas, related problems, and a review of reformative measures. The literature on urban administration reveals that the area of road traffic safety has not received adequate attention. Therefore, this is an exploratory study to bring out the salient features of prominent traffic-safety-related issues. The study is based on both primary and secondary data. The secondary data is in the form of published reports by the international, national, and local agencies in addition to government orders and police laws. For first-hand information, the researcher administered 500 questionnaires to assess the perception of road users. Further, 50 traffic police personnel who were involved in the field work were interviewed to gain insights into operational-level problems.

The chapter is comprised of three parts. Part I deals with the growth of urban traffic, road safety, and focuses on characteristics of road traffic in India. Part II discusses the role of traffic police in road safety in the city of Hyderabad metropolis. Further, it reviews the enforcement measures, operative mechanisms, and perceptions of road users and police personnel. Part III contains the conclusions and suggestions of the study.

Road Safety in India

India is a populous country and occupies second position in the world with a population of 1210 million. Although, modern India is a country with a predominantly rural population, there has been a progressive increase in urbanization. Independent India has brought about remarkable changes in urbanization. According to the 2011 census, urban population had increased to 31.16% or 377 million by 2011, from 17.61% or 62 million in 1951. The number of one million-plus cities also increased to 53 from 5 cities during the same period. Hyderabad city is the sixth largest metropolitan in India.

Contemporary urban life in India is throwing many challenges to its public administration, its policymaking, and law enforcement. These have become formidable concerns for modern public administration in India. One such concern, posing a threat to the security of urban life, is the remarkable increase in the vehicular population in urban areas. India has experienced a tremendous increase in the total number of registered motor vehicles, which increased from around 0.3 million on March 31, 1951 to around 142 million

Table 14.1   Road Accidents in India

Year	Number of Road Accidents	Number of Persons Killed	Number of Persons Injured
1970	14,800	14,800	70,100
1980	153,200	24,000	114,000
1990	28,200	54,100	255,000
2000	351,999	70,781	405,200
2011	497,686	142,485	511,394

Source: Ministry of Road Transport & Highways, Government of India, New Delhi, 2011.

on March 31, 2011.* This is a rise of 460%. The one million-plus cities occupied 40,382 thousand of motor vehicles on March 31, 2011. Among these cities, the Hyderabad city had the fourth largest number of registered motor vehicles and recorded highest compound annual growth rate of 12.30% during 2001–2011. The impact of liberalization in the wake of globalization since the 1990s had significantly added to this growth. Further, the total road length in India has also increased significantly from 399,000 km in 1951 to 423,600 km in 2008.[†]

Expansion in the road network, surge in motorization, and a rising population of a country contribute toward an increase in the numbers of road accidents, injuries, and fatalities. According to official statistics,[‡] 497,686 road accidents were reported during 2011 in India. The number of persons killed in road accidents was 142,485, or an average of 1 fatality per 3.5 accidents, and 511,394 persons were injured. However, this is an underestimate, as not all injuries are reported to the police. The situation in India is worsening, as shown in Table 14.1. This is partly due to the increase in number of vehicles on the road and partly due to the absence of a coordinated official policy to control the problem.

Table 14.1 shows that road traffic accidents have become the single largest threat to human life in the urban areas. Between 1970 and 2011, the number of accidents increased by 4.4 times and was accompanied with 9.8 times increase in fatalities and 7.3 times increase in the number of persons injured. This is with the backdrop of more than 100-fold increase in the number of registered motor vehicles and close to a fourfold increase in the size of the road network. Approximately 142,000 people are killed in road accidents and 511,000 people meet with serious injuries every year in India, causing an

---

* Road Transport year Book, 2010–2011, Ministry of Road Transport & Highways, Govt. of India, New Delhi.
† Basic Road Statistics of India, report, 2010, Ministry of Road Transport & Highways, Government of India, New Delhi.
‡ Report on Road Accidents in India, 2011, Ministry of Road Surface, Government of India, New Delhi.

annual social economic loss of Rs. 55,000 crores (US$550 billion).* Further, the study found that during 2011, one accident took place for every 285 vehicles and for every 1038 vehicles one person was killed. Every hour almost 16 persons are killed on Indian roads. A significant decline in the number of accidents per 10,000 motor vehicles is discernible from 814.4 in 1970 to 35.1 in 2011. This decrease was as a result of concerted and coordinated road safety efforts made by the government to minimize road accidents.

Causes of Road Accidents

Figure 14.1 presents the causes for road accidents in India during 2011.

The analysis of accidents by cause shows that the drivers' fault is the single most important factor responsible for accidents. Drivers' fault accounted for approximately 77.5% (3,085,806 accidents) of total road accidents during 2011. It appears that the lack of awareness in road safety and proper driver training is the principle cause of such traffic accidents. The fault of the cyclist and that of the pedestrian appears to be of marginal consequence accounting for approximately 1.3% and 2.4%, respectfully, of the accidents. The accidents caused due to defects in the motor vehicles also accounted for 1.6% of the total road accidents. Lack of road safety strategies and the allocation of funds for implementation are vital reasons for increasing road accidents in the country. Further, the statistics and personal observation of the researcher also indicates that negligence in following road safety rules and road-user behavior to be the main cause for road accidents and a contributing factor in approximately 77.5% of the cases. The above discussion reveals that Indian

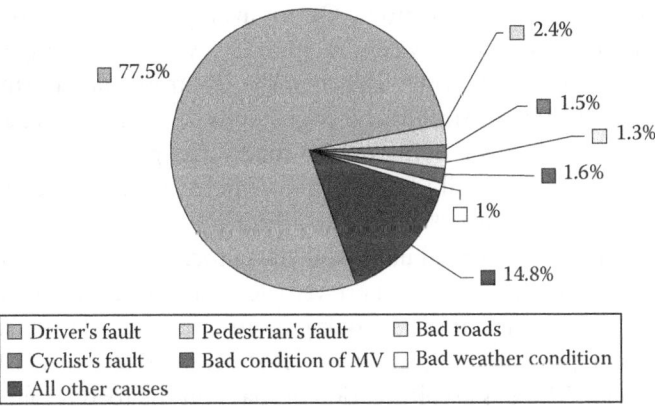

Figure 14.1 Causes for road accidents in India during 2011.

* Road Accidents in India 2011, Report Ministry of Road Transport & Highways, Government of India, New Delhi. July, 2012.

roads are highly unsafe for road users. The government needs to pay attention to peruse the matter very seriously to improve the road safety situation.

Road safety is a multisectoral and multidimensional issue requiring a multipronged approach at various levels. The government has taken a few steps to improve safety for road users, which include enactment of National Transport Policy, approval of a National Road Safety Policy, established the National Road safety Council, and also suggested to all State/UT governments to set up State Road Safety Councils and District Road Safety Committees. The government has adopted a multipronged strategy to address the issue of road safety based on the four E's of road safety viz: (1) education, (2) enforcement, (3) engineering (roads as well as vehicles), and (4) emergency care. In addition, the strategy includes the establishment of driver training institutes and the tightening of safety standards of vehicles such as helmets, seat belts, power-steering, and rear view mirrors. Despite many steps taken by the government, the absolute number of fatalities and road violations are still very high.

General Characteristics of Indian Traffic

After discussing the growth of urbanization, traffic growth, and road accidents in India it is necessary to throw light on the characteristics of Indian traffic.

First, Indian roads are characterized by limited width and length. The Indian Road Congress has recommended 20% of the land available in any metropolis to be allocated for roads. The minimum width of the roads is put at 100 ft (30 m). In most of the metropolises, the road length and width do not conform to these specifications. On an average percentage of the land allocated for roads stands between 5% and 15% with the average width at 30–40 ft (10–13 m), which is 60% less than the recommended norm.

Second, the vehicular traffic is heterogeneous in nature. There are no less than 25 types of vehicles moving on the roads. The physical dimensions of these vehicles vary drastically. Some of the vehicles, for example, trucks and buses, occupy more than 50% of the width of the road and thus become a cause of concern for both road users and law enforcement.

Third, the potential speed of these vehicles is also of different variations. A number of vehicles are of slow-moving nature like man-driven carts, animal-driven carts, and bicycles; and these vehicles are mixed with fast-moving modern vehicles. There is no bifurcation of space on the road for fast-moving and slow-moving vehicles.

Finally, a large number of vehicle drivers are averagely educated and the minimum qualifications prescribed for driving license holders is the ability to read and write at least one Indian language out of those specified in the

VII schedule of Indian Constitution and English.* This limited knowledge of English does not enable drivers to understand the complexities involved in traffic rules and regulations. In other words, a lack of awareness of rules is a major attribute of Indian traffic, which comes through in the current trial and error method in driving.

Road Safety Legislation

The Motor Vehicle (MV) Act of India 1988 and Central Motor vehicle rules 1989 are the principal legal instruments of the country through which road transport is regulated. In addition, Municipal Corporation, Urban Development Authorities, and State Road Transportation Corporation Acts also influence the road traffic system in metropolitan cities. However, the MV Act of 1988 represents an integrated approach toward traffic administration throughout the country. The Road Transport Authority (RTA) and state police are empowered to enforce the MV Act. Technically speaking, the RTA has exclusive jurisdiction over the traffic management. However, the State Police Department is empowered by a system of convention and usages to exercise control over traffic.

The MV Act of 1988 empowers an officer of the rank of police inspector, has prosecution powers and is able to check driver licenses and registration. Under the Indian Police Act of 1861, the police officials exercise wide-ranging powers including imposition of fines and the collection of penalties from traffic violators. In other words, exercising control over the traffic regulations and enforcement to facilitate orderly movement of traffic and action to prevent and investigate road accidents are a police responsibility.† The chapter will explore the functioning of traffic police in providing safety and security on roads in the Hyderabad metropolis of India.

Hyderabad Metropolis

Four hundred and twenty one years old and the historical city of Hyderabad is the sixth largest metropolis both in terms of population and area in India and first largest city in the state of Andhra Pradesh. It is recognized as a metropolis and given the status of a Megacity by the central government in

---

* The Hyderabad Metropolitan Development Authority was formed by an Act (GO Ms. No. 570 MA, dated September 25, 2008) of the Andhra Pradesh legislature in the year 2008, with an area of 7100 km² under its purview and merged Hyderabad Urban Development Authority (HUDA). It is the second largest urban development area in India after the Bangalore Metropolitan Region Development Authority (8005 km²).

† Indian Police Act 1861, Section 31—stipulated that "it is the duty of the Police to keep order on public roads, streets, thoroughfares, ghats, landing places and all other places of public resorts and to regulate assemblies and procession."

September, 2007. The transformation of Hyderabad as a metropolis began in the late 1950s, with the formation of Hyderabad State in 1951, later Andhra Pradesh state in 1956 and Hyderabad becoming its capital. Large-scale industrialization, particularly in the public sector, took place in the early 1960s. In the late 1960s and early 1970s, a large number of important educational, research, and training institutions were set up in and around Hyderabad city. Since mid-1990s, massive development has been taking place in the areas around Hyderabad city in the field of information technology (IT), biotechnology, and sports infrastructure, creating new employment opportunities and thereby, triggering expansion of townships. The city has established itself as a center for sunrise industries such as IT and accounts for 10% of IT exports for the country.

The city of Hyderabad is located on the crossroads of the rivers, Krishna and Godavari in the Telengana region, and lies on the convergence of national and state highways, trunk, air, and rail routes, which link it with other metropolitan centers and key centers of importance in the country. The well-developed national and regional railroad network criss-crossing the city improved the access of Hyderabad to a number of key growth centers within and outside the state. Hyderabad has excellent domestic and international air links to the major metros of India and important international destinations in southeast Asia, Middle East, Europe, North America, and other countries. The emergence of new economy industries has catapulted Hyderabad to a prime position in India.

Demographical Growth

From the beginning, Hyderabad city population has been cosmopolitan in nature, plural, and multicultural in composition. After independence, various factors have turned Hyderabad into a point of attraction for the people of various walks of life. These included political activity, industrialization, trade and commerce, religious festivities, cultural growth, the spread of higher education, and growth of media and entertainment.

As a consequence of all these developments, the city of Hyderabad registered continues growth in its population. The present Hyderabad Urban Agglomeration (HUA) consists of the Hyderabad core city (Police Commissionerate area), 12-peripheral municipalities, Secunderabad Cantonment, Osmania University, and other areas (shown in Figures 14.2 and 14.3). Table 14.2 presents the details of population growth of HUA including core city of Hyderabad.

The population of the HUA increased from 27.1 million in 1981 to 75.59 million in 2011. The growth of population was more than 50% during the 1981–2011 period, 27% during the 1991–2001 period, and 44.57% during the 2001–2011 period. However, several well-established urban components of the city are located well beyond the urban agglomeration. Therefore, it has

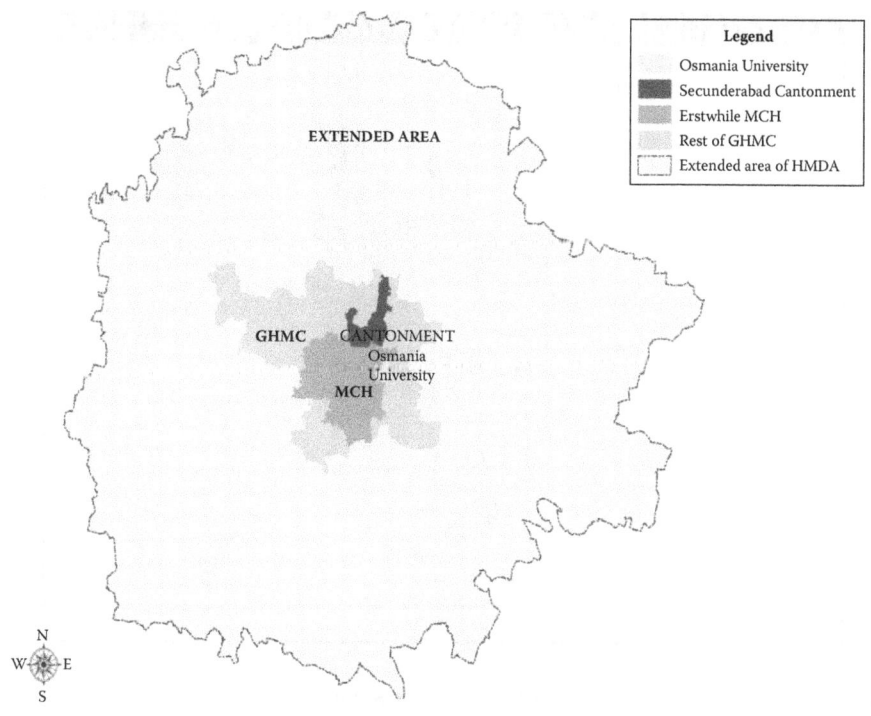

Legend

Osmania University
Secunderabad Cantonment
Erstwhile MCH
Rest of GHMC
Extended area of HMDA

EXTENDED AREA

GHMC   CANTONMENT
Osmania
University
MCH

N
W   E
S

Source: Comprehensive Transportation Study (CTS),
Hyderabad Metropolitan Development Authority (HMDA) Reports, 2012–2013.

Figure 14.2 Hyderabad Metropolitan Development Authority area.

absorbed immigrants from all over the world and its population has constantly increased. The transportation system has had to accommodate this growth. As discussed, many government agencies are involved in road safety. These include police, urban local body, Road Transport Authority (RTA), district collectorate, and the Urban Development Authority. But, as identified in Table 14.2, there is a lack of uniformity in the jurisdictions among these administrative units. For instance, the Hyderabad city police has a jurisdiction of 172 km^2 (Figure 14.3), the district administration jurisdiction is 217 km^2 including the Cantonment Board, which is governed by the district collector. The Municipal Corporation of Hyderabad (MCH) became the Greater Municipal Corporation and its jurisdiction was extended to 630 km^2 from 172 km^2 in 2007, due to merge of surrounding urban local bodies. The Hyderabad Metropolitan Development Authority jurisdiction also expanded to 7100 km^2 in 2008 by merging of erstwhile Hyderabad Urban Development Authority, HADA, CDA, BPPA.[*]

In view of the rapid urbanization, expanding surrounding areas, and extending jurisdictions of various development agencies, problems of law and order and crime also increased. To tackle these problems for

[*] Cyberabad (Metropolitan area) Police Act, 2004, dated. July 3, 2004.

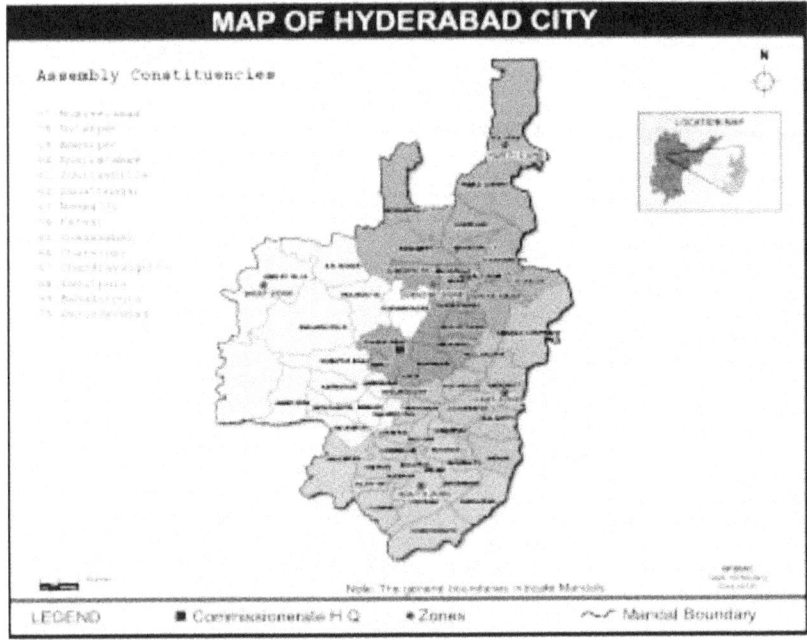

Figure 14.3 Hyderabad City Police Commissionerate area.

Table 14.2   Population Trends in Hyderabad Urban Agglomeration and Jurisdictions

Component	Area (km²)	Population (Lakhs)				Density (2011) (per km²)
		1981	1991	2001	2011	
Hyderabad core city (city police)	172	21.0	30.5	36.3	37.97	23,315
SCB	040	1.35	1.71	2.06	2.13	5,325
Hyderabad district	217	22.35	32.21	38.36	40.10	18,479
Surrounding 12 municipalities	458	3.8	9.9	17.0	27.99	2,267
GHMC*	**630**	**24.8**	**40.4**	**53.3**	**68.09**	**25,582**
Others	148	2.3	3.2	4.0	7.57	5,236
HUA	778	27.1	43.6	57.3	75.59	9,715

Sources: Census Reports, Government of India, New Delhi, India, 2001 and 2011.
SCB, Secunderabad Cantonment Board; GHMC, Greater Hyderabad Municipal Corporation formed in 2007.
* GHMC area includes Hyderabad core city area and surrounding 12 municipalities area.

administrative convenience and geographical background, the government established a separate Police Commissionerate to cover the Hyderabad metropolitan region, which excluded the Hyderabad city area. As a result, due to lack of uniformity in the jurisdiction and coordination among these units, the administration generated confusion and faced many problems in policy making and implementation, especially in traffic management. The scope of the present study covers the Hyderabad core city area that has a high population and density. Table 14.3 presents the growth of population of the core city since the formation of the State of Hyderabad in 1951.

Table 14.3 reveals that the population of Hyderabad city increased from 1,083,00 to 4,010,000 between 1951 and 2011. The decadal growth rates increased from around 10% in 1961 to 40% in 1991, and declined to around 10% by 2011 due to spread of the population over surrounding areas. However, the density of population continued to increase from around 5,500 to 23,315 km² between 1951 and 2011.

Vehicular Growth

Urban growth, both spatially and by population, puts heavy pressure on traffic growth. It is a well-known fact that, Hyderabad has witnessed fast growth in all respects. This growth is quite alarming to say the least, as the transport system from time to time is not able to keep pace with the growth of the city. Prior to 1956 (formation of the State of Andhra Pradesh), the transport system was mostly depended on slow-moving vehicles like *Tongas and bull carts* on one hand, and *rickshaws and bicycles* on the other. After 1956, there was a change in the mode of transportation of people. Animal-driven vehicles disappeared and fast-moving vehicles increased.

Today, Hyderabad city roads and lanes are littered with as many as 25 types of vehicles. Many of which are fast-moving mixing with slow-moving traffic. The common sight today is that as one type of vehicle tries to overtake the other types, causing the traffic flow to turn particularly chaotic. At the time of the

Table 14.3   Population Growth of Core City, Since 1951–2011 (in Thousands)

Year	Population	Difference	%	Density per km²
1951	1,083,624	—	—	5,429
1961	1,191,687	108.053	9.97	5,970
1971	1,682,537	491.850	41.27	9,748
1981	2,251,089	567.472	33.81	13,042
1991	2,945,939	694.930	40.01	17,068
2001	3,632,586	686.647	23.30	21,046
2011	4,010,748	378.162	10.41	23,315

Sources: Census Reports, Government of India, New Delhi, India, 2001 and 2011.

formation of the State of Andhra Pradesh in 1956, the vehicle strength in the city was only 7133. However, by 2010, the strength of the traffic had increased to 2.3 million. Table 14.4 gives the details of decadal growth since 1956.

Table 14.4 reveals that since the formation of the State, the growth of traffic has been more than 100% in each decade. During the year 1956, the number of vehicles was 7,133 and within 4 years by 1961, it had risen to 15,000 vehicles, the rate of growth being 110%. From 1961 to 1981, the growth in number of vehicles was between 110% and 150%. However, between 1981 and 1991, the number of vehicles increased fourfold. In 1991, the number of vehicles was 518,000, and had risen from 88,270 in 1981, with the growth rate for this period being more than 487%. By 2001, the number of vehicles had risen to 1,327,000. Almost more than 800,000 vehicles were added by 2001 and another 998,000 by 2010. The average increase was 80,000 vehicles per annum. Table 14.5 presents the annual growth rate of vehicles between 2001 and 2010.

Table 14.4   Decadal Growth of Vehicles, Since 1956 (in Thousands)

Year	Total Strength	Growth	Growth (%)
1956	7,133	—	—
1961	15,000	9,776	187.13
1971	38,000	23,000	153.33
1981	88,270	50,270	132.28
1991	518,258	429,988	487.12
2001	1,327,287	809,029	156.10
2010	2,326,028	998,741	75.25

Source: Records of Office of the Hyderabad Regional Joint Transport Commissioner, State Road Transport Authority (RTA), Government of Andhra Pradesh, 2012.

Table 14.5   Growth of Vehicle during Years 2001–2010 (in Thousands)

Year	Major Road Length	Total Vehicle Strength	Growth of Vehicles	Growth (%)	Vehicles per km²
2001	235	1,091,734	—	(−)1.04	5,588
2002	235	1,183,309	91,575	23.49	6,350
2003	235	1,281,923	98,614	57.88	6,791
2004	235	1,399,532	117,609	14.25	7,758
2005	235	1,527,470	127,938	9.52	8,497
2006	235	1,681,520	154,050	10.08	7,155
2007	235	1,847,429	165,909	8.37	7,841
2008	235	1,947,099	99,670	5.39	8,285
2009	235	2,049,900	102,801	5.27	8,723
2010	235	2,326,028	276,128	5.66	9,897

Source: Records of Office of the Hyderabad Regional Joint Transport Commissioner, State Road Transport Authority (RTA), Government of Andhra Pradesh, 2012.

Table 14.5 reveals that the number of vehicles has been showing a rapid growth, but the road length growth has remained static. The total major road length in Hyderabad city is only 235 km, or 6.5% of the total area and most of the roads and footpaths are encroachment by the hawkers. By the end of 2010, the total number of motor vehicles registered was 2,326,028 compared to 1,091,734 in 2001. The growth rate between 2001 and 2010 was more than 113%, which was a yearly average vehicle increase of 123,429. Further, Table 14.5 shows that the growth rate of vehicle density has been increasing exponentially. The density of vehicles per square kilometer had increased to 9897 in 2010 from 5588 in 2001. Table 14.6 presents details of the share of different categories of vehicles in the city during the year 2010.

Presently, the main forms of transport in the city are two-wheelers, cars, auto-rickshaws (three-wheelers), and public transport that comprises mainly of buses. Table 14.6 reveals that there are approximately 362,090 cars and more than 75,163 auto-rickshaws, which operate in the city and a phenomenal 1.73 million plus two-wheelers. With two-wheelers touching more than 1.7 million, the auto-rickshaws growing by three times with a similar increase in strength of cars. Almost 96% of these vehicles are privately owned and operated. Public transport occupies very meager strength of only 0.81%. In the absence of public transport growth, the demand for auto-rickshaws (private transport carriers) is on the increase. This mode of transport carries a million commuters a day. This means a very high utilization of auto-rickshaws in the absence of other satisfactory means of public transport. As a result, frequent traffic jams and accidents are increasing in the city. Further, it has been observed that the average journey speed of vehicles in 2010, decreased to 12 kmph from 18 kmph in 1981.

Discussions with the traffic police chief reveal that their goal is to increase the average speed of the vehicles to 35 kmph by 2021. Taking into account that the traffic authorities have prepared an action plan to improve the average

Table 14.6 Share of Vehicles during the Year 2010

Categories of Vehicle	Total Strength	Share in Total Strength	Vehicles per 1,000 Population
Motor cycles	1,730,079	74.67	382.67
Motor cars/jeeps	362,090	14.84	76.05
Stage carriage (buses/ mini buses)	18,800	0.82	4.24
Goods vehicles	95,856	4.35	22.27
Taxi	33,935	1.55	7.96
Auto rickshaws	75,163	3.34	17.11
Tractors	1,518	0.06	0.30
Others	8,587	0.35	1.82
Total	2,326,028	100.00	512

Source: Records of Office of the Hyderabad Regional Joint Transport Commissioner, State Road Transport Authority (RTA), Government of Andhra Pradesh, 2012.

speed of the vehicle, the researcher also emphasizes that they should work with the vision of the "Traffic and Transportation" for Hyderabad city, which is to provide a safe and reliable transport system. This traffic system is to be sustainable, environmental friendly, and to significantly improve the share and quality of public transport service that would improve traffic safety.

It could be thus summarized from the above analysis that one in every three persons in the Hyderabad city is the owner of a vehicle. At least 756 new vehicles are entering the city roads daily, indicating the increase in the affordability of the city dwellers. The high and steady growth in vehicles in conjunction with the increase in population, static road length, and decreasing average vehicles speed has resulted in high traffic volume on all types of roads.

Heavy Traffic Volume Locations in the City

To reduce the traffic congestion, it is necessary to identify the pockets where there is more congestion. Such an effort requires a scientific approach. The researcher has undertaken rides along with police to identify such areas where there is heavy concentration of traffic. This was designed as a field study to make use of participatory observation. The details of the study are as follows. This study was conducted during the first week of July 2010. The study lasted for five continuous working days. The researcher visited the following important junctions and used stop clock method of F.W. Tailor,* a count of the vehicles was conducted. The findings of the study are given in Table 14.7.

Table 14.7 indicates that the study intersections of Hyderabad city have heavy traffic volumes of more than 20,000 vehicles per hour. It may be stated that, the other areas also may contain certain pockets, where there is heavy traffic volume. Many reason can be attributed for increasing traffic volume, these are lack of road pavement markings, construction of footpaths and cycle tracks, bus bays, parking spaces, and insufficient road width and length. Apart from this encroachment of pavement, footpaths are another vital problem for traffic congestion on the road. The government should put efforts into reducing the traffic volume to provide safe movement of vehicles.

Method Adopted to Reduce Traffic Volume

It has been found that several methods are adopted to reduce the traffic volume. The methods adopted include the imposition of restrictions on four-wheelers from entering in central business district, banning of three-wheelers in the city center areas, construction of flyovers, foot over bridges, and the collection of entry fees and parking fees. A discussion with officials of the traffic and

---

* Tailor, F. W. (1903). *Shop management*. New York.

Table 14.7 Volume of Vehicles Counted per 1 Hour

Study Location	Intersection	Vehicles Volume per Hour
1.	Khairatabad	31,142
2.	M.J. market	30,122
3.	Afjal Gunj	29,332
4.	Chaderghat	29,231
5.	Koti	28,732
6.	Patny center	28,267
7.	Lakdikapool	27,362
8.	Ameerpet	23,345
9.	RTC × Road	22,363

transportation section of MCH* reveals that, Hyderabad city administration has adopted some of these methods in a phased manner. Flyovers for instance are being constructed in such areas where the traffic volume is more than 10,000. However, it may be stated that, at present there are no flyovers in such areas where there is heavy traffic volume (Table 14.7). The existing flyovers are constructed in areas where the traffic volume is within manageable limits.

Further, it may be noted that the increase in the number of cars has caused a number of problems. First, space occupied by the cars is disproportionately higher than other vehicles. This has caused traffic congestion and frequent traffic holdups. Second, air pollution has also worsened. Third, it is general knowledge that roads get congested during peak hours (8:00 am–11:00 am and 5:00 pm–7:00 pm). Traffic management personnel find it highly difficult to clear the traffic jams during such periods. To ease this situation, the government should deploy more human resources to regulate traffic flow and establish more traffic police stations to monitor observation of traffic rules. However, these aspects are not easily accomplished due to financial constraints. Finally, the government needs to improve infrastructure facilities, for example, constructing new roads, foot over bridges, subways, and flyovers. Needless to say that, the creation of such structures requires heavy financial outlays and the government is finding it difficult to meet this requirement because of the paucity of funds.

Road Accidents in Hyderabad Metropolis

Road traffic safety is an important component of the traffic and transportation mechanism. Road traffic accidents in the Hyderabad city were recorded by the traffic police up to the year 1981. Subsequently, the law and order department has taken over the responsibility of recording the accidents. The road accident trend for last 10 years is presented in Table 14.8.

* Reddy, N. V. S., Managing Director of Metro Rail Hyderabad (former additional commissioner, traffic and transportation, MCH, Hyderabad).

Table 14.8   Road Accidents Trend between 2001 and 2011

Year	Road Accidents	Deaths	Injuries
2001	2618	405	2841
2002	3039	411	3115
2003	3427	451	3373
2004	3525	419	3643
2005	3088	344	3741
2006	3477	426	3874
2007	3420	544	3220
2008	3342	518	3205
2009	2990	481	2908
2010	2797	494	2662
2011	2651	441	2528

Source: Hyderabad City Police. Traffic Branch. Statistic archives retrieved from http://www .htp.gov.in/Statistics.html.

Figure 14.4 explains that every year the accidents rate has decreased slowly since 2006. Moreover, the death rate due to accidents is stable between 400 and 500 per year. In addition, the number of injuries also is increasing every year with one person killed every 24 hours and one person is injured every 160 minutes. Out of every 10 persons killed in road mishaps in the state, one is from the city. The study establishes the fact that the roads are highly unsafe in the city. Until December 2011, 2651 accidents have occurred in Hyderabad city alone, in which 441 persons were killed and 2528 injured. The Hyderabad city has registered the highest number of accident cases as compared to other metropolises.

Table 14.9 shows that 78% of the accidents in the city are due to the fault of drivers. The present study has conducted fieldwork to elicit the opinion of the road users through the questionnaire method. It has found that out of 500 people surveyed, 342 respondents (68.4%) were license holders without a prior proper driving test being conducted, and 138 (27.6%) were driving without holding a driver's license. This means, the lack of proper training and the issue of improper driving licenses is a prime reason for the increase in the road accidents.

This discussion reveals that Hyderabad roads are highly unsafe. Reasons include the lack of traffic infrastructure facilities on one hand and the lack of proper traffic awareness among road users on the other, are the vital problems of road safety. However, efficient traffic enforcement will bring safety and security on the roads of Hyderabad to reduce violations and accidents. Police are playing a vital role as a traffic enforcement agency to regulate traffic systematically.

Police in Road Traffic Safety

Police, it has been observed, are the most visible arm of the government as it deals with such vital social issues as protection of life and property

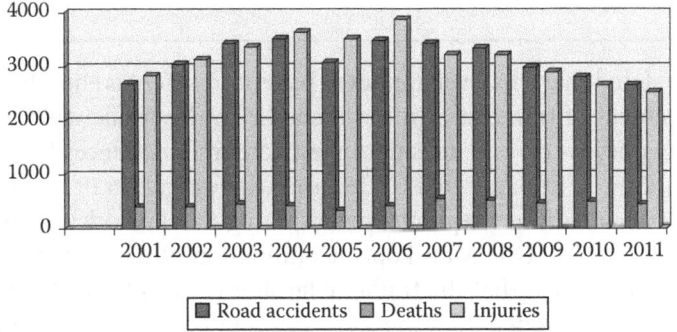

Figure 14.4 Comparison of road accidents.

Table 14.9 Causes for Road Accidents in the City during 2010

Driver's fault	78%
Bad roads	15%
Vehicle conditions	7%
Total	100%

Source: Hyderabad Police. Traffic Branch. Statistic archives retrieved from http://www.htp .gov.in/AccidentAnalysis.htm.

and the administration of justice. Within the various police functions, control of automobiles is one of the most visible police functions. Law and order and traffic control are two inseparable functions. In fact, the police Act does not make any distinction between the traffic related offences and other criminal acts. However, the traffic function is organized into a separate branch, which functions in close association with law and order branch. Hyderabad city traffic branch is headed by an officer of the rank of additional commissioner of police who is drawn from the senior Indian police service cadre.

At present the entire city of Hyderabad has been divided into 2 traffic districts, 6 traffic divisions, and 23 traffic police stations for better traffic control and enforcement by the police. The present strength of the traffic police is 1174, including 1 additional deputy police commissioner, 2 deputy police commissioners, 2 additional deputy police commissioners, 7 assistant police commissioners, 20 inspectors, 3 reserve inspectors, 121 sub-inspectors, 21 RSIs, 206 head constables, and 791 traffic constables. In addition, 871 home guards were also deputed to the traffic branch to support in traffic regulation. Important functions of the city traffic branch is to regulate traffic movement, enforcement of traffic laws under the MV Act and City Police (CP) Acts, traffic education, and coordinate with other concerned agencies for better traffic control.

Traffic

It may be stated that whatever applies to law enforcement is equally applicable to enforcement of traffic law. In Hyderabad city, the traffic wing looks after only regulatory work, and does not investigate traffic offences like fatal road accidents (304-A Indian Penal Code cases). Investigation of traffic offences cannot be separated from regulatory work, as regulatory work has a bearing on traffic offences. The One Man Police Commission of Andhra Pradesh State (1984) recommended that the traffic wing should be entrusted with investigation of all traffic offences.* The same opinion has also been expressed by the traffic personnel. But, action has not been taken by the government to provide powers of investigation of accident cases to the traffic police. Efforts should be made by the government to assign accidents investigation responsibilities to strengthen the efficiency of the traffic enforcement authorities to provide safety on the roads. The traffic police should emphasize management of the safe and smooth flow of traffic, the minimization of the incidence of accidents, effectively prosecute traffic violators, conduct accident investigations, and lay greater stress on road user education.

In regulating urban social life in Hyderabad city, city traffic police play an important role. Its concern can be seen during the morning and evening (peak) hours especially in the context of school children's rush and the heavy thrust of office goers. On an average, the operative employee of the traffic police is too busy to talk to others during morning peak hour. During peak hours the police constable cannot afford to move away from their place of work. On festive occasions the role of the traffic police becomes very crucial.

Traffic Violations

The traffic police of Hyderabad city, while employing the techniques have been imposing penalties and collect sizable amounts as the compounding fee under the MV Act and CP Act. The details of which are given in Table 14.10.

Table 14.10 shows that every year traffic offences are on the rise. During 2007, more cases were registered due to new safety devices such as wearing a helmet and using seatbelts being made compulsory. But it has been observed that after 2008, these rules were not being implemented seriously due to pressures from various groups. During 2010, the number of cases increased to 2,766,459, the reason being the introduction of e-challan system (electronic ticketing system) and programmable device applications (PDA) to enforce violations. Under the newly introduced e-challan system, 1,085,652 and 1,448,710 cases were registered during 2010 and 2011. By 2011, almost 5 million (4,782,670) cases were registered. The discussions with police officials reveal

* Report 1984, "The One Man Police Commission of AP," Chairman, Sri. K. Ramachandra Reddy, Govt. of AP. Recommendation 15.48, p. 181.

Table 14.10   Traffic Offences under Motor Vehicle Act and City Police Act during 2007–2011

Year	MV Act Cases	CP Act Cases	Total Cases
2007	2,214,145	10,074	2,224,219
2008	1,662,514	26,000	1,688,514
2009	1,818,273	18,988	1,837,261
2010	2,766,459	31,280	2,797,739
2011	3,333,961	1,448,710	4,782,671

Source: Hyderabad Police. Traffic Branch. Statistic archives retrieved from http://www.htp .gov.in/Enforcement.html.

that only a meager number of cases are being registered due to the shortage of personnel. However, special programs were conducted against drunken drivers, irregular number plates, and vehicle documents to control traffic violation in the city. According to the traffic police chief,* around 9000 cases were registered against drunken driving between January and September, 2012. All these violators were given counseling and prosecuted by the court.

Strategies Adopted by the Police

The following strategies were adopted by the traffic police of Hyderabad metropolis to improve their enforcement performance to minimize traffic violations and to ensure better public safety in the city.

- The Hyderabad traffic police introduced the e-challan system (e-ticketing) during 2007 for better traffic enforcement. E-challan is a noncontact enforcement system to curb violations and implement stricter traffic discipline among the traffic commuters. E-challans are generated with photo evidence. There are two types of e-challan, one is with surveillance cameras (CCTVs), which automatically takes the violation photos that will be printed on the challan itself. The second type is with the use of digital cameras, the officer will take a snapshot of the violation in the field. These photos will be stored for record purposes. The status of e-challans can be verified from the website (www.htp.gov.in). In India, Hyderabad traffic police is the first traffic department that has developed the e-challan system with photo evidence and online payment facility.
- The e-challan system significantly reduced the burden of the traffic officer to catch violators and issue them a challan notice, but it was found that only 30% of the violators responded to the e-challans and paid the penalty. To overcome this problem, PDA devices were

* Additional Commissioner of Police (Traffic), Hyderabad city, press release dated, October 12, 2012.

introduced in 2009. The PDA devices were connected to a central server that retrieved the history of challans issued for any vehicle in context, and issued challans on the spot to the violator. These PDAs have helped traffic officers to increase the collection of fines.

- CCTVs were provided at 150 important traffic junctions to iden-tify violators like triple driving, signal jumping, cell phone driving, defective number plates, and one-way entry. The surveillance cam-eras were increased to 350 during 2012 and many more new junc-tions were brought under the surveillance camera system.
- To control vehicles speed, the police have introduced speed laser guns in the city. Speed violations are captured through the laser gun camera that records the speed of the vehicles.
- Traffic command center was started by the city traffic branch. The surveillance cameras, new traffic signaling system, automated red light violation system, e-challan system, and all other existing soft-ware in the surveillance camera control room. These systems will all be integrated under a new project called the Traffic Command Centre and all the systems will work in harmony with each other with additional features to automatically generate e-challans and other video analytics for the traffic violations.

In summary, the data clearly indicates that the problem of road safety has been increasing, due to vast increase in vehicles and the lack of sufficient police strength. Consequently, it became a vital challenge for traffic officers to maintain discipline on the roads and to minimize traffic offences. Unless there are increases in the traffic strength, the technology will not be sufficient to overcome this problem.

Disproportionate Increase in Vehicle and Police Strength

The total present strength of the city traffic police is 1174 and the strength of the home guard is 871. It may be observed that the sanctioned strength of the police has to be increased from time to time. It is necessary to state that the sanctioned strength is linked to the population of the vehicles and strength should be raised in accordance with the rise in the strength of the vehicles. It may be necessary to examine this aspect. Table 14.11 contains the data regarding increase in the strength of the sanctioned and vehicular traffic.

Table 14.11 reveals that the vehicular strength increased during the period 1995–2010 by more than 261%, whereas the strength of police has increased by only 38.77%. The ratio of police to vehicles was 1:654 during the year 1995 and decreased to 1:1701 in 2010 (vehicular strength has been increasing and police strength remains static). This is a percentage decrease of 160.09%. This means that the work pressure and burden on police officers, especially field enforcement personnel, has increased. As a result, the intention of drivers to

Table 14.11   Growth in Police and Vehicle Ratio

Year	Police Strength	Growth	Vehicle Strength in Thousand	Growth in Thousands and %	Police Vehicle Ratio	Growth
1995	846	—	553	—	1: 654	—
2010	I174	328 (38.77%)	1997	1444 (261.12%)	1: 1701	1047 (160.09%)

follow rules is declining and violations are increasing in the city. Discussion with the constabularies has revealed the fact that if the vehicle ratio increases to more than 500, it may affect badly on the performance of the enforcement of traffic laws, including proper regulation of traffic. However, there is no particular scientific methodology to fix the strength of the traffic police personnel. In view of this, efforts may be made by the government to maintain the standard ratio of police and vehicles for efficient performance and enhance road traffic safety activities on urban roads to minimize road accidents and traffic jams.

Police Perception

Most of the people working in the traffic branch at different levels are not willing to remain in the traffic branch. In this connection, the researcher has interviewed 50 traffic police personnel of subordinate services who are actually involved in the traffic regulation activities. Those interviewed included 10 sub-inspectors, 15 head constables, and 25 traffic constables covering 23 traffic police stations within the city.

Forty-three of 50 (more than 86%) police personnel expressed their unwillingness to continue in the traffic branch. During the interaction with the personnel, the researcher has found various reasons for such an attitude, including the following:

- The serious health problem faced by the officers on account of high levels of air and noise pollution. Traffic personnel standing at traffic junctions have reported serious impacts on hearing abilities. According to the Apollo Hospital doctors, it has been discovered that 76% of city traffic personnel of the operational wing suffer from "noise-induced hearing loss," which is a permanent disability.* Further it was found that the traffic personnel who have put in more than 6 years of service have been the worst affected.
- No fixed working hours and a lack of proper facilities to the personnel.

---

* Apollo Hospital Jubilee Hills Hyderabad has conducting a hearing assessment test for odd traffic cops in the city since 2002–2005, under the supervision of the Dr. E.C. Vinay Kumar, Head ENT Department.

- Work pressure has been increasing due to static strength.
- Lack of support from other concerned agencies.
- Lack of accident investigation activities.
- Lack of promotional benefits in the organization.
- They are not permanent base staff of the traffic branch; therefore, they are not serious about their duties.

Road Users Perception

This research included a survey of selected road users to elicit their perception of the role and performance of the traffic police. A sample of 500 road users was surveyed at random, covering all the traffic police stations of the city. Of the entire sample, only 22.6% (113) were satisfied with the traffic safety measures of the police and an overwhelming 77.4% (387) were dissatisfied.

The dissatisfaction with traffic control by the traffic police was by and large uniform across all the traffic police station areas. It has been found that the road users blame the traffic police for the disorder and mismanagement, although they are not the only agency responsible for the state of affairs. This could be owing to the fact that the traffic policeman is the only agent physically visible on the road and the road users consider him or her responsible.

Quite a number of road users (328 or 65%) felt that the traffic police try to execute wrong priorities like collecting penalties for violation of rules, for example, being in possession of papers or wrong driving, instead of ensuring smooth traffic movement by bringing about order into an otherwise disorderly, congested, clogged vehicular movement or non-movement.

It would be instructive to carry out a survey of the road user's perception of their own allegiance to rules and norms that ensure smooth traffic without the police having to enforce the same.

Conclusion

The paper identifies the various sources of disequilibrium responsible for the chaos on the city roads. The unplanned growth in population, the expansion of space, and the tremendous increase of vehicular strength together with the stagnant road length, are the prime reasons for the unruly behavior of vehicles on the road. The traffic police is the only visible arm on the road to control traffic, but the minimum facilities to be provided for the field personnel are deteriorating with time. The multiple agencies concerned with road traffic safety and the lack of coordination among them, adds to the problem. The agencies responsible for allowing vehicles and drivers on the road are not effectively functioning, which is leading to a greater increase in road fatalities. The result of the traffic management system being part of the overall police administration makes it a temporary agency that lacks seriousness and belongingness, which would aid toward a smooth flow of traffic. For that reason, the government should make every effort for a better road traffic system that will help to ensure greater public safety in the city.

Suggestions

The following measures may assist in strengthening the road traffic safety in the Hyderabad city and metropolis:

1. A separate coordination body with uniform jurisdiction should be established for policy making and implementation of road traffic safety activities.
2. Comprehensive legislation covering all aspects of road traffic administration such as traffic enforcement, traffic engineering, and traffic education is needed. The traffic police may be given powers to implement the provisions of the proposed legislation.
3. Traffic police are made responsible for the registration and processing of the road accident cases.
4. Traffic police personnel strength should be increased to release stress and work burden on existing field staff.
5. Traffic police personnel should be motivated with sufficient facilities to function efficiently and effectively.
6. There is a need to modernize and improve the technology to strengthen the traffic enforcement function and to relieve officers from the burden of routine duties so as to concentrate on traffic planning and control.
7. In view of the findings that the traffic administration suffers from a financial crunch, 50% of the proceedings related to fines and penalties imposed on road users may be assigned to traffic police. Besides, project-specific special funds could also be released to strengthen engineering and educational aspects.
8. A good network of roads and an efficient mass urban transport system makes significant contributions to improving the working efficiency of a city and its environs. A poor urban transport system not only constraints urban economic growth but also degrades the public's quality of life through congestion, pollution, and accidents.
9. Improve the quality of crash investigation and of data collection, transmission, and analysis.
10. Finally, the study feels that the participation of people is the most effective solution to ease the traffic problem in the city.

References

Census Reports. (2001). New Delhi, India: Government of India.

Census Reports. (2011). New Delhi, India: Government of India.

Crime Reports of Andhra Pradesh. (2010). State Crime Record Bureau. Hyderabad, India: AP Police.

Crime Reports of Andhra Pradesh. (2011). State Crime Record Bureau. Hyderabad, India: AP Police.

Comprehensive Transportation Study (CTS) Report. (2011). Hyderabad Metropolitan Development Authority (HMDA). Hyderabad, A.P.

Global Status Report. (2009). *Road safety. Global plan for the decade of action for road safety 2011–2010*. Geneva, Switzerland: WHO, UNO.

Hyderabad City. (2008). Development plan, JnNURM, reports. New Delhi, India: Ministry of Urban Development, Government of India.

Hyderabad City Police. Traffic Branch. Statistical archives retrieved from the http://www.htp.gov.in/Enforcement.html.

Hyderabad City Police. Traffic Branch. Statistical archives retrieved from http://www.htp.gov.in/AccidentAnalysis.html.

Hyderabad Police. Traffic Branch. Statistic archives retrieved on August 31 2014. http://www.htp.gov.in/Statistics.html.

Hyderabad Regional Joint Transport Commissioner, State Road Transport Authority (RTA), Government of Andhra Pradesh, 2012.

Ministry of Road Transport & Highways. (2011). *Road accidents in India*. New Delhi, India: Government of India.

Ministry of Surface and Transportation. (2011). Government of India, New Delhi, India: Government of India.

The central motor vehicle rules. (1989). Ministry of Road Transport & Highways, Government of India, New Delhi. New Delhi, India: Deepak Publishers.

The Hyderabad City Police Act, 1348-F. (1940). Hyderabad, India: Law Publication.

Year book (2011–2012). Road Transport. Transport Research Wing, Ministry of Road Transport & Highways, Government of India, New Delhi.

Conclusion

15

As concluding remarks, this chapter offers an overview on the dynamics and effects of police reforms through the lens of the contributions included in this book, and also expands on other related considerations that are critical in understanding the underlying forces that build police reforms. As mentioned in the "Introduction," the relation between socioeconomic developments, violent crime, and policing is complex and characterized by a plurality of factors that may impact police reforms. More precisely, this chapter will address the sources of police reform, types of reforms, factors influencing the dynamics of police reform, and impact of reforms as well as challenges that emerge in postreform eras. Finally, this chapter identifies the critical components of a research agenda of police reforms that consider violent crimes and socioeconomic developments.

This book provides several case studies and the theoretical background necessary to identify five main sources of changes that can trigger or weaken police reform: economic, political, technological, criminal, and leadership/managerial factors. Each chapter in the book addresses police and criminal justice system reform topics that impact economic developments and violent crimes. For example, Chapters 11 and 12 illustrate that the corruption of public officials is highly disruptive to the legal economy, erodes citizens' confidence in the public system, and increases unfairness in the distribution of financial opportunity. Corruption of police officials can also lead to abuse of power that translates into police brutality, intimidation, and the use of lethal force. In Chapter 2, we see that when police organizations choose to integrate new technologies, they inject investment in the private sector and stimulate the economy through research and development. For example, some police technology can contribute to reducing the risk of violence by offering a broad range of nonlethal solutions that de-escalate a dangerous situation. Chapters 10 and 12 show that when police organizations implement reforms that support democratic values and keep a distance from political patronage, it contributes to a more stable society where citizens are less exposed to violent crime or political violence and can therefore have access to individual economic freedom. By adapting to criminal changes through knowledge-based reform, police are able to curb criminal violence that disturbs the stability of communities and creates economic losses. Finally, in Chapters 3, 5, and 7 we find that the adoption of innovative leadership initiatives and management models that aim for more efficient police practice can be instrumental in reducing the cost of public policing.

In addition to providing the opportunity to reflect more thoroughly on each of the identified aforementioned sources of police reform, this book places a primary emphasis on the economic perspective by considering police reforms as a consequence of economic fluctuations and as a vector influencing economic developments. For instance, Chapter 1 provides key examples in which economic booms, urbanization, and expansion of trade activities require in-depth changes in the ways that police are protecting commercial transportation routes. In the same vein, Chapter 14, written by Adki Surender, illustrates the challenges and reforms faced by police departments in charge of transportation infrastructure in a megacity needing road safety and transportation security. The example provided by the author shows the importance of integrating police participation in road and traffic management. It shows also how the safety and security of motorways are key concerns for urban development as well as for the vitality of local and regional economies. It is now part of any modern policing mission to increase public safety on roads as well as to develop and implement new strategies that decrease accidents and mortality rates.

Further, an economic downturn can have a critical impact on police agencies by considerably reducing public funding for security and safety resources, which demand police forces to restructure and develop new crime prevention strategies. However, Chapter 1, written by Frederic Lemieux, shows that violent crime rates are not impacted equally in all cities. The findings show that the globalization level of a city is the best predictor of the variation in homicide rates across large cities. In the wake of major financial crises and a potential downsizing of police forces (as seen in the aftermath of the great recession in 2008), these results also indicate that crime prevention strategies deployed by police officials should consider the influence of macroeconomic factors for the sake of efficiency in allocation of resources. Conversely, we saw that the downsizing of the public security sector can also lead to major reform by stimulating the private security sector and by opening the market to new players, which offer complementary and new services to citizens. The "rebirth" of private policing happened during the second half of the twentieth century when the budget of public police agencies started to shrink in most advanced democracies (Johnston, 1992).

In addition to the economic factor, police organizations can be deeply influenced by politics or impact politics. According to Bayley (1995), the nature of a government is indistinguishable from the police, who reflect that government. In general, the maintenance of order and law enforcement activities are often politically driven—a condition for both democratic and nondemocratic countries. The government and the state craft and enact laws that police agencies enforce. For instance, the formation of regulating bodies tasked with the mission to enforce laws contributes to the stability of the economy, reliability of justice systems, fairness in the application of laws, and compliance to state regulations. States that are unable to govern properly through their institutions and implement transparent "checks and balances" often generate fertile ground for corruption and the abuse of power.

In Chapter 12, Johanna Berning and Moses Montesh scrutinize the roles and functions of agencies in South Africa in enforcing newly developed strategies targeting corruption. The authors conclude that from a strategy and policy perspective South Africa seems to be on the right path, but the application and implementation of the anticorruption strategies by enforcement agencies are problematic. The authors assert that the cyclical establishment and dismantling of anticorruption agencies by the government undermines the overall strategy and is mainly the result of a lack of political vision in that matter. Also, in Chapter 11 Setlhomamaru Dintwe examines the effectiveness of the anticorruption programs deployed by the South African government to decrease pervasive corruption patterns in the public sector. The author concludes that several critical elements prevent the government from achieving its objectives of minimizing corruption. Among them, the author identifies bureaucratic secrecy, the absence of checks and balances, protracted rule by one political party, administrative inefficiency, and complex decision-making procedures. Finally, in Chapter 10 James F. Albrecht provides a comprehensive analysis of the challenges faced by law enforcement agencies and the justice system in Kosovo in a postconflict era. The author concludes that several government officials are former military commanders suspected of being involved in war crimes or having relations with criminal groups. The author also mentions the lack of leadership and vision from Western countries involved in the reconstruction of Kosovo, which were mainly motivated by national interest.

These aforementioned chapters show how political laxity and corruption of government officials represent key factors that degrade the overall state's ability to govern, maintain trust and transparency with citizens, and eventually establish its legitimacy. Despite an apparent well-thought strategy, law enforcement agencies and the justice system in Kosovo as well as South Africa seem to face considerable difficulty in carrying out reforms due to a deficit of political will (national and international) and to persistent dishonest practices within government institutions (cultural and individual). Ultimately, it is undeniable that weak institutional governance, corrupted practices, and the inability to enforce laws can adversely affect an economy in several ways: (1) erosion of foreign assistance programs due to anticorruption policies at the national and international levels, (2) shrinking of foreign private investments due to the cost of bribes and risk of sanctions, (3) favoritism in trade and commercial activities due to nepotism in political appointment, (4) nonenforcement of contracts due to corruption of police officials, (5) emergence of an underground economy due to the lack of legitimate opportunities, (6) organized crime activity due to lower risks from the justice system and protection from public official bribery schemes, and

(7) money laundering being encouraged due to the lack of checks and balances and dysfunctional (if not absent) financial monitoring mechanisms.

It would be false to assume that political laxity and corruption of public officials is a plague that is only thriving in newly industrialized countries or emerging democracies. For example, the New York Police Department was the object of two extensive investigations for corruption in the 1970s (Knapp, 1973) and the 1990s (Mollen, 1994). Both commissions were mandated by the mayors of New York to investigate alleged pervasive corruption within the police rank and file. The Knapp Commission (1973) found that petty corruption associated with bribes, gratuities, and kickbacks was rampant and deeply ingrained in the cultural background of the department due to the reinforcement of deviant values by senior police officers ("grass eaters"). Also, the commission found that a smaller group of police officers was engaged in premeditated and aggressive behaviors that generated the opportunity to shake down pimps and drug dealers ("meat eaters"). Twenty years later, Judge Milton Mollen found out that the grass eaters were less pervasive; but the commission pointed out that the face of corruption in New York was characterized by brutality, theft, abuse of power, and active police criminality. In 1993, similar corruption activities were disclosed when 12 police officers (the "dirty dozen") from the Metropolitan Police Department in Washington, DC, were convicted of accepting thousands of dollars to protect and secure shipments of narcotics. In 1999, the Rampart Division of the Los Angeles Police Department was the object of an inquiry regarding an alleged act of violence and corruption. More than 70 police officers were under investigation for several crimes, including unprovoked shootings, unprovoked beatings, planting of false evidence, framing suspects, stealing and dealing narcotics, bank robbery, perjury, and cover-up of evidence.

These police corruption cases in the United States also show that illegal opportunities could have a significant political impact by destabilizing local and state governments. One commonality in these cases is the political impact of police corruption scandals. In these cases, the police commissioner often had to resign while political opponents used the police scandal to spin off political attacks against the administration in place. In all cases, police misconduct led to critical reforms in law enforcement oversight practices and changes in the political landscape. Other famous cases in Australia, Canada, and England show similar outcomes regarding police reform and the subsequent political impact.

A third important source of police reform is the emergence and implementation of technologies. For example, the implementation of patrol cars and police radios had a significant impact on police responses to calls from citizens. On the one hand, patrol cars provided the opportunity to decrease the response time by sending police resources faster to crime scenes. On the other hand, police radios provided the opportunity to better dispatch resources and transmit useful information related to a situation. These technologies were instrumental in modifying police practices in servicing communities.

Another critical impact of technology on law enforcement occurred when police in Western countries started to use more computerized systems to store and organize the information collected. Today, police reports and queries about suspects are all made through computers and mobile devices. Moreover, the computerization of police organizations has provided fertile ground for the development of new crime prevention strategies. By applying technology to data analytics, many law enforcement agencies are now able to produce high-end analysis that provides better understanding of crime distribution in time and space through geo-mapping and predictive methodology.

In the same vein, Christopher Vas makes the case in Chapter 2 that to integrate the growing complexity and the uncertain nature of socioeconomic development, police organizations should employ more preemptive and preventive crime strategies by adopting a technology-driven approach that is based on social network patterns. According to the author, it is vital for law enforcement agencies and the criminal justice system in general to leverage social media to engage with the community and comprehend better social trends as well as collective behaviors. The ultimate goal of such an approach is to reduce uncertainty and improve the capability of authorities to serve the population by early detection of complex trends that can lead to crime and disruption of social order. The contribution of Christopher Vas is pushing the boundaries of existing predictive policing methods by incorporating a broader perspective centered on the use of raw data related to social, economic, and political phenomena affected by technology-based crime.

Using a different approach, in Chapter 6, James Lewis explores how police agencies investigate crimes committed, although computers need to be better conceptualized and understood. By discussing the modus operandi of some cybercrimes such as theft of valuable information, the author argues that police may sometimes misconstrue the nature of an offense by confusing white-collar crime with, for example, industrial espionage. Through research-based education and practical demonstrations, the author shows how various types of cyberespionage may be easily concealed if investigations are based on the proper conceptualization of the crime and the proper adoption of search techniques.

The work of James Lewis leads to the fourth source of police reform: change in crime. Throughout the recent history of police, changes in crime patterns (such as cross-border criminal activity, acts of extreme violence, and computer crimes) have required police to transform their practices by increasing information sharing, investing in highly trained units (SWAT), and acquiring new information technology talents. Also, evolution in the conceptualization of crime (such as white-collar crime, organized crime, and globalization of threats) has led police agencies to change their policy by adopting new strategies on targeting criminals (high profile), categorizing serious crime (harm done to society), and understanding the characteristics of criminal activity through analysis (social network analysis, link analysis, etc.). Changes in crime patterns usually require critical revisions of police know-how, while a change in crime conceptualization emerges from an evolution of police knowledge on crime.

Evolution in police know-how and knowledge is usually channeled through research, education, and training activities. Police training and academia have made advances in the past 40 years or so to provide a cross-pollination of opportunities related to applied research and crime analysis. In Chapter 8, Jonas Hansson examines the impact of academically oriented police education with a strong scientific emphasis on police students' perception. The research conducted by the author contributes new knowledge about teaching and learning in police training. As pointed out by Hansson, training that provided concrete examples and a sense of professional relevance guided students to understand the larger picture through concrete experience, reflective observation, abstract conceptualization, and active experimentation, which combines practical and theoretical elements. Such training is central to prepare the next generation of police officers to develop and integrate new knowledge about policing and criminal issues.

Following the same perspective, Johan Bertilsson and collaborators discuss in Chapter 9 the opportunities, experiences, and challenges of having research collaboration between police authorities and universities. The authors strongly suggest that police–university collaborations must be reciprocal, not only to foster academic knowledge in a police academy and in training but also to integrate a police perspective in applied academic research. For example, seasoned police professionals can assist scholars in the production of scientific knowledge that clearly addresses the practical needs of law enforcement. Reciprocally, police organizations should include scientific knowledge and learning activities in a training curriculum to educate police officers to be critical when presented with reports and novel scientific studies, as well as to be able to detect possible flaws and shortcomings before the implementation of new strategies or tactics.

Finally, the last identified source of police reform comes from management and leadership initiatives. Police and criminal justice administrations in general can generate deep changes by developing new approaches to security problems. For example, the adoption and implementation of new policing models are often advocated and led by senior leaders in police organizations and the justice system. During the past 40 years, law enforcement agencies experienced several changes in police management models, with some adopting community-based policing and others preferring problem-oriented policing or intelligence-led policing. Also, many agencies are trying to integrate drastically opposed policing models that provide both aggressive and passive crime prevention strategies. In Chapter 4, Stephen B. Perrott provides an analysis of the resistance of numerous police officials to concede that community-based policing models are now outdated and must be abandoned. More precisely, the author argues that more aggressive and intrusive forms of policing practices are widely used by law enforcement since 9/11 despite the fact that most police organizations openly affirm to being community oriented. According to Perrott, this double discourse generates sharp dissonance with police recruits and incongruence with the public perception of police roles in the community. Putting an end to this confusing divide between rhetoric and practice in police management models can, according to the author, be instrumental to initiate productive discussions about new directions for policing in modern democracies.

In Chapter 7, Colette Squires and Darryl Plecas review and assess a new initiative deployed by the Abbotsford Police Department, British Columbia, Canada, to address gang-related violence. Inspired by similar initiatives implemented in the United States, the police's multidimensional program integrates a broad range of tactics and strategy by mixing approaches such as intelligence-led and problem-oriented policing with an emphasis on intensive deterrence strategies. More precisely, the program includes tactics aiming at disrupting gang activity and fostering community engagement through actions that limit access of gang members to services and shops, prevention strategies that provide support to parents and that target gangs' recruitment schemes, and proactive interventions. According to the authors, the results of this multidimensional policing approach showed an astonishing decrease in violent crime within the 2 years after its implementation (no homicides).

The correctional system has also encountered deep internal changes regarding how punishment is administered. During the twentieth century, the correctional philosophy evolved and different models were developed and adopted: retribution, rehabilitation, and restoration. Each of these models has been challenged by the evaluation of existing practices and implementation of innovative programs. In Chapter 5, Keith Robinson and collaborators evaluate the shoplifting restorative justice program sponsored by the Chilliwack Restorative Justice and Youth Advocacy Association, British Columbia, Canada. The findings demonstrate the effectiveness of restorative justice for shoplifting cases, in contrast to those processed through courts. The authors suggest that the success of this restorative justice program should open a discussion on extending its application to other relevant sectors of the Canadian justice system, including repeat and adult offenders.

Finally, management and implementation of reform through a new national strategy can be inadequate or incomplete. In Chapter 13, Moses

Montesh and Johanna Berning make the case that youth crime prevention strategies in South Africa need to be addressed more specifically. The authors point out the need for leadership in the criminal justice system to recognize and implement youth crime prevention strategies. Also, the authors point out other factors indispensable for the success of such a strategy: government leadership, socioeconomic development/inclusion measures, cooperation/partnership programs, sustainability/accountability, knowledge-based policy making, and interdependancies between national and international crime trends. In this particular case, the authors conclude that the National Crime Prevention Strategy does not provide adequate perspective, leadership, and initiative on youth crime.

It is important to note that these sources of police reform are not mutually exclusive as they are very often complementary and their effect is additive. For example, the CompStat management philosophy in the 1990s, which was a revolutionary approach for police performance based on comparative statistics, was implemented because of the convergence of computerization of police (technology), need for police accountability on crime reduction strategies (politics), evolution of knowledge on crime patterns from the Broken Window Theory (Wilson & Kelling, 1982) on urban disorder and crime (crime pattern), adoption of an alternative management approach to community-based policing (leadership/management), and the resource allocation efficiency during a period of budget restriction (economy).

Peter Johnstone also points out this complex interaction between different sources of police reform in Chapter 3 by arguing that the evolution of policing in America is not the sole consequence of Sir Robert Peel's conceptualization of modern policing. The author explores several police models throughout history that have influenced the American police system. For example, the chapter contends that the American policing history was influenced by the English metropolitan police, French gendarmerie, Roman vigilante, contemporary twelfth-century Norman tax collectors, and private detectives from French prisons.

Another critical aspect of police reform is the context in which it happens. On one side, reform is often imposed on law enforcement and criminal justice systems through political pressure and public opinion. In general, these types of reforms happen in the wake of scandals related to a waste of resources, corruption, an abuse of power, and police brutality. On the other side, desired reforms usually come from inside the organization and are supported by upper management or the rank and file. The underlying elements of desired reforms are typically aligned with cultural features specific to the police profession. For example, more aggressive police management models (e.g., intelligence-led policing) might be more desired than passive models (e.g., community-based policing) because of cultural values attached to the role of police officers as "crime fighters." In that case, it is more likely that the implementation of reform will be championed internally. Another point of view on this perspective is suggested by den Heyer (2013), who points out that law enforcement agencies and police leaders can either shape their own future (proactive or desired reforms) or adapt to the changing, complex environment where they evolve (reactive or imposed reforms).

This book also highlights several factors that can affect or challenge the implementation of police reform. In many occasions, authors have mentioned the lack of senior leadership or political interest as being a critical issue for executing successful police reform. Also, elements of reform have to transcend the training and education of police officers to change mentalities and to impact values that are deep rooted in an obsolete cultural framework. Another important factor is the understanding and integration of cultural diversity that defines the various professional subgroups composing police organizations. The tensions, differences, and work realities of sworn officers versus civilian employees; gender divide; management staff versus "real" police professionals; investigators versus patrol officers; and racial divide can be critical organizational features that can derail or unsettle reform processes. Finally, public opinion and the role of the media can also have a critical impact on police reform processes as they can shape a platform that is characterized by negative rhetoric, witch-hunting, and political interferences that can antagonize key stakeholders and potentially ruin the chances of the successful implementation of significant changes.

As concluding remarks, we would like to point out that this book provides strong insights into foundational elements for a research agenda on police reform and on its impact on economic developments and armed violence. First, this field needs more systematic international comparative analysis on the impact of reform in law enforcement on economic development and violence, for example, measuring the effect of adopting a specific model of policing or implementing a particular technology on reduction of violence, cost of crime, and efficiency of public policing. The field of policing and public safety lacks, in general, international comparative research. Second, it is critical to produce a body of evaluative research that assesses, with methodological rigor and systematic analytical processes, the impact of police reform on economic development and violence. Third, there is a need to adopt a case study approach to scrutinize in more depth change management strategies used in police reforms and implantation of strategic initiatives in law enforcement and the justice system. Finally, because several chapters in this book point out issues with political leadership in implementing reforms in law enforcement and the justice system in general, it would be essential to support research aiming at understanding better how police leaders and senior public officials manage the politics of reform. Such research would be instrumental in generating knowledge about effective leadership under pressure and effective policy development in organizations facing crisis.

References

Bayley, D. (1995). *Patterns of Policing: A Comparative International Analysis.* New Brunswick, NJ: Rutgers University Press.

den Heyer, G. (2013). Shape or adapt? The future of policing. *Salus Journal 1*(1), 41–56.

Johnston, L. (1992). *The Rebirth of Private Policing.* London, United Kingdom: Routledge.

The Knapp Commission Report on Police Corruption. (1973). *Commission to Investigate Allegations of Police Corruption and the Cities Anti-Corruption Procedures.* New York: George Braziller.

Mollen, M. (1994). *Commission to Investigate Allegations of Police Corruption and Anti-Corruption Procedures of the Police Department.* New York: City of New York.

Wilson, J. Q., & Kelling, G. L. (1982). Broken windows: The police and neighborhood safety. *Atlantic Monthly, 249*(3), 29–38.

Chapter Abstracts 16

Chapter 1: Economic Recession and Homicide Rates in Globalized Cities: A Cross-Sectional Analysis

Frederic Lemieux

This research examines the relationship between international economic trends and crime rates in large urban areas. More precisely, it examines the influence of the recent economic recession on violent crime in globalized cities. The outcomes of this research provide a better understanding of the influence of macroeconomic phenomena (international recession and globalization) on crime trends in large cities. To define guidelines for future public policies, this research scrutinizes the preventive and deteriorating factors—associated with the "globalized nature" of selected large cities— that could directly and/or indirectly affect crime rates during a recession period. According to this economic perspective, crime rates can be considered as a performance measure, which could be used to assess the aptitude of local governance to curb the negative impacts of an international economic downturn.

Chapter 2: Generating Insight from Foresight: Emerging Challenges for Law Enforcement Policy Makers

Christopher Vas

The landscape of law enforcement is constantly changing given the uncertain times that we live in. The emergence of new technology and social media are paving the way for new forms of connectedness among individuals, communities, and societies more broadly. This chapter links the macro global and micro societal trends using a law enforcement and criminal justice perspective for better planning and strategy in policy making. Acknowledging the growing complexity and uncertain nature of socioeconomic development, the central argument of this chapter is for a need to transition from traditional approaches of law enforcement toward preempting and preventing crime by adopting a technology-driven societal network-based modus operandi.

Chapter 3: Real Influence of Sir Robert Peel on Twenty-First Century Policing in America

Peter Johnstone

There is a widely held view authored in the majority of U.S. criminal justice textbooks that the overwhelmingly major influences on policing in America have been Sir Robert Peel and the Metropolitan Police Act of 1829. The chapter explores this position and suggests that the influence of Peel is important but represents only one part of a far more complex policing history for the United States that draws in part from seventeenth-century Paris, France, and evolved in England with the adoption of the word "police," which was more by accident than choice, around 1720. Over the course of the following 100 years, and frequently to the ignorance of the British political elite, England subsumed a number of European policing models alongside the uniquely English marine insurance detectives so that by the end of the eighteenth century the Fieldings, Colquhoun, and eventually Peel all recognized that elements of the French policing model were advantageous and applicable to England. The chapter argues that it is the product of these modern developments alongside public and private law enforcement responses of greater antiquity that were transported, in stages, and absorbed into the policing landscape of the United States. In effect, twenty-first-century policing in America is the result of a complex and multifaceted policing history influenced by an English metropolitan police, a French gendarmerie, a Roman vigilante, a contemporary twelfth-century Norman tax collector (who acted as a part-time peace officer), and private detectives from French prisons.

Chapter 4: Burying Community-Based Policing to Protect Democratic Law Enforcement

Stephen B. Perrott

Over the last two decades, Western police forces have experienced significant innovations, most notably CompStat, homeland policing, and intelligence-led policing, while simultaneously coping with the fallout from 9/11, a radically new type of public protests, and a societal shift toward a neoliberal political backdrop. Despite these changes, the policing institution clings stubbornly to the three-decade-old zeitgeist of community-based policing. To many, these innovations are simply add-ons or complementary to community-based policing. It is argued here that this is an erroneous conclusion, and a rationale is offered as to why police forces are motivated to adhere to the community-based policing mantle despite evidence to the contrary. The analysis concludes with the contention that there is a need to come to terms with the death of community-based policing if we are to retain an open, consent-based type of policing consistent with the values of Western democracies.

Chapter 5: Pre-Charge Restorative Justice and Its Effect on Repeat and Adult Offenders

Keith Robinson, Darryl Plecas, Colette Squires, and Kim McLandress

Whereas most Canadian community-based restorative justice groups focus primarily on pre-charge cases for first-time young offenders, an examination of shoplifting cases from a restorative justice program provides surprising and positive results for repeat and adult offenders, compared with similar offenders processed through traditional justice. In comparison, the results for first-time young offenders are much less remarkable. This examination suggests that pre-charge restorative justice may have greater efficacy and potential for repeat and adult offenders than previously considered by those who reserved it as a low-level response for first-time youth offenders only.

Chapter 6: White-Collar Cybercrimes: Cyberespionage

James Lewis

Techniques and trends in cybercrime investigations are motivated by past experiences and lessons learned from actual events. Traditionally considered a white-collar offense, cybercrimes are committed by individuals encompassing all levels of socioeconomic status. More than 25,000 Internet-related crimes are reported each month to the Internet Crime Complaint Center, and it is estimated that many more go unreported. When cybercrimes involve activities that gain access to sensitive information about an adversary or a competitor for the purpose of gaining an advantage or when they involve matters pertaining to national security, these actions may be classified as cyberespionage. Research-based education and practical demonstrations are the focus of this chapter, and the chapter exhibits how various types of cyberespionage may be easily committed and concealed.

Chapter 7: Death by a Thousand Cuts: The Abbotsford Police Department's Multidimensional Program for Gang Suppression

Colette Squires and Darryl Plecas

Between 2005 and 2010, gang violence escalated in the Lower Mainland region of British Columbia, Canada, resulting in unprecedented levels of gun-related homicides and street violence. The Abbotsford Police Department employed a comprehensive array of tactics and strategies to create a multidimensional gang suppression strategy that resulted in zero homicides in 2011 for the city

of Abbotsford. Analyzing their work in light of other focused deterrence programs, this chapter provides a detailed description of the history, rationale,
and methods of and the lessons learned from "Death by a Thousand Cuts."

Chapter 8: Traditions in Basic Police Training Programs: An Interview Study among Swedish Police Students

Jonas Hansson

Police training and higher education in the United States, Australia, and
Europe are coming closer together. This chapter focuses on one European
country, Sweden, where academically oriented police education with a strong
scientific basis is being discussed and implemented. Police students begin
basic training with assumptions about what they need to learn to handle
their future work. These beliefs and the educational culture that they encounter during their training, which can be more or less academically oriented,
affect their learning. The purpose of this study was to analyze Swedish police
students' opinions about the teaching and lessons that they receive during
basic training. This study contributes new knowledge about teaching and
learning in police training. Eight interviews were conducted with police students in their final semester at the Basic Training Program for Police Officers
in Umeå, Sweden. The sampling was based on the participating students'
learning styles, using a Swedish version of Kolb's Learning Style Inventory.
Furthermore, a hermeneutical approach was used in the analysis of the interviews. The findings show that the students' sense of professional relevance is
significant and positively affects learning.

Chapter 9: Opportunities and Challenges of Research Collaboration between Police Authorities and University Organizations

Johan Bertilsson, Peter Fredriksson, Lars-Folke Piledahl, Mans Magnusson, and Per-Anders Fransson

This chapter discusses opportunities, experiences, and challenges of having research collaborations between police authorities and universities. The
growing complexity of society presents a number of challenges to police
authorities around the world. Criminality and terrorism exist in new forms
and use new mediums such as the Internet, and criminal organizations have
extensive resources to develop new kinds of drugs aimed at bypassing present regulations. Hence, the world of law enforcement faces the challenge to
continuously address new demands.

Collaborations between police authorities and universities can provide a base for mutual exchange of recent scientific discoveries and instigate new research projects within areas of special relevance for law enforcement and society. Simultaneously, such cooperation provides opportunities for law enforcement personnel to gain experience in general scientific methods and procedures. This is of increasing importance in a knowledge-based society. For example, based on firsthand experience, the police are particularly well suited to define problems that need attention from different scientific, social, and legal perspectives. Universities, on the other hand, are experienced in effecting research projects aimed at creating required solutions, training new students in the process.

Chapter 10: Rule of Law and Justice Administration in Kosovo: Evaluating the Challenges in Policing a Postconflict Developing Democracy

James F. Albrecht

More than 10 years after the final Balkan conflict, in which thousands of innocent civilians were killed and a few hundred thousand were displaced, the government of a self-proclaimed independent "Republic of Kosovo" continues to move toward a functional democratic government and eventual European Union membership. Under the supervision of international actors, most notably the United Nations, European Union, and United States, Kosovo's government administrators continue to be mentored and supported into shaping a free democracy and creating a credible rule of law system. When examining the law enforcement and justice mechanisms, much has been accomplished in creating professionally functioning actors, but both local Kosovo Police and international law enforcement professionals are still plagued by overwhelming caseloads involving government-sustained organized crime, war crimes, and corruption. The identified successes and challenges in establishing and coordinating the rule of law in Kosovo will provide insights into similar issues faced by other postconflict developing democracies across the globe. Finally, a number of recommendations are proposed to move Kosovo into a more effective democratic future.

Chapter 11: The Shortcomings of Anticorruption Program in Addressing Public Corruption: A Forensic Criminological Case of South Africa

Setlhomamaru Dintwe

The new democratic dispensation brought about a realization of the levels of corruption within the public service of South Africa. It encompasses understanding the causes of corruption on the one hand and calculated responses in countering corruption on the other. Although corruption may have been rampant even before the first democratic elections were held in 1994, a call for accountability and transparency, which became synonymous with democracy, removed a dark veil that covered the unbecoming actions of mainly public servants in democratic South Africa. Although this chapter acknowledges the presence of corruption during the apartheid era, its crux is whether the programs employed after the democratization of South Africa proved to be adequate in turning the tide against the scourge of corruption. The aim of this chapter is therefore to establish whether the anticorruption programs employed by the South African government encapsulate the internationally accepted elements reminiscent of anticorruption programs worldwide and whether this strategy is effective enough to thwart public corruption.

Chapter 12: Analysis of South African National Anticorruption Agencies

Johanna Berning and Moses Montesh

To address problems of corruption in South Africa, the government launched South Africa's National Anti-Corruption Program in 1997. This was followed by the adoption of the Public Service National Anti-Corruption Strategy in 2002 and the promulgation of the Prevention and Combating of Corrupt Activities Act 12 of 2004 as well as the Prevention of Organized Crime Act 121 of 1998. As a result, a number of agencies were established with different mandates. This chapter seeks to unravel the roles and functions of a number of South African agencies such as the police, Asset Forfeiture Unit, Special Investigating Unit, Office of the Auditor General, Public Service Commission, Directorate of Special Operations, and Directorate for Priority Crime Investigation.

Chapter 13: Need for a Youth Crime Prevention Strategy for South Africa

Moses Montesh and Johanna Berning

Preventing crime has been a priority for all government departments in South Africa, and it culminated in the launching of the National Crime Prevention Strategy (NCPS) in 1996. The NCPS emphasises the prevention of crime, rather than entirely relying on the criminal justice process to arrest and convict offenders. It is also based on the idea that the South African

Police Service alone cannot reduce crime. The NCPS has been reviewed on two occasions, but it has failed to properly address youth crime. Although the NCPS has laid a foundation that provides regulations to various relevant departments to develop strategies that are aligned with existing approaches so as to avoid duplication of services, youth crime prevention is still a problem. This chapter seeks to analyze the NCPS, as well as proposing a separate youth crime prevention strategy for South Africa.

Chapter 14: Policing and Urban Road Traffic Safety in India: With Reference to the Hyderabad Metropolis

Adki Surender

With the increasing urbanization, industrialization, and advancement of science and technology, traversing long distances has become the order of the day. According to World Health Organization (WHO) reports,* each year nearly 1.2 million people die as a result of road traffic collisions, that is, more than 3500 deaths a day. It is noted that 90% of road traffic deaths occur in low- and middle-income countries, which claim less than half of the world's registered vehicle fleet (48%). India is a leading country in this phenomenon. In spite of road safety receiving international attention and support, the results presented in WHO reports shows that much more needs to be done especially in developing countries like India. This chapter examines the major road safety issues confronting India, especially in the Hyderabad Metropolis.

---

* *Global Status Report on Road Safety: Time for Action.* Geneva, Switzerland: World Health Organization, 2009. http://www.who.int/violence_injury_prevention/road_safety_status/2009.

IPES Story

International Police Executive Symposium (IPES), www.ipes.info

The International Police Executive Symposium was founded in 1994. It enjoys a Special Consultative status with the United Nations. The aims and objectives of the IPES are to provide a forum to foster closer relationships among police researchers and practitioners globally, to facilitate cross-cultural, international and interdisciplinary exchanges for the enrichment of the law enforcement profession, and to encourage discussion and published research on challenging and contemporary topics related to the profession.

One of the most important activities of the IPES is the organization of an annual meeting under the auspices of a police agency or an educational institution. Every year since 1994, annual meetings have been hosted by such agencies and institutions all over the world. Past hosts have included the Canton Police of Geneva, Switzerland; the International Institute of the Sociology of Law, Onati, Spain; Kanagawa University, Yokohama, Japan; the Federal Police, Vienna, Austria; the Dutch Police and Europol, The Hague, The Netherlands; the Andhra Pradesh Police, India; the Center for Public Safety, Northwestern University, USA; the Polish Police Academy, Szczytno, Poland; the Police of Turkey (twice); the Kingdom of Bahrain Police; a group of institutions in Canada (consisting of the University of the Fraser Valley, Abbotsford Police Department, Royal Canadian Mounted Police, the Vancouver Police Department, the Justice Institute of British Columbia, Canadian Police College, and the International Centre for Criminal Law Reform and Criminal Justice Policy); the Czech Police Academy, Prague; the Dubai Police; the Ohio Association of Chiefs of Police and the Cincinnati Police Department, Ohio, USA; the Republic of Macedonia and the Police of Malta. An annual meeting on the theme of "Policing Violence, Crime, Disorder and Discontent: International Perspectives" was hosted in Buenos Aires, Argentina on June 26–30, 2011. The 2012 annual meeting was hosted at United Nations in New York on the theme of "Economic Development, Armed Violence and Public Safety" on August 5–10. The Ministry of the Interior of Hungary and the Hungarian National Police hosted the meeting in 2013 in Budapest on August 4–9 on the theme of "Contemporary Global Issues in Policing". The 2014 meeting on "Crime Prevention and Community Resilience" will take place in Sofia, Bulgaria on July 27–31.

There have been also occasional special meetings of the IPES. A special meeting was cohosted by the Bavarian Police Academy of Continuing Education in Ainring, Germany, University of Passau, Germany, and State University of New York, Plattsburgh, USA in 2000. The second special meeting was hosted by the police in the Indian state of Kerala. The third special meeting on the theme of "Contemporary Issues in Public Safety and Security" was hosted by the commissioner of police of the Blekinge region of Sweden and the president of the University of Technology on August 10–14, 2011. The most recent special meeting was held in Trivandrum (Kerala, India) on "Policing by Consent" on March 16–20, 2014.

The majority of participants of the annual meetings are usually directly involved in the police profession. In addition, scholars and researchers in the field also participate. The meetings comprise both structured and informal sessions to maximize dialogue and exchange of views and information. The executive summary of each meeting is distributed to participants as well as to a wide range of other interested police professionals and scholars. In addition, a book of selected papers from each annual meeting is published through CRC Press/Taylor & Francis Group, Prentice Hall, Lexington Books and other reputed publishers. A special issue of *Police Practice and Research: An International Journal* is also published with the most thematically relevant papers after the usual blind review process.

IPES Board of Directors

The IPES is directed by a board of directors representing various countries of the world (listed below). The registered business office is located at Norman Vale, 6030 Nott Road, Guilderland, NY 12064 and the registered agent is National Registered Agents, 200 West Adams Street, Chicago, IL 60606.

President
Dilip Das, Norman Vale, 6030 Nott Road, Guilderland, NY 12084. Tel: 802-598-3680. Fax: 410-951-3045. E-mail: dilipkd@aol.com.

Vice President
Etienne Elion, Case J-354-V, OCH Moungali 3, Brazzaville, Republic of Congo. Tel: 242-662-1683. Fax: 242-682-0293. E-mail: ejeej2003@yahoo.fr.

Treasurer/Secretary
Paul Moore, 125 Kenny Lane, West Monroe, LA 21294. Tel: 318-512-1500. Paul@ipes. info.

Directors
Rick Sarre, GPO Box 2471, Adelaide, 5001, South Australia. Tel: 61-8-83020889. Fax: 61-8-83020512. E-mail: rick.sarre@unisa.edu.au.

Tonita Murray, 73 Murphy Street, Carleton Place, Ontario K7C 2B7 Canada. Tel: 613-998-0883. E-mail: Tonita_Murray@hotmail.com.

Snezana (Ana) Mijovic-Das, Norman Vale, 6030 Nott Road, Guilderland, NY 12084. Tel: 518-452-7845. Fax: 518-456-6790. E-mail: anamijovic@yahoo.com.

Andrew Carpenter, The Pier, 1 Harborside Place. Apt 658, Jersey City, NJ 07311. Tel: 917-367-2205. Fax: 917-367-2222. E-mail: carpentera@un.org.

Paulo R. Lino, 111 Das Garcas St., Canoas, RS, 92320-830, Brazil. Tel: 55-51-8111-1357. Fax: 55-51-466-2425. E-mail: paulino2@terra.com.br.

Rune Glomseth, Slemdalsveien 5, Oslo, 0369, Norway. E-mail: Rune.Glomseth@phs.no.

Maximilian Edelbacher, Riemersgasse 16/E/3, A-1190 Vienna, Austria. Tel: 43-1-601 74/5710. Fax: 43-1-601 74/5727. E-mail: edelmax@magnet.at.

A.B. Dambazau, P.O. Box 3733, Kaduna, Kaduna State, Nigeria. Tel: 234-80-35012743. Fax: 234-70-36359118. E-mail: adambazau@yahoo.com.

IPES Institutional Supporters

IPES is guided and helped in all the activities by a group of Institutional Supporters around the world. These supporters are police agencies, universities, research organizations, and similar instiutions.

African Policing Civilian Oversight Forum (APCOF; Sean Tait), 2nd floor, The Armoury, Buchanan Square, 160 Sir Lowry Road, Woodstock, Cape Town 8000, South Africa. E-mail: sean@apcof.org.za.

Australian Institute of Police Management, Collins Beach Road, Manly, NSW 2095, Australia (Connie Coniglio). E-mail: cconiglio@aipm.gov.au.

Baker College of Jackson, 2800 Springport Road, Jackson, MI 49202 (Blaine Goodrich) Tel: 517-841-4522. E-mail: blaine.goodrich@baker.edu.

Cyber Defense & Research Initiatives, LLC (James Lewis), P.O. Box 86, Leslie, MI 49251. Tel: 517 242 6730. E-mail: lewisja@cyberdefenseresearch.com.

Defendology Center for Security, Sociology and Criminology Research (Valibor Lalic), Srpska Street 63, 78000 Banja Luka, Bosnia and Herzegovina. Tel and Fax: 387-51-308-914. E-mail: lalicv@teol.net.

Fayetteville State University (Dr. David E. Barlow, Professor and Dean), College of Basic and Applied Sciences, 130 Chick Building, 1200 Murchison Road, Fayetteville, North Carolina, 28301. Tel: 910-672-1659. Fax: 910-672-1083. E-mail: dbarlow@uncfsu.edu.

Kerala Police (Mr. Balasubramanian, Director General of Police), Police Headquarters, Trivandrum, Kerala, India. E-mail: JPunnoose@gmail.com.

Molloy College, The Department of Criminal Justice (contact Dr. John A. Eterno, NYPD Captain-Retired), 1000 Hempstead Avenue, P.O. Box 5002, Rockville Center, NY 11571-5002. Tel: 516-678-5000, Ext. 6135. Fax: 516-256-2289. E-mail: jeterno@molloy.edu.

Mount Saint Vincent University, Department of Psychology (Stephen Perrott), 166 Bedford Highway, Halifax, Nova Scotia, Canada. E-mail: Stephen.perrott@mvsu.ca.

National Institute of Criminology and Forensic Science (Kamalendra Prasad, Inspector General of Police), MHA, Outer Ring Road, Sector 3, Rohini, Delhi 110085, India. Tel: 91-11-275-2-5095. Fax: 91-11-275-1-0586. E-mail: director.nicfs@nic.in.

National Police Academy, Police Policy Research Center (Naoya Oyaizu, Deputy Director), Zip 183-8558: 3- 12- 1 Asahi-cho Fuchu-city, Tokyo, Japan. Tel: 81-42-354-3550. Fax: 81-42-330-1308. E-mail: PPRC@npa.go.jp.

North Carolina Central University, Department of Criminal Justice (Dr. Harvey L. McMurray, Chair), 301 Whiting Criminal Justice Building, Durham, NC 27707. Tel: 919-530-5204/919-530-7909; Fax: 919-530-5195. E-mail: hmcmurray@nccu.edu.

Royal Canadian Mounted Police (Helen Darbyshire, Executive Assistant), 657 West 37th Avenue, Vancouver, BC V5Z 1K6, Canada. Tel: 604-264 2003. Fax: 604-264-3547. E-mail: helen.darbyshire@rcmp-grc.gc.ca.

Edith Cowan University, School of Psychology and Social Science, Social Justice Research Centre (Prof S. Caroline Taylor, Foundation Chair in Social Justice), 270 Joondalup Drive, Joondalup, WA 6027, Australia. E-mail: c.taylor@ecu.edu.au.

South Australia Police, Office of the Commissioner (Commissioner Mal Hyde), 30 Flinders Street, Adelaide, SA 5000, Australia. E-mail: mal.hyde@police.sa.gov.au.

University of the Fraser Valley, Department of Criminology & Criminal Justice (Dr. Irwin Cohen), 33844 King Road, Abbotsford, British Columbia V2 S7 M9, Canada. Tel: 604-853-7441. Fax: 604-853-9990. E-mail: Irwin.Cohen@ufv.ca.

University of Maribor, Faculty of Criminal Justice and Security, (Dr. Gorazd Mesko), Kotnikova 8, 1000 Ljubljana, Slovenia. Tel: 386-1-300-83-39. Fax: 386-1-2302-687. E-mail: gorazd.mesko@fvv.uni-mb.si.

University of Maine at Augusta, College of Natural and Social Sciences (Mary Louis Davitt, Professor of Legal Technology), 46 University Drive, Augusta, ME 04330-9410. E-mail: mldavitt@maine.edu.

University of New Haven, School of Criminal Justice and Forensic Science (Dr. Richard Ward), 300 Boston Post Road, West Haven, CT 06516. Tel: 203-932-7260. E-mail: rward@newhaven.edu.

University of South Africa, College of Law, School of Criminal Justice (Prof. Kris Pillay, Director), Preller Street, Muckleneuk, Pretoria, South Africa. E-mail: cpillay@unisa.ac.za.

University of South Africa, Department of Police Practice, Florida Campus (Setlhomamaru Dintwe), Christiaan De Wet and Pioneer Avenues, Private Bag X6, Florida, 1710 South Africa. Tel: 011-471-2116. Fax: 011-471-2255. E-mail: Dintwsi@unisa.ac.za.

Index

A

Abbotsford, 118, 122–124
  changed intervention creation, 131–132
  education and awareness, gang
    suppression, 124–130
  enforcement-oriented prevention,
    132–140
  gang suppression strategy, 145–147
  inform and mobilize, community,
    130–131
Abbotsford Bar Watch, 131
Abbotsford Police Department (APD), 118
  Census Metropolitan Area data,
    136–137
  gang-related homicides statistics, 146
Abuse of power, 222
ACAs. *See* Anticorruption agency
Accidents. *See also* Road accidents
  in India, 264
African Union Convention on Preventing
    and Combating Corruption, 225
AFU. *See* Asset Forfeiture Unit
Ahtisaari Plan, 186–187
À la carte services, xxxv
ALFA 802.11 wireless USB adapter,
    external, 112
ANC Youth League, 231
Anticorruption agency (ACAs), 236–239
Anticorruption law, 238–239
Anticorruption programs
  public corruption, 199–200, 213
    character of, 205
    consistency and visibility of
      sanctions, 209–210
    corruption incentives, eradication,
      208
    degree of, South Africa, 204–205
    manifestation of, 202–204
    political will, 211–212
    public awareness, 207–208
    public perceptions, comprehension
      of, 205–206

  rationale, 200–202
  reforming government bureaucracy,
    210–211
  in South Africa, xlii
Apartheid, legacy of, 253
APD. *See* Abbotsford Police Department
Asian economies, 21
Asset Forfeiture Unit (AFU),
    229, 235, 236
A.T. Kearney's Global Cities Index, 9–10
Attacks of 9/11, 68–70
Attack vector
  challenges in compromising systems,
    114–115
  college students' objectives, 109–110
  egress of stolen information, 111
  methods demonstrated, 110–111
  previous field research, 111–112
  wired attack vector using dark network
    technology, 113–114
  wireless attack vector using USB
    connected devices, 112–113
Auditor General Act, 228
Automobile industry, 262
Awareness, gang suppression, 124–130

B

BackTrack 5 software, 112–113
BAC levels. *See* Blood alcohol concentration
    levels
Bar Watch program, 130–131
Batch file, 112
Battle of Seattle, 70–71
Becker's model, 3
Bill of Rights, 234
Black bloc tactics, 70
Blood alcohol concentration (BAC)
    levels, 170
Bootable Debian-based thumb drive, 114
Borderless crime, 17, 32
Boston's Gun Project and Operation
    Ceasefire, 120